HOUSE OF EXILE

EVELYN JUERS

House of Exile

The Lives and Times of Heinrich Mann
and Nelly Kroeger-Mann

FARRAR, STRAUS AND GIROUX

NEW YORK

FARRAR, STRAUS AND GIROUX
18 West 18th Street, New York 10011

Copyright © 2008 by Evelyn Juers
All rights reserved
Printed in the United States of America
Originally published in 2008 for the Writing and Society Research
Group at the University of Western Sydney by the Giramondo
Publishing Company
Published in the United States by Farrar, Straus and Giroux
First American edition, 2011

Library of Congress Cataloging-in-Publication Data
Juers, Evelyn, 1950–
    House of exile : the lives and times of Heinrich Mann and
  Nelly Kroeger-Mann / Evelyn Juers. — 1st FSG ed.
        p.   cm.
    ISBN 978-0-374-17316-6 (pbk. : alk. paper)
    1. Mann, Heinrich, 1871–1950—Exile.   2. Mann, Nelly—
  Exile.   3. Authors, German—Biography.   4. Authors, Exiled—
  Biography.   5. Authors' spouses—Germany—Biography.
  6. Exiles—Germany—Biography.   I. Title.

PT2625.A43Z686 2011
838'.91209—dc22
[B]

                                              2010046560

Designed by Harry Williamson

www.fsgbooks.com

10 9 8 7 6 5 4 3 2 1

FOR IVOR, SAM AND BEN, WITH LOVE

CONTENTS

Part One

Now That It's Broken

Blink of an Eye

Approaching from a distance, hand in hand like lovers, the tall blonde and the old gentleman both called out to him – Brecht! He turned towards them and waved. The Californian sun glinted from his glasses like the sword of Zorro. It was early morning. Heat and the scent of jasmine hung loosely all about the marketplace. Sunlight played upon the unreal splendour of the fruit and vegetables. Not quite real. Some people claimed the produce of this country lacked character, it always looked much more promising, bigger, brighter, than it tasted. Especially apples. They complained that there were certain things – gooseberries, for instance – which you could not get at all. Asparagus only came in cans. And who had been able to buy chanterelles since they'd left Europe? On this day in the summer of 1944, just before the German generals' attempt on Hitler's life, the news had sped like wildfire through the community of European exiles in Los Angeles that a farmer from the north was selling berries at the market. Not just strawberries, blueberries, raspberries, blackberries, there was also a small supply of gooseberries. At the head of a line of people anxiously waiting to be served, Bertolt Brecht chewed on his El Capitán Corona. Fond of sayings and slogans, he proclaimed that the early bird catches the *vorm*, and money talks, and proceeded to buy up all the golden berries. Oh yes, they were ripe enough to eat. Striding across the plaza towards Nelly and Heinrich, he stopped here and there to divide the loot, handing *Gänsebeeren*, as he jokingly translated from the English, to friends who had missed out. – Ah, here comes the man who loves gooseberries, someone said in a heavy accent, referring to one of Chekhov's stories, casually, as if Russian classics were still common currency, as if Brecht had just crossed Berlin's Savignyplatz and was offering summer berries from a cone-shaped paper bag. Finally he scooped a great mound of amber fruit into Nelly's basket. He gave them each, Heinrich and Nelly, a translucent gem to taste. – One for Adam and one for Eve, he chuckled. The proof of the pudding. And crushing a berry against his own palate like an oyster, announced triumphantly that it was delicious, the real thing, not a hybrid, and that he was no gooseberry fool.

It could have happened.
It had to happen.
It happened earlier. Later.
Nearer. Farther off.
It happened, but not to you.
WISŁAWA SZYMBORSKA, 'COULD HAVE'

Several months later, on Sunday 17 December 1944, at home at 301 South Swall Drive, Los Angeles, in the not yet broken dark-ness before dawn, the outline of a bowl of fruit on the window-sill, its curves – a hand of bananas Nelly had bought earlier in the week, grapes, some pears – reminded Heinrich of Brecht's generosity and of their animated exchange that day at the mar-ket, when they'd all had new information about friends in trouble, jailed, people killed, and shocking rumours of the progress of the war. Oh the terrible disgrace! They'd switched between languages,

Stachelbeeren, Stacheldraht, Stacheln, barbs. – Barbarians! Brecht had exclaimed. But that moment, which Heinrich tried to conjure up, now faded.

It left nothing before his eyes but a silhouette of fruit backlit by a gauze of curtains, grey on grey. He was a very old man shrinking from the night, from this terrible night, the worst night of his life.

He was no longer sobbing uncontrollably. He felt numb. Unable to focus. Did he doze? Briefly? Perhaps he was dying? His only physical sensation came from the bridge of his spectacles pressing on his nose. He made himself take them off, and rubbed his eyes. Did he then recall or did he dream? That when they were children his brother had once worn a peg on his nose for a whole day, until a blockage in the plumbing was fixed and the stench the household had to endure was gone.

Heinrich sat very still inside the folds of his suit. Inside the immaculate whiteness of his long-sleeved shirt. His wife had washed it, hung it out, brought it in, ironed it as he watched her through the open door, and placed it on a hanger, smoothing it with the flat of her hand, tugging each cuff into shape. This image and the thought of her absence was too much to bear. He was crushed with grief. He sat deep inside the maculations of his own soft skin and felt minuscule. Like a grain of sand. His mind searched for a place to go, where it could escape.

In Lübeck. In summer. In the garden. In the scented air. Where it was warm and still. A red dragonfly – *Sympetrum vulgatum*, the vagrant darter, how strange to remember it – hovered over the fountain like a hawk. Dragonflies fed on mosquitoes; mated in the air; this one settled for a moment on the leaf-blade of a stand of purple irises. Blackcurrant and prickly gooseberry bushes grew against the garden wall. He sat in the shade of the walnut tree. From an open door someone called his name. – Children, how far did we get with this? he heard his mother ask.

A change in the weather. A wind came up, and suddenly clouds like great grey waves were being swept along. The boy looked up, following their crazy script. Just then a grain blew into his eye and he rubbed the irritation with his fist until the billowing sheet of sky that he'd been watching flashed red from too much rubbing, and his eye burned with pain. He took up his pencils, blindly, and the sketches he'd made. With one lid shut, the other squinting sympathetically, he felt his way along the wall until he reached the door.

The old man did not want to enter. He knew that there was no going back. For one thing, this house at Beckergrube 52 no longer existed, it had been destroyed during the British raid in 1942.

Lübeck, a member of the once significant Hanseatic league of Baltic ports, lies on a low-crested island between the rivers Wakenitz and Trave. Even in the long decline since its peak of power in the fourteenth century, with its trademark late-Gothic gateway, the Holstentor, and the towers of St Aegedien, St Jakobi, St Katharinen, St Marien, St Petri, and the Dom, rising above stepgabled merchant-houses that line narrow streets and foreshores, the town always retained the demeanour of an independent trading centre. During the night of 28–29 March 1942, by the light of a nearly full moon, deemed *excellent visibility*, more than half of Lübeck's buildings were destroyed and hundreds of people killed and injured; 234 aircraft had split into three waves of attack to drop more than 400 tons of bombs. In retaliation, it is said, the Germans opened a Baedeker tourist guide to England, selected several sites of historic significance, and bombed Bath, Exeter, Canterbury, York and Norwich.

But of course, innocent of what the old man knew, the boy had already gone into the house, there was no stopping him. He was splashing his face with water, telling his sisters no, no, that he hadn't been crying, that it was just a bit of dirt. And so the old man followed his childhood self, unseen.

– How far did we get? their mother asked again. On sofas and chairs they sat in an attentive circle, while she opened a volume, resting it on the lid of her desk. To read to them, she often stood up, and so it almost seemed like a sermon in church, or a lesson in school. It might have been in the early summer of 1886, when he, Heinrich, was aged fifteen, Thomas (whom they called Tommy) was eleven, Julia (called Lula) was nine, and Carla, sitting close to her eldest brother, was only four years old. Always inclined to theatrical pranks and gestures, they had picked flowers that morning and had assembled for the reading, with Carla wearing an extravagant crown of pansies. Tommy had plaited it, Lula had pinned it to her sister's curls. Now they waited in mischievous silence, until their mother looked up from leafing through the book and broke into a smile. – Ah yes, she said. Here we are . . . *she wore a little wreath of pansies.*

Then she continued . . . *and there were more pansies on the black ribbon winding through the white lace at her waist* . . . They were spellbound by the scene of Kitty, Anna and Vronsky at the ball, by the quadrilles, waltzes and mazurkas. But some minutes into the reading they noticed, one by one, the intense concentration etched on Carla's petalled brow. She had folded one leg up against her chest, her slender arms encircling her knee. This was how she always sat, in her own embrace. And for a few seconds more, she held her pose, deepened her frown, delighted in her audience, before she too, not exactly knowing what was funny, burst out laughing.

An actress, Heinrich thought. Years later, this is how he would begin his tribute to his sister . . . *She was an actress.*

As far back as each of them could remember, their mother had read to them. Folktales, Mörike's *Peregrina* poems, Goethe, E.T.A.

Hoffmann's sinister stories that made their hair stand on end, or Theodor Storm's sentimental ones awash with wind, sand, sea and mist, where the moon swam from its cloud cover, and where in summer on wooden benches in the shade of linden trees young boys listened to the chronicles of old men's lives. As soon as she discovered new books for herself, thrilled especially by heroines who were themselves readers of the same novels she had lined up on her shelves, she read selections to her children. They were captivated as much by their mother's dramatic ingenuity – she could be a haughty princess, or one of Fritz Reuter's roughest peasants speaking dialect – as by the language, crisp or languorous, the spin or tease of verse, the ever-new suspense of stories they'd heard a dozen times before.

Tommy wanted to know how characters clung to life. He held a toy soldier tightly in his hand. To live, to live on and not die, like Frederick the Great who had inspired his troops to persevere. One day, the novelist Thomas Mann would write that *all the heroism lies in enduring, in willing to live and not die*. At the end of the reading hour he often became aware that his mouth had stayed *a little open and his eyes were half closed*, that the rhythm of his mother's voice echoed in the warm, gentle pulsing of his blood as it coursed through his body; there was a wavelike rushing in his ears.

Even more memorable than these sessions in the library were the bedtime stories Julia told her children, who half reclined on pillows before sleep, or sat on the floor of her room as she dressed to go out. Tommy fastened her pearls. Heinrich sketched. For herself Lula dreamed of ruffled dresses and festivities. And Carla played with a collection of fans, fluffing their feathers or tracing their painted landscapes with her finger. All the while, intrigued by the romance of their family heritage, they listened closely to their mother's childhood reminiscences.

———

The fourth child of Maria da Silva, of Portuguese-Brazilian descent, and Johann Ludwig Hermann Bruhns, a North German coffee and sugar merchant, Julia Mann was born Julia da Silva Bruhns in 1851, while her parents were en route between the Brazilian coastal towns of Angra dos Reis and Paraty. She was not yet five when her mother died in childbirth in 1856, seven when she, her sister, brothers and father made the two-month journey to Lübeck, where the girls, under the guardianship of their widowed German grandmother, were to be educated. Obliged to attend to his business in Brazil, her father bid her a sad farewell and returned to South America with his sons. Through death she had lost her beloved mother, and then through distance that seemed as sundering as death, father, brothers, home and language. Julia mourned as only a child mourns, with an unwavering fidelity to all she'd lost.

Later she re-created for her children what she always longed for. She coaxed their limber imaginations to the doorways, windows and verandas of her childhood home, the Fazenda Boa Vista, to look in one direction across the Bay of Paraty, in the other, along a dense wall of forest. She asked them to choose which way to go, towards the sea or jungle, and so to select their favourite stories.

To convey the allure of the sea, she would tell them she was fishing for words, prompting her audience to call out colours – sapphire, turquoise, emerald, ink – with which to paint the water, where it lapped onto pale sand, where they waded, swam, then deeper, where they rowed. Shells and rocks, she incanted, ships, islands, the horizon. Silver at dawn, copper at dusk. Within this glistening shorescape, she unfurled a series of adventures made even more incredible by the occasional appearance of a powerful sea-goddess or a temperamental, shape-changing serpent.

Their mother said that when she was very young she had heard the beat of the green heart of the jungle. Monkeys, parrots, toucans, hummingbirds, orchids, flowering climbers, glass-winged insects, with every retelling the bounty was augmented. Each of the children entered their mother's trancelike pact of remembrance, and claimed an affinity with this closely woven tapestry of sound and scent and light. Lula and Tommy thought that their darker colouring most closely matched their mother's, and Tommy convinced himself of a special mutuality, that *certain exotic racial characteristics in his external appearance had come to him from her*. They were unaware that in order to enhance her own romantic image of herself, she dyed her hair. Many years later, writing *Death in Venice*, he might still have wiped his brow with his pocket handkerchief when imagining – on his hero's behalf – crouching tigers, creeping tendrils, rising sap, and a *hairy palm-trunk thrusting upwards from rank jungles of fern, from among thick fleshy plants in exuberant flower* . . .

Carla was sure that she closed her eyelids, fringed with long black lashes, just as her mother did, slowly, to be transported to faraway places and fabled lives, daughter like mother.

Heinrich had no need for special claims. When he was born, 27 March 1871 (the year Germany became a nation), named Luiz Heinrich, nicknamed Heine, his mother was barely out of her teens, and for four years he was her only child. He was the first of all his siblings to hear her laugh out loud like a schoolgirl, or whisper conspiringly, play Chopin, or sing Lieder, sweetly, to herself. The first to learn that she sometimes disappeared into a terrible tumescence . . . of what, he did not know . . . of melancholy . . . and that his childish kisses and embraces made her sigh, but that he could not console her. In equal portions, their relationship combined intimacy and distance. *I sit in front of her desk, playing with a small bronze box, its lilac lining effusing a magical scent.* In this box, or perhaps in another, he found feathers, shells, tiny rings made from the tailtip of an armadillo, a little black ragdoll she called the *negrinho*, and most curiously of all, a leathery hand-sized purse which was the large dried flower of the golden chalice vine, *Solandra maxima*. A neat circle of holes pierced near its mouth was threaded through with faded velvet ribbon; it was full of clinking foreign coins.

Some objects are the shape of thoughts. Some thoughts illuminate the dark, like swamp lights, constellations, lines of narrative. In Los Angeles, in the dead eye of night, without conscious effort, Heinrich Mann sketched his childhood. He was a boy stretched out in a summer garden, daydreaming, picturing the adult world just outside his reach. A woman who resembled his mother turned away from a man, an officer with a sword at his side. Who was this man? Was she rejecting him, or flirting? Was it a game? Water spurted from a fountain, unambiguously. There was a walled garden, a house, and inside the house, a baby in a cradle. From courtship to consummation and conception, to birth, his own birth, or one of his siblings', in one round scene.

The old man remembered how as a boy he had once watched his parents as they dressed for a party, a masquerade. *My father is a foreign officer, with a powdered wig and sword, I am immensely proud of him. As the queen of hearts Mama flatters him more than ever.* His father – Thomas Johann Heinrich Mann, called Henry – always wore softly textured suits, and a small flower in his lapel. He was a grain merchant, head of the family firm, and a senator; a pillar of society with many civic responsibilities. He made, lost and regained fortunes. He was a man, Heinrich later said, who was unfamiliar with the idea of creative genius outside business hours, and who believed that his experience and status would one day pass to his eldest son.

Although the boy liked to read the newspaper across his father's shoulder, and to accompany him on walks through town or rides into the countryside, he was a dreamer. He was too impressionable. When he watched marionette performances, or when his mother read him Theodor Storm's story about a puppet theatre, *Pole Poppenspäler*, another world entered his imagination, and like its hero, *a single glance at the stage sufficed to carry him a thousand years back in time*. When his parents took him to a real theatre, he could not see the phantom line between life and art, and during the performance, deeply enchanted, he made a racket calling out warnings to his favourite actor about to be ambushed on the stage, and had to be taken home.

Germans love puppets and anarchic fools. In the form of man-children, *savants*, jovial tramps, blockheads, they are what you grow into if you don't conform, outsiders that embody obscenity, contempt, ridicule, rebellion, transgression. Known as Till Eulenspiegel, Münchhausen, Kasperle, Hans Wurst. Goethe was inspired by the figure of Faust when as a child, season after season, he watched the folk-character of the same name, comical, grotesque, in the popular routine of bantering and bargaining with his Punch-like sidekick. His contemporary Heinrich von Kleist found in the marionettes' mechanical flow of movement a superior form of dance, unachievable by humans shackled by physical and existential heaviness from the double burden of gravity and self-consciousness. The more Romantic the writer, the greater the conviction that the marionette replicates not life but its essence, its signature, that within their wooden core the dolls carry a spark of soul. No matter that the glint from the puppets' dark pupils can be explained as light catching the metal head of a tiny nail, of the kind that cobblers use to fasten together the upper and lower leathers of a shoe. A favourite in the Mann household was Hoffmann's tale *Der Sandmann*. The story's protagonist Nathanaël was the victim of his own imagination. As a child he was overcome with a terror of the fabled Sandman, who prowls at night to steal the

eyes of wakeful children. As a young man he suffered from his misplaced and unrequited love for a doll-like creature. Like myriads
of eyes, dark meanings lurk in every corner of his life and their
burning gaze drives him to madness and death.

Heinrich and Tommy, Lula and Carla, and later their youngest
brother Viktor played with marionettes at home, and with model-
theatres for which the figures and scenery came as sheets of paper
cut-outs that had to be assembled. The conventional *Papiertheater*
repertoire included operas like *Lohengrin* and *The Magic Flute*
and plays by Shakespeare, Goethe, Schiller and Kleist, which the
children received as Christmas gifts. They were also inspired to
create their own plays. The writing of scripts, the painting of back-
drops, the drawing and cutting-out and colouring-in of figures, the
placing of them on stands, the invention of sound effects – dried
peas or lentils in a carton for rain, or for applause – followed by
rehearsals, and family performances, kept them happily occupied
throughout the long Northern winters.

Inside the mighty church of St Marien, not far from their home,
a thirty-metre-long eighteenth-century copy of a fifteenth-century
fresco of the Dance of Death impressed all who saw it. Created
in 1463 – after the plague had ravaged Lübeck's population several times – the twenty-four life-sized representatives of social rank,
from pope to empress, duke, doctor, merchant, maiden and newborn child, are invited by a troupe of black skeletons to join hands
in a dance, a farandole. The Black Death as punishment for earthly
sins. But who leads in this *danse macabre*? It is the worldly dancers,
with their flourishes of colour and choreography, who are keeping
time, who are the death-defying custodians of life and energy.

Nonetheless Thomas Mann later claimed that he and his
brother were strongly influenced by the shadowy atmosphere of
Lübeck, where twisting Gothic alleys and hidden corners seemed
to be haunted by something very old and pale, emotionally de-

formed, spiritually diseased, a remnant of the hysteria of medieval times. He said Lübeck was the city of The Dance of Death. Hans Christian Andersen, who visited St Marien in 1831, thought he detected ironic smiles on the skeletons' faces, and was moved to write a story about a boy called Christian who asked for paper reproductions of figures from the Dance of Death to play with. Most likely, for the Mann children, those images in all their ambiguity would have provided rich material for theatrical productions and night terrors. The church fresco was destroyed in the bombing of 1942.

When Heinrich painted scenery for family performances, he thought that one day he'd become an artist. The puppet theatre also nurtured Thomas's fantasies. Here he served his apprenticeship for the craft of writing and gave himself a foretaste of the hot glow of success. In one of his earliest stories, 'Der Bajazzo' ('The Dilettante'), he transposed a pastime normally shared with his siblings, into one of intense solitude, as if he'd been an only child. The narrator describes his favourite childhood activity, of creating, directing, acting out an opera alone behind the locked door of his room, where he plays every part, from librettist, to usher, to members of the audience conversing before the show. He even cuts a hole in the paper-curtain for his paper-actors to see if the performance is well attended, which of course it is. He tries to conduct the orchestra, sing the different voices, and play various instruments, all at once, there is great applause, and as concert master he takes a low bow to thank the players and the audience. At this point he could only imagine a full house, but the large numbers of people, sometimes several thousand, that later attended his readings and lectures would count among his greatest adult pleasures.

Their mother's desk did not have a lock, and every morning before going to school Heinrich placed his small violin inside, high enough for Tommy not to reach it. It should have been a safe place. He later wrote that the instrument was his joy, or the promise of joy one needed to look forward to each day. But when he returned he often found that it had been played, or rather played with, since sometimes it was damaged, with loose or broken strings and scratches. He wondered who helped his brother take it out and then replace it. When this happened once too often, Heinrich raged. His behaviour was met with dark looks and sharp words from his mother. One day he came home to find his violin in pieces. He cried. You see, his mother said, it no longer matters if it was yours alone or if it belonged to both of you, now that it's broken. Complex reasoning for a young boy to comprehend.

The brothers were tied by bonds of love and jealousy. There were fallings-out, short and long periods of not speaking to each other, followed by peace. Tidal forces of affection. During one of the family's summer holidays in Travemünde, a seaside resort fifteen kilometres from Lübeck, to cut the ice, Heinrich raced Tommy to the shore and deliberately fell over in the sand to let his brother win. Then they dipped their toes into the blue-green water – measured in degrees of coldness, even on the hottest day – and daring one another, they both plunged into the waves.

Two hundred fifty rivers drain into the glacial basin of the Baltic Sea; as the largest volume of brackish – in some parts almost fresh – water on the planet, it contains only about a quarter of the salt of oceans. It was once a lake and has been a sea for a scant 7,000 years; now it is related to the North Sea, and distantly, to the North Atlantic, via narrow straits. Sudden wind changes and violent storms make it hazardous for ships; on its bed there are more rotting, rusting wrecks than in any other sea on Earth. Heinrich told his younger brother, as they dived into the viridescent waves, about a marine landscape of ships' hulls, broken masts, treasure chests and cannonballs, crusted with shells, flagged with fluorescent algae. He said that the Baltic was a cemetery. That swimming further out, they must be careful not to touch the bottom with their feet, for fear of kicking up old bones; that the water of the Baltic tastes like blood.

In Los Angeles, in the not yet broken darkness before dawn, Heinrich cast pencil markings across a new page of his sketchbook: 1886, he calculated, May or June, when their mother began to read *Anna Karenina* to them, for soon afterwards they were on holiday, and the book, unfinished, had been left at home.

Travemünde in July and August was a place of milk-washed skies, sand like silk against the skin, shells picked up and left randomly on windowsills and gateposts. Everyone rose early and retired late; with a Nordic thirst for light and warmth, accumulated over too many months of winter, they lavished themselves with sun. At the water's edge was the familiar line-up of bathing machines which one entered clothed and exited by a short ladder, temporarily amphibian, for health from seawater and sea air. From the promenade, and from a maze of manicured gardens, with the crunch of pebbles underfoot, came bursts of laughter and sounds of calling to acquaintances, in a great variety of dialects and languages. Holidaymakers wearing mostly white, men with straw hats, women twirling parasols, strolled, or gathered with contagious leisure, against the backdrop of the hardly incongruous row of picturesque Swiss chalets, or the *Musiktempel*, or the *Kurhaus*, where one sipped salt water. On the beach children chased raucous seagulls, and with Lilliputian spades built forts and castles; with their bare hands they dug wet sand, urgently, to make channels and as the water rushed in and out, and the walls threatened to collapse, they hurried to secure them; if someone wilfully destroyed these masterworks, there were slaps, kicks, howls, tears.

A youth carrying a book might slink towards the dunes to read or daydream, unsure of his status in society, while others of his age rehearsed the arts of courtship in every little way. Two or three young people walked in the direction of the lighthouse and the *Brodtener Steilufer*, a cliff from which great chunks, trees even, sometimes fell into the sea; at its base was a narrow strip of sand, a renowned treasure trail for fossil hunters, leading between Travemünde and the fishing village of Niendorf.

Along slowly darkening paths some who stayed out late followed the rituals of glow-worms – wingless female beetles, *Lampyris noctiluca* – that lit up their bodies to attract the unilluminated flying males.

Like many others, the Manns probably hired an open carriage for excursions to villages further along the coast, Niendorf, Timmendorf, Scharbeutz, where they would eat freshly smoked fish for lunch, herring, sprats, or eel. They stopped to buy berries from a farmer's stall, and the old coachman took a nap while they picked great bunches of blue lupins that grew beside the road, and strawflowers from a white-gold carpet covering the dunes. As they headed back to Travemünde for dinner, fields on one side, sea on the other, Lula coughed from the dust kicked up by the horses, and Heinrich noticed that Carla was almost asleep against his chest, that Tommy was sunburnt.

Light and shade flickered hypnotically as the carriage rolled through a forest of beech trees. The coachman told stories. Not only amber washed up on these shores, he said, but people too, the living and the dead. He recounted the terrible storms he'd experienced in his lifetime. The worst by far were the winds that caused the great flood of November 1872, when it seemed as if, in the black of night, the sea would altogether claim the land. Trees bent like straw, buildings were destroyed, others filled with sand, people and animals drowned, those who had managed to climb onto roofs felt the walls collapse below and were set adrift. As the water subsided, survivors were found in treetops and boats on meadows far from the shore.

Going further back in time, the coachman thought it was the summer of 1837, he was a young man then, courting the innkeeper's daughter, and he remembered that travellers on their way by ship to other Baltic ports had to wait for the wild weather to abate before continuing their journeys. The wind was so powerful that a beehive was tossed high into the air and carried to an island with its swarm intact. For days the inn was full of restless people, pacing, smoking, drinking; not a rowdy bunch at first, but they grew irritable as the conditions worsened. He remembered one man going to Riga who was increasingly impatient with the delay, intolerant of the crowded space, red with anger; how the volume of his voice rose from his chest, producing rapid streams of curses; how he slammed the wooden benches with his fist. To calm him, the innkeeper showed him a book which absorbed the man so completely, he was seen musing, making notes, tapping rhythms on the table. When the storm passed and it was time to continue their journey, his wife had trouble rousing him from his concentration. The fellow's name, the coachman revealed as he pulled up at the hotel entrance, was Wagner.

And the book the innkeeper had brought him was *Till Eulenspiegel*, which he'd immediately thought would be a perfect subject for a quintessentially German comic opera. Richard and Minna Wagner were going to Riga, where he was to take up the position of musical director at the German Theatre. The Wagners' return journey in 1839, with their Newfoundland dog, was even more eventful. Minna was pregnant, and having lived beyond their means in Riga, they were travelling in a great hurry across borders, without visas, to escape their creditors. At one point their coach overturned, and as if the trickster Eulenspiegel himself was at work, Wagner landed in a pile of dung. Man, woman and dog crawled through high grass to reach the dinghy that would take them to their ship. Minna later found she had miscarried. They expected to be in London in a week, but the trip took almost a month. Tempestuous weather blew the small merchant vessel far off course; it was driven onto rocks that tore off its figurehead, and the sailors, familiar with the legend of the fleeing Dutchman, suspected that the Wagners might be the harbingers of great misfortune. Wagner's opera based on this experience premiered in 1843. It was a great success.

In early September 1886 the Manns arrived back in Lübeck, bright-eyed and tanned, with bunches of everlasting daisies, *Immortellen*, rustling on the girls' wrists and bursting from their hatbands.

Heinrich was a reader. When he was very young, he was given a volume of enticing tales and images that danced through his dreams at night; this was his first literary love. But he'd left the book at his grandmother's place, and somehow it disappeared before it could be truly savoured. *Over the years I asked for and was given many other books, but never that one . . . Much later, when it was time to choose books for my daughter, I remembered the one I'd lost. Curiously, I always avoided buying that one for her.* Little did he know then that more than once, going into exile, he would have to abandon his entire library. There's a photo of him aged about fourteen or fifteen, with his fingers firmly placed between the pages of a book, as if, in mid-narrative, he'd only granted a few moments of his time to the photographer. It's easy to imagine that after the family's return from their holidays, he picked up the page-marked copy of *Anna Karenina* that had been left behind, and even before unpacking his bags, settled in a corner to continue it.

Around that time in Lübeck the lure of books occupied another child in quite different circumstances. Passing between Beckergrube and the station, the Manns would have known the Lindenplatz pharmacy owned by Siegfried Mühsam. Well-respected in the town, he had been a soldier at the battle of Königgratz, Prussia's decisive victory over Austria in 1866. He presided over a household at once conservatively Jewish and passionately Prussian; he kept his sword always by his bedside; a cane hung off the back of his chair, ready to strike anyone who slouched at the dining table. He was an example of what psychologists later identified as *black* or *poisonous pedagogy*, entrenched in hierarchical cultures like nineteenth- and twentieth-century Germany, where parental love and basic human empathy were suppressed for the sake of a communal order that required discipline and obedience. Mostly it was his son Erich (born 1878) who received corporal punishment, for laziness, and all the misdeeds that an intelligent child, tested by too many rules, might invent. Like Thomas and Heinrich, who later said that their formal education had been a painful experience, in fact, a question of survival, Erich Mühsam attended the Katharineum school, and also like them, he was not a good student. He reacted against the unrelieved strictness of his upbringing by developing a profound hatred of authority, and was expelled for expressing Socialist ideas, although he managed to finish his education elsewhere, and then to study pharmacy. He later became a committed anarchist and writer, and an admiring reader of the work of Heinrich Mann. Of his childhood Mühsam said . . . *They knew that I loved to read books. I never received any presents, and when it was discovered that at night I secretly got out of bed and went to my parents' bookcase, taking copies of work by Kleist, Goethe, Wieland, Jean Paul, the bookcase was locked and I was deprived even of that one chance to satisfy my deep desire.*

It was a time when desire, more arousingly than ever, must have draped its glossy peacock-feathered cloak across this town.

On 15 September 1886, Sigmund and Martha Freud, newly married, travelled from Hamburg to Lübeck, where they stopped for six days, going on to Travemünde for a further two, before their return journey to set up house in Vienna. It seems too sober an itinerary for the honeymoon of the century's most famous sexual theorist, but years before, Freud had had a drug-induced prophetic dream of trudging forlornly through the countryside, seemingly forever (their long engagement!), eventually coming to a seaport whose medieval-fortress gateway he recognised as Lübeck's Holstentor, flanked by two sturdy, cone-roofed towers, through which he entered, triumphantly. No mention of the gateway's iron *dentata*. And Martha's perspective was not recorded.

A little later, 1889 or 1890, only a few steps from the Holstentor – via the Puppenbrücke, the bridge of dolls – Lübeck's Lindenplatz became a site of yearning for Thomas. This neighbourhood was the home of his schoolfriend Armin Martens, the son of a timber merchant. In the novella *Tonio Kröger* (1903), portraying Martens as Hans Hansen, Tonio (who was Thomas) named what he loved best: *the fountain, the old walnut tree, his violin and the sea in the distance, the dreamlike summer sounds of the Baltic Sea.* He loved *his dark, fiery mother, who played the piano and the violin so enchantingly.* And he loved *Hans Hansen, and had already suffered a great deal on his account.* For it seemed that *whoever loves the most is at a disadvantage and must suffer.*

Heinrich on the other hand followed his youthful curiosity by visiting the Pension Knoop in a laneway near St Aegidien for his first experience of what he later called *normal sensual bliss. Cherished memories . . .* It was also around this time that he was seduced by his cousin, a young woman in her mid-twenties; they had a brief affair.

The difference between the brothers was already set. Thomas would be the one who laboured at his craft. His aesthetic, and his experience of sensuality, lay in attenuation. He would one day tell his wife that his favourite word was *Sehnsucht*, longing. Heinrich would indulge, engaging all his senses in the art of living, producing his work in hot flushes of creativity. With the result,

21

Thomas thought, that Heinrich's writing was altogether too excessive, and too often shamelessly erotic.

Travemünde, 1889. An unpredictable blue-grey sky. Through an open window, the heady pungency of pine from scattered stands of trees, orchestral strains from the pavilion in the centre of the town. Encouraged by the anonymous publication of one of his stories in the *Lübecker Zeitung*, Heinrich spends most of his seaside holiday writing. When two more pieces are accepted for publication, he decides he will become a writer and tells his parents he does not see the use of staying on for his final year of school. A writer! Nothing will persuade him to return to school, and so they try to steer their headstrong eldest son – he was eighteen now – towards an apprenticeship in the book trade. In fact, he would have done anything to cut loose from Lübeck, he would even have become a pimp, he later boasted to a friend.

Those early autumn days when Heinrich knew he would soon be leaving home, he and Carla, now eight, spent the evenings reading together, whatever took their fancy, Heine, Tolstoy. The light fell only on the book. While he read she was mostly silent. She inhaled the words. Her lids closed on certain passages, as if locking an image or idea into herself. Go on, she'd say, go on. She wanted the narrative to flow, no stops, no comments. She said that listening to him, she felt suspended, as from a cloud, watching the world below.

Heinrich left Lübeck on 28 September 1889 for Dresden, where the Manns had relatives, to join a firm of booksellers, *von Zahn und Jaensch*, Schloss Strasse 24. It was an auspicious time for him, as the very next day one of his stories appeared in *Die Eisen Zeitung*. The apprenticeship was disappointing from the very beginning. He did not like having to stand all day, keeping accounts, filling out order-forms, sorting books on shelves, or the extended working hours of the Christmas season. It was all immeasurably boring. To his astonishment the worst books, the ones he thought publishers should be ashamed of, were the ones that sold out in just a few hours. In his letters to Carla, he would pun on his employers' names, joke about Jaensch, send her verses that made up *unjaenschlich* to rhyme with *unmenschlich* – inhuman – or compare his experience to *schlimme Zahn-Schmerzen*, a bad tooth-ache, confessing that every day he felt like pulling out. To make her laugh.

Young would-be writers were setting out in all directions. Franz Kafka in Prague, and David Herbert Lawrence in Notting-hamshire, both started primary school. At this time in Paris, André Gide climbed the stairs to the sixth floor of a house in the rue Monsieur-le-Prince, to a large unfurnished room, and dreamed of placing his writing desk by the window with the entire city spread out below; an event momentous enough to be the first diary entry in what would become his greatest work, his journals. A few months later he wrote, *I suffer absurdly from the fact that everybody does not already know what I hope some day to be . . . that people cannot foretell the work to come just from the look in my eyes.* In America the teenage Willa Cather escaped the small town of Red Cloud by moving to Lincoln, where she prepared for university and for a writing career, immersing herself in literature and languages. One of her earliest stories was about a musician who migrated from Bohemia to Nebraska; when his violin broke, he shot himself.

At the bookshop in Dresden, Heinrich had two hours off for lunch to explore the cake shops and tobacconists along Schloss Strasse. Weekends he visited the art gallery, where he disliked Hol-bein and Dürer and loved Rubens and Van Dyck. To spend the money he'd earned, he went to taverns, dance halls, the opera, ballet, theatre. Brothels at ten marks a night. He was puzzled by his outbreaks of *pathological sensuality*, as he called it, but thought love must be the highest form of happiness, followed by literary success. He referred to his own attempts at writing as *Erguss*, ejaculation. He read more than ever, forgettable contemporary writers, as well as Storm, Fontane, Kleist. And Poe, who made his flesh creep. Never quite convinced by the idea of pure fiction, he grappled with the notion of the *real* as opposed to the *believable*, and always returned to Heinrich Heine, whom he loved above all others, and with whom he must have identified: his aversion to studies and regular employment, his struggles to prove himself a writer, his urge to travel. Heine's uncle once remarked that if the stupid boy had learned something worthwhile, he would not have had to write books.

His first Christmas away from home was spent with his relatives, drinking champagne, eating oysters and roast goose, and no doubt smoking good cigars. From Lübeck he received a box of presents that included opera glasses, stationery, cigarettes and books. A friend sent him some marzipan. He was never homesick.

In 1890 Heinrich completed a novella, *Haltlos* (To Stop at Nothing); his grandmother died; and that year his youngest brother Viktor was born. His father wrote to tell him that these were serious times, and it was important to secure one's future through hard work, independence and the circumspection of one's needs, concerned that if his son did not make an effort to establish himself in a career, opportunities would pass him by. He went home for a few weeks in the summer, and was back in Dresden by the end of July. His parents visited him in November. But the atmosphere at work worsened, and he expected to get fired. He had discovered Nietzsche, the radical content, the dynamic style, urgent, sketchy: he called him the greatest modernist, and asked for *Thus Spake Zarathustra* for his birthday. By the beginning of April 1891 he had sent a six-page letter of explanation to his father, and had left Dresden and moved to Berlin to work as a volunteer with the publisher Samuel Fischer.

Berlin made a grand impression; he took in everything, cafés, museums, in the evenings he sometimes walked for hours between Potsdamer, Leipziger and Friedrich Strasse, looking for the right woman. He identified his tripartite self as the sensualist who acted on impulse and was running riot, the intellectual who weighed up the consequences of actions and had of late become rather atrophied, and the voyeur who kept a keen literary eye on the other two. Soon Nietzsche's prophetic voice was getting on his nerves. He explored ideas associated with Symbolism. It seemed his life had only just begun.

His father, who in his letters to his son was always concerned about the tyranny of time, was ill, and Heinrich went home for six weeks in the summer. In August he wrote a poem for his mother's 40th birthday, recalling the magic of her voice when she read to her children, and thanking her for the great gift of an artistic sensibility that she had passed on to him.

Heinrich was twenty, Thomas was sixteen, when their father died in October 1891, aged fifty-one. He had warned his wife to be strong with her children and if she weakened she should read *King Lear*. In his will he gave instructions to liquidate the family firm, since neither of his sons was interested in taking it over. He requested that his eldest son's choice of a literary career should be discouraged. Heinrich later claimed, and perhaps it was only a fantasy, that in his last moments the dying man said he wanted to help him. He interpreted this to mean that his father wanted to help him to become a writer. Perhaps he'd taken this supportive sentiment from the biography of Heinrich Heine, whose father worried how his son could succeed as a poet while Goethe's name was on everyone's lips.

The Mann family might then have remembered Hoffmann's

story of the Sandman, with its protagonist Nathanaël declaring that the death of his father was the most terrible moment of his youth. It accorded with Freud's claim, that a father's death was the most important event in a man's life; Freud told a friend that since the time of his own father's death he had felt thoroughly uprooted. It is well known that for Nietzsche, who was only four years old when his father died, the experience left him deeply unsettled for the rest of his life, as the idea of the father grew large and became pervasive. Wrestling with this ghost, Nietzsche, who was named Friedrich Wilhelm after the paternal figure of the Prussian king with whom he shared a birthday, tapped into what was the era's greatest challenge: breaking loose. Freud argued that the primary love children feel for parents must necessarily be repressed as they grow up. Otherwise there would be no argument with the past, no independence, no moving forward; but always *the force of the original current continues to exist*, preserved in the great powerhouse of the unconscious.

Not long after Heinrich returned home that year for what must have been a sorrowful Christmas, he became very ill, suffering a lung haemorrhage. For the next few years he moved between sanatorium-regimes in Berlin (Dr Oppenheim's), Wiesbaden (Heilanstalt Lindenhof) and the Black Forest, packed in furs and blankets and exposed to the elements on snow-covered balconies in winter, or taking naked sunbaths in the summer, exercising, walking. From autumn 1892 until spring 1893 he was in Lausanne, where he rowed on the lake, returned to Nietzsche, read French literature and made short trips to Geneva (for love) and Montreux (for the casino). Most often he stayed in Riva on Lake Garda at the clinic of Dr von Hartungen that was much frequented by writers and artists, including Nietzsche and Rilke; Kafka was there in 1909 and 1913.

In April 1893, in a state of *raptus sexualis*, as he called it, there was a jaunt in Paris, followed by a brief final return to Lübeck in May. All the while he pondered over what was healthy, what was sick. He increased his reading, and with great determination to hone his skills, he wrote reviews and short articles, and began work on a novel, *In einer Familie* (In One Family). For the Manns a chapter of their lives was closing. In the summer of 1893 Julia Mann moved the family south, to Munich. It had all happened in the blink of an eye.

Alone and shivering, for the sun had still not risen, in Los Angeles the old man might also have remembered one winter afternoon in Lübeck in the 1870s. It was already dark. The gas lamps were lit. A distant doorbell to announce someone entering a house. Then *the little boy, who is me* saw the ice-glazed side street leading down the hill, a perfect place for sliding, and such a great temptation that he tore himself away from the hand holding his. He slid steeply, one foot slightly forward, arms outstretched for balance, he flew with the thrill of speed. Unable to stop, he approached the crossroad, where a woman suddenly stepped out in front of him. She was wrapped-up against the cold, and she carried something under her shawl. They collided, fell, and he heard something shatter, a plate or bowl. But it was dark, he was frightened, and he ran away. Only to be pursued for days and nights by his conscience, as he imagined she was very poor and the dish he broke contained the only food she and her family had to eat that day. To make amends, the boy thought he must give the woman all he owned, his toys, his books.

In the house of exile where the old man sat, a bell rang, followed by the sound of something breaking.

The Gaze

According to Heinrich, all seemed to be going well for his youngest sister, Carla – Carla Augusta Olga Maria Mann, born 23 September 1881 – until she turned nineteen. *For years, in her ungainly adolescence, she stretched out on the sofa, devoured bread with sausage and entire collections of lending libraries, and afterwards, with her arms crossed behind her head, gazed at the ceiling, speechless, enchanted.*

Sometimes, when she fell asleep to dreams of radiance, her lashes fluttered for a moment, so that Heinrich, who was fascinated by his sister, might have wished to touch her cheek, or when she woke, to call her his *papillon*, but evidence of such fleeting moments of endearment has not survived. Shapely and golden-haired, with a penchant for tragedy and travel, and the desire to wear elaborate hats, at the age of nineteen she got up from the sofa to become an actress. A restless career that took her away from her family and their social circle. Despite her abilities, she discovered that acting required constant renewals of energy and resilience. It was like walking – she thought of her mother's stories of her childhood in Brazil – through water or jungle, where each step forward closed the path behind without a trace.

Between engagements she continued to read novels. Like Flaubert's Emma Bovary, Carla *had an enthusiastic veneration for all illustrious or ill-fated women*, catching sight of herself in characters such as Tolstoy's Anna Karenina, or Fontane's Effi Briest, who was herself bewitched by the magnificent heroines in the novels of Sir Walter Scott.

She soon found that her stage roles would not come to life unless she invested them with extra substance from deep within her own reservoir of raw emotion. She developed a talent for extremes of comedy or tragedy, but with each performance, whether playing the lead, or as a parlourmaid, it seemed to her that she was scooping up and handing out parts of herself. Sometimes exhaustion caught up with her, followed by disappointment. When her acting fell flat, she was repulsed by her failure and what she took to be, increasingly, her lack of fire, lack of commitment, lack of substance. She read fiction, poetry and drama, more fervently than ever in her youth, rehearsing an extravagant repertoire of roles in front of mirrors or in her head, while going about ordinary chores, making tea, polishing her nails, or being measured by the milliner for a new hat. And so she collected parts that offered a great range of emotional responses, for the future, when she might be called upon to play them.

Once, as Ophelia, in a small provincial theatre production of *Hamlet*, she caught a cold, with bronchial complications, and was replaced for the remainder of the season by an understudy who drew great applause. For Carla this produced another in a series of small melancholies that she added to her string and wore: her black pearls. She recuperated slowly, just in time to attend the play's last night. When everyone had left the theatre, she gave her best performance to an empty hall, watched only by the skull that Hamlet had interrogated so convincingly. It would be her trophy. Back in her room, with her chilling companion, she recalled childhood fears brought on by stories her older siblings told, especially their rendition of Hoffmann's tales, like the story of the Sandman that her brother Thomas read with a creepy voice by candlelight, perfecting his pitch of terror, so that she screamed and screamed, and they were all astonished, even the cook who rushed from the kitchen, to hear such a sound – piercing, grotesque – from such a little girl. It still made her shiver to think of it, that story's persuasiveness of trickery and evil. One image in particular had left its mark, of thousands of pairs of glasses piled up high, which start to flash and flicker and stare like eyes, and they become eyes, shooting blood-red glances at Nathanaël, the young man tortured by his own misguided vision.

So Carla called the skull Nathanaël. Each summer she visited her family, and each autumn she joined a different theatre company. Wherever she set up her temporary home, the skull would be placed prominently, on a chest of drawers, a desk, or a chair, under a light, next to a vase of flowers. It was an eccentricity that shocked some of her visitors, who twisted their mouths or showed their teeth in mockery of the dead. Heinrich thought the skull belonged to his sister's peculiar mix of weariness and whim. But for Carla, in her loneliness, it represented something more. It was the gaze that might be filled with meaning, distances that might be crossed, infinitudes of self, astonishment, intensity, a scream. Nathanaël, she would say, like a mother speaking of her child, was no ordinary skull.

In fact, long before she acquired it, it had been sawn in half, presumably to remove and examine its brain before burial. More strangely though, and perhaps for some ornamental purpose, the two halves had been carefully realigned, with the discreet addition of a set of hinges and an inset base of light-toned polished wood. And so it continued to function as its biological origins intended. A kind of vessel, Carla joked.

Most of the time she made an effort to be sociable with her fellow actors. But she was an outsider who preferred solitude to nightly gaieties and promiscuities. Theatrical gossip passed her by. One evening, however, with the company in high spirits, buoyed by a splendid opening night – they had had the audience laughing, sobbing, endlessly applauding – she joined her friends, clinking glasses all around to a première that promised great success. They were loudly drunk and competing with their tall tales of dramatic mishaps, a backdrop or a dress on fire, a swallow dropping luck on King Lear's head, and the more unusual props they had encountered: portraits that sneezed, frogs in goblets, drooping papier-mâché swords, a skull in which wasps had nested and another that opened like a box. Each incident and item invited commentary. The skull that doubled as a receptacle, it was rumoured, was fitted with a set of finely crafted silver hinges that sometimes caught the stagelights, and from its eye sockets cast a fearsome flash. It had once belonged – in the most intimate sense of belonging, someone laughed – to a man called Solander. – Who was he? Carla asked. They did not know. In this town no one visited her in the attic rooms where Nathanaël kept watch, and so the skull remained her secret. When the season finished – this time the plays, and her roles in particular, had pleased the critics – she once again moved on.

In the train she found herself sitting opposite two young men, almost identical in suit, hat, voice and glasses. It was hot in the carriage, airless, and as she fanned her face, they produced an orange which they peeled and divided into segments. The talk she overheard was so learned, and each burst of citrus fruit so pungent, the piece they offered her so refreshing, that she felt inclined to ask, without any further introduction, if the name Solander meant anything to them. Side by side, ankle to ankle, knee to knee, they sat, one flinging his head sideways when he spoke, the other leaning forward. – Yes, indeed! They did not seem at all surprised. They were botanists, travelling to Berlin, where they would be cataloguing . . . redesigning . . . The train sounded its whistle, entered a tunnel, and Carla missed their words. – But Solander? she asked again. Of course they knew who he was . . . a Swedish naturalist who accompanied Joseph Banks and Captain James Cook between 1768 and 1771 on a voyage round the world. Carla accepted another piece of orange and made herself comfortable, one hand resting on the hatbox she had placed beside her on the vacant seat, the other lightly fanning. The men admired the fan, finely painted with a landscape of a palm-fringed beach. – Daniel Solander was born in 1733, the sideways-flinger began. – February 19, the forward-leaner continued, in Piteå, northern Sweden, very near the Arctic Circle.

Eight months before Daniel's birth, the botanist, taxonomist and adventurer Carolus Linnaeus, also known as Carl von Linné, had briefly visited Piteå. He was delighted with its geography of coastline, rivers, rocks, lakes, sandy meadows, sheltering forests. He kept a journal, and noted, *immediately on entering the town I procured lodging, but had not been long in bed before I perceived a glare of light on the wall of my chamber. I was alarmed with the idea of fire, but on looking out of the window saw the sun rising, perfectly red, which I did not expect would take place so soon. The cock crowed, the birds began to sing, and sleep was banished from my eyelids.* That was in the summer of 1732. It was the Solander family who had provided Linnaeus with a room. After a few days collecting plants, insects, notes and impressions, including the discovery of an unusual coral-rooted orchid, *Orphrys corallorrhiza*, as well as the shocking sight of the bloody, quartered body of a man which had been placed in a wheelbarrow by the front door of a nearby house – it was explained as customary punishment for incestuous liaisons – he continued on his tour.

In Piteå, young Solander's grandfather was the local vicar, his father was headmaster at the school. The boy grew up in a house full of learning and music. He left in 1750 to attend one of Europe's leading centres of scientific research, the university at Uppsala, where he boarded at the home of his uncle, a professor of Law. Solander soon came under the spell of Linnaeus, now a charismatic teacher and the universally celebrated author of the *Systema Naturae*. Published in 1735, it was a classification of plants according to their perceived male and female characteristics. Just as Linnaeus as a student had stuck closely to the tutorship of Dr Celsius, Solander spent most of his time with Linnaeus – the *Herr Archiater*, as he was respectfully addressed – his chosen mentor, who by his own admission *cherished him as a son*. The young man assisted the master with the gathering and labelling of plants, wrote pamphlets on the Linnaean method, and accompanied him on numerous botanical expeditions. Like Linnaeus in his youth, he went to Lapland. And like him, some say, he even adopted the habit of wearing a green coat, though in a less vibrant shade.

Independently, Solander established a large library and his own impressive hoard of botanical and other natural specimens, whatever he could find, not least the skeletons and skulls of birds and small animals. It is not known if he was ever tempted to augment his private treasure by simply taking a seed or a cutting from the vast collection of the *Princeps Botanicorum*. In any case, everyone knew that Linnaeus kept a close watch over every sample that he gathered, ordered, owned. Solander often spent mealtimes with Linnaeus and his family: a wife, of legendary ferocity; their son, Carl; and four daughters, the eldest Elisabeth Christina, or Lisa Stina, as she was called, then Louisa, Sara Stina, and the baby, Sophia. In prayer, the master always thanked God for giving him the greatest herbarium in the world and the greatest knowledge of the world of Nature. In the evenings the intimate circle of family and *apostles* compared their notes, on petals and pods, mosses and insects. They discussed the very latest evidence of the interdependence of species, and with great excitement, the grand vision of establishing all the plants of the world in the Linnaean gardens on the Baltic.

Occasionally Solander returned home to his family in Piteå. But he preferred, even in his holidays, to stay with the master's household, as in the summer of 1758, which he spent at Hammarby, their newly acquired farm south-east of Uppsala. That year Solander was twenty-five. And Lisa Stina was fifteen. Of all Linnaeus's children, she expressed the keenest interest in the study of plants, of animals and their habitat, often accompanying her father and his entourage into the rich surrounding landscape of forest, field and wetlands.

It was a glorious summer, laden with the promise of new discoveries that usually continued well into the last long hours of daylight, and beyond. One evening, walking by herself at twilight, Lisa Stina witnessed a strange phenomenon. Orange, red and yellow nasturtiums, in clumps that cushioned the borders of a path leading to the dark domain of trees in one direction and to the house in the other, appeared to trigger from one flower to the next a series of sparks. It was inexplicable and a little eerie. The following night, she and Daniel strayed from a group that had set out to hunt moths, and found themselves alone, in silence, at the edge of the forest. Lisa Stina waited for the flowers to display their radiance, and suddenly it happened. Thin threads of brilliant light sped comet-like along the ground. Solander could not believe his eyes. But the face of the young girl, whose hand now held his, confirmed that it was not an illusion.

The train steamed into the night. Carla was spellbound. The narrators' voices dropped to an audible whisper, conspiring with the gathering-in of darkness. – Go on, she urged.

Every evening at Hammarby, Daniel and Lisa Stina waited to watch the flowers lose colour, grow grey, and black. And then the rush of fires. Were the plants still or moving when the radiance took place? Were they perhaps reflecting light from other sources? Or was it after all a trick of the eye? Could eyes transmit light as well as receive it? Other questions came into their heads much later. Did the flashes signify the beginning or the end of something . . . sparks into life or vanishing points?

The weather cooled and the days shortened. Soon the family would be packing up to return to town. From the open doors of the summerhouse, quite alone in semi-darkness, they indulged their curiosity one last time. They exchanged pledges and spoke of plans for future collaboration, travel, publications. Torches, and then some voices, approached their hideaway. It was the moth-hunting party returning from its final expedition and passing the pavilion. Inside, the young couple kept very still and thought they'd not been seen. But moments later Linnaeus himself called out their names. For weeks, noticing that they were drawn to each other, he'd kept a careful eye on them.

He had something to show them. It was a moth, a noctuid for the ever growing collection of *Lepidoptera*, quite drab, until it spread its wings and disclosed the unexpected glory of its yellow underwing. – Oh, how beautiful! What will you call it? his daughter asked. – *Noctua pronuba*, he answered readily, smiling. Lisa Stina and Daniel both blushed. They had had a classical education and knew that in Roman lore the Pronuba were guardian spirits that presided over the good fortune of young brides.

Carla's wide-eyed attention indicated that she did not expect the narrative to end there.

The French call this moth *la Fiancée*, the sideways-flinger commented. In German, with less dazzle, it's known as *Hausmutter*. Daniel Solander believed Linnaeus was more than merely a taxonomist. The master was a man of neat perspectives, that was true, but there were also his insights, intuitions, and in matching names to nature, as in his search to discover underlying truths, he was a thinker and a kind of poet. In his high estimation of his mentor, the forward-leaner assured Carla, Solander was not alone. The great Goethe had cited Linnaeus, alongside Shakespeare and Spinoza, as a major influence on his own work. The vastness and variety of plants Goethe had seen and read about, made him wonder about the possible existence of an archetype, *the primordial plant amid this multitude*; to discover it would require not science alone, but *Anschauung*, a technique which combined observation and intuition: the gaze.

And in Königsberg, the two botanists continued with a flurry of excitement, there lived a short man with a large head, Immanuel Kant, the philosopher who, not unlike Linnaeus, aimed to overtake illusion and superstition, in order to call things by their proper names. At exactly half past three Kant's solitary daily walk took him as far as a row of linden trees, and when he reached his destination, before turning to go home, he nodded sharply, as if in agreement above all with himself. At that time he was one of many asking the big questions, about a single evolutionary source or unifying purpose. Each day as he walked and thought, he came closer to the truth. Kant acknowledged Linnaeus as a fellow traveller, even in those uneasy years when their countries, Prussia and Sweden, were at war.

In England Linnaeus's reputation reached mythical dimensions. And when he was invited to send a representative to London, for the principles of the *Systema Naturae* to be taught and more effectively applied in English scientific circles, without hesitation he chose Solander, who left Uppsala in the spring of 1759 for an overland journey to Skåne, where he would lodge with a cousin, before continuing by ship. But in Skåne Solander fell ill with what was called Uppsala Fever, or malaria, and so his onward journey was delayed. From his pharmacopeia he treated himself with infusions of cinchona, the bark of a South American tree, an appropriate remedy since it contained quinine. He also made a point of avoiding damp and swampy places. Sometimes he felt better, thinking that the fever had run its course, and he ventured out to collect plants and insects, samples of which he sent to Linnaeus, including *Scolopendra*, or millipedes. He regretted, he wrote the Herr Archiater, that *I have not been able to find the true Scolopendra electrica*, the kind that glowed. He'd collected a similar species, *but have never been able to see a shine in the darkness*. Solander knew Lisa Stina would be asked to read the letters to her father, and as he wrote he imagined he could hear her sigh. From the sandy soils of Skåne he also sent some speedwell, of which the outer cup, the calyx, seemed *most specieux*.

On 14 May 1760, about a year after he'd set out, and now at last on his way to England, Daniel Solander wrote to Linnaeus that he'd been to the port town of Elsinore – here Carla interrupted the story's flow with a little cough and her hand brushed lightly across the hatbox – the port of Elsinore, the narrators continued, where he said he *found nothing of note*.

At Uppsala Solander had left behind an incomplete doctoral dissertation and his *greatest wealth*, an extensive collection of books, plants and other specimens. He had bid everyone farewell with the assurance of a speedy return. When he finally arrived in London at the end of June 1760, he received the news that his father had died the previous month.

In England, one thing led to another. Someone assumed that he was Dr Solander, and so the title stuck; he was much in demand. The Seven Years War was still being fought, with Sweden on one side and Great Britain on the other. Europe bristled with colonial ambitions. English ships were returning from all over the world carrying zoological and botanical cargo, with great expectations of its commercial potential. In London, a host of scientists was busy investigating these treasures as soon as ships docked and specimens were unloaded. In Sweden, they thought themselves lucky to have someone as reliable as Solander in London, to snap up what was new and send it home – or as Linnaeus put it with an undisguised collector's greed, *to get to the garden what is wanting.*

The botanists leaned towards Carla; their voices lowered to a confidential tone. It appears that Solander's travel, and other expenses, were supported by a substantial stipend and that he was sent to England on an even more clandestine mission than the spying out of plants; indeed, that he was also gathering intelligence to benefit the development of Swedish industry. In any case, life in London's highest scientific and intellectual sphere, where before long he was well ensconced, was costly, the money he'd been allocated was not enough and he wrote to his benefactor with requests for more. To make matters worse, Linnaeus's own demands for plant samples, and to be kept informed, more often than not went unfulfilled. The master became increasingly frustrated with the new independence of his pupil. Was the young man severing their ties? He urged Solander to apply for the vacant Professorship of Botany in St Petersburg, closer to home, but Solander procrastinated and let the opportunity pass. Possibly letters were written and lost, or written and destroyed. Did the novelist – the sideways-flinger could not recall his name – the novelist who attended a weekend party in a country house, smelled smoke during the night, and following his nose had rushed in the direction of Solander's rooms to find the doctor burning balls of paper, crumpled letters, did he get the picture right? Did he see him, as he said, cast flaming spherules off his balcony into the night? It is generally thought that in October 1762, Solander had sent what would be his second to last letter to his mentor, containing special greetings to Lisa Stina.

Meanwhile, that same year, Elisabeth Christina Linnaeus had written and published *The Gaze of the Nasturtium*, a short botanical description of *Tropaelum majus*, from the Latin *tropaeum*, a trophy. She mentioned sitting alone at night in the summerhouse at Hammarby, noticing how flowers in the nearby courtyard were repeatedly radiating light, and that she brought this phenomenon to the attention of her family and friends, including her father; that they were all amazed, her father suggesting that the enigma might belong to the experimental field of physics, rather than botany. She said she'd thought it odd, that when she looked at the flowers without blinking, the sparks stopped. *I leave it to scientists with eyes sharper than mine to comment on these findings*, to men whose research leads *to palaces filled with the wonders of the world*. A fair conclusion, since many of Linnaeus's apostles had been sent on voyages of discovery, and those left behind waited anxiously to hear what great knowledge these men encountered. What would they bring back? It was a hazardous quest, and many did not return at all. Women also longed to travel. And some did. It's said that to make things easier for themselves, they sometimes disguised themselves as men.

Lisa Stina studied her face in the mirror. She had pinned her dark-blonde plaits tightly around her head and put on her brother's hat. Her brown eyes glistened with intrigue.

It's well known that one day in the summer of 1762, Immanuel Kant read Jean-Jacques Rousseau's *Emile*, and quite out of character and just that once, completely absorbed in the story, he missed his three-thirty walk to the linden trees and back. Except for a portrait of Rousseau, those who visited him have reported that Kant's rooms were entirely free of decoration. People travelled great distances to see Kant in Königsberg. They had heard that if they knocked at his door when he was about to sit down to lunch, he might ask them to join him, because he liked company when he ate his midday meal.

It is less well known, perhaps even apocryphal, that in the spring of 1764, a handsome young man arrived, a Swedish botanist, and despite the fact that he refused to take off his hat on entering the house, he was invited in. The two talked about plants, about unexplained occurrences in nature, about intrinsic, relational and perceived phenomena; and about even larger mysteries, the creative principle, which the visitor, drinking wine until his cheeks glowed and his brown eyes sparkled, said he thought lay in spontaneity, and – the excitement of the moment coursed through his veins and he could not stop the chain of thought – and that God, freedom and immortality are convertible, one into the other; that these are felt by us as powerful forces, of attraction and repulsion, which produce . . . illuminations! And the youth asked Kant if on a hot summer's night he had ever seen the nasturtium flower's flashing gaze.

Reaching the linden trees on his walk that day, the philosopher, who rehearsed his afternoon thoughts as a sportsman might run his daily mile, nodded as he always did, but then people passing thought they also saw him smile, as if something perplexing – a small trick of fate, like an endearment – had briefly brushed his face.

Brown eyes, dark-blonde plaits. Without adornment, and yet bright as a sunbeam, that's how Solander must have remembered her. In 1763 he was working at the British Museum, in charge of the natural history collection. The following year he was made a member of the Royal Society. It is not known whether he was informed that in July 1764 Lisa Stina had married a Swedish army officer, or if he ever found out that about a year later, with her newly born daughter, she had left her husband, and wings clipped, returned to live in her parents' home. In London, Solander had become firm friends with Joseph Banks, a man of wealth and scientific acumen, and as a team they joined Captain James Cook's 1768 expedition to the South Seas, with the purpose of reaching an ideal vantage point in the southern ocean to observe the transit of the planet Venus across the sun.

On board the *Endeavour*, heading towards the east coast of South America, marine specimens, which Solander called *sea products*, were caught, identified and illustrated, and often handed on to the cook. Scientists and draughtsmen sat around a large table, Banks studying books of earlier voyages, Solander sorting a miscellany of material collected at their first port of call, Madeira, and pressing plant samples between the pages of Addison's commentary on Milton's *Paradise Lost*. A few days after crossing the Equator they saw luminescence in the water, produced by a species of *Medusa*, or jellyfish. They wondered if radiance was designed by nature as a lure or a deterrent.

Unexpectedly the forward-leaner burst into quotation . . . *it is less the horror than the grace / Which turns the gazer's spirit into stone* . . . saying it was from a poem by Shelley, 'On the Medusa of Leonardo da Vinci in the Florentine Gallery'. He took a deep breath, as if something had been laid to rest. Then he resumed the narrative.

After months at sea, their arrival in Rio de Janeiro in November 1768 was at first a great relief, followed by disappointment. The ruling viceroy was suspicious of them. In an age of fierce colonial competition, he could not accept that this was a purely scientific expedition. And so only the captain was permitted to go ashore. Banks and Solander, having familiarised themselves with Brazilian plants in British collections and in books, were at fever pitch, anticipating an abundance of novelty and beauty just beyond their reach. They did not wear the restrictions lightly and began to scheme. When it was announced that the ship's surgeon could also go ashore, he took Solander along, dressed as his assistant. Once he'd set foot in town, Solander managed to bribe a guard to accompany him to the outskirts, collecting plants and insects while listening to stories of botanical wonders he would never see. Each blossom picked, it was declared, had a brighter, more fragrant, or more poisonous cousin growing one day's journey to the north or the south, each tiny bird flirting with a flower was only a gigantic duplicate of its minuscule prototype flitting in the foothills of mountains inaccessible to man.

Having glimpsed a small fraction of the abundant flora and fauna of the place, and left to imagine the rest – the seeds he might have collected and taken home – at night Solander dreamed repeatedly of thresholds he had never crossed, and of Sweden, where it was winter. Snow slid heavily off branches. Women wrapped in woollen shawls struggled against an icy wind to carry their children, their baskets, their bundles of kindling. There was one with brown eyes, dark-blonde hair; she carried books; on their spines the golden letters spelled out titles in Latin, German, English. The winter before he left, they had shared music and laughter, sleigh rides, the heat of the fireplace, and the work that Linnaeus set before them. From this same dream he woke drenched in sweat night after night; a recurrence, perhaps, of the malaria he suffered after leaving Uppsala, when his departure from Sweden was a journey into exile. But was this exile imposed or voluntary? In a fit of longing, Solander shrugged off hesitation and confusion, and before leaving Brazil to sail into uncharted waters, he would try to make contact one more time. He wrote and sent his last letter to Linnaeus, dated 1 December 1768. It expressed his regret at postponing *an obligation that I always had imagined would become my greatest pleasure, had I only just once been honoured with one single line from the one I hoped wanted to show me that friendship, if not prevented by others . . . the amiable Herr Archiater's eldest daughter . . . my senses hardly are able to function . . . when I recall the one who I thought would make me happy.*

The two narrators noticed tears in Carla's eyes. They were surprised at the impact of their tale.

The continental masses of the northern hemisphere made the existence of southern counterweights a probability. But who would discover them? Who would claim them? A patriotic mission – for new colonies and commodities – now filled the *Endeavour*'s sails. The men on board watched the sun bed the horizon in a hundred ways. They counted constellations from Rio to Cape Horn, Botany Bay (where, according to the artist Sydney Parkinson, *though it was the beginning of winter when we arrived, every thing seemed in perfection*), Batavia, the Cape of Good Hope, and London. It was July 1771 when they relished the exquisite pleasure of return, salt-tongued, fin-eyed, diminished in number. Many men had died, including Parkinson, two other artists, Alexander Buchan and Hermann Sporing, and the astronomer Charles Green. The copy of Diderot – *Les Bijoux indiscrets*, perhaps, or *Le Fils naturel* – that was found on board, unclaimed, its pages harvested by rats, must have belonged to someone who did not make it back. The survivors were mindful of what might have been. But they were also enriched, everyone agreed, by the journey. Rumours that they were bringing an extraordinary collection of natural specimens, new *wonders of the world*, had preceded them, and when they stepped ashore as from the pages of a book, it was the botanists that were celebrated even more than the captain.

The train in which Carla and her narrators travelled would soon reach its destination, and so they hurried the story to its end.

Linnaeus died in 1778. Before his death he had an elm cut down and oversaw his coffin being made from its timber. Solander never returned to Sweden. He never published his findings. Eventually, seven plants, two species of fish and a petrel were named after him. He died in May 1782 of a cerebral haemorrhage. Lisa Stina had died just a few weeks before. After his death a number of unopened letters from his mother were found among his belongings. Some scholars believe that he broke off communications with both

Linnaeus and his mother when he learned, from an undetermined source, that he had always been ineligible to marry Lisa Stina, because Linnaeus was his natural father.

The great visionary Emanuel Swedenborg, who set out to find the soul of creation inside the radiant chink he glimpsed between the material world that was infinitely divisible, and the indivisible spiritual world, had died in London in 1772, and Solander's coffin was placed next to his in London's Swedish Church. In 1816 Swedenborg's skull was stolen, then replaced by a substitute, which was also stolen. It may be surmised that Solander's remains did not stay undisturbed; indeed, before his burial, his skull had already been sawn in half by one of his own good friends, the surgeon John Hunter.

Carla gasped. The train came to a halt. The forward-leaner and the sideways-flinger stood up as one. They gathered their coats and bags and offered to help Carla, who had remained in her seat, with hers. Her hand tightened around the handle of the hatbox, she smiled and thanked them for their wonderful narration. She wished them luck. They bowed. A cleaner who had seen the piles of orange peel told them sharply to get moving so that she could do her job.

When she travelled, Carla carried Nathanaël in her hatbox. The skull also served as a keepsafe for a much darker secret.

Love and Death

When Heinrich arrived in Florence in the late autumn of 1893, it was love at first sight. *Never have I seen so many beautiful things in one place.* His window opened to a view of the river and the old bridge. He was writing in German, speaking Italian and reading mainly French literature, with a strong taste for neo-Romantic, neo-Kantian explorations of the mind: passions, irrationalities, impulses, erotica, dreams and terror. Like D. H. Lawrence's character Aaron Sisson (a few decades later), *the magic of Florence at once overcame him . . . And he felt that here he was in one of the world's living centres . . . a perfect centre of the human world.* Heinrich looked forward to receiving a regular income from his inheritance, 160 marks per month, starting in March 1894, and he intended to travel to Bologna, Venice, Milan, Genoa, Nice, Marseille, Paris and Berlin. For the next twenty years he would keep moving between Italy, France and Germany. Whenever he returned to Munich, his mother cooked buckwheat, specially ordered from a Lübeck grocer, for the porridge Heinrich liked to eat for supper.

From 1895 to 1896 he was editor of a staunchly conservative publication, *Das 20. Jahrhundert* (The Twentieth Century), to which his brother also contributed. One might call it a misguided experiment in the youthful search for identity, for he soon distanced himself from this short but nonetheless embarrassing phase, and claimed he had never believed in the magazine's right-wing Germanic, anti-Semitic premise.

Intermittently in the 1890s, Heinrich and Thomas lived together in Italy. When required to state their profession, they called themselves *giramondi*, globetrotters. While Heinrich immersed himself in the naturalism of Emile Zola's work and savoured the emotional spectrum of the novels of Paul Bourget, Thomas read Schopenhauer and the Russian classics. In the hot summer and autumn of 1897, staying at the Casa Bernardini in Palestrina, they talked about writing a novel together, provisionally called *Decline*, for which Thomas began collecting family history and anecdotes. Throughout his life, circling his origins with a love-hate compulsion, Thomas would return to Lübeck, both in person and in his writing. Perhaps he was trying to compensate for what was lost. He felt the severance from his past, and later from his homeland – his sources – much more deeply than his brother. Years later, when he acquired a painting of young men bathing, titled *Die Quelle* (The Source), by the Expressionist painter Ludwig von Hoffmann, it became one of his most treasured possessions, especially during his years of exile. For Thomas the months with his brother in Italy were just an interlude, and the Italian sky was always much too blue. He returned to Munich, where he inherited some of his parents' furniture; slept in the bed in which he was born; wrote his epic *Buddenbrooks – Decline of a Family*. Meanwhile Heinrich cultivated a Nietzschean state of homelessness and a Dionysian sensibility. For him Italy was a land of wonders, overwhelming, surprising, excessive, where he felt *like the Arabian seafarers of 1001 Nights, who enter a mysteriously deserted city, and whose senses are so much sharpened by this extraordinary experience, that they slow their step at every street corner, in anticipation of what they might encounter.* He became an aficionado of the kind of extravagant, wasteful beauty, *unnütze Schönheit*, that appears in dreams, except that in Italy it was all very real.

In his writing Heinrich wrestled with the ethics of seduction and excess. By 1900 he had published the novel *Im Schlaraffen-land* (The Land of Cockaigne), a social satire that exposed modern greed. The book attracted some attention. But then *Buddenbrooks* was published in 1901, and it was Thomas Mann who reaped fame and prosperity; he would claim that with this book, its literary rendering of the Manns and Lübeck, he had achieved as much for his hometown as his father had done as one of its leading citizens. Suffering nervous exhaustion, presumably made worse by sibling envy, towards the end of 1901 Heinrich went to the sanatorium in Riva, where he picked himself up again by beginning work on *Die Göttinnen* (Goddesses), his trilogy about a woman who re-invents herself, in turn, as Diana in search of freedom, as Minerva pursuing creativity, and as Venus in love. He hoped that with its baroque elaboration, its proto-expressionist *delirium of sexuality, colours, adventures which will take the reader's breath away*, this new work would be a great success.

In those days actresses were responsible for their own wardrobe, and in October 1902, Carla packed her bags, including several hatboxes, said her goodbyes in Munich, and caught a train which took her far from home. Zittau was a manufacturing and mining town in the very south-east of the country, close to the Czech and Polish borders. It was her first engagement; it was understood that she would have to work her way from the cultural margins to the centre. She had been hired to play the sentimental lead. The plays? Lessing, Schiller, Goethe, some Shakespeare, but mostly comedies and melodramas.

At the door of the theatre, she tried to compose herself, looked down at her shoes; they were covered in dust and neatly symmetrical, like the wings of a moth. Her large hat cast a circular shadow, in which she stood as if trapped in an arena. With her eyes fixed on her distant, dusty shoes, she felt vertiginous. Keep moving, she told herself and took a deep breath. Someone opened the door. And trembling slightly, she stepped across the threshold.

She sought the limelight; she thrilled easily to new challenges and was always well rehearsed. Fired by the conviction of her own emotions, this is how Heinrich pictured her on stage, *the upper part of her body thrown back and arms stretched out in front, delivering her intoxicating lines.* Carla soared as high as she knew she would then fall low. Did she laugh like a heroine from fiction, *a rich wanton laugh*, especially in the boisterous atmosphere after a show, when *the champagne frothed over the rim of her delicate glass and onto the rings on her fingers*? When Zittau gossip reached her ears, she heard it said that she'd been fooling round, and that she drank champagne even at breakfast time.

Travel, new relationships and careers separated the family. Nonetheless, their paths often crossed. They visited their mother in Polling, in Bavaria, where she now lived with her youngest son Viktor. Or spent the summers together in the mountains. The brothers also met more frequently at the sanatorium in Riva. Heinrich published *Die Göttinnen* in 1903, its intensity influenced, he claimed, by Flaubert's *strong, sculptural style* and Stendhal's *tear-away passion*. That same year Thomas brought out a volume of stories which included one of his best, the autobiographical *Tonio Kröger*. As their publications increased, the brothers' habit of discussing their latest projects gave rise to tensions about ownership. Heinrich, for example, believed a substantial share of *Buddenbrooks* had come from him. He thought that if they had gone ahead to work jointly on the project, it might have been a strange book, but one in which their father would have recognised his *house*; on the other hand, he later conceded that no one but Thomas could have written it. Questions of sameness and difference – a kind of mimetic anxiety – surfaced throughout Thomas Mann's life, as much an aspect of his craft, as it was inherent to his relationship with his brother. Rowing together on Lake Garda, with their competitive instincts aroused, Thomas accused Heinrich of stealing a number of his words and phrases.

A lively correspondence flourished between Heinrich and Carla, which he would say later, was one of his very greatest enjoyments. As she described for him the world of the theatre and her adventures, he freely transcribed her life into literature. His novel *Die Jagd nach Liebe* (The Hunt for Love) was completed in the summer of 1903, based on Carla's letters from Zittau. Reading the book, she instantly recognised herself in the protagonist Ute Ende, a hard-working actress who was neither especially talented nor successful, with a skull that kept her company in an attic room high above the town. In perfect register with Carla's image of herself, *Ute seems to set great store by all that's pathological*, she wrote to Heinrich. *I'm not fundamentally lacking character; however, something seems to be constitutionally not quite right. People who, with all their might, resist being swallowed up by sadness or misfortune, seem strange to me. Those who simply collapse, mentally and physically, are the only ones I can play. And of course those who are thoroughly hysterical, or indisputably sick. The same applies to Ute, doesn't it?*

Here was a *Doppelgängerin* for her collection, all ice and fire, created from the original by her brother. And in the novel he portrayed himself as Claude; Ute and Claude were like brother and sister; their relationship was sexually charged. If one reads significance into names chosen by authors for their characters, Claude is *un homme claudicant*, a man impaired, or deterred, by a *Liebesverbot*, a taboo. Heinrich Mann had described the hunt for love as a primal quest linked to an ancient dilemma. How does one love one's female self? One's sister?

We might ask: as Goethe loved Cornelia, Heine loved Charlotte, Flaubert loved Caroline? As Edvard Munch loved his sister Sophie? And Robert Musil could only imagine that he might have loved his sister Elsa? To the death, the end, *das Ende*? Musil sometimes wondered what it would have been like if Elsa, who died in infancy before he was born, had lived; whether she would have been the person closest to him; or what if he had died instead? In his story 'Typhus' (1887), Chekhov wrote about the same conundrum, about a young lieutenant who survives a fever, only to find that while he was sick, his sister had caught the disease from him and died.

It was windy outside. A door swung on its hinges. The old man looked up and down the stairwell of their house in Lübeck until it faded from view. In his chair in a room in a house in California he sobbed with grief. Oh, the empty stairs. Orpheus descending to fetch Eurydice. Returning alone. The sacrifice! Oedipus dragging one leg behind, limping down a corridor, opening a window, smashing a vessel. Pandora's *pithos*, the honey vase they said was full of demons. The breaking sound. Picking up the pieces one by one. Tolstoy's Oblonsky dreaming of glass tables that sang and *some little decanters that were women*.

Carla admired Heinrich's work. She had no problems with its risky content nor with its montage structure, its breathless pace. A few years later she told him, *your books are absolutely dense with people and experiences that I recognise. I don't think there's another writer anywhere who incorporates into his work his sketches from life as much as you.* But if *The Hunt for Love* was intended as an allegory, this was not how it was received. Most people read it literally. One critic likened it to a brothel. Worse still, the book deeply offended his family. His mother was upset about the revelation of the heroine's – her daughter Carla's – indignities. Thomas, asserting his own literary identity by putting his brother's work in question, wrote to tell Heinrich that he thought the novel was morally and spiritually corrupt. It was also taken as a *roman à clef* that targeted Munich high society, particularly the set frequented by his sister Lula, who had married Dr Joseph Löhr, fifteen years older and the director of a bank. Full of self-reproach, Heinrich made a note on the back of his brother's letter, that the portraits of Carla and himself were indeed too depraved, and concluded that he might as well give up writing altogether.

In 1903 Thomas also had portrayed Carla, in a story drawing on Ovid's Daphne and Apollo, called 'The Wardrobe'. He describes his sister's radiance, her long hair, dark eyes, and her mannerisms, how she liked to sit with one leg pulled up, her slim arms slung around it in an embrace; he notes how her skin shone as it stretched across her knee. His heroine appears ghostlike through the doors of a wardrobe. She looks at the narrator but does not see him, *ohne Ausdruck, unergründlich und stumm*, without expression, beyond reach and silent. Like all those who are cursed with exile, she has stories to tell. But the listener misinterprets their appeal. He experiences them as manifestations of his own sexual desire. He touches her. The magic dissolves. The woman disappears. And each time she returns, she must first find her voice again, and painfully regain the ability to speak. Her narratives always end in tragedy.

In March 1904 Carla, who was working at the theatre in Düsseldorf, confessed to Heinrich that in recent times she'd had experiences she'd rather forget. She'd thought of going far away, to Russia. *I really don't like thinking about my future. I will let it come crashing down on me and will try to bear it as best I can.* But then she'd met a man called Alfred Flechtheim. Born in 1878 in Münster, he was the son of a wealthy grain and fodder merchant and was expected to follow in the family business. He had other ideas. On trips to

Paris he came across Cubist and Expressionist works of art, which he began to collect. At first he stored the paintings in his parents' basement, where his mother turned the Picassos and Braques towards the wall, in case they frightened the maid. When Carla met Alfred he was a young man not yet independent of his family's grip. The story of this relationship provided Heinrich with material for a novella in 1906 and a play in 1911, both called *Schauspielerin* (Actress).

A grey ostrich feather on a large Parisian hat complemented Carla's white coat and white lace shawl. Looking past the rim of her hat, she saw standing before her *a young man, tall and dark-haired, slim-featured, olive-complexioned, self-possessed, with a long, accentuated nose.* (In profile he bore an uncanny resemblance to Fra Bartolomeo's portrait of Savonarola, of which her brother Thomas was so fond.) They were introduced to each other. *He leaned slightly forward, towards her, and seemed to resume an intimate conversation with her, as if they had just been briefly interrupted.* The men she found attractive, and to whom she in turn appealed the most, were always Jewish. Alfred, she called him Fred, claimed to be the great-nephew of her favourite poet Heinrich Heine.

Carla was very proud of her beautiful hands; she polished her nails with a small square of *chamois* leather. Alfred told her she had the hands of a madonna. They discussed Oscar Wilde, Jakob Wassermann, Heinrich and Thomas Mann, immersed themselves in literature, religion, ethics, poetry. They drank champagne. He smoked cigars. He loved the language of her eyelids, the stray strands of hair that played around her face, and when she brushed her hair right back, he said *I see the faces of your brothers.*

He often went to Brussels, to the stock exchange. *The same evening he'd be back in his room – with its black silk wallpaper and light-coloured furniture – reading. He was always reading, and liked to quote from books.* Carla listened, *her chin resting on two fingers, her lips slightly parted.* He never yielded to her charms entirely, believed sex was primitive; he wished to transcend it; their friendship would thus be of a higher order, Platonic, uncorrupted. And yet the space between them sparked with possibilities. *Chandeliers, and the candles on the table, sent out strangely shimmering waves of light; she had the impression that the flowers bending outwards from the vase gazed into the mirrored surface of the cutlery as if into the clearest of pools. She ate little, and without awareness; taking his words as delicacies instead.*

In a black lace dress, the one he said showed off her fair-haired beauty to its best advantage, she received his last-minute telegrams, always with apologies for unavoidable absences. She sat alone by lamplight, reading his favourite books. Was it aesthetics or something else, she wondered, that formed his views on love? Would this become merely another link in her chain of dangerous liaisons? (*Schlimme Liebschaften*, Choderlos de Laclos's *Les Liaisons dangereuses*, was translated into German by Heinrich Mann the following year.) There was an outdoor festival, where her friends told her they'd seen Flechtheim with another woman. Carla was pouring champagne at the time. It overflowed. When they pointed out a couple in the distance, she laughed; it wasn't Fred after all. But she had surprised herself with a sharp pang of jealousy and realised that she loved him, that she was deeply in love.

Love is a place, Freud suggested, where *a considerable amount of narcissistic libido overflows on to the object . . .* where *the ego becomes more and more unassuming and modest, and the object more and more sublime and precious . . . until . . . the object has, so to speak, consumed the ego. Traits of humility . . . and of self-injury occur in every case of being in love.*

How thin you are! said her friends and family. How pale! Time was configured with the exquisite pleasures of desire and the pain of attenuation. It was like love, and it was mutual. *They both suffered springtime like a sickness. The flowers she had worn pinned at her breast in the evening still pursued him with their scent the next day.* Every move, every whisper became tinged with expectation. Each withdrawing was like a needle-stitch of death.

At night she couldn't sleep. *She paced the rooms, her arms pressed tightly in a self-embrace . . . and she undressed in the dark, that the mirror would not reflect her scorned limbs, which she lowered into bed, heavy, useless, miserable, as though she was casting them away.* If only I'd be offered more challenging roles in the theatre, she thought, if only someone came along to pluck me out of this despair. At the end of April 1904 Carla wrote to Heinrich that she needed a person to hold on to her in the event that she took a few steps too close to the banks of the river Rhine. If only Alfred were strong enough to stand up to his father's ban on marriage to someone outside the Jewish faith. None of these wishes were granted, and one unhappy night, fraught with bad thoughts, Carla knew she had to leave. It was a moment of clarity, the kind that cuts through murky heartache with a single ray. Some people will torture you to death with their selfish sensibilities, she thought, and by the summer she had left Alfred and Düsseldorf, to make a new start in another town. But the affair had left its mark.

In *Actress*, the novella based on Carla's experiences, Heinrich once again addressed the idea of forbidden love. Flechtheim is the protagonist Harry Rothaus, a name-change that stressed *Flechte* (in the sense of an eruption of the skin) as *Rot*, a redness, an irritation; and the suffix *-heim* (home) became the less cosy *-haus* (house). There is also something of Heinrich in the character of Harry. The work continued his brother-sister dialogue and his hunt for love. Carla told him that if the book was successful, her misery in Düsseldorf would have been worthwhile.

After short appearances in Kassel and Reichenberg, Carla's

next long engagement, for the winter season 1904–1905, was in Königshütte, a small town in Upper Silesia, where the air was full of coal dust and sometimes it was so cold that the actors had to perform in fur coats and boots. In October 1904 Thomas was engaged to Katia Pringsheim, and in early December Carla wrote to Heinrich that she would not be attending their brother's wedding because she had not been invited, *except by Mama, which doesn't really count*. She also mentioned that since she did not have rehearsals that day, she had been to synagogue; that she'd like to learn Hebrew, and perhaps he could find a rabbi to give her lessons when she came to Riva in the summer. Jakob Wassermann was now her favourite author and she'd read everything he'd written. Thomas and Katia were married in February 1905, and neither Carla nor Heinrich attended the wedding.

Early in 1905 in Florence, Heinrich met and fell in love with Inés (Nena) Schmied. Born in 1883 in Buenos Aires, she resembled his mother in that she was of South American and German descent. She was training to be a singer, but also hoped to become an actress. He thought that the circumstance of meeting at the right moment was Everything and that Everything was strange and fateful. *So now I'm also someone who can happily think of love! I remember too well how I'd always believed that for me an intimate relationship with a woman was impossible.* This was a productive year for Heinrich. He published a book of essays, another of stories, and the novel *Professor Unrat*, filmed much later, in 1930, to international acclaim as *Der Blaue Engel*, The Blue Angel. As if foreshadowing Marlene Dietrich's famous role as Lola Lola, Inés told him that she wanted to play the lead when *Professor Unrat* was adapted for the stage. He began work on another novel, *Zwischen den Rassen* (Mixed Blood), an attempt, he confessed, to translate himself into the feminine.

He told Inés that everything about her enchanted him, he only had to say her name to feel euphoric, he memorised her letters, fanned himself with her fan, which *has kept some of the scent of your perfume*.

Carla visited Heinrich in Florence at the end of April 1905. I imagine that they strolled through markets, gardens, churches and museums, and inspired by the vitality of Florentine street life and statuary, Michelangelo's *Dawn*, Donatello's *Bacchus*, or caught in a misty spray from cherubic fountains in the Boboli, they discussed the aesthetic ambiguities of flesh and stone, and the future. He said that his sense of homelessness made him a writer. She said her home was the stage.

They watched the river from its banks, and from the open *loggia* of the Ponte Vecchio, where they stopped at stalls, inspected pieces of coral, turquoise and gold jewellery; they bargained, purchasing a delicately carved cameo of two joined hands. They walked up the Via del Monte alle Croci, up the wide stone steps ending at the terrace of the church of San Miniato, and when they arrived, puffed and hot, bells rang, lifting their spirits even higher than their breezy hilltop destination. Opposite were rocks, woods, villages, villas. They saw the road leading to Fiesole where unforgettably, years ago he had first heard a barrel organ play the melody from Puccini's *La Bohème*. Their view swept across a terracotta sea of roofs to the Duomo, the tower of the Signoria, San Lorenzo; he pointed out the landmarks, the winding Arno with its bridges, the broad plain, the distant *mezzaluna* of the Apennines. Near and far were vineyards, olive groves and the long black brushstrokes of cypresses rising from their shadows.

The geometric green and white marble facings of San Miniato al Monte, the Romanesque church some think the finest of its kind in all of Italy, intrigue the eye, teaching it to make connections: exterior to interior, body to spirit, frame to passage, the alternation of blind and seeing arches, the building's intricate game of openness and closure. They attached themselves to a guided tour. Miniato, they heard, was a rich Armenian merchant prince, who served in the Roman army, was denounced as a Christian and subjected to a series of tortures, all of which he miraculously survived. On the gallows, as protection against the weapons hurled and shot at him, an angel clothed Miniato in a cloak of brilliant light. When he was decapitated, legend has it that he picked up his head and reattached it to his body. He died a martyr in a cave nearby. The church bears his relics and his name. The tour moved on. The guide took up position at the end of the nave, where on the left, he pointed, there is a chapel that contains the tomb of an especially virtuous and celibate cardinal about whom it was said – Carla listened attentively all the while to Heinrich's translation – that he lived in the flesh as if he were free of it. That is no small achievement! she commented. Which he translated for the group, and their laughter was all the louder for its echoes. The view from San Miniato is at its very best at dusk, when with a lingering passion the river holds the sun's reflection. Before returning to the city, they visited the nearby cemetery, where they found the grave of Carlo Lorenzini (called Il Collodi), the inventor of Pinocchio, the puppet boy who was a famous liar.

After dark they joined the life of the tavernas and piazzas. One evening they were invited to a masquerade. The weather had turned cold, and well wrapped up against the wind, they arrived at a candlelit villa. Was it Heinrich who lifted her hooded cloak from her shoulders, speechless to see Carla dressed as Anna Karenina in a black-velvet gown trimmed with lace, pansies in her hair and pearls around her neck? Did she say laughingly she would dance with every officer of the local regiment, but would save the last dance for him?

Tensions arose when Heinrich introduced Carla to Inés. Around the end of May, brother and sister left for Riva. Inés stayed in Florence; for a few days in July, she met Heinrich secretly in Abetone. In August, Inés asked him to send her Plato's *Symposium* and Burkhardt's history of the Renaissance. She was living in Fiesole, where she loved to go for long walks alone. This was frowned on by the locals. *Now I don't know where I can go anymore and it makes me very sad. It's really too stupid being a woman . . . at times deep down I feel like a man in disguise. Uncomfortable.* She also mentioned her frustration, that while she spoke many languages, she could not express herself well enough in any one of them. When the question of her career came up, Heinrich tried to encourage her. *The songs, Nena, that you have inside you, will be sung.* He told her that he was pleased that she was such a good singer, and not a *Literatin*, a woman who pursued literature, as that was a type he abhorred. She replied that she was very sorry he did not like women writers, since it was her greatest wish to be one; she thought that perhaps she'd misunderstood what he meant by the term *Literatin*.

In September, Carla began work at the theatre in Flensburg, another border town, this time in the very north of the country, near Denmark. She rented rooms in the house of a butcher called Ipsen. Among a great many parts, she played Jessica in *The Merchant of Venice*, the lead role in Lessing's *Emilia Galotti*, Louise in Schiller's *Kabale und Liebe*, Faust's Gretchen, and Othello's Desdemona. The reviews were mixed. A critic thought that as Gretchen she was only convincing in the mad scene. As Emilia, especially at the tragic self-destructive end, one critic praised her great success, while another thought otherwise. Carla suffered from headaches and throat infections. Her last performance on the Flensburg stage was in April 1906. Until mid-May, there was a short engagement in Nürnberg, where she had a silent part as a prostitute in Frank Wedekind's *Totentanz* (Dance of Death). She made a pilgrimage to Fürth and Zirndorf, places associated with the life and work of Jakob Wassermann.

Heinrich loved forests, altitude, fresh air and hiking. He spent much of the summer with Inés and her mother at the Jungborn sanatorium in the Harz mountains, where the earth was thought to contain healing properties. He wrote his sister that he was eating mainly fruit and she replied, *I hope Jungborn or whatever it's called does you good. Lying on the ground in the rain might be beneficial, but I wouldn't be sure of that, and it can't be good for everyone. If you catch a cold, you must stop.* Carla, Heinrich, Thomas, his wife, Katia, and their baby daughter, Erika (born November 1905), then spent the late summer together in Oberammergau in the Bavarian Alps.

In August 1906, Inés again wrote that she envied men their freedom and mobility. *I often feel as if I'm stuck in a snail shell.* This notion kept surfacing. During a brief visit to Berlin in September, her room seemed like a cage. She harboured a great desire just to stroll aimlessly through the city. *Impossible!!!* Because before she went anywhere, she had to make herself presentable, though truly she was happiest when she paid no attention to her looks. *If I were a man I think I'd always walk around with my hands in my pockets, whistling. Why can't I be a man?* She told Heinrich that she was very conscious that he wanted her to behave like a lady, and asked if, in this respect, he was aware how much he was expecting of her, since to be a lady meant that one needed a stylish coiffure, whereas she preferred to fix her hair absentmindedly while she read philosophy. Later that month, it's not known if for medical or cosmetic reasons, she had an operation on her nose. Inés Schmied to Heinrich Mann, 17 September 1906: *You know, I have a great fear of life, of life itself, do you understand?*

Periodically Heinrich suffered from asthma, for which he took homeopathic medicine; he only felt well while he was writing; was fearful of the idea of aging; in the autumn of 1906 he was again sick from nervous exhaustion. He travelled continuously, often for his health; to Berlin and Bremen in November 1906, Munich in December, Riva in April 1907, Bavaria in June, Riva again in

September, Milan in October, Munich and Berlin and Königsberg in November. He had begun work on *Die kleine Stadt* (The Small Town), a novel about music, passion and power, set in Italy. Published in 1909, it was a commercial failure; but it would always be his favourite book.

Inés returned to Buenos Aires for over a year. There are photos of her in the jungle during an expedition to the Rio Confuso. In June 1907 she wrote to Heinrich that she had to tell him the truth. *I'm not much of a bourgeois young woman. My need for independence keeps growing stronger.* Four months later she told him that she loved him as much as ever, but that she was still too restless to get married and needed to be alone: *let me go.* Heinrich received a letter from her father to say Inés had shed a few tears and was convinced she could not get married, that she first had to achieve something, and that she had written a play; and then another letter urging marriage and asking Heinrich to discourage her from pursuing a stage career; her father thought her voice lacked strength. He advised his daughter that she should marry the excellent Dr Enrique Mann as soon as possible; if she did not, she would probably live to regret it.

Heinrich spent that summer as the only guest at an inn at the foot of Monte Grappa. There was a rose bower in the garden where he ate polenta and looked out at a blue sky, a deep, Venetian blue, such as he thought he would never see again.

From 1906 to 1907 Carla worked in Göttingen. Sometimes she had excellent reviews. But one rather venomous critic described her as *a young actress who spent her bored existence lying around on chaises longues, waiting with heroic desire for a millionaire to appear, while she manicured her exquisite hands.* It was noted that in the course of a performance Carla's wig had slipped without her being in the least aware of it, thus undermining the play's climax. In *Die Jagd nach Liebe*, Ute calls the audience an apocalyptic beast and says if she does not become a great and famous actress, things will end badly; she aims to work in Berlin; she tests the power of her voice on mountaintops and against the crash of thunder. Now Carla told Heinrich, *I still want to do serious work and achieve something great.* To study one of her parts more closely, she visited a mental asylum; there she was deeply affected by an inmate, an old woman who worried about where she was going to live when the world ended. From May to September 1907 Carla worked in Metz.

Heinrich announced his wedding plans, for June 1908, to his family. His mother called him a peculiar fellow, when she heard he and Inés had already been engaged for eighteen months. *So your fiancée sings?* Thomas responded. *In public? Then you'll be leading an itinerant existence? I'm not sure if I should wish that upon you!* Thomas and Katia, Heinrich and Inés, as well as Carla, holidayed together in Venice. Carla was in high spirits. Someone had brought a copy of Wassermann's *Caspar Hauser* and they took turns reading it. But Inés was unhappy; she found Thomas, especially, to be cold and indifferent; when she borrowed a book by Fontane, he asked for it back before she'd finished. Did she complain to Heinrich that the atmosphere was oppressive, even a little creepy; did Carla enter the room, overhearing, and explain that it was Tommy's *northern soul . . . das Nördliche*, quoting *Effi Briest*? And while Thomas spent the time writing, perhaps already preoccupied with the feverish ideas that later became *Death in Venice*, did his brother make a grim discovery? Maybe Carla had placed the skull Nathanaël on the windowsill, looking out, and some guests passing below saw it and complained to the hotel's manager. Carla had gone for a stroll, white coat, white boots, white lace parasol, and Heinrich had let himself into her room to remove the offender. And inside its cavity he found a small package tied all around with string. When he asked her about it – a private moment in the lobby, while the others had not yet come down for dinner – she replied mischievously that it contained her life savings, and tried to divert him with a little lecture on the age-old use of crania . . . painted, gilded, drilled, as relics, trophies, warnings. But he insisted that she must tell him more. What was in the parcel? Enough cyanide to flatten an entire regiment, she confessed. Had she really requested it from Flechtheim as a parting gift? Her brother was shocked. She assured him she had kept the poison in its wrapping since she received it, explaining, that simply to possess it sharpens the mind. Did she mimic the maiden from Lübeck's Dance of Death, one arm circled up, the other down, making an S, saying that it kept you on your toes? Heinrich had to take her at her word.

The marriage was postponed. Heinrich and Inés spent the summer apart. He went to Riva. Perhaps in response to his hopes for a good income from the novel he said he had to finish it before their wedding, she reassured him that *Die kleine Stadt* would be extraordinary. She asked him to send her a copy of *Caspar Hauser*, which she did not get to read in Venice; told him that all she was suffering from was a cold, not to keep bothering her with homeopathic remedies and not to believe everything Dr von Hartungen said. She looked forward to seeing him, although she dreaded being persuaded to take all sorts of cures. By late 1908, and the beginning of 1909, there was unease. It seems that Heinrich opposed her wanting to become an actress. She told him that she'd never love anyone as she loved him, but his relatives were right to think that she was not the marrying type; she was terrified by the idea of family life. There was one last attempt to save the relationship, when they all met at Thomas and Katia's summerhouse at Bad Tölz; but Thomas kept his face averted when he spoke with Inés and his tone was disdainful; for her it was a nightmare. In December 1909 Inés wrote to Heinrich, *You must understand that you were born in North Germany and I in South America. How is that supposed to work?* She said she'd like to remain friends.

After her disappointment with Flechtheim, Carla was involved with a fellow actor called Leo Landau, the son of a Galician rabbi. *Why do I always end up in these adventures? I hardly recognise myself. I'm really crazy.* There may have been other affairs; not much is known. For three seasons from September to April in 1907–1908, 1908–1909, 1909–1910, she lived and worked in Mulhouse in Alsace, where she thought she was *la femme la plus jolie, la plus chic et la plus gracieuse*. She had fallen in love with a man called Arthur Gibo. For him she toned down her style of dress and adopted polite mannerisms. Sweetly, she accompanied him on the piano, while he played the violin. For his health she bought nicotine-free cigarettes. In a letter to Heinrich, she described the suicide attempt of another actress, who had tried to strangle herself with her own long hair.

When the relationship became more serious, the Gibo family moaned. Not a daughter-in-law who's an actress! They not only rejected her, but actively conspired against her. Carla and Arthur were engaged against his parents' wishes. They threatened to disinherit him. He proved too weak to withstand the pressure. Rumours circulated, accusing Carla of an affair with someone else, followed by denials, proof, confession, tears.

Her fiancé wavered. They parted, made up, and parted again. Arthur was exhausted, said he no longer knew what to think or do, told her not to be surprised if he took a little cyanide: *I see nothing but the end – la fin, das Ende – to end everything, death.* She was broken, cried for hours at a time, and even then she clung vehemently to the demands of this most difficult role she had invented for herself. She now held up her own faithfulness as a personal doctrine, reasoning that even if he failed her completely, if he abandoned her, it could only fortify her love. Carla had entered a battle she was not prepared to lose.

Like some of the heroines of the books she'd read, and none the wiser, she became ensnared by the clinging fabric of her own reasoning, and desperately sought relief from this self-made stranglehold. To prove the strength of her conviction, she planned to score one more point, on the assumption that nobody doubts a person who is dead. She travelled to Polling, where her mother lived.

Cyanide is most effective on an empty stomach. Carla would have skipped breakfast; locked the window and the door of her room; removed the tiny parcel from inside the skull. It was the height of summer. She may have heard her mother talking with a neighbour or the song of a bird; rocked herself, with the momentum of someone who dreams of death; picked up the cup to wash down the poison as it burned her mouth and throat; let herself go.

Heinrich was spending the summer in the Tyrolean Alps. One morning, it was the last day of July, just as he was setting out to walk, he heard a woman's voice calling him by his first name, which in these parts nobody would have known . . . Luiz, Luiz . . . insistently at first, and then receding, as if a gust of wind had brought the voice and a light breeze was taking it away. He answered as he turned around, but saw no one and continued on his walk, disturbed.

Carla died at their mother's home, on Saturday 30 July 1910. A telegram was sent just before seven o'clock the next morning. It reached Heinrich when he returned from his walk. It read: *Please tell Mann, carefully, that Carla has had an accident and he should come.* Heinrich believed she had called to him from a fracture between life and death.

After Carla's death the family found that her possessions were few: books, a distinctly elegant but not extravagant wardrobe, some jewellery, a journal of twenty notebooks, a hatbox containing the skull, and some bits and pieces, handbags, hairbrush, make-up, handkerchiefs. Did she perhaps, with a cynical dash of wit, also keep her letters in an old biscuit tin, like Emma Bovary's faithless lover? For Arthur she left a note saying she loved him, that she had betrayed him only once, but she loved him all the same; on the envelope her mother noted that these were *my dear child's last written words*.

The night before her funeral she was dressed in white lace, and Ophelia-like, there were flowers in her long fair hair; petals, leaves and tresses, intertwined; a sprig (of Aphrodite's myrtle?) in her hands.

Heinrich kept a vigil. His torment was grafted on the words he'd been reading in her letters and diaries all day. He fell into an uneasy sleep where he saw her, *in a transport of heroism which made her almost gay, she ran down the hill and across the cow-plank, hurried along the path, up the lane, through the market-place, and arrived in front of the chemist shop*. Snow began to fall, and horse-drawn sleighs pulled up. More women emerged, crowned with myrtle, dressed in white, their faces veiled by crystals clinging lacelike to their features. They walked barefoot in the snow. Wedekind's Lulu, Heine's Mephistophela, death-maidens, *femmes fragiles*, exiles. All the women who were his sister joined hands and led a *danse macabre* down the hill. It was a very steep descent. Suddenly they halted. They gazed up at the black windows of the chemist shop. A bell rang. And he knew they could not be saved. His nostrils filled with the cyanide scent of bitter almonds.

The old man was drenched in sweat and tears. Had he dreamed of the death walk, the eternal wandering to which the souls of suicides are said to be condemned? Such rubbish! Superstition! Angrily he shook these clawing notions from his brain, took up his pencil, turned the page.

In his memoir, decades later, Heinrich wrote about *the actress* who had once been and would always remain his soul mate. He saw her *unfold* before his eyes, as if she were still alive, every part of her, arms, legs, neck, the sound of her voice, the expressions of her face, and how she'd once said to him that he, in his writing, created characters, but that in her case, she was her own creation.

When Carla died, Thomas could not stop crying. He was hurt. Didn't she know that *all the heroism lies in enduring, in willing to live on and not die*. He regarded Carla's suicide as a selfish act that betrayed their family's solidarity. It loosened the bond. What would happen to them now? He was afraid that they would drift apart. Like his sister Lula, he fretted that the manner of Carla's death might tarnish the family's social standing. It seems as if this fear overshadowed their grief. But Lula must have mourned her sister's death, which added greatly to her own burdens: an unhappy marriage, drugs, affairs, all hidden behind a respectable façade. Was she a reader too? Did *the heroines of the books she had read, and that lyrical legion of adulteresses . . . sing in her memory with sisterly voices that enchanted her?* She took her own life, seventeen years later. Did she, like Effi Briest, dream of a red glow? Did she, like Emma Bovary, look into the mirror to farewell herself?

Their mother's pain had no end. And yet she understood her youngest daughter's act. For the gravestone inscription she chose lines from Mörike that she had come across in one of Carla's notebooks: about death as an ethereal transformation, where pain and passion and the darkest melancholies are dissolved in an omniscient light.

The death notice referred to *our dear daughter, sister, sister-in-law and bride*, and included the *bridegroom* Arthur Gibo in the list of mourners; the funeral on Tuesday 2 August 1910 was attended by a small group of family and friends. When her possessions were distributed, who offered to take Nathanaël? One day Heinrich received a small parcel from his mother. It contained a square of chamois and a note: *she used this for her manicure.* Carla's notebooks have disappeared.

———

In August 1910 Sigmund Freud met Gustav Mahler in Leiden. They discussed Mahler's marital problems, caused by the fact that his wife, Alma, was also a composer and that he had forbidden her to work. Freud diagnosed unresolved oedipal issues.

That year, the relationship between Heinrich and Thomas worsened. It was also the year when Alfred Flechtheim got married; he promptly spent most of his wife's substantial dowry on paintings and sculptures, and went on to become one of the early twentieth century's most influential art dealers. While Carla had not made it to the Berlin stage as an actress, Heinrich Mann's play based on her life, *Schauspielerin*, premiered there on 6 November 1911, with Tilla Durieux in the lead role.

Heinrich broke off contact with Inés Schmied, or she with him. She went to Berlin to study acting. She never married. In 1912 she gave birth to a daughter; lived in Munich in the 1920s, and from the 1930s, in Ascona, Switzerland. Inés died in 1976 in a hospital near Lago Maggiore, aged 92.

For Thomas, *after a succession of cold, wet weeks a premature high summer had set in.* On his walks near his home in Munich, he often passed the cemetery, where he discovered *the face of death*, with its *air of imperious survey.* He was increasingly confident that he was on the right track as a writer and like his hero Gustav Aschenbach, experienced *an extraordinary expansion of the inner self,* which in turn expressed itself as *a youthful craving for far-off places . . . It was simply a desire to travel; but it had presented itself as nothing less than a . . . hallucinatory force.* Towards the end of May 1911 he was in Venice; the novella *Tod in Venedig* (*Death in Venice*) was published in 1913, to phenomenal success.

In February 1913 Franz Kafka was correcting *The Trial*. An important process, he thought, because *the story is like a real birth that issued from my body covered in dirt and slime*, and so it was up to him to clean it up.

Heinrich continued to live in Italy, France and Germany. Social insights and radical questions now became more emphatic in his work. Essays such as 'Geist und Tat' (Thought and Deed), published in 1911, warned readers that without democracy, people would seek salvation from their leaders, would believe in supermen, while their own development remained dangerously stunted.

From 1911 to 1913, Heinrich was involved with a married woman, Edith Kann, a relationship that inspired the play *Die grosse Liebe* (Great Love; again with Tilla Durieux), and during the rehearsals he met another actress, Prague-born Maria (Mimi) Kanová. His friend, the writer and publisher Wilhelm Herzog, has pointed out that in the essay 'Flaubert's Monologue', written around this time, Heinrich has Flaubert express his own despair: how was it that in his forties he was still unattached and lonely? Heinrich told Mimi that until now everything had broken in his hands, he needed someone who was patient with him, and hoped she would be the one.

Visiting Goethe's house in Weimar one summer night in 1912, Franz Kafka experienced a rush of recognition in the present moment from everything he'd read about the place in the past, as if the poet were still alive. This was instantly contradicted by the darkness of the windows and the empty rooms. He went on to spend time at the Jungborn sanatorium in the Harz mountains (where Heinrich had stayed and about which Carla had been so sceptical). Kafka felt a bit queasy at the sight of so many naked bodies lying in the grass, strolling with umbrellas, riding on hay carts, climbing up ladders to pick cherries with little baskets on their arms; old men without a stitch of clothing, jumping over bales, or racing across the meadow in the rain, like wild beasts. A naked nobleman told him he was composing an important piece called *For My Sword*; Kafka noted that out of respect for the man's social status he did not dare to look at him since neither of them was wearing any clothes. One wonders what he was looking at instead, feet perhaps, he'd always liked feet. It was a strange place, where people did breathing exercises to straighten crooked toes, and gymnastics to increase the size of their penises. On his return to his hut one night – everyone lived in healthy timber huts – he found a glass of water under the table, sandals behind the mirror, a chamber-pot on top of the cupboard, and most disconcertingly, Flaubert's *Education Sentimentale* inside the pillowcase, a wet face-cloth and an ink bottle in the bed.

In November 1913, Kafka wrote that he deliberately went to red-light districts because he was excited by the mere act of walking past prostitutes, and by the distant but nonetheless real possibility of choosing one. The hunt for love. In *A Berlin Chronicle* (1932), Walter Benjamin remembered how *whole networks of streets were opened up under the auspices of prostitution*, leading to *an obstinate and voluptuous hovering on the brink . . . beyond this frontier lies nothingness*. Kafka had torn off the glove of his fiancée, Felice Bauer, to kiss her hand; a few months later, by July 1914, the engagement was broken off. That month, with Europe on the verge of war, he travelled to Lübeck, where he stayed in a hotel run by a dwarf, with cluttered walls and dirty linen; followed by a day in Travemünde; he walked barefoot on the beach and suspected people thought this was indecent; then on to Marienlyst, with his friends Ernst Weiss and Johanna Bleschke (she would change her name to Rahel Sanzara and become an actress and a writer), who were always bickering. In *The Eyewitness*, a novel about the war which he started while they were on holiday, Weiss would write that *at one blow there was no longer a Europe. Boundaries were sealed, and blood flowed all over – in the North, in the East, in the South, in the West.*

Heinrich and Mimi married in August 1914 and settled in Munich. Like Carla she loved hats; like Inés she was not really accepted by the rest of his family; like Katia she was Jewish, though from a very different milieu. At first Heinrich helped her get parts in the theatre, but she soon gave up acting, to concentrate on housekeeping and typing up her husband's manuscripts. Heinrich was diagnosed with a weak heart and did not have to serve in the army. Their daughter was born in 1916, named Carla Maria Henriette Leonie Mann, and called Goschi for short. A proud father, Heinrich was frequently seen walking, or stopping at cafés, with Goschi in her pram. Their circle of friends in Munich included Frank Wedekind, Erich Mühsam, Lion Feuchtwanger. And Wilhelm Herzog, who described Heinrich Mann at age forty-five, looking like a nobleman from an El Greco canvas, with his long, narrow face, heavy eyelids, dark-blond goatee, in his bearing rather unapproachable, like a distinguished diplomat.

Mühsam noted that on 20 September 1914, he'd been at the Torggelstube, a wine bar, where everyone was ecstatic over the victory against the Russians at Tannenberg. Except for Heinrich Mann, who asked, *What's the use of victories? Winning and losing are just concepts. How can a country win if it is hated by the rest of the world?* Mühsam, who visited the Manns for coffee in November and found Heinrich's anti-war rage undiminished, was very poor. His father had sent him a parcel containing his bar mitzvah presents: gold cufflinks, a kitschy tie clip, some old silver coins, and had included a box of cigars and a sausage, and from his siblings cigarillos, woollen gloves, gingerbread, chocolate and cigar scissors. Some of these items he would share with friends, the rest he'd try to sell in order to have enough money to live for about a month. His father died on 20 July 1915, and Mühsam returned to Lübeck for the funeral, only to find that the old tyrant had made his will conditional: his son was to return to work as a pharmacist or marry a Jewish woman; otherwise he would have to wait for his inheritance until he turned sixty. *What child has not had reason to weep over its parents?* Nietzsche's Zarathustra asked.

Thomas (also exempted from active service) defended the Reich. He believed the war was an expression of national honour. Upholding the ideal of Frederick the Great, he wrote newspaper articles about the heroic potential of Germany's militarism.

Heinrich was appalled, both by the nation's and his brother's delirium. He stood out against it, a fairly lonely public figure. In 1914, his novel *Der Untertan* (The Underling) began serialisation in a literary magazine, but as an anti-German satire it was quickly censored and not published until the war was over. Undeterred, he continued to place himself publicly in opposition to the war, and followed with an essay on Zola, published in November 1915 in the monthly *Die weissen Blätter* (its editor, René Schickele, had to move the magazine to Switzerland in 1916). This essay recalled the Dreyfus scandal and Zola's *J'accuse*, to argue as passionately for democracy as it denounced all forms of repression, especially in the latest manifestations of nationalism and patriotism. Wedekind wrote to congratulate his friend. In the autumn of 1915, Walter Benjamin was in Munich and quite by chance attended a reading by Heinrich Mann, who sat on the stage in front of a brightly coloured Futurist painting. Benjamin liked Mann's *very spiritual, sonorous, low voice*, and his *great, fertile ideas*, especially his conclusion with respect to war, that there were two kinds of people, those who wanted happiness and those who wanted power.

Thomas regarded the Zola essay as a personal attack on him and his views. Although they lived not far from each other in Munich, communication between the brothers ceased completely. Much to their mother's anguish, the rift would last until 1922, when Heinrich was in hospital, suffering from influenza, appendicitis and peritonitis, and his condition was described as serious. Thomas sent a card and flowers.

Throughout his early travels, Heinrich collected postcards of his favourite artworks. Only a few survive, their corners torn and marked by a succession of drawing pins. One such card is of Raphael's *Madonna del cardellino* (1506), which hangs in the Uffizi in Florence. It is a triangular design with Mary seated in the centre and at her knees her young son, on whom she bestows a loving gaze, and his brother-in-spirit, St John the Baptist. In her hand she holds an open book. The two boys play very gently with a goldfinch, one holding the bird, the other stroking it. After Raphael had given the painting as a wedding present to a friend, it was damaged in an earthquake, broken into several pieces, and then restored.

Points of Origin

I was born on June 20, 1887, in Hanover. As a child I had a little garden with roses and strawberries. Hanover and Hannover, one hen in English, two hens in German, a clever teacher could have told young Kurt Hermann Eduard Karl Julius Schwitters – what a name – who lived with his parents in Veilchenstrasse. Violetland, he called it, and called himself Kuwitter, Ku short for Kurt of course, but also *Kuh* a cow, and *wittern*, a foreboding in the cow's nostrils, *Wetter wittern*, a change in the weather, things to come. When Kurt wet himself as a child he was locked in the bathroom. When he watched other boys destroy his garden, a hill he'd made, a pond, the roses, the strawberries, he was so upset that he had an epileptic fit. He was sick for two years. In 1919 Herwarth Walden published Schwitters' 'Anna Blume' in the magazine *Der Sturm*: a poem about an ordinary girl, *ungezähltes Frauenzimmer*, uncounted, untold, Anna-nonymous, who is like a flower. She wears her hat on her feet and walks about on her hands, she has a pet bird, the poet loves her. A heroine, a hero.

Boldly Schwitters took an axe to the ruling idea of commerce – *Kommerz* – cutting it in two, stealing its *end* to make art from rubbish. From broken and discarded material he made collages and assemblages of serene melancholy beauty that he called Merz, with the resonance of *Erz* (ore), *Herz* (heart), *Scherz* (joke) and *Schmerz* (pain). During a visit to Berlin, he came across Döblin, who was on his way to the Café Gumpert where he liked to sit and write amidst noise and bustle.

(Bruno) Alfred Döblin was born in 1878 into an impoverished Jewish merchant family in the Pomeranian town of Stettin. Alfred would later say that they were exiled from their little paradise when his father abandoned them. At the age of ten he arrived in Berlin with his mother and four siblings, to live with relatives. He became a doctor (general practice, psychiatry, obstetrics), a writer (one of his earliest works was a novella called *Astralia*) and co-founder of the magazine *Der Sturm*. He described himself as pale, skinny, shortsighted, with grey-blue eyes, an overbite and a strong, long nose paralleling the angle of his forehead. A smoker. He said he was never a good dancer. In 1912 he married Erna Reiss, who had been a medical student; a few months before his marriage, his son from his relationship with a nurse, Frieda Kunke, was born. Interior monologue that sets a furious narrative pace and moments of arresting ecstasy define his writing, which at the time was labelled *cinematic* and *Expressionist*. Connoisseurs compared him to James Joyce. In his novel *Berlin Alexanderplatz*, the definitive German epic of early twentieth-century urban life, Döblin wrote, *aber die Hauptsache . . . but the main thing about a person are his eyes and his feet. You have to be able to see the world and to walk towards it.* He regularly ran into Roth.

(Moses) Joseph Roth was born in 1894 in Brody, also the birthplace of Freud's mother, a Galician border town where everyone was from somewhere else and people spoke Russian, Polish, Ukrainian, Yiddish and German, often, a Brodyan has told me, all at once. He never saw his father (the eyes), who took off before he was born (the feet). He later said that if he had a son, he'd always keep an eye on him. Joseph went from school in Brody to university in Lemberg (Lvov) and Vienna. When war broke out he served on the Eastern Front. In 1920 he arrived in Berlin, where he found that *sometimes a ride on the S-Bahn is more instructive than a voyage to distant lands. Experienced travellers will confirm that it is sufficient to see a single lilac shrub in a dusty city courtyard to understand the deep sadness of all the hidden lilac trees anywhere in the world.* As a writer he moved through towns and cities, navigating and narrating like the great expeditionaries who once explored the globe. He was always well-dressed, a Viennese dandy sporting special items from his collection of walking sticks and watches. He knew everyone, everyone knew him. One day, about to cross the Nollendorf Platz, he stopped to tip his hat and speak to the exotic Lasker-Schüler.

Elisabeth Schüler, who became Else Lasker-Schüler, liked to say she was born in 1876 (but the year was 1869) and also that the place was Thebes in ancient Egypt (not Elberfeld near Wuppertal). She descended from a line of rabbis and (she claimed) women poets. She arrived in Berlin in 1894. Her second husband was the composer and writer Georg Levin (born 1878, Berlin); she persuaded him to change his name to Herwarth Walden. She led an unsettled existence. In her world, the sky was golden and the stars were blue, and this blue was also the colour of loss and desire. In her poem 'Homesickness' she wrote: *I don't know the language of this cold land, / nor its rhythm. / Even the passing clouds are incomprehensible to me.* Her lover, the poet Gottfried Benn, declared her Germany's *grösste Lyrikerin* – greatest woman poet – of all time; she placed Benn just a little lower down the scale, calling him the Kokoschka of poetry. Referring to her thorns, the writer Rudolf Jakob Humm wondered how this little *gooseberry* could have produced such sublime poetry. In 1920 Bertolt Brecht heard her read her *good and bad poems, excessive and unsound, but some very beautiful.*

Eugen Berthold Friedrich Brecht, later Bertolt Brecht, was

born in 1898 in Augsburg. Observing him at play, his mother thought he would grow up to build bridges. His parents showered him with books. As a child he had a nervous disposition and often stayed home from school, where he'd once been given a bad mark for displaying too much imagination. Studied medicine, played the guitar, read Wedekind and Kipling, wrote poetry and plays, and after several short stays in Berlin, moved there in 1924. He always tried to satisfy what he called his daily diet of 2–3 pounds of crime fiction and claimed that he'd read all the books from all the lending libraries around. For his literary pursuits he sometimes took passages from other writers without acknowledging the sources. Just like Shakespeare, he'd argue, Shakespeare was also *an acquirer*. Herwarth Walden and the much feared critic Alfred Kerr, among others, drew attention to Brecht's citational practice. The culprit responded by saying that it was in fact too early to respond to the charges, because he took plagiarism very seriously and still hoped to achieve great things in this largely neglected field of literature.

The most dangerous liars, Brecht soon discovered, were people like Joseph Goebbels. Born in 1897 in Reydt, into a working-class Catholic family, he had a deformed foot which he never stopped thinking about; it exempted him from military service. It's said that in his youth he was not an anti-Semite, that his first fiancée was Jewish. He loved his dogs, his mother, and Christmas, was interested in pantomime and modernism, received a PhD in literature in 1922, wrote a novel, became the Nazi Minister for Propaganda. The doctor – he always insisted on the title – who doctored the truth.

There was no problem with lies as such, Brecht argued, only with their intended meanings. His friends understood. Born in 1890 in Berlin as the son of a Jewish merchant, Kurt Tucholsky was a lawyer and a writer who saluted Brecht's habits of literary appropriation and referred to them with intellectual nuance as *an-*

ticipations. In other words, it wasn't only where an idea or quotation came from that mattered, but rather how it was reinvented and projected into new significance. Language was a common fund.

Walking the streets of Berlin in the early years of the twentieth century, they would have felt the city's sequined resonance, sweet spring and fungal autumn, dust from roadworks, soap smells, cooking, blood, tyres and cigars, small waves lapping at the water's edge. Some had experienced the war first hand. Döblin was a medico on the Western Front (where a dashing Alfred Flechtheim fought in the cavalry). The pacifist Tucholsky was conscripted, and like Roth who volunteered in 1916, was sent to the Eastern Front; he later wrote *I did everything not to get shot and not to shoot*. Mühsam was jailed for organising opposition to the war. Others watched and listened. They read between the lines of news reports. Peered past the slogans and the clichés, into doors and windows. Around red geraniums in pots. Between the slats of half-closed *Jalousien*. Through white lace curtains. And to their horror, looked into six hundred thousand widows' eyes, to find dark reflections. They saw themselves and registered the devastation. An economy in ruins, almost two million German soldiers dead, more than four million wounded and disabled. Estimations varied between a total of fifteen and eighteen million deaths for both sides together, the Allies and the Central Powers, with psychiatric casualties too vast to count.

When Heinrich Mann's novel *Der Untertan* (published in English in 1947 as *Man of Straw*) was finally allowed to appear in December 1918, it sold 80,000 copies in a week. Overnight he became one of the country's most outspoken social activists. The target of his satire was Germany's obsession with social hierarchies. By grafting the figures of a superior (the Kaiser) and his subordinate (his *Untertan*, underling) into one despicable protagonist,

Diederich Hessling (sounds like *hässlich*, ugly, hateful), for contemporary readers it must have been as if with a single blow Mann's book demolished the double-headed evil of imperialism and subservience. In cities like Berlin, where now on streetcorners the legless sold shoelaces and the blind sold matches, in the immediate postwar vacuum when ideologies, parties and factions scrambled for power, with speeches, mass demonstrations, a short-lived revolution, arrests, assassinations, this book struck a chord with readers trying to fathom Germany's outrageous self-deceptions and destructive urges. Tucholsky noted that even Rosa Luxemburg and Karl Liebknecht, murdered in January 1919, their bodies thrown into the Landwehr Canal, hadn't understood that they were like sea gods consumed by their own waves. The season changed. Chestnut trees dropped their blossoms. At Versailles in June 1919 the peace treaty was signed in the Hall of Mirrors. Women gained the right to vote. Heinrich Mann was uplifted by the success of another book, his essay collection *Macht und Mensch* (Power and People, 1919). Mühsam was again in gaol, while Albert Einstein, Tucholsky and Lasker-Schüler, among others, campaigned for his release. The birth pangs of a new era. And that great sardonic baby, the Weimar Republic, was born.

From towns and far-flung provinces and other countries, people flocked to the metropolis in the thousands. They chose Berlin because it reflected their dreams more brightly than any other place. In the trains, women chatted anxiously about their destination and the chance of finding work there, as typists or shop assistants, as ticket sellers or rubbish collectors, as postal or factory workers. Or in the theatre? You'd have to be lucky! Most of them would be happy just to have a job. They travelled with baskets on their laps or bundles at their feet, wore headscarves or at best, modest hats. In wonderment they arrived at railway stations which Roth likened to cathedrals, to try their luck on the doorsteps of the city that Benjamin described as sacred text. Walter Benjamin, born 1892, Berlin. But the newcomers were more likely to experience it as Döblin saw it, a constantly expanding human mass, *an unpoetic city, not very colourful but very real.*

From my forays into the past I often return with little more than a clutch of names and dates, cold facts. I pick through them like someone looking for coins in the pockets of an old coat, blindly feeling for unexpected details to emerge, blunt or buffed or dented, that will clink together, pay my fare, take me to yet another point of origin.

Like Schwitters' Anna Blume, Nelly Kroeger was an ordinary girl with a special spark. Heinrich Mann loved her, his brother despised her. Recreated from a slim harvest of available facts, here is her story.

In northern Germany the winter of 1897–98 was so mild that spring flowers appeared at Christmas time. In the small Schleswig-Holstein town of Ahrensbök, Bertha Margaretha Elise Westphal (1873–1957), who already had one child (Elsa Emma, born 21 July 1895), gave birth to Emmy Johanna at 3 pm on 15 February 1898 in the house of Noah Troplowitz, where she was employed as a maid. Instead of frost and snow, the countryside was lit up with patches of violets and primulas.

As for Emmy Johanna's humble lineage, from church records it's been possible to establish that her mother Bertha's parents were married on 13 May 1870 in the round-bellied late-romanesque stone church in Pronstorf in the Bad Segeberg district of Schleswig-Holstein. Bertha's father, Heinrich Detlef Westphal, a carpenter (born 12 December 1842, died 24 March 1896 in Neuberg near Ahrensbök), was the son of Johann Christian Westphal, a forest bailiff, and Anna Margaretha Catharina (née Meier); Bertha's mother, Elsabe Magdalena (born 11 August 1839), was the daughter of Hans Joachim Fick, a farm worker, and Lucia Margaretha (née Engel).

The father's name does not appear on Emmy's, nor on her sister's, birth certificate. Possibly her father was Noah Troplowitz, born 11 January 1858 in Gleiwitz, now Gliwice, on the river Klodnitz, a provincial centre in the industrial region of Upper Silesia, which was incorporated into the German Empire in 1871 and is now part of Poland. Apple, plum, cherry and pear trees lined the roads leading to the town. The local summer fruit made excellent liqueurs. In the early twentieth century Gleiwitz had a population of over 60,000 and boasted foundries, distilleries, breweries, mills, brickworks, glassworks, trams, theatres, a hospital, two orphanages and a synagogue. By 1923 it had the brand-new Seidenhaus Weichmann, a textile emporium designed by the modernist architect Erich Mendelsohn. The local Jewish community was patriotically German. On 31 August 1939, when Nazi propaganda was in its stride, German soldiers dressed up as Polish soldiers and attacked the radio station in Gleiwitz. This charade led to Nazi 'reprisals', to the invasion of Poland the next day, and to the start of the Second World War. Equidistant from Warsaw, Prague, Vienna and Berlin, for a moment Gleiwitz was centre stage. Then the Eastern curtain dropped again. The town was about 50 km from Auschwitz and became one of the subsidiary sites of that concentration camp.

According to a Troplowitz descendant now living in Argentina, the family's residence in the Gleiwitz area has been documented from the late seventeenth century. On one branch, Scholim Jacob Troplowitz (1752–1820) and his wife, Helene Freund, had at least eight children, including one son named Salomon (1789–1869), a wine merchant, and another named Enoch (also called Heinrich, 1795–1874), a livestock trader.

The wine merchant Salomon Troplowitz's son Simon Ludwig (also known as Louis, 1825–1913) was the builder of the Gleiwitz synagogue, which opened in 1861. By all accounts it was magnificent. It was destroyed during Kristallnacht, 9 November 1938. Simon Ludwig was the father of Oskar (1863–1918), who studied pharmacy in Breslau, gained a PhD in chemistry, physics and botany, did a year of military service, and then moved to Hamburg. In 1890 Oskar Troplowitz bought Paul Carl Beiersdorf's pharmaceuticals factory in Altona and modernised it. He created the first marketable toothpaste Florisal, later Pebecco, and the adhesive bandage Leukoplast. In 1911 he purchased the patent for the emulsifier Eucerit, to form the basis for a new range of cosmetics and medicines, including the moisturiser Nivea. Oskar also collected art. He owned significant paintings by Max Liebermann, Auguste Renoir, Alfred Sisley. Picasso's *Absinthe Drinker* hung above his desk. After his death in 1918 his collection was donated to Hamburg's Kunsthalle.

Oskar's great-uncle the livestock trader Enoch Troplowitz (1795–1874) married Sophie Schefftel (1796–1859) and they had eleven children, including a son called Isaak Salomon (1828–1911) who married a woman called Marie Rose. Their son Noah Troplowitz also became a trader, left home as a young man, made his way west and settled in Ahrensbök, a small town near Lübeck with a weekly horse and livestock market. In 1887 he married (Dorathea Helene) Johanna Stegemann; they had four children (a son who was killed in WWI, another called Heinrich, then Minna born 1891, and Otto born 1895). It is not known whether as second cousins who moved in very different social circles, Oskar in Hamburg and Noah in not-too-distant Ahrensbök ever saw each other in those years. Noah Troplowitz died 28 March 1931, his wife in 1939.

The warm winter of Emmy's birth was followed by an exceptionally cold, wet summer. In about 1900 Bertha and her young daughters moved to Niendorf, by country road less than 20 km from Ahrensbök, where she married Nicolaus Wilhelm Heinrich Kröger, a fisherman, and since fishermen often practised a second trade, also a carpenter. The couple worked hard to make ends meet. Together they had five more children: Annie, Hedwig, August, Käthe and Walter. Their stepfather adopted the two Westphal girls in 1920, when they officially changed their name to Kröger. Then sometime in the mid- or late-1920s, Emmy Johanna changed her first name to Nelly and in 1939, with her marriage to Heinrich Mann, she became Nelly Kroeger-Mann.

There's a biographical novel by Joachim Seyppel called *Abschied von Europa* (1975) – Farewell to Europe – that is the story of Heinrich and Nelly Mann as told by two fictionalised narrators (a barely disguised Seyppel and his researcher-lover); it takes its title from a chapter of Heinrich Mann's memoir *Ein Zeitalter wird besichtigt* (1945). The book is flawed, largely because the author-narrator is far too keen to puff his own story and compete for attention with his subjects. Nonetheless Seyppel must be credited with proposing that Nelly's father might have been Noah Troplowitz. To gather evidence from those still left alive in the early 1970s he travelled to Ahrensbök, where he spoke with Troplowitz's son (and possibly Nelly's half brother) Otto. And then to Niendorf, where he met Nelly's half brother Walter Kröger. He didn't learn much from these encounters, and when it was published, his book's slurs alienated both families. But in a photo of Nelly as a child, which he claimed to have been given by the Krögers, he thought he'd found what he was looking for: a strong facial resemblance between Nelly and Otto, reinforced, he believed, by the discovery that Nelly was not a natural blonde. I have not been able to locate the photo in any archives, and when I wrote to Seyppel asking what had happened to it, he said he was very sorry, he could not remember.

I contacted Noah Troplowitz's granddaughter and her family and visited them in Ahrensbök in 2004. They were wonderfully hospitable but had no further insights into the puzzle, not even rumours. Nor did they negate the theory of Nelly's paternity. They said Noah's wife was very domineering – often stern, sometimes histrionic – and they thought it was quite possible that for a time Noah might have found affection elsewhere, and that he might indeed have fathered the maid Bertha Westphal's child, or both children, Emmy and Elsa. They gave me a copy of a photo of Noah Troplowitz which shows a resemblance to photos I've seen of Nelly. It was likely that Bertha was dismissed, either when the misdemeanour was revealed, or if the mistress of the house had suspected it all along, when the situation was no longer tenable. On the other hand, her departure might have been on her own initiative. It's now not known if Nelly was ever told who her real father was. But she was aware that Kröger was not her father and that she was born in Ahrensbök, which was named as her place of birth on her marriage certificate in 1939. When I spoke about this to Nelly's niece, Walter Kröger's daughter, over an iced coffee at Hamburg's Alsterpavillion, she said that although it was never discussed, the family assumed that Nelly's father was the man in whose house in Ahrensbök her grandmother Bertha had been employed.

In Niendorf fishermen had always occupied the top rung of the social order, venerated because they earned their livelihood in often treacherous conditions. They caught cod, flounder, herring, sprats, eel and perch, and their wives worked just as hard, setting out at midnight twice a week to sell fish at the Lübeck market. It all began to change in the late nineteenth century, when like its neighbours Travemünde to the east and Timmendorf to the west, Niendorf discovered its appeal to summer visitors, pale cityfolk desperate to have a month or so of sea and sand and sun.

Roads were improved, a promenade was built, pine and spruce trees were planted to stabilise the dunes. Cafés sprang up, and rooms-to-let, hotels with restaurants, a park, a reading room, tennis courts, baths, bathing machines, a train line, a pier for steamships that serviced ports up and down the Baltic coast. While the appearance of the village and the local economy kept improving, the fishermen were in trouble. They needed the beach for their boats and to unload their catch, but the smell of fish and screaming gulls spoiled the atmosphere for tourists. When the music pavillion was completed on 1 August 1914, the military band playing at the opening was called away to war in mid-performance. Development stopped. It was not until 1920 that the harbour and the Aalbeek, a willow-bordered stream which had once caught Napoléon's eye as an ideal refuge for his warships, were improved to provide moorings for local fishing boats.

Loosely based on Nelly's childhood and youth, and partly set in Niendorf, Heinrich Mann's biographical novel *Ein ernstes Leben* (1932), published in English as *A Hill of Lies* (1934), is a modern fable of innocence and experience. His heroine Marie Lehning grows up in poverty. *All the seasons except winter seemed almost like strangers to the child. Cold and stormy weather ravaged the desolate shores of the Baltic sea in winter*. Storms visit her as nightmares all year round. Summers, by comparison, *seemed magical and not quite believable*. In Mann's view, while the winter-side of life forges Marie's inner strength, it's her spark of sunniness – her goodness and empathy – that sets her apart and will never be extinguished.

This is what the locals told me. When the pinecones opened it meant the sun would shine. Windswept grasses, elms, beeches, poplars, and by the river and the lake reeds and rushes, curtains of willow, coils of fern. Children roamed, with great bunches of primula, woodruff, speedwell and buttercup to place in jars on windowsills at home. Emmy must have known all the birds and their habitats. Seagulls, ducks, woodpeckers, siskins. Near the cemetery, if she stayed very still, she could follow the undulating flight of a golden oriole. It was shy and hid in the canopy of the highest trees. Its harsh call alternated with the sweetest song. In August ceps appeared on the mossy forest floor, as did their poisonous doubles. Some mushrooms were silky to the touch, some bled when they were bruised. And if you went to the forest after dark you saw the blue-green glow, the mysterious emission of light from living things where honey mushrooms grew on rotting stumps.

Emmy attended the newly opened school in Niendorf from 1904 to 1912. Even if at first she was easily brought to tears and was called crybaby by the other pupils, she soon adjusted and did well. She was taught that in 1810 Napoléon's troops had occupied the village, that the nearby lake, the Hemmelsdorfer See, marked Germany's lowest geographic point, that the pirate Störtebeker had his hideout here. She could say the names of oceans and continents by heart, could recite even the longest poems without stumbling, her voice rising with the thrill of stringing words into significance. Her bold handwriting was held up as an example of perfection. She enjoyed the privilege of borrowing books from the teacher's own shelves, and before long she'd read them all. It's possible that she found one on a park bench, forgotten by a visitor, that it was *Effi Briest* and she kept it in a small suitcase under the bed she shared with Elsa. Reading it, there was much she did not understand. An older husband spooks his young wife into submission and drives her to despair and death? At night she retold the story to her sister. The novel opens on an idyll, a mother and daughter sit together sewing next to a majolica bowl full of gooseberries. This was the storyteller's starting point. After that the two girls let their imaginations roam, playing the action backwards and forwards, asking which of the characters was to blame for the final tragedy, talking about love and its rumoured consequences, as much as all the details of Effi's wardrobe, down to the gloves and petticoats and buttons on her boots. They took the narrative into their own hands and plotted escapes for the heroine. In one version they dressed her as a sailor who finds employment on a merchant vessel bound for Australien, where endless opportunities for adventure and happiness present themselves. Emmy confessed that when she first heard about this continent she thought it was called *Ausstrahlen*, radiance, because the teacher said it was a bright place where summers never ended. But she could not quite believe in its existence and dreamed instead of living in Berlin, going to museums and the zoo, sitting in the corner window at Kranzler's café and reading novels by Sir Walter Scott, just like Fontane's Effi.

At the end of each tourist season the hotels and rented rooms in Niendorf emptied very suddenly, as if the cityfolk had had enough of aimless strolling and sitting around. Then groups of local children gleaned for treasure on the beach. You'd see them scavenging in small groups, one or several at once dashing ahead to claim a coin or a piece of jewellery that had been hidden for months, uncovered now by the great gusts of autumn wind that lashed the sand against their legs. They also collected *thunderbolts*, which were 100-million-year-old petrified remains of squid, and black and white *firestones*, said to bring luck and if placed inside a coop, to encourage hens to lay more eggs. Sometimes, after an easterly had blown, they found amber. Once they came upon a leather-bound volume plump with moisture. Its ink had run, its ragged pages fluttered just like the fanned-out feathers of a dead seagull's wing nearby. They dug a hole. It seemed right to say a prayer and bury bird and book together, summer magic lightly spun.

Growing up in a small community that was dependent on the sea and land, Emmy would certainly have witnessed hardship, including death and destruction caused by extreme storms and floods in 1904, 1908 and 1913. The fact that fishermen often did not know how to swim made it all the more precarious. After an especially severe battering from the elements she would have stood in awe with others at the base of the Brodtener bluff that rose above the village, to inspect great chunks of fallen land. She may also have lost a sibling. In Heinrich Mann's novel the accounts of three such deaths – by drowning, rape and murder, and the consequences of a self-induced abortion – must surely be an exaggeration of the facts. It seems he purposely departed from truth to accentuate the destitution from which his heroine struggles to escape. Marie Lehning's father is not a fisherman like Emmy Kröger's, but a drunken day labourer too often unemployed, who is washed away in a flood, along with their house, leaving the family to fend for itself. Marie pitches herself against poverty, illness and death, against her mother's weary lament that they'll end up in the poorhouse, and against personal and social injustices, including an illegitimate pregnancy, all heaping up before her to form a hill of lies. When her child is abducted, its rescue becomes her most courageous fight. This, Henrich Mann believed, was a story that needed to be told, a serious life – *Ein ernstes Leben*.

The piecing together of Emmy Kröger's biography now depends largely on Heinrich Mann's and Joachim Seyppel's books and their mix of truth and factual misalignments, some anecdotes, and a small amount of archival material such as letters, bills and photos. For example, woven into Mann's novel is a love story between Marie Lehning and her childhood friend Mingo Merten, who went to sea. I've been able to discover that Mingo was the family nickname of Emmy's youngest brother, Walter, but other than the transference of names, it has not been possible to identify this character and he may have been fictional. When I began my research there were only a few members of her family remaining, and either they knew very little or they were reluctant to talk. Because so much of all this evidence is inconclusive, I started to look for Emmy elsewhere. I believe I've found her reflection in the biographies of others.

In 1919 Emmy Johanna Kröger responded to the future as birds reply to light with song. She was twenty-one, had plucked her eyebrows into swallows' wings and coloured her lips rose-red, wore good shoes, silk stockings, an elegant suit, a hat as à la mode as growing up in the country and the postwar year allowed. She was blonded, curled, tall, striking. Carrying a mixed summer bunch of expectations and an old suitcase with her initials EJK on the inside of the lid, containing a change of clothes and the tools of her trade, an excellent pair of scissors, tape measure, thimble, needles, pins, thread, as well as some books, she had left her home in Niendorf and now stepped onto the platform at Berlin's Lehrter Bahnhof, placing her feet firmly on the ground. Keep your feet firmly on the ground, my girl, they'd said to her as they waved goodbye. Emmy entered an ocean of sound that rolled along boulevards and swelled between buildings, it drew her into a maze of asphalt, cobblestones and bricks. *Berliners have no time*, Tucholsky wrote in 1919, *Berliners are mostly from Posen or Breslau and they have no time. They're always running, phoning, arranging meetings, arriving out of breath or a little too late, then rushing off to the next appointment.* She felt the pulse, followed the rhythm of shoes on the pavement and the hum and clang of traffic, the festive ringing of tram bells, and was surprised to hear her own voice in this new place, asking for directions. *She set out with the idea of conquering Berlin. She felt courage because she had a goal, even if this goal remained nameless.* That's how Heinrich Mann described this moment of her life.

It's been suggested that she found accommodation somewhere in the north-east of the city, in the area near Lehrter Station where she first arrived. In the beginning, as she walked through the streets, her new impressions must have appeared like handfuls of gold to a beggar. Newcomers like Emmy memorised road names, tram destinations, advertising slogans, opening hours, prices, headlines, and felt richer not only by what they discovered but also by all that they imagined still to be attainable, just beyond their reach: some explored museums and department stores, and looked around the lobbies of hotels. Perhaps she coaxed herself into a small amusement, by asking a waiter in a restaurant to show her the menu, pretending that on the strength of it she'd reserve a table for the evening; and if he was respectful, bowed, wished her good day, she would have realised that despite her village origins, she possessed a certain credibility and metropolitan charm.

She must have begun her apprenticeship as seamstress in Niendorf, and completed it in nearby Lübeck; probably she'd already started to earn a salary; she arrived in Berlin with enough money to rent a room. Did she then find work in a factory, or in one of the city's numerous tailoring businesses? Did she get off on the right foot, or did she make mistakes? Called to a grand hotel – the Adlon, the Esplanade – to attend to the guests' wardrobe alterations and repairs, and having worked hard late into the night, did the young seamstress get lost and wander through the hotel's maze of corridors trying to find the exit, passing a lineup of shoes put out for cleaning, and one pair caught her eye, almost new, the right shade of blue, her size exactly? Did she put herself in other people's shoes? Or like the needle she plied, was she more focused, had she covered the table in her room with felt, acquired a sewing machine and an iron, and set up independently as *Damenschneiderin*, a ladies' tailor, more than a mere seamstress, to create detailed, made-to-measure garments for clients who could afford such luxuries? If the material chosen by the customer was cut in a certain way, she could make up two pieces, the second one for herself. She might soon have numbered among Berlin's best-dressed, but of course she did not mix with those who did the counting. Or did she make hats? Because many years later she had cards printed, that stated her profession as *Modistin*, milliner. In that case, she might have begun by working at the hat factory near Spittelmarkt.

A decade later she knew the city well and loved it, and so in those early years she must have explored it on foot in her free time, witnessed the mingle of life in every quarter, taken shortcuts through hidden laneways, crossed bridges with views that opened out, looked up at stucco façades and at the green copper dome of the Hedwigskirche, entered chilling church interiors, and gazed into the dizzying distance of the Kurfürstendamm, which started at the Gedächtniskirche and, as they said, went on forever. When the foreign minister Walter Rathenau was murdered in June 1922, most likely she joined the thousands that lined the streets on the day of his funeral and wept. She might have been especially drawn to certain places, like the round reading room of the Staatsbibliothek or the Dutch paintings at the art gallery. Perhaps she stopped in front of a portrait – warm flesh tones against browns, wine reds – because its subject looked like she would step out of the frame towards her, and from then on continued to visit Rembrandt's *Woman at an Open Door* as one might go to see a friend, and overheard an expert say this woman's pose belonged to the prototype of depictions of sixteenth-century courtesans. Perhaps she rode a bicycle to outlying palaces, villages, lakes and forests; returned from these excursions with mushrooms or apples from a tree that overhung a wall; brought home a kitten that seemed lost and hungry; carried it in her pocket, gave it a name. And with a Sunday crowd she climbed the 247 steps to the viewing platform of the Siegessäule, the triumphal column rising 67 metres from the centre of the Königs Platz, to look across the greenery of the Tiergarten on one side, across the dome of the Reichstag in the other.

Or made her way to the top of Berlin's only hill, once covered by vineyards, the Kreuzberg, to trace from its summit avenues in all directions, railway lines, canals mirroring the sun. And saw the city as a giant skirt that she herself was wearing, its red and green moiré pleats gathered to the place where she was standing. At a high point in my life, she must have thought.

Some of the money she earned she sent home, the rest she spent on rent and food. Books were bought or borrowed. If *Madame Bovary* had fallen into her hands, I imagine what she would have loved most was its intimacy, the heroine confiding in her greyhound much like her own conversations with her cat, and she too *waiting for something to happen. Like a shipwrecked sailor she scanned her solitude with desperate eyes for the sight of a white sail far off on the misty horizon.*

We know that she made friends easily. Many years later, when she was no longer living in Berlin, she remembered that the happiest time of her life was during those sultry summer evenings on the Kurfürstendamm, when she strolled arm in arm with a girl-friend and sometimes a young man would pass, speak to them, and together they went dancing. Perhaps that was how she met Werner Schmidt; he was handsome, a bank clerk, well dressed, well mannered. Well, well, well . . . she could hear her mother's tone of voice. From the moment he had introduced himself, she knew she'd caught sight of a white sail on the horizon. She'd been reading Goethe, so she called him Werther. Seyppel claimed he was shown a photo of the couple, with *Emmy and Werther* written on the back.

Together Emmy and Werther ate chocolate. They saw Greta Garbo in *Love.* It was based on *Anna Karenina* and in the audience the women's handkerchiefs were soaked with tears. Some films were far too sinister. After *Dr Caligari's Cabinet* the feeling of terror stayed with her and she could hardly sleep. They preferred comedies. According to Tucholsky, the most famous person of the time was not a politician, a scientist, an opera singer, or even the great Garbo, but a Mr Charlie Chaplin, who walked like no one ever walked before and who often looked a little sad, a philosopher-comedian *who's made everybody laugh at least once, Parisians and Londoners, all Americans, and Australian sailors, Chinese cinema goers and now also German ones.* They bought tropical fruit or shared a jar of local pickles, as the mood demanded. Champagne, chablis. He taught her to play tennis and to drive. She discovered a passion, as much for Werther as for driving fast. It was easy to confuse the two. He bought flowers, weekly, daily, sweets, and one day, a ring. Told her she looked too good for words, and that her best colour was red, dangerous red, which she understood to mean that she would be the one taking all the chances.

There was a joke that hems were rising even faster than inflation. Shapely legs in silk stockings were all the rage, jazz, cinema, new styles of art, alongside hunger, riots, theft, and apprehension about what each next day would bring, great bundles of banknotes in suitcases, in pillowcases, in prams. Probably, as happened to thousands of others, Werner Schmidt lost his job. In any case, one day her sun-bleached sail – her white-collar worker boyfriend – left. Perhaps they quarrelled; perhaps she kicked him out; perhaps the news of her pregnancy and the prospect of responsibility blew him away.

Emmy gave birth to a healthy baby. It is not known if it was a girl or (as in Mann's novel) a boy. Now fewer people could afford a seamstress. We might suppose that in order to pay the rent and also to pay a woman who lived nearby to look after the child, she had little choice except to return to working in a factory, and when the factory closed down, she thought of packing up and going home to Niendorf. The sea air would do them good.

But she stayed on, gave herself another chance, changed her

name to Nelly because it sounded more modern; the double-m in Emmy was too heavy, too steady, like someone who had both feet on the ground. A double-l was lighter, *leichter*, *heller*. With a name like Nelly you could turn somersaults, you might even fly. Ten years' experience serving drinks and a stack of golden references, she must have told the manager at the Kakadu Bar, a popular haunt near the Kurfürstendamm. And he must have been uncertain if it was true and so hired her on the spot, because in an atmosphere of rapidly shifting values, where people bought and sold whatever they could, falsehoods dressed as truth had become good currency. Emmy, who was now Nelly, knew she could tell a lie with an engagingly honest glow. It was a kind of talent.

She was soon promoted from barmaid to work the room as *Animierdame*. *Animieren*, to animate or stimulate. A hostess who moved from table to table, sat with customers or danced with them, all to ensure a steady sale of alcohol, who understood political gossip, personal woes, and when to exchange whispers for another round of drinks. All bars have regulars, shy or loud or tragic people, a man who'd lost his family in a fire, another who always arrived saying he was as thirsty as a pond and with his look of sheer desperation made everybody laugh. Her own drink was diluted and she knew how to clink glasses, say cheers in a dozen languages, without ever taking more than just a sip or two. I like to think she also knew where to draw the line – a fine line – between this job and a related trade that took place when the bars closed. In those smoke-filled places when the music lost its volume and a singer trailed the last furry notes of song, arguments dwindled, fists took a comically wide aim and missed their mark, you heard the shuffle of shoes on the dance floor, the scrape of chairs before they're swung through the air to end upside down on tables. The stale warmth inside was marbled with cool streams of night air as couples slipped out into the dark. Opened doors were quickly shut again.

Despite attempts by some writers to paint Nelly's Berlin years – her whole life, in fact – garishly, promiscuously, there is no evidence that she ever worked as a prostitute. Quite the contrary, if we accept Heinrich Mann's portrait of her. He insists that even in the most compromising situations she stuck to her principles. In any case, earning a living and looking after a baby would have been exhausting enough. So let's assume that in the early hours of the morning she went home alone from the Kakadu to her lodgings at Kantstrasse 156 and when the wind and rain came beating from the north, that she imagined she could smell the sea and on such nights, turning the key in the lock, was overcome with homesickness. But it was important for her that she had a job at all and that it paid well. Her child was cared for. According to Heinrich Mann's depiction, *when its mother entered the room and came near, despite the dark, it stretched out its little arms to be lifted up.* This was the truest love, she would have thought as she carried her baby to her own bed.

In the afternoons, groups of children spilled from nearby doorways to play. They turned skipping ropes, sailed walnut-shell and newspaper boats in the gutter after rain, or swung by the crook of their knees from carpet rails. They carried bags of clay marbles, grey, blue, silvery, speckled pink, like birds' eggs. They had special ones made of glass called cat's-eye or comet, which they rolled in their palms or held up to the light like precious stones, as they negotiated the rules of the game. You dug a hole in the ground by turning round and round on your heel, then you smoothed the rim, took the agreed number of steps away, drew a line with a stick, knuckled down, and shot. On a visit to the museum a guide told me that marbles of stone, clay, porcelain or glass were sometimes found in the ancient graves of children. I've read that scientists now have evidence that before its infinite exaggeration, its *inflation*, the universe was the size of a marble.

The children called to her, stopped their games, gathered round, admired her elegance and fussed over the child dressed up in hand-embroidered summer cottons, or a sailor suit, or coloured wools and quilted coats in autumn. When Nelly gave up making clothes for others, she continued sewing and knitting for her child and herself. Towards the end of the year, it was already snowing, she invited the gang, as she called them, to her room for a party. She sat them all along the bed, covered the table with a bright cloth, served them hot chocolate in tall glasses she'd brought back especially from the bar, and little cakes. They sang out rhymes that made them shriek with laughter; her child clapped and asked for more. At dusk she sent them home with gingerbreads she'd bought, with *My Darling* and *Good Luck* in pastel icing.

The coughing started. Everyone, it seemed, was unwell or affected by the illnesses of others. Children and the elderly suffered most; stories of people dying, of malnourishment, tuberculosis, flu, crept into talk in bars and on the street. Behind the closed doors and wintry windows of apartments, neighbours listened warily to each other's hammering chests, moans, sobs and silences. In his poem 'Vision in White' Brecht wrote, *At night I am woken up, bathed in sweat, by a cough which strangles me. My room is too small. It is full of archangels.* Only a few of the neighbourhood gang now sat in stairwells and doorways, and even they had dull eyes, runny noses, sunken cheeks. They told her if someone she knew was ill or had not gone to work or school that morning. The woman caring for the child suddenly had enough to do to look after her own family. Nelly stayed home and cooked soup for those too sick to care for themselves.

She had planned to return to Niendorf for Christmas, had packed and was ready to leave the next day. But then her child lost its appetite and grew pale, whimpery, lethargic. She took it to the doctor, was given some medicine, told to go home and come back if things got worse. During the night the child's fever rose. It tossed and twisted in her arms. As it quietened, gradually, she tried to hold off her own drowsiness. Had they then both fallen asleep? And for how long? She looked down at the little face. No breath, no heartbeat. The grey hand of daylight was reaching out for her. She shrunk away. It was as if a great rock was lodged in her throat, it would not be swallowed and she choked with grief. In her embrace of the child, her body firmed like a shell. She could not move and lost the thread of time. When voices called, fists drummed on the door, and eventually when people burst into the room, she could not speak. They carried her away like that, on a stretcher, her dead child locked very gently in her arms.

Where did they take her? To the Bethanien Hospital in the Kreuzberg district or to the labyrinthine world-within-a-world of the Charité? She was injected, her armour crushed, her arms and legs unbent. But the drug was too strong. For weeks the patient laboured between coma and consciousness. Always on reaching the surface, she sank back, dragged down by a terrible weight. On the ocean floor she crawled into a cave to sleep. When she finally managed to stay up for breath, she protested against further medication. She cried and cried. Until the chaotic burden of grief and guilt lifted enough for her to see she was not as ill as others. She helped them by listening and with small acts of kindness.

One evening, while grey boiled fish was being served for dinner, and all the noses in the ward twitched from the unpleasant smell, she called a young doctor to her bedside. She had something to tell him, she said. A man sat in a restaurant (Nelly raised her voice for everyone to hear), a man with his face very close to the plate in front of him. He was mumbling and whispering, shrugging his shoulders, rolling his eyes, as if in conversation with the fish he had just been served. The waiter was amused and called the manager, who called the cook, and together they watched their eccentric customer. Then they walked over and asked the man what on earth he was doing, talking to the fish like that. I was inquiring for news from the river, the man answered. And what did the fish say? asked the cook with a sly grin. He told me, replied the man, that he had no news from the river because he'd been lying around in your kitchen for too long.

The entire ward, doctors, nurses, patients, roared and cackled. The applause of cutlery on metal trays made a great din. The protesters sent their fish back to the kitchen. That same day Nelly was discharged. Someone handed her flowers from a bedside vase. A nurse took the trouble to iron her dress and polish her shoes.

The sky hung low. The city she crossed was still blanketed with snow. Her heels tapped the pavement, fracturing the thin ice that had formed on puddles. Looking down she saw neon lights and the fragments of her thoughts reflected in the splinters of ice and in the shiny leather of her shoes. Let's say that's how it was. We know that Nelly carried a deep sadness with her all her life. We know she lost a child, but not the circumstances.

Lehrter Bahnhof. The touch and smell of metal. A winter's crowd. She was going home to Niendorf. In the compartment the only empty seats faced away from the direction of the train. Never mind, she chose a window seat and settled down, took off her gloves, unbuttoned her coat but kept it on, loosened her shawl. With a clicking murmur the train left the city centre and its outskirts, heading north-west, picking up speed, racing its shadow. Through the window she watched ravens foraging in fields, some from reason, some from memory. Snow-capped furrows. Barren branches lit by a moonstone sun.

With her eyes on the horizon, she recalled the same journey home last summer, when she'd seen white-flowered potato crops, creek-fed meadows, horses grazing, brown and white cows assembling for milking at two-thirty, she remembered looking at her watch. Bad Wilsnack, Wittenberge, the Elbe River, the bridge, red poppies, wind-combed wheatfields, purple borders. A gypsy caravan. The dark buildup of clouds, the bilious light heralding a summer storm. Swallows flying low, their sweeping dance, thunder and the spectacle of lightning. A downpour followed by its parting gift of dripping, glistening freshness, replenished rivers, brimming troughs, wet timber barns. Lupins, geese, a bicycle propped against a fence, another lying on the ground. The train had tunnelled through closely woven foliage, ferns like lace, the luminous green of linden, the black of firs, and sped through Ludwigslust, a drift of seeds where a prince once built a castle and pursued the pleasure of the hunt. Golden bales. Brahlstorf, where she'd seen storks flying to their nests. She'd heard it said that stork mothers pull out their own feathers to keep their young warm. The nests were empty now because storks spend the winter in Africa and return to their northern breeding grounds in spring, often to the same nests near human habitation. Villagers are thankful for this; they take it as a sign of trust and wisdom. The messenger bird, and according to legend, though voiceless, a great storyteller. Folklore also speaks of the transmigration of souls as birds. Tales of babies born in swamps. Beaks like forceps. As a child you'd repeat a verse to ask the stork to bring you a brother or sister.

The light was fading. Wet snow began to fall. Last summer the child sat on her lap as she pointed out the cows, a farmer's cart, two horses head to head. Naming things, as in the pages of a picture book. She could still feel its weight against her thighs, standing up, urging to press its chubby palms and then its nose, forehead, cheeks, mouth against the glass. Now tears fell on her hand. She turned away from the other travellers and leaned her arm high against the windowpane, as if to look more closely into the darkening winter landscape. But the window had become a mirror and in its frame, returning Nelly's gaze, was a woman in an open wine-red coat and matching turbaned hat, a white woollen shawl draped across her shoulders, head tilted, threshold eyes, simple pearl earrings, dim flashes of gold, a ring, a bracelet. Rembrandt's mistress-wife, Hendrijke Stoffels, the *Woman at an Open Door*, her passing reflection like an X-ray of a painting that reveals other compositions. Until sleet dashed against the glass and threw the warm tones into abstract disarray. Nelly saw that the seat opposite had been vacated and she changed over, facing forward now, in the direction of the speeding train.

In Hamburg she stayed with relatives. Her older sister, Elsa, had met her future husband, Wilhelm Bodenhagen, while she worked as a nurse during the war. He'd been a soldier in France and was wounded. According to their son Harry Bodenhagen, there were *three bullets in his head between the two brain lobes. At first he was stacked with the dead, but then a doctor saw no decomposition, he was treated. Lost his hearing. After the operation he was sent to a hospital in Hamburg where a nurse helped him back to life. She was Elsa Kröger.* They married and by the end of 1926 had migrated to America. Old Mrs Bodenhagen missed her son and daughter-in-law and was happy to have a visitor; she gave Nelly soup and bread and a warm bed for the night.

The next day at the Hauptbahnhof, as she waited for the Lübeck train, the small suitcase with her initials on the inside of the lid must have been taken by mistake. She hadn't noticed, and when the train doors opened and people stood up to board, she absent-mindedly picked up a similar-sized bag standing by her feet, and only later realised it was not hers. It contained an apple and a fruit knife side by side, a woman's woollen dress, a tin of Nivea, some knitting, and a romance novel called *Einsame Seelen* (Lonely Souls), from a fiction series for housewives. Her own bag, with the baby clothes she was going to pass on to relatives, was lost. There was nothing to be done. She ate the apple and opened the book, not at the beginning but at the place earmarked by its previous reader, and read on. Chapter VI. *Was the marriage of the prince and princess a happy one? This question could not be answered with a definite 'yes' or 'no'; it was not worse or better than hundreds of others.* Whenever Nelly looked up from her reading she saw groups of women whose lips never stopped moving as they swapped stories and advice. When the train stayed at Oldesloe station for too long, the passengers grew restless, moved around, leaned out of windows. Probably someone lying on the track again, they said.

Even more than family and friends, in Niendorf it was the liminal world of the beach at dusk in winter that Nelly sought as her companion landscape. She pulled her scarf tight and pushed into the wind. Her shoes caught on wrack and washed-up netting. The fishermen's dogs ran circles, danced on their hind legs, fetched sticks for her. She waited for the lights to appear along the bay. At home mother and father still called her Emmy. They did not know how to talk about the loss of her child and the breakdown she'd suffered. She helped with the household chores. In a burst of energy when the sun momentarily came out, she washed all the windows of the house until they sparkled. But soon she'd heard every detail of village news three times over. The talk was all about marriages, deaths, a ship lost at sea, and a small town further east along the Baltic coast that had been completely covered by the sand of wandering dunes, so that only the tip of the church spire was visible. No doubt she'd also been the subject of gossip at the local gathering place near the harbour, that they called the hill of lies, Lügenberg. An old man who used to sit there on an upturned barrel once told her that acorns and beechnuts cannot grow where they fall in the dark shade of the parent tree, and that there's a bird, a jay, that secures its species' future food supply by picking up those seeds and flying off to plant them in open places further afield. The bird doesn't just drop the seeds at random, but selects a site and pushes each seed deep into the soil. It was time to return to the city, Nelly thought.

Whenever they met for lunch, Tucholsky's great respect for his friend Heinrich Mann was replenished. Their discussion inevitably swerved towards one question, whether intellectuals – writers – can have an effect on politics and on the course of history. Years before, in an essay on Voltaire and Goethe, Heinrich had written that the novel was the natural medium of democracy, the equaliser, the space in which the entire world could be revealed in all its great and small humanity, connectedness, complexity. He was no longer sure. At once a sceptic and an idealist, he now wanted to know who their readers were. Who are we writing for? It was an urgent matter, and he wondered if instead of satire and polemics, he should be producing simple fables that could sway the masses. But it was becoming all too difficult. Heinrich confessed he often thought about packing his bags and going to Brazil.

In different parts of the city Döblin, Schwitters on a brief visit, Roth, Lasker-Schüler and Brecht stepped out, looked up at the sky and opened their umbrellas. Brecht turned up his collar, pulled down his cap. Schwitters picked up the tram tickets other people dropped. Their paths crossed, hello, how are you, at the Nollendorf Platz, the Alexander Platz, the Jannowitzbrücke, the Pariser Platz, where they asked aloud about the times, about tidal waves of history and its backwash of debris. They talked about commerce, everyone did, movies, the latest play they'd seen or written, the latest gossip. Brecht's devilish cigar glowed as he insisted that Thomas Mann's *Magic Mountain* was flawed by the cheapness of its irony. Döblin agreed and added that Mann's writing was too neat. Roth bought a sausage with mustard and the all-weather sausage seller instantly became the hero of his next story. If Walter Benjamin had come along, there might have been an argument. He liked *The Magic Mountain* because it was an experiment, a curious hybrid, not neat at all, it offered literary criticism in the form of a novel, and this was a brave move, not to be sneezed at. He could not abide Lasker-Schüler, although he liked her work. She was dressed as Jussuf, Prince of Thebes, an outfit for which she'd been arrested several times in Munich, and presented her friends with feathers from her turban. Birds of a feather. But Benjamin was nowhere to be seen; he was heading for the Prinzessin, a café downstairs, brothel upstairs, where from 1924 to 1925 he worked on *The Origin of German Tragic Drama*, keen to keep himself separate from the city's literary cliques.

On 5 December 1925, Goebbels was in Lübeck, charmed by this picturesque old Hanseatic city under snow. It brought *Buddenbrooks* to mind. The Holstentor, harbour, churches, the painting of the Dance of Death. *I am rejuvenated*, he wrote in his diary; *I can't stop thinking about Thomas Mann*. In September 1926 he visited Berlin, walked through the streets at night, called it a pit of sin. He'd expected to find the country's élite, he complained, and found only the *Israélite*, and the so-called *jeunesse dorée* was only the *jeunesse isidorée*. There was work to be done; two months later he moved to Berlin, and if he was chased out of working-class areas like Moabit, it spurred him all the more. He was convinced that Charlie Chaplin was a Jew, Greta Garbo a goddess. In 1930 he re-read *Buddenbrooks* and noted in his diary that it really was a pity about the author.

Historical mantras about Weimar Germany are so well chanted they almost do not bear repeating, and yet there's always a kind of thrill in noting, for example, that Ernest Hemingway, Thomas Wolfe, Stephen Spender, Christopher Isherwood and Vladimir Nabokov were among the writers who dipped their pens in Berlin's atmosphere at this time, that more than ever, this city was a great attraction. In 1927 its population rose to four million, it spoke a fanfare of languages and as many varieties of German as there were spawnings of the fatherland on the map. Those who already lived there did not leave. The new hopefuls, hungry for a taste of modernity, arrived by train, by bicycle, on foot, family members took turns to carry the youngest and pushed their belongings towards the city in baby carriages. Once there, often they were too far from their points of origin to return home. And instead of a slice of the metropolis, they settled for its crumbs. Masses of people cast themselves into a growing tide of malnutrition. Food, a bed and work was what they needed. Most remained unemployed, many became ill.

Soup kitchens and welfare organisations were set up to rescue people from complete despair. It's possible that Nelly volunteered to work with Rote Hilfe, a charitable branch of the KPD, the German Communist Party, that offered financial, legal and practical assistance to the poor. There is no evidence that she ever joined the party. As a sympathiser she met others who were equally outraged at the social injustice, poverty, squalor, sickness all around them, and mindful that the country was edging closer to a political abyss. One of Nelly's best friends was a young man called Rudolf Carius. Born in Berlin 15 October 1907, Rudi was almost ten years younger than Nelly, and a good deal shorter. His father, Fritz Carius, was a barber, his mother, Martha, was a worker, the parents divorced in 1928. He was trained as a precision engineer, *Feinmechaniker*, and by 1925 he was a member of the German metalworkers union. He lived in the Charlottenburg quarter of the city, perhaps already then, as later, in Wallstrasse. His daughter told me that he was very much in love with Nelly. Little is known of the early history of the relationship, but it seems they were lovers first and always remained friends.

Warmth is ebbing from things, Walter Benjamin wrote in *Ein-*

bahnstrasse (*One-way Street*; completed 1926, published 1928). It was true. People could not afford heating at home and sought comfort in bars. There was a theory that whenever the Western world became an unhappier and more uncertain place, the patronage of public bars increased. At the Kakadu, Nelly no longer diluted her own drinks. A new kind of customer appeared: men and women who returned there every night as if to a robbers' cave, laying out their haul of political intrigue, facts and hypotheses which were held up to be authenticated, weighed and graded. These bars were the bases from which anti-Fascists organised hideouts and vantage points, blockades and demonstrations.

In the late afternoons before going to work at the Kakadu, Nelly sat in cafés. At the Bellevue, or the Romanisches, or as she'd once imagined, in a corner window at Kranzler's. The book she was reading now was a translation of the English classic *The Bride of Lammermoor*, and from time to time she looked up from the text. Outside a massive river of pedestrians swept along the pavement. Inside the café there was laughter, rising discussions, the patrons peppering their speech with foreign exclamations, *Yes sir! Oh c'était possible!* When the place started to liven up like this, Nelly closed the novel and the copybook in which she'd been writing, and prepared to go. *If only the smoke from my cigarette and the ink of my pen flowed with equal ease*, she heard someone say quite distinctly and she looked around. A shock of hair, steel-rimmed glasses, moustache. The man hunched at the next table appeared to be rehearsing his thoughts aloud as he wrote them down. Then he looked out the window, slowly turned to Nelly and asked if she'd ever put her ear to the ground to listen to all those feet hitting the pavement? At that moment a man on crutches passed by, then a boy with a bicycle, a pregnant woman pushing a small child in a pram. Nelly said that it was the march of democracy. The pedestrian polka, he laughed, moving his chair across to her table and ordering two more coffees. Only someone who travels the road on foot understands the power it commands, he said, speaking like a prophet. She tried to lighten his intensity. Oh, I walk a lot, I love it, but what I'd love most would be to fly, she said.

She told him how a jackdaw with an uncanny resemblance to the philosopher after whom the street in which she lived was named, tapped its beak on her window one day, and again the next. She placed some food on the sill. Kant also fed birds, she said, he liked to watch them and thought to fly must be the ultimate freedom. Her bird was now tame. She called it Vogel. Crows are vermin! Dirty thieves! a neighbour had yelled from the white-spotted balcony below. Then they're real Berliners! she'd yelled back.

He shook his head. He pointed to her notebook. He said that the simple reader never discovers those parts of himself that are opened up by the text – he took a sip and held the cup aloft, as if the suspension of this act would usher his thought to its conclusion – because the simple reader is easily distracted and follows the movement of his own mind in the free flight of daydreaming. Only the hand-copied text can be fully understood, it connects with the soul of the person who is writing it down. She nodded. She understood the connection between reading, writing and walking. But she was expected at work, and gathering hat, coat, gloves, books, she prepared to leave. Blue eyes, he noticed. If colours have an infinite range of nuances, and single colours flit from form to form like winged creatures, blue was the colour he always noticed, that he could not ignore. It was a colour that gave depth to other colours, and always made him think of dreams. She extended her hand, at once to introduce herself and to say goodbye. Nelly Kröger. He stood up and knocked an empty cup, saucer and some cutlery crashing to the floor. The percussion instruments, Nelly laughed, to save his embarrassment. His name was what?

She had only heard a part of it, not sure if it was the first or last. He pointed to her book. Walter . . . Sir Walter Benjamin, historian, fabulist. A handshake, and she said she was sure their paths would cross again.

In December 1928, in a newspaper article, Brecht nominated James Joyce's *Ulysses* as one of the best books of the year. In October 1929, Döblin's *Berlin Alexanderplatz* was published. For many it was too modern, dynamic, even dangerous. For those who knew better, the book's apparent dissonance was magnificently orchestrated, a contemporary form of the Baroque, as Brecht would later describe Döblin's oeuvre, with echoes of Joyce, Rabelais, Fielding and Sterne. Its protagonist Franz Biberkopf experienced freedom as a fearful state of exile, and returning to Berlin after he'd been in prison, he asked: Where do I go now?

It was a loaded question.

The Adventure

Affectionately, friends and comrades called her Nelke and on her birthday delivered a large bouquet of red carnations to her door. They were all more than a little in love with this tall blonde with sky-blue eyes.

In January 1929, Nelly Kröger no longer worked as *Animierdame* at the Kakadu. Her group favoured the more intimate depths and generous glasses of another bar. So that was where she found a job, as hostess at the Bajadere.

She had also moved from Kant Strasse to a small apartment with more light, in Leibniz Strasse. Apart from the bed and the wardrobe, she furnished it with a red upholstered chaise longue, an ottoman and an oriental rug, a dressmaker's dummy in one corner, in the other a tabouret bearing a dwarf palm in a brass bowl. There was a fireplace, and many mirrors which kept catching and casting out green curtains, white wall angles, pale winter sunbeams and licks of flame. Mirrored palm fronds quivered all around the room.

Nelly ranged widely in her reading, insatiably, through newspapers, pamphlets, histories, comics, crime fiction, even atlases. Below the window stood a modest desk with five books arranged between two miniature wine-barrel bookends: *Effi Briest*, and in translation, *The Bride of Lammermoor*, *Madame Bovary*, *Anna Karenina*, as well as a thin paper volume of a play she had just discovered, Ibsen's *Hedda Gabler*. These five were her special books, that she re-read often and worried over. Books with hooks, she called them.

When she moved from Kant Strasse to Leibniz Strasse, Nelly transported her two tame jackdaws, Vogel and Vogelfrau, in a large ornamental cage borrowed from a friend. For a few days she kept them locked inside. Then she let them out into the room. A few days more and she opened the window, leaving it ajar despite the cold, to introduce them to the new windowsill and outside ledge, placing food on both. Each new set of possibilities produced intonations of muted argument and sweet agreement between Vogel and Vogelfrau.

One evening, hurrying across town before work to return the borrowed birdcage, Nelly stopped to help a woman in a wild-looking fur who had fallen on the pavement. Another woman, more elegantly dressed, intervened. Nelly moved aside and watched their strange performance. Then the two drove off. It was only on her way back, passing the same spot, that she noticed the parcel which the fur woman had clutched. Its soaked wrapping paper was almost indistinguishable from the dirty snow piled along the street edge of the pavement. She picked it up and took it home. Inside it was an exquisite slip, which she washed with Sunlight soap and hung up to dry.

In January 1929, via Harwich and the Hook of Holland, Leonard and Virginia Woolf, Duncan Grant, Vanessa Bell and her son Quentin, aged eighteen, arrived in Berlin, at a station which to their horror was not mentioned in the Baedeker guide. They had come to hear music and see art, and to visit their friends Harold Nicolson, who worked as a counsellor at the British embassy, and his wife, Vita, who was spending Christmas and the New Year with him.

Leonard refused all invitations to Harold's dizzying rounds of diplomatic cocktails and dinners. Instead, guided by Vita, who happily escaped from her husband's social obligations, the group of visitors spent their first evenings struggling through grey snow and tundra winds, moving in a line – wolves with bells, someone joked – between their base at the Hotel Prinz Albrecht and a string of restaurants that might, but often did not, have a large enough table at such short notice. Vanessa suspected they were not very successful in their searches for dinner because they looked odd, with their long English faces, alternately tense and childishly hilarious from the adventure. Virginia, in particular, was a sight; being hungry without knowing it, she seemed more than usually disoriented. The city of London occupied her mind so fully, there was no space for Berlin. At the restaurant door Leonard would usher Virginia ahead of everyone else to get her out of the cold. She was dressed in a coat borrowed from her mother-in-law, which she said was *like the pelt a sheep wears when it's been left on a high mountain alone for too long – an old sheep*; her shoes covered in mud, her cheeks alarmingly red, her chignon coming undone. Vanessa thought her sister looked like a sketch, lines hastily captured on paper, intimations of a great work.

They were to stay a week. After the initial, exhausting efforts at tourism, walking everywhere and getting lost in what Virginia later described as an immeasurably mediocre place, too sprawling, ugly, cold and noisy, they found meagre comfort when they decided to take their meals at the Hotel Prinz Albrecht's restaurant.

That winter, one in fifteen of Berlin's inhabitants suffered from an especially severe influenza. Amidst the sniffing, sneezing, watery-eyed masses, Leonard worried about Virginia, who displayed bursts of intense nervous energy, presaging illness. Waiting for Vita, she would not sit still, rushed forward when she heard a call, knocked over a pot plant and scooped up the soil with a teaspoon, forgot, and seconds later stirred her cup. With the taste of earth in her tea, in the lobby of the Hotel Prinz Albrecht, where many of the faces were buried noisily in plain or bordered handkerchiefs, Virginia probably caught the flu. Or so Leonard thought. But there were other occasions, of which he was not aware, when her immunity was loosening its hold. Waiting, he ordered a tray of cognac, which was called up from the cellar with a great deal of pomp, the bottle dusted off, its complex liquid poured sparingly and sipped from glass balloons, to warm throats and calm nerves.

Three years later the Hotel Prinz Albrecht became a favourite place for National Socialist meetings and rallies. Five years later the SS Reichsführer set up his headquarters there. Its cellars became dungeons for imprisonment, interrogation and death.

Virginia lost her gloves. So the band of English tourists made their way to Leipziger Platz and entered Wertheim's department store, where from an overwhelming selection, she chose a new pair in red leather, which gave her an idea, and she insisted on taking time to browse, saying she would meet them all half an hour later. Left alone, she quickly found her way to the lingerie section. Touching linen, batiste, charmeuse and various grades of satin and silk, she decided in a flash to purchase something rare, in silk muslin. Rose? No, it was too fleshy, too predictable; not lilac either, and certainly not black or white. This blue! It had to be. She shivered from the thrill of resolution. It was a gift for Vita; and light as a feather, it might be carried unnoticed in her coat pocket until she had a chance to present it. Quentin watched her make the purchase. He had been asked by Leonard to keep a protective eye on his aunt and remained well hidden behind an armoury of stockinged legs, brassieres and corsets.

The group reassembled at the Romanisches Café, unaware of Joseph Roth rushing past them out the door, or Heinrich Mann writing at his regular table, close to the one at which they were being seated. They ordered coffees, except for Virginia, who announced that she was ravenous and kept changing her mind – Bienenstich, Mandeltorte – eventually selecting a large slice of Schwarzwälder – like that gentleman is having, she pointed discreetly. Heinrich, eating a cherry, nodded politely. She also asked for hot cocoa with mountains of cream.

The next day Leonard wondered if Virginia would prefer to take the morning off to rest in bed. She said no. The week was coming to an end. At some point, he told her, he would have to schedule a meeting with a couple of his political contacts, in a bar or a café.

But that last day the group was swept off again on a full itinerary by Vita, who had a car. Leonard wanted to see one of the poorer suburbs. So they drove to Wedding, where they parked and went for a walk, watched by faces from tenement windows, doorways and archways. Feeling feverish, Virginia began to peel off her hat, gloves and coat, until she was advised against it by the others. Vanessa noticed that her sister sought out and ran her hot hands across any cool, metallic surfaces within her reach, doorknobs, buckets, some empty milk cans, fence posts and carpet rails. They soon found themselves deep within one of the district's courtyard labyrinths. Virginia slid her fingers along the links of an abandoned dog chain, and across a screen of shadows she tossed a playful glance at Vita, who stepped back quickly as if to let it drop. Returning her ungloved hand to its coat pocket, Virginia wondered if icy satin would not have been a better choice for the intended slip. On their way back to the car, Leonard gently tugged her back from the contours of a chipped enamel chamber pot standing forgotten on some stone steps.

They visited the Hallenbad, to marvel at its artificial waves, then drove to Potsdam to see Frederick the Great's Sanssouci, the paintings, the mirrors, and the clock that had stopped at the exact moment of his death, the avenue of mulberry trees leading to the New Palace, their shoes on the gravel like the scroop of silk, the Shell Room's opalescence. Back in Berlin they cut briskly across the wintry cheerlessness of the Tiergarten. Their feet and wind-lashed faces ached. When they returned to the hotel in the late afternoon, Leonard made some phone calls. At seven? At the Bajadere? Let's see . . . Joachimsthaler Strasse? Kleist Strasse? The concièrge sketched directions on a piece of hotel stationery.

Bayadères, Virginia announced, are women of the Orient. According to Flaubert, and he would know, the mere word inflames the imagination. *Bayadères*, she set the word afloat, *odalisques* . . . as Leonard took his leave.

Vanessa, Duncan and Quentin were slumped in leather arm-chairs, Duncan yawning, Quentin reading *Buddenbrooks*. Vita asked them where they should eat that night. They shook their heads. They had no intention of going anywhere. Let's eat at the Funk-turm, Virginia called out from the foyer where she had said good-bye to Leonard. And then again, projecting her voice towards the high ceiling of the hotel lobby . . . we'll eat at the Fuck Turm!

In their hats and furs, and in high spirits, Vita and Virginia ventured out alone. As they stepped into the sleety night, Virginia laughing at her own exuberance, her imagined liberation, turning round and round with arms outspread like wings, she slipped and fell into a pile of snow.

Virginia sat in the gutter, amazed. Her red gloved hands held a small package. Something precious, Nelly thought as she crossed the street. She set down the large, ornately wrought birdcage which she had been carrying, and offered to help. She held out her hand to Virginia, who asked meekly if the empty cage was meant for her. At that moment Vita leaned across to lift her friend back onto her feet – she received a passionate embrace and it seemed that she too would lose her footing.

Vita regained her balance. In her handbag she kept a revolver; it belonged to her father, who had died recently. She pulled it out, so that only Virginia would see it, pointed it at her and told her sternly to stand up and get into the car. Sitting very still in her monstrous fur in a fast-melting pile of black snow, Virginia looked stunned, as if in fact she had been shot. The streetlight struck her red gloved hand, now grasping the coat across her chest, and Nelly, who had also caught a glimpse of the gun, thought it was blood welling to the surface and jumped forward. Once again Vita stepped in. Virginia smiled very slightly as she was ushered into the car and waved as they drove away. She did not know that Vita had also inherited her father's hoard of bullets.

At the Funkturm they ate duck. Virginia was so pleased to have Vita to herself and not, as she would later write, *Vita in black trying to be a diplomat's wife with Harold to pull the strings*, which she thought was always a pathetic sight. High above the gemstones on black-velvet night, the elation she had felt before, had felt earlier that day, returned. She imagined she was dancing, being danced, a tango, a two-step, a waltz, in the tower's searchlight turning round and round. (In his novel *Despair*, Vladimir Nabokov would describe the Funkturm's nightly ritual as *a luminous twitch; the wild lunacy of a revolving searchlight*.) She recollected a late English spring, the notes of nightingales and frogs, the frogs drumming. A cool, moist, metallic beat. Like a pulse, she thought. Like life, *vita*. And she declared her love.

At that very moment, Vita pushed a piece of shot from her tongue to her lips. She exhibited it on the palm of her hand, signalling to the waiter with the other, to make a complaint. This distraction brought Virginia's crescendo to a halt. Too much suppressed randiness, Vita thought, and managed for herself a subtle extrication from the plot. On the way back to the hotel she talked ceaselessly. Political gossip. Scientific discoveries. *There is a kind of mouse,* she told Virginia, forgetting that it was Virginia who had told her this, *which turns forever, because its ears have no spirit level.* Later on Vita would refer to this evening as a moment when Virginia gave startling and disturbing expression to her feelings.

Virginia remembered the slip, which she had lost in the snow. She remembered her mother, Julia, on her deathbed and that kissing her was like kissing cold iron.

To prevent seasickness on the way home, Vanessa offered her sister a dose of Somnifène, which caused her instantly to fall into a deep sleep. Leonard carried her, dead-bear fashion, over his shoulder, from ferry to train to taxi to bed. She was suffering from the combined effects of the drug and the flu, reducing her to a state of extreme physical and mental weakness. Leonard believed the excitement and exertion of their Berlin jaunt had taken its toll. He had suspected, he reminded the others, that she was already unwell when the drug tipped the balance.

The worst to endure, she knew from past experience, would be the headaches, the terrible pain through which she was obliged to crawl and claw from day to day in order to survive.

Virginia was bedridden for almost a month and unable to put pen to paper for another month. When her strength returned, she wrote to Vita. *It's so odd to have gone straight from all that movement, and big houses, and street signs and wine and Vita to lying alone in bed up here.* And again. *How you frightened me that night on the pavement.* She closed her eyes. *I see you with extreme distinction – well anyhow it was worth the week with you. I think of the tower and the lights and the waves and the shell room at Sans Souci and you, and you –*

The bird was back in her cage. *This is what makes one serene – these secret thoughts.* She often returned to that other place, perplexed *how the ugliness of Berlin remains with me.*

One morning, between waking and sleeping, she experienced a sensation of being washed by tides of light like water, but at the same time like the colours of speech and the flow of words. *One ought to invent a fine narrative style*, she thought. The sun rose. Birds chirped. *I feel on the verge of some strenuous adventure.*

She wondered who her reader would be.

Many scenes have come and gone unwritten . . . that summer, walking through a shady clearing, she saw a flower that looked at first like the eye of a bird. Carrying a bunch of furry-stemmed sky-blue speedwell for the vase on her desk and reflecting on what one of the village women had said – dry it in the shade, steep it, boil it briefly, two cups a day; bird's-eye, cat's-eye, speedwell, some call it veronica after the saint or hebe after the goddess; cures fevers and heals wounds – it crossed her mind – how absurd, it seemed completely unconnected – that one of the bills that came in after Emma Bovary's death was a three-year subscription to a lending library. She smiled. Bird's-eye, cat's-eye, authors playing tricks. For a brief moment she hoped the cerulean shade of speedwell might illuminate the most obscure lives and the very darkest places.

The windows were wide open. The sun shone in. Heinrich Mann and Nelly Kröger watched the antics of the two jackdaws with amusement and a glass of wine. They had just met. From afar Puccini reached their ears, and it made them laugh out loud when the birds picked up some strains of *La Bohème*. Nelly sat on his knee. She wore nothing but a blue silk slip. It was the summer of 1929. It would be an adventure.

Worlds Apart

*O*ne might criticise Th.[omas] Mann on the ground that he reminds one of a boy who has practised self-abuse and later becomes the head of a family . . . what does his problem child, Castorp, do in all that time on the Magic Mountain? Obviously he masturbated! But M. removes the private parts from his characters as if they were plaster-of-Paris statues. ROBERT MUSIL, *DIARIES*

Musil once thought he might *construct a person from nothing but quotations*.

Thomas and Katia Mann now had six children: Erika was born in 1905, Klaus in 1906, Golo in 1909, Monika in 1910, Elisabeth (called Medi) in 1918, and Michael (called Bibi) in 1919. After a long rift, the brothers Heinrich and Thomas Mann were reconciled in 1922. *Dear Heinrich . . . now we're over the mountain and will choose a better road, – together, if you want that as much as I do.* Their mother died in 1923. Thomas Mann's *Der Zauberberg* (*The Magic Mountain*) was published in 1924. Their sister Julia died in 1927.

In 1928 Heinrich separated from Mimi. They were divorced in November 1929; Mimi received 500 Reichsmark and thereafter Heinrich was required to pay 300 RM monthly, as well as provide for his daughter's clothing and education. Mother and daughter were given continued use of the household goods, furniture, books (legally they were his) and remained in their apartment. He moved to Berlin. There he had been involved with the actress and cabaret star Trude Hesterberg, who was usurped in her ambition for the lead role in *The Blue Angel* by Marlene Dietrich and in Heinrich Mann's affection by the young woman he met in a bar on 17 June 1929, Nelly Kröger. Thomas Mann was awarded the Nobel Prize in Literature on 12 November 1929. Heinrich spent the beginning of 1930 in Nice, some of the time with Nelly. In March they attended a pre-release showing of the *The Blue Angel* in a small cinema on the Promenade des Anglais; it premiered 1 April 1930 at the Gloria Palast on the Kurfürstendamm and became an instant international success. In France it seemed as if Heinrich Mann was known by every head waiter as *l'auteur de l'Ange Bleu*, while in higher circles he was regarded as a leading representative of the Weimar Republic, a tireless exponent of democracy, an advocate of the fledgling idea of the United States of Europe, speaker at conferences, member of various committees, signatory of numerous petitions. Everyone invited him to give readings from his work; he even made an appearance in a Berlin department store.

At the Grand Hotel in Aix-les-Bains in August 1930, Willa Cather, who built her narratives from chance encounters, met Flaubert's niece Caroline, now Madame Franklin Grout.

At the end of 1930, as the best book of the year, Döblin nominated Robert Musil's *Der Mann ohne Eigenschaften* (*The Man Without Qualities*), the first part of which had just been published, and Musil nominated Döblin's *Berlin Alexanderplatz*.

Nineteen thirty-one. Like many contemporary writers, Virginia Woolf wanted to capture the lives of ordinary people, to discover what went on behind veils of anonymity, *the thing that exists when we aren't there*. It was more difficult to achieve than she'd expected. On Monday 2 February she believed she was close to finishing *The Waves* (first conceived as biography, then as autobiography, then as a novel, and originally called *The Moths*). *Never have I screwed my brain so tight over a book.* She finished it on Saturday 7 February. *I wrote the words O Death fifteen minutes ago, having reeled across the last ten pages with some moments of such intensity and intoxication that I seemed only to stumble after my own voice . . . and I have been sitting these 15 minutes in a state of glory, and calm, and some tears . . .*

On 27 January 1931 Heinrich Mann was elected president of the literary section of the Prussian Academy of the Arts. But far from letting it all go to his head, he remained a pessimistic optimist, an optimistic pessimist, depending on the weather, who took nothing for granted and believed that by a sheer trick of fate his life could easily have taken, and could still take, an entirely different set of paths. Celebrations for his sixtieth birthday were held at the Academy on 28 March, with supper and speeches. At one point the chairman made a slip, referring to Heinrich as Thomas. In his own congratulatory speech, Thomas described his brother as a cultural paragon, a sentiment echoed by the poet Gottfried Benn. Speaking for an audience that represented an entire generation of German writers, he called Heinrich Mann the master who had made them all, and Flaubert's heir, and he praised the brothers Mann for the *phosphorising* effect of their work on German literature and culture. His exuberance no doubt received a dignified reply. In June Heinrich stayed at the Salzburger Hof in Bad Gastein. He wrote his brother that he hoped to spend some time with him this summer, suggesting Thomas could meet him and his daughter somewhere near Salzburg in July. He then planned to be on the Baltic coast in August, so they could also get together there. If all else failed, they'd see each other in Berlin in autumn. Thomas was in Lübeck in September, for his old school's four hundredth anniversary. In late October Heinrich delivered the eulogy for his good friend and hiking companion, the Austrian doctor, novelist and playwright Arthur Schnitzler. In a newspaper article in December he wrote that it was possible the Germans would now let the National Socialists get the upper hand, because they heard the beckoning call of the abyss, that it was a call the Germans heard fairly often.

On Sunday 28 March 1931 Virginia was surprised by her sadness at the news of the writer Arnold Bennett's death. He had drunk tap water in Paris and contracted typhoid. In April the Woolfs travelled to Montaigne's birthplace at Castillon. On their way home, at Le Mans, Virginia refused an ice-cream, remembering what had happened to Arnold Bennett. Thursday 28 May she described her headache as *flashes of light raying round my eyes, and sharp pain*. She wrote it was so bad that *if it were not for the divine goodness of Leonard*, she would have thought of death. In early June she dreamed of the writer Katherine Mansfield, of meeting her and shaking hands while knowing she was dead. Towards the end of June she had an idea for a book, *a voyage round the world . . . partly the result of Leonard saying if we go to America we should . . . go around the world*, and someone suggesting that she should write an *Orlando* of her tour. In July she talked to friends about *being in the cage*. She had a visitor who raised *her cup of tea six times to her lips but always thought of some new parenthesis or qualification and put it down untouched*. On Friday 17 July she gave the finished manuscript of *The Waves* to Leonard to read, and worried that he might not like it. Two days later he told her it was a masterpiece. At the beginning of October Harold Nicolson wrote to her to say the same, *The Waves* was a masterpiece. To herself she noted that if the book is anything *it is an adventure which I go on alone*. She found it odd that reviewers should praise her characters *when I meant to have none*. When the book sold well, its author was perplexed *that people can read that difficult grinding stuff*. Vanessa was overcome by its beauty. Vita found it dull. At the end of October Virginia commented that Leonard had spent ten years writing a book called *The Deluge*, just published, which was not getting a good response, and now he thought his work had been a waste of time. In November the novelist E.M. Forster called *The Waves* a classic. Virginia continued to suffer from headaches. Her friend Lytton Strachey was very ill.

Nineteen thirty-two. On Friday 1 January, Virginia wrote *O these dogs – that's my present curse. And one must learn to overcome it somehow. This irregular sharp bark is the devil. Ear stoppers?* But she found it difficult to write with earplugs. Strachey died 21 January 1932. Virginia wrote literary criticism, hoping that it would lead to a burst of fiction. At their house in Rodmell, in Sussex, Thursday 24 March was *the loveliest spring day: soft: a blue veil in the air torn by birds voices.* She was *glad to be alive and sorry for the dead.* In May the Woolfs went to Greece, to Corinth, Mycenae and Delphi, where she wore a silk dress, took off her shoes, and ate a bread roll with honey. Returning home, *just for a moment England and Greece stood side by side, each much enlivened by the other.*

A weekend of bliss in the form of uninterrupted sleep and reading at Rodmell in June, *with the may tree like a breaking wave outside; and all the garden green tunnels, mounds of green.* To celebrate, Virginia bought herself a desk and Leonard bought a beehive. The bees swarmed and hung *in a quivering shiny brown black purse* off a tombstone. *We leapt about in the long grass of the graves . . . the whole air full of vibration: of beauty, of this burning arrowy desire . . . the quivering shifting bee bag the most sexual and sensual symbol.* One night in July the Zeppelin passed *with a string of light hanging from its navel.* One evening in August while watching the flight of a white owl, she fainted, not into unconsciousness but into a great pain that pounded in her head like the galloping of horses. She was left hovering *like a most solicitous mother, over the shattered splintered fragments of my body,* and reflected on the possibility of sudden death in the midst of daily life, such as laughing or feeding the fish in the pond.

———

Kurt Hiller was born 1885 in Berlin. His father was a manufacturer of ties. He studied law and philosophy in Berlin, Freiburg and Heidelberg; his PhD examined the legalities of individual rights, specifically in relation to suicide and sexual practice. He was a pacifist, a gay and human rights activist, and a publisher. As a writer he was a founder of literary Expressionism, and with Carl von Ossietzky and Kurt Tucholsky, one of the most frequent contributors to the major left-wing weekly *Die Weltbühne* (founded 1905 by Siegfried Jacobsohn as *Die Schaubühne*; banned 1933). It featured Ernst Bloch, Lion Feuchtwanger, Erich Mühsam, Else Lasker-Schüler and Ernst Toller, among others, swelling its list of contributors with the pseudonyms of its regulars: Tucholsky's included Kaspar Hauser, Peter Panter, Theobald Tiger, and Feuchtwanger sometimes posed as J. L. Wetcheek.

Hiller considered Heinrich Mann to be the father of German literary activism, and in an article titled 'The President' (*Die Weltbühne*, 9 February 1932), he made the point that while Mann was clearly a leftist he stood above party politics, his thoughts were in touch with his feelings, and he was someone who could see the bigger picture. He argued that Mann could provide the unity so urgently needed by the left if it was to defeat the build-up of right-wing forces, and was the perfect candidate for Reichspräsident, the leader of the Weimar Republic, to challenge Hindenburg (and Hitler) in the March elections. If Heinrich Mann, who again spent several months at the beginning of the year in France, was flattered by this proposal, he did not take it very seriously at the time; years later he told his brother that it would not have been a bad idea.

In the first years of their relationship Heinrich and Nelly did not appear together in public, he was often away, and she retained

her job, her apartment, and her circle of friends. Despite their independence, they spent as much time as possible in each other's
company. When he was in Berlin she cooked his meals and typed
his manuscripts. On 15 February 1932, Nelly signed a copy of *The
Blue Angel* and sent it to her sister in America.

People said that Nelly was a storyteller. She often captivated
Heinrich with colourful accounts of her life. Whenever she produced another installment or embellished one already told, he
urged her to write it all down. Early in 1932, while he was in
France, this was the task she set herself. We can imagine that she
concentrated, that to test the sound of the words as they poured
onto the page, she spoke much of it aloud. Her birds tapped
across the parquet floor, scratched the floral carpet in search of
hidden seeds, and cocked their heads at her soliloquies. She must
have worked briskly, revising, retyping, to hand him the complete
manuscript when he returned to Berlin.

He was astonished. He read the work in one sitting. Nelly
busied herself and waited anxiously for his comments. When he
finished, he said it was extraordinary, it was almost a novel. What
do you mean by a novel! It's my life! Nelly replied. But she beamed
with pride at his praise and said that now she wanted to sell her
life. All over again, she joked. And she asked him which publisher
he would recommend. He told her he'd have to think about it.

What happened next? Perhaps one morning, not long after he
had read her work, she woke up to find him at his desk, deeply absorbed in writing. She was puzzled at his urgency, and noticed he'd
been up for hours, as the room was already cosy with a blazing fire
and an aroma of coffee hung in the air. They kissed. His hand
passed across the silk surface of her dressing gown, and where the
gown fell open, slid in to touch her sleepwarm skin. She asked
what he was writing. He pointed to the fireplace. But she did not
understand. He told her he had burned her manuscript and was

rewriting it. In Nelly's own account of this scene – filtered through second-hand reports – the details differed a little, but the climax was the same. She claimed that Heinrich read her manuscript, and still wearing his reading glasses, with an enigmatic smile, he dropped the pages into the fire. It was all so matter-of-fact. She asked what he thought he was doing, and did not know whether to laugh or cry. He explained that it was an important story and that it must be told, but as the Life and Times of Nelly Kröger, a complete unknown, it would never be published in the present climate. It was a serious life, he added, and that would be its title, *Ein ernstes Leben*. And since it was not right for him simply to put his own name on her manuscript, he was rewriting it. The book was finished in July and I like to think that she told him she thought her version was the better of the two, and that he agreed.

In June the chancellorship had passed to Franz von Papen, but he was never in control of the tragedy unfolding on the German stage. One sharp observer, Count Harry Kessler, noted that Papen *has the air of an irritable billy goat trying to adopt dignity and wears for the occasion a silk-lined black jacket, Sunday best. A character from* Alice in Wonderland. In July Kessler wrote, *while we spent Sunday driving through the lovely countryside, the unbridled, organised Nazi terror has again claimed seventeen dead and nearly two hundred wounded as its victims.* Assaults. Murders. Bombs.

Nelly recognised herself in Heinrich's heroine Marie Lehning: hair dyed blonde, eyebrows pencilled, the long stride of her walk, and like Marie she was loyal and she was smart. She did not mind the novel's digressions from the truth, satisfied that the tough lives of the fishermen and their families had been brought to the fore. It was all there, the spectre of the sea and of unemployment, the men's too frequent consolation of a glass of schnaps, and the women's infinite burden of child-bearing, child rearing and housework. When Marie moves to Berlin, navigating a minefield of corruption, she finds work in a bar called The Harem which was just like the Bajadere with its artificial flowers, posters of exotic destinations and women in leggy poses. We don't know how Nelly ended her own story, but its new author, struggling to compose the final pages, might have looked up from his writing and told her that she deserved a happy ending, a new beginning, and in a fairy-tale flourish, he punished the bad and rewarded the good. The heroine was arched between biographical truth and fiction like an acrobat whose supple spine describes a backflip, semicircular, and when she rights herself, it's the present moment, 1932 up close, and an Austrian clown, as Heinrich Mann called Hitler, has already entered the arena and started unpacking his sinister bag of tricks.

A beast claimed the earth. Its boots marched through the land, its knife-hands stabbed the sky. In November 1932 the Nazis won the votes. Some said smugly that history was being made. No no no, others replied in horror, the beast would soon be dead. Heinrich Mann's *Ein ernstes Leben* was published that same month. It was to be the last book of his to appear in Germany for over a decade. He told Thomas, these days you could no longer expect literature to influence politics, but you had to keep believing that chaos could still be sorted out, as it is in fiction. He was touched by his brother's response to the book and told him, *you've just proved once again that at every moment of my life you have been my closest ally.* He confessed that he had probably written the book too quickly, and that he had trouble with the ending, because when *the self-contained idyll of the first chapters was over, it was impossible to stand above the consequences – the dissolution as you put it.* His aim, Heinrich said, was to show the present moment infused with criminality. But he could not fix the focus on what was immediately before him. He knew only that throughout an ever-worsening situation the heroine had kept her inner strength and that was the story's meaning, if it had any meaning at all. He'd done his best. As with all his work, he was keenly aware of its imperfections. In a review, his friend Maximilian Brantl wrote that the book showed how now everything depended on the best judgement of ordinary people like Marie Lehning because the country had been abandoned by the gods.

In a strange gesture of defiance that might also look like blindness, Heinrich bought new furniture, including a desk and matching chair made of ash, with tapestry upholstery, the armrests carved with lionheads, and on 1 December 1932 he moved to 61 Fasanenstrasse, Berlin W15. How had Nelly and Heinrich spent their Christmases? She in Niendorf with her family, he in Munich with his daughter, worlds apart? Was this the first Christmas they celebrated together, with their closest friends? Did the snow fall softly, did ice crystals bloom on all the windowpanes, did Nelly stock the kitchen with extra butter and eggs and flour and spices to bake honeycake and gingerbread and stollen? Did she cook the most delicious meal, wear the most elegant gown, receive a precious gift, kick off her shoes to dance? Was the hall filled with the scent of pine needles and candlewax, did every room flicker magically with chandeliers and candlelight, did the guests leave drunk with the best wine and jokes and music? Was it a grand Christmas?

Nineteen thirty-three. Hitler became chancellor on 30 January. The same day Walter Mehring published a long poem in *Die Welt-bühne* called 'The Saga of the Giant Crab', warning that *once the crab-dictator's in, a reign of unrelenting woe will come upon us while we track, never forward, always back.* That night an SA torchlight procession snaked triumphantly through the Charlottenburg quarter of Berlin. In Wallstrasse, a Communist stronghold, the locals threw flowerpots and the Nazis opened fire, killing one of their own, Sturmbannführer Hans Eberhard Maikowski, a gardener and anthroposophist in his early twenties, as well as police chief

Josef Zauritz. They blamed the Communists. Altogether fifty-six people were charged. Nelly's friend Rudi Carius, who lived with his mother at 52 Wallstrasse, where the deaths occurred, was suspected as one of the snipers. It's not clear whether he went into hiding immediately, or if he initially complied with the police, to report every day. One writer has claimed that after his escape Rudi was sentenced to death, in absentia. A state funeral for Maikowski was held in Berlin Cathedral, attended by Hitler, with speeches by Göring and Goebbels broadcast to the nation. Wallstrasse was re-named Maikowski Strasse (it is now called Zillestrasse), and at what was once number 52, a commemorative Hans Eberhard Maikowski fountain and plaque were installed (they are no longer there). After the war, ex-SA men who were there that night revealed that following orders, an SA man had shot Maikowski, because on the one hand the party had found him difficult to control, and on the other, they could make a martyr of him, so killing two birds – Maikowski's nickname was 'red rooster' – with one shot.

When Hitler became chancellor, a group of leftist writers called a meeting to discuss what could be done; Brecht said he was ready to act, but requested a bodyguard.

Thursday 5 January, Virginia reminded herself that she wanted to ask Nora Darwin, editor of her grandfather Charles Darwin's diary, about Jemmy Button. She finished writing *Flush*, the biography of a dog, and started on *The Pargiters* (later to be called *The Years*). Sunday 15 January, *a cloudy, goose wing day with silver shields*, she described the physical sensations and pain of writing, which varied from book to book, how one work had increased her heartbeat and another had stiffened her neck muscles. *What connection has the brain with the body? Nobody in Harley St. could explain* . . . That day she and Leonard brought home their new car, a silver-green Lanchester. The following week they went to the ballet, but Virginia admitted that *I can't keep my wits at the ballet; can't*

throw a ring round so many wild horses – music, dancing, decoration: and
so hop on my perch, and merely make parrot noises of appreciation.

Jemmy Button, born circa 1815 on one of the islands of Tierra
del Fuego, was bought for a shiny mother-of-pearl button, and
with three others, Fuegia Basket, Boat Memory and York Minster,
was brought to England in 1830. It was said that he liked to wear
gloves and well-polished shoes, and showed great sympathy for
anyone in pain. Boat Memory died in England. In 1831 Charles
Darwin was on board the HMS *Beagle* that returned the other
three Fuegians to their home. Beguiled by the endless unfolding
of natural phenomena, of sameness and difference between species, and despite the fact that he suffered from seasickness, Darwin spent five years travelling, collecting, discerning. The passion
never ended. In his retirement he cultivated fifty-three varieties of
gooseberry in his garden in Kent. *See how different the leaves of the*
cabbage are, and how extremely alike the flowers; how unlike the flowers of
the heartsease are, and how alike the leaves; how much the fruit of the dif-
ferent kinds of gooseberries differ in size, colour, shape, and hairiness, and
yet the flowers present very slight differences.

In Germany, differences grew beyond coherence. All flirtatiousness between language and ideas grew wan. Subtleties died.
For three days in February, advertising pillars throughout Berlin carried placards signed by Albert Einstein, Heinrich Mann
and the artist Käthe Kollwitz, appealing urgently to Socialists
and Communists to form a united front against the Nazis. In a
speech on 10 February Hitler attacked democracy. By 15 February Heinrich had been expelled from the Academy of the Arts.
His apartment was under surveillance day and night. Sunday 19
February he attended a concert and dinner where all the guests
were keenly aware that it was the very last of such occasions; even
the host had packed his bags and had ordered the removalists for
the next day. When it was time to leave, the French ambassador

André François-Poncet shook Heinrich's hand and in a coded but nonetheless clear message, offered him diplomatic protection: he said, *if you cross the Pariser Platz, my door will be open.* Like Mann, he believed that European peace depended on an alliance between Germany and France. His friend Harry Kessler said François-Poncet wasn't an ambassador, he was a missionary. *Some sort of fate has brought him back to Germany, over and over again . . . In Germany he awakened to the life of the mind. Germany is the country which always attracted him most.* If François-Poncet saw the writing on the wall, there was no doubt that Heinrich had to get out of the country as soon as possible.

He'd started writing a biography of Henri IV of France, and sorted through his manuscripts, taking only what he needed for his work in progress. Nelly helped him pack. They decided that she was not in any immediate danger, and so would stay behind to close up their apartments and settle their accounts. Later, remembering his newly furnished rooms, Heinrich wondered at his own lack of anticipation of the looming crisis. Nelly's clearheadedness helped him escape quickly and inconspicuously. On 20 February she bought a train ticket to Frankfurt for the following day, and checked in a small suitcase. The next morning he dressed with his usual sartorial attention, shirt, suit, meticulously tied bow tie, woollen scarf, hat, coat, gloves. He might have stopped for a minute to consider . . . what? Whether to wear a brand-new pair of shoes, still in their box, or a more comfortable older pair? When he left on 21 February he carried only his umbrella and his briefcase. At the door he turned to look at his desk. What had he forgotten? Gently Nelly pushed him out into the hall. Their steps echoed in the stairwell, as if dozens of people were heading for the door at once. Outside the temperature was well below freezing. Did she hold his arm tightly, as they moved as one along the icy footpath, and repeat his travel plan to him several times, unsure if he was listening? She used to say to her friends that when Heinrich took a tram, she always had to tell him exactly how many stops to count and where to get off, otherwise he would keep going – deep in thought – until he reached the terminal.

The Anhalter Bahnhof was known as the Gateway to the Blue Beyond. Two figures above its entrance symbolised day and night, one looking into the distance, the other with its eyes shut. With every step shadowed by the pain of separation, they made their way through the swarming crowd and walked up and down the platform until it was time for Heinrich to board the train and for Nelly to remain behind. She suppressed her sobs and the constriction of her throat locked up her words. They must not make a scene in case they were being watched, and so offered each other little more than a polite farewell, cracked whispers, with the assurance that they would see each other soon. The train rolled off and headed south. It really was as if she'd turned him to face in that direction, wound him up and off he went. He spent the night in Frankfurt, continued to Karlsruhe the next day, 22 February, changed a hundred Reichsmark into francs, and crossed the bridge over the Rhine – he called it the Rubicon – to Strasbourg, never to set foot in Germany again.

It has often been recounted that at the very moment when Heinrich crossed the Rhine, the police arrived at 61 Fasanenstrasse, and that when they did not find him they searched, looted and destroyed the apartment, and then boasted that he'd been arrested. I have recently established contact with Rudolf Carius's daughter, who offers a postscript to this crucial moment. Heinrich Mann phoned Rudi and a few other friends just before he left and told them to come and take whatever they could carry. Nelly had the keys. In the time between Mann's departure on the morning of 21 February and the arrival of the police the next day, Rudi managed to remove the desk, desk-chair, a marble writing set and numerous books, including the collected works of Schiller, Goethe, Lenau, Körner, Shaw, and Shakespeare, three volumes of Zille, Zola's *Germinal* and *Thérèse Raquin*, and Dostoyevsky's *The Brothers Karamazov* and *Crime and Punishment*. What was left would later be claimed by the landlord in lieu of unpaid rent.

Heinrich travelled to Toulon, where he met his old friend, the Berlin-born critic and publisher Wilhelm Herzog. Wrapped in coats and scarves they drank *pastis* on the windswept terrace of a small hotel and talked about the last few days. Far from sadness or defeat, Herzog noted in Mann a tone of incredulity, even amusement. It covered up the fact that if he had not escaped in time, his fate would have been the same as that of others: on 27 February the Reichstag burned, followed immediately by an emergency decree suspending constitutional rights, and the mass arrests of political opponents, who were imprisoned, tortured and killed.

Over the next decade, half a million Germans left their country. With foresight Tucholsky had gone into exile years before; Roth left Berlin for Paris on 30 January 1933. Thomas and Katia Mann left Munich on 11 February; he delivered his Wagner lecture in Holland, Belgium and France; then they went to Arosa in Switzerland, where he began to write the diary that would become the record of his exile. On 28 February Döblin left with his wife for Switzerland, their sons following the next day; they then went on to Paris. With his wife, the actress Helene Weigel, Brecht also left that day for Prague, Vienna and then Switzerland, where they met Döblin and Feuchtwanger. Having made sure that his pets were safe, while preparing to escape, with the train ticket in his pocket, Erich Mühsam was arrested on the night of 27–28 February. Walter Benjamin stayed a few more weeks, departing 17 March. Heinrich Mann's former wife, Mimi, and their daughter Goschi left Munich in March to live with Mimi's parents in Prague; the contents of their Munich apartment, including furniture and books, were seized. On 19 April, after being beaten in the street in Berlin, Else Lasker-Schüler immediately boarded a train for Switzerland; because she arrived in Zürich with nothing, she had no choice at first but to sleep on park benches. When, after the expulsion of his friends and colleagues, Gottfried Benn chose to remain in Germany and was elected head of the poetry section of the Academy of the Arts, Thomas Mann's son Klaus wrote him an open letter: outraged, he said that Benn had let down young writers like himself, who once looked up to him.

The results of the Reichstag election on 5 March gave the Nazis 288 votes, with 120 for the SPD and 81 for the KPD. Dachau concentration camp was opened two weeks later. After Heinrich's departure, Nelly's life became a frenzied web of bureaucratic ends which she had to tie on his behalf, while maintaining contact with Rudi and others of their circle who'd gone into hiding. The city was rife with rumours. People she'd known had disappeared. Knocks on doors went unanswered. Her phone was tapped. When she was followed, she deliberately exhausted her pursuers on erratic trails across Berlin, as much to protect her friends as herself.

She was arrested several times. Once, under suspicion of trying to withdraw money from Heinrich Mann's account, which was now blocked, she was kept for interrogation at the police station for three days. They thought that she was preparing either to send the money to him or to deliver it personally. She was indignant and called their bluff by demanding to speak directly with the police chief. It was a dangerous game she played. As hostess at bars like the Kakadu and Bajadere, and as Heinrich's mistress, she was well connected across Berlin's social strata, and through her network she had access to a wealth of secrets which their original owners would rather not see publicly revealed. Blackmail was one of her options. And when things got too sticky she could also call on someone who seems to have been both a close relative and an SS officer to bail her out. In her letters to Heinrich, for fear they might be intercepted, she did not disclose the officer's name, but referred to him in code as Ningo. A character called Mingo appeared in *Ein ernstes Leben*, and this was also the nickname of her youngest brother Walter, who had joined the SS, and he may well have been the one who helped her. In the end it was agreed that a certain amount of money from Heinrich Mann's account did in fact belong to her, the sum of monthly payments owed to her as his housekeeper. But Mann was required to authorise the payment.

When Nelly was released, she feared her cover could be blown at any moment. When a friend who knew that she was being watched and had already been in trouble phoned to ask her to deliver a manuscript to Mr Herzog in France, she wondered if this was a setup. While Nelly seemed strong to others, who continued to depend on her, her mind filled with anxieties and her defences crumbled. Perhaps she opened her eyes one morning and no longer knew how she would face the day. Perhaps she hardly slept. She sought medical help, but the drugs she was prescribed only made things worse, causing headaches, nausea, dizziness. On 29 March she fainted and falling, hit her head. A psychiatrist who examined her concluded she was suffering from a nervous breakdown, and told her that it was not the best time – historically speaking – to be going crazy; now more than ever it was important to have your wits about you; his own family had already left the country and he'd be leaving soon. She should do the same. He wrote her a doctor's certificate which issued a warning, to whom it may concern (in other words, anyone trying to interrogate or arrest her), that any aggravation to the patient would lead to a deterioration of her condition with possible fatal consequences. He asked her if she had anyone to look after her. Over the next few months she kept this piece of paper with her at all times.

Thomas Mann had always been extremely uncomfortable with any kind of separation or departure. This feeling was now intensified to the point of panic. He knew that doors had closed on one part of his life – Germany – and that he would need to reinvent himself. His deep sense of loss led to fever-like symptoms, when his body shook with fear and pain. He suffered badly from insomnia. He took pills, Luminaletten, to get him through the day, and to sleep at night, Adaline with peppermint tea, and Phanodorm, among other products. He chose to read Tolstoy's *War and Peace*. Tuesday 21 March he saw in the *Neue Zürcher Zeitung* that in Germany Jewish lawyers and doctors were being removed from public office, and Communists, Socialists and Jews were being sent to concentration camps. He received letters warning him not to return home. When he met with fellow exiles and they talked inexhaustibly about the criminality and repugnant insanity, the sick sadism of those in power in Germany, he needed Adaline, Phanodorm and chamomile tea to help him sleep. He and Katia knew they were lucky to be out of the country when the disaster struck; it would have been much worse if like so many others they had been forced to flee across the border without notice.

On 1 April, SA and SS troops marched through the streets of Berlin to enforce the boycott of Jewish businesses. Nelly was still sick and one of her sisters came to take her home. From Niendorf she wrote a number of letters to Heinrich. Addressing him formally as Herr Mann, she told him about her misadventures: how she extricated herself from the clutches of the police and after closely checking her calculations the officials had agreed to pay the amount Mann supposedly owed her. Otherwise his bank account remained blocked and nothing else could be retrieved. He must send his permission to the police chief, with a copy to her. This was very important. Or should she leave for France immediately? She hoped his daughter Goschi was no longer in Germany, since there was a great danger she might be arrested in order to lure him back. In a postscript she said that life was shit.

On 4 April she wrote again to say so many bank accounts were frozen that now each written appeal took a long time to resolve, and again stressed the importance of the two letters Heinrich needed to send, one for the police chief and a duplicate for her, as that way she was more sure to get results. She worried that her Berlin apartment had been broken into, and asked him to send her enough money for the return fare to Berlin, since she'd arrived in Niendorf without a penny. She was restless to leave, but was still unwell, and waited anxiously for his reply.

One letter surviving from that period is undated. Nelly told Heinrich that it wasn't easy to be calm. She'd managed to rest a little and to think things through. Some of their mail had obviously gone astray. She was angry to be left alone in this messy situation, hampered and harassed by officials, while he was oblivious to it all and much too slow in responding to her requests for various forms and letters that were necessary if she was to get anything done at all. Now she needed his consent to terminate the rental agreement on his apartment. Her efforts had landed her in a great deal of trouble. First she had to dodge grubby remarks regarding her claims that she was his housekeeper. Then she had a hard time convincing the authorities that Heinrich Mann's income was not as high as they supposed and that he had not been able to pay her for her work for two whole years. She'd explained to them that any publishers who had not gone broke over the last couple of years were nonetheless in great financial difficulties and could not pay their authors. In order to obtain as much money as possible from the account, she'd tried to tell them that Mr Mann wanted to provide for her until she found a new job. But it didn't work, since they still suspected her of being his mistress and of trying to get the money for him. She said she caused quite a scene, but it made no difference.

Her apartment had been wrecked and the neighbours looked at her with a mix of mistrust and pity, as a constant stream of brownshirts and police from the department of criminal investigation came and went. The police chief said Heinrich Mann's conduct was treasonable and they would not rest until he was caught. Nobody told her the exact nature of the charges against him. They whispered things she didn't hear. All the backstabbers were emerging from the shadows and she could not bear to think how it had come to this. She hoped it was only gossip, not real accusations by people they had once considered to be friends and who now seemed out to destroy them. The slander and the bureaucratic grind were too much to bear; she had lost weight; her face was so thin she could hardly find it in the mirror. She would not stay in Berlin a moment longer and was uncertain what to do next. Get a job; or move in with her sister and brother-in-law, Käthe and Emil Säbel in Lübeck, where Hitler had been made an honorary citizen. For now Heinrich should address his letters to Marie L. (using Nelly's fictional double Marie Lehning), c/o Säbel. She was tempted to leave for France without delay.

She'd signed the letter and then resumed it, because the mail had just arrived with a copy of the authorisation he'd sent to the police chief, which was so complicated she feared it would simply disappear into a bureaucratic file. She was frustrated, reiterating that what she needed was a very simple note to take to the bank in person in order to deal with the matter on the spot. She reassured him that everything else had been settled, but she could not give details of her arrival, fearing that her travel plans would be discovered, in which case all her nightmares would turn out to be real.

Mid-April, Heinrich wrote to Thomas to tell him he was staying at the Hôtel de Nice. He said he'd read newspaper reports that
Göring had denied he was trying to wipe out the intellectuals. One
could only hope those Nazi bandits had a guilty conscience and
that their lies and crimes would be uncovered. The worst thing
was that the rest of the world wanted to believe that the Nazis'
main agenda was their fight against communism, and the persecution of Jews did not fit this picture. In the South of France friends
were arriving from Berlin, looking ten years older than when he'd
seen them last.

Saturday 1 April in Lugano, Thomas read in the papers that
in Germany Jewish shops were being marked with yellow stars.
He heard that his publisher, old Samuel Fischer, needed strong
medication to help him sleep. Thomas was concerned that he did
not have a passport, and about the diaries he had left behind in
Munich. If they were discovered and made public, there would
be terrible – perhaps fatal – consequences. Was he suggesting
that if the contents were revealed, he would have to kill himself?
Brecht was also in Lugano, but Thomas declined an invitation to
get together. A letter from his brother overflowed with hatred for
the thugs in power in Germany.

In March Virginia rejected an honorary doctorate from Man-
chester University, which meant that *I need not emerge from my fiction
in July to have a tuft of fur put on my head*. It was the finest spring
she had ever known – *soft, hot, blue, misty*. In the Letters page of
the *TLS*, George Gissing's son objected to an essay Woolf had written about his father, and she replied. *I am sorry . . . I have left out
three dots to indicate that the words 'with a cart' are omitted. Otherwise the
quotation is accurate. I also regret that I may have led the reader to suppose
that Gissing dined off lentils a year after he had given up eating them; still
got up at five when he had stopped getting up at five; took six books to a
bookseller when in fact he took only two; referred to a fog and a landlady*

when there was not a fog or a landlady; and used the phrase 'as he died' instead of 'two days before he died'. Such mistakes do not seem to me . . . of a serious nature. But I apologise for having stated that the Gissings had *'to scrape together what education they could get'* when it appears that there was no shortage of money for educational purposes. Regarding her work on *The Pargiters*, she told herself she must be *bold and adventurous. I want to give the whole of the present society – nothing less: facts as well as the vision.* She was aiming for a combination of two different styles, *The Waves* and *Night and Day*, but wondered if that was possible; *there are to be millions of ideas but no preaching – history, politics, feminism, art, literature – in short, a summing up of all I know . . .* Walking in Hyde Park, Virginia and Leonard ran into George Bernard Shaw, who talked and talked, and then asked if he was keeping them, and touching her arm, asked if she was cold. Afterwards, she said she thought Shaw liked them, but Leonard told her that Shaw did not like anyone. Saturday 29 April, they met the conductor Bruno Walter, one of Thomas Mann's closest friends, who was almost insane with despair about what was happening in Germany.

As Heinrich Mann's mistress and as a Communist sympathiser, Nelly's circumstances became dangerous. Did she also know Troplowitz was her father and did this increase the danger? It's unlikely that she made any more trips to Berlin, and it's uncertain if her attempts to have some of Heinrich's money released were successful. With the help of her family, she made plans to escape. Her brother Audi (August) would take her via Sassnitz to Denmark on his fishing boat, then she would travel via Copenhagen and Brussels to the South of France. Nelly asked Rudi, who had been in hiding for months, whether he wanted to come too.

After Karl Marx and Karl Kautsky, Heinrich Mann's name was third on a list of authors issued on 9 May to Fascist student groups. Many young people were disenchanted with their elders, and what a great symbolic game the new government now encouraged them to enact: to play with fire! On the evening of 10 May on the Opernplatz opposite the university in Berlin a bonfire was lit; bands played patriotic songs; uniforms – SA, SS and Hitler Youth – were de rigueur. Then in support of a cultural policy that was nationalist, racist and anti-modern, in the hour before midnight, books were passed along a chain of hands and thrown into the flames, in synchronicity with similar events on the Römerberg in Frankfurt, the Königsplatz in Munich, the Schlossplatz in Breslau, and in front of the Bismarck column in Dresden. Goebbels and his young deputies ceremoniously denounced each writer with a *Feuerspruch*, a fire speech. *In the fight against decadence and moral decay! In the fight for discipline and common decency within the family! I submit the work of Heinrich Mann to the fire.* And so Nelly Kröger's story, *Ein ernstes Leben*, was flung into the flames (for the second time, as Nelly might have noted). Radio broadcast the events. With great satisfaction Goebbels announced that the age of overdetermined Jewish intellectualism was now past.

In some cases, as with Heinrich Mann, one book was chosen and destroyed to symbolise a writer's entire oeuvre. In other cases, as with the satirist Walter Mehring, a number of books were destroyed. Throughout May and June, thirty German universities participated in this dark-age ritual. Later, books were pulped rather than burned and the paper was re-used to publish Nazi-sanctioned works. Other authors whose books were burned or were eventually banned included Henri Barbusse, Bertold Brecht, Alfred Döblin, John Dos Passos, Albert Einstein, Lion Feuchtwanger, Sigmund Freud, André Gide, Maxim Gorki, Ernest Hemingway, James Joyce, Franz Kafka, Helen Keller, Alfred Kerr, Irmgard Keun, Egon Erwin Kisch, Klabund, Jack London, Klaus Mann, Carl von Ossietzky, Marcel Proust, Erich Maria Remarque, Joseph Roth, Arthur Schnitzler, Ernst Toller, Kurt Tucholsky, Jakob Wassermann, H.G. Wells, Emile Zola, Arnold Zweig, Stefan Zweig.

Thomas Mann's name was not added to the list for several years. On 16 May libraries and bookshops received a warning to remove 131 authors from the shelves; twelve of them, including Heinrich Mann, were marked with a cross and identified as especially dangerous. By 1934 the list cited 4,100 books and publications. If banned books were found in random raids, the shopowner could be charged with high treason. Copies of all banned books were to be kept locked in the so-called poison cabinets of city and university libraries.

Katia and Thomas headed for France, where they would be reunited with their children. At Les Roches, Fleuries Thomas felt the aphrodisiac effect of being near the sea, was bitten by mosquitoes, read Tolstoy and took tablets to help him get to sleep. In the bathroom mirror he discovered that his hair had greyed. On 10 May they arrived in Bandol; since leaving Munich, this was their tenth stop after Amsterdam, Brussels, Paris, Arosa, Lenzerheide, Lugano, Rorschach, Basel and Les Roches. On 19 May, Thomas was relieved to find that a suitcase with his diaries had been delivered to his room. Heinrich had also arrived. Over the next weeks, on the terraces of harbourside cafés, in the garden of the Grand Hotel, or on short excursions, the brothers discussed their situation. Thomas was amused that Heinrich's Lübeck accent had reappeared with age, and envious that his brother managed to drink half a bottle of red wine followed by two glasses of cognac every night, as well as several coffees throughout the day, without being any the worse for it. He observed that physically and emotionally his brother was the more tenacious of the two of them; he thought the mere fact that he lived alone attested to an inner strength. But Heinrich had been receiving treatment for his nerves, and was taking homoeopathic phosphorus as a digestive aid. He told Thomas about Nelly Kröger, that she had been his *housekeeper* in Berlin and that he missed her terribly; she was being persecuted for her association with him and he was making arrangements for her to come to France.

The Manns' Munich bank account was appropriated by the German government. Thomas worried about the future of his family, his six children, and each discussion with Heinrich, Wilhelm Herzog or the Feuchtwangers only increased his anxieties. When he heard about the arrests of Ossietzky and Mühsam he noted that although he'd never had much to do with them he felt sick at the thought of what they faced. Night after night he took Adaline and Phanodorm. In Paris Harry Kessler had heard the same rumours about the Nazi maltreatment of prisoners. *For days and weeks they are mentally tortured and thrashed three times a day, morning, noon, and night. But what gets the victims down more than anything . . . is that they are forced to watch the ill-usage of their fellows. That induces complete breakdown.*

In May the Woolfs went to France and Italy. At Vienne Virginia watched the face of a woman embroidering green silk. At Charpentras she spoke to a servant girl, who admired their car and told them she would love to travel. They passed through Rapallo, an indolent orange-blossom world of English spinsters that she called Miss Cotton and Miss Thread. At Leirici, *very full of the breaking of waves*, they saw the house where the poet Shelley lived and the balcony where Mary Shelley had stood looking out to sea. Thoughts of Shelley's drowning and his body being burned on the beach. Then Siena, with a view *like a line of poetry that makes itself*; there they met two more people, a blue-eyed woman who wrung her dusty hands, and by the river a melancholy fisherman, both lamenting that they were too poor to travel. Virginia read Henry James and admired him for *driving his spoon deep into some stew of his own – some swarming mixture*. Abbeys and basilicas in the Tuscan countryside. A stonebreaker, an old woman, a man with a mule. None of the locals looked at the view. She recorded Friday 19 May in Piacenza, and then, *it's a queer thing that I write a date. Perhaps in this disoriented life one thinks, if I can say what day it is . . . Three dots to signify I don't know what I mean.* They crossed the Apennines. Sunday 21 May, visiting D. H. Lawrence's grave in Vence, they saw his *phoenix picked out in coloured pebbles.* Back in Vienne she noticed the odd angles of people's legs – men in urinals, children at play – and how the present moment was being drawn apart by the idea of going home. Followed by the anticlimax of returning. In London at the end of May, she wondered if what she experienced as depression was for others a normal state.

On Thursday 1 June, still in Bandol, Thomas marked the beginning of his birth month, his favourite time of the year. Heinrich praised his nephew Bibi's performance on the violin and this pleased Thomas. In the afternoon light the brothers walked along the coast; over coffee Heinrich told Thomas he'd heard from Nelly, and that she'd broken down from the strain of her recent experiences. When Thomas was sick with flu, Katia rubbed his chest with eucalyptus oil. News of political developments, and his private worries, increased his depression.

The Brechts set up house in Denmark. Bertolt Brecht needed to walk while he worked, and wherever they lived his wife made sure that he had his own large room for pacing.

In July in Bandol the Mann brothers continued to share their daily promenade and meals. Sometimes they joined others, the Schickeles, Meyer-Graefes, Zweigs, Feuchtwangers, or Heinrich's good friend, the elegant, monocled, chivalric Dr Oscar Levy, who was the British publisher of Nietzsche. One day Heinrich strolled to the pier alone and let his thoughts drift out to sea on the colours of an oil slick, its opal spectrum breaking up, rejoining. But it was hot, he had one too many glasses of red wine for lunch, felt sleepy, returned to his apartment, took a nap. And then? In the manuscript of his memoir, written many years later, there's a note in pencil. It describes how one day in the year 33 he experienced total happiness. *At the seaside town of Bandol, near Toulon, the door of my holiday apartment opens and my wife enters. She had followed me into exile, for her it was even more a place of exile, more foreign than it was for me . . . Without any sense of danger she had tracked across Europe. She had found me, stood before me. That was the greatest expression of human affection I have ever received. In all truth a moment of pure happiness . . .*

Their reunion must have occurred on or before 20 July, because that's when Thomas noted in his diary that Nelly had arrived. Thereafter he recorded many instances of meetings with his brother, without mentioning her name; he swam every day; he discussed his political ambivalence with his daughter Erika, acknowledging that on the one hand he had chosen exile and on the other he had not spoken out against the Nazi government because he was keen to protect his publisher and to ensure that his books would continue to be sold in Germany.

Forest fires, flies and mosquitoes in the South of France and a heat wave across Europe. Throughout August the ever-increasing circle of exiled writers and their families gathered at readings and *monstrous* garden parties, described by Sybille Bedford in her biography of Aldous Huxley. *It was a broiling afternoon; tea and drinks flowed. Petit fours melted in the sun.* While some wore shorts, *Heinrich Mann, even more stiff and formal than his brother, arrived in a high collar and black coat . . . Only Feuchtwanger circulated, making the round of the younger and more attractive women telling them about his latest sales figures . . . What struck the Huxleys was the regard some of them had for themselves.* Bedford also noted the presence of Heinrich's *Junoesque mistress.* It was a convivial summer; they took photos, like the one of Heinrich Mann and Lion Feuchtwanger at the latter's villa in Sanary, with the date, July 1933, in Nelly's handwriting on the back. Heinrich Mann's name now headed a list of so-called traitors that included Einstein, Feuchtwanger, Toller and Tucholsky, who were all stripped of their German citizenship and whose property had been confiscated.

In August Virginia was exhausted from the effort of living *in two spheres*, the novel and life. She struggled to continue writing. By the end of September her *summer is put away folded up in the drawer with other summers*.

Thomas re-read *The Fall of the House of Usher*, and remembered that his own protagonist, Hanno Buddenbrook, had quoted from that story. He enjoyed his daily swim in the Mediterranean more than ever. Their daughter Erika found a house for them in Zürich, which Heinrich thought was too close to Germany. In a Czech paper, Joseph Roth denounced the publishers who remained in Germany. Thomas must have felt implicated; he referred to Roth as an alcoholic who'd only gained status from his emigration. But by now his children Klaus, Erika and Golo had told their father he must publicly declare his opposition to the Hitler regime. Katia, on the other hand, supported her husband's reticence, since one of his books was about to come out and it would not be right to cause trouble for their German publisher. Tuesday 12 September he tried to think through his dilemma while walking first with Katia and then alone. Lightning lit the sky. When he returned home he found that Heinrich and Nelly had arrived for dinner, exasperating his tiredness and nervousness. He thought Nelly was *very common*. French papers reported that a German newspaper publisher and WWI veteran, who was arrested by the Nazis, had been returned to his family in a coffin, and that after being fired from his post, a German professor of psychiatry had committed suicide. Friends told Thomas that Heinrich was sick with worry about his brother's decision to live in Zürich. Thomas found this curious, and at their farewell party he was touched by his brother's concern. He wondered if he'd made the right decision, and felt depressed. Wednesday 27 September they moved into Schiedhalden-strasse 33, in Küsnacht near Zürich.

Brecht was in Sanary for a month from 17 September to 17 October, staying with Margarete Steffin at the Hotel La Plage; they were working on *The Threepenny Opera*. After meeting with Heinrich Mann, he thought Mann was imitating Victor Hugo in exile and dreaming of a second republic.

In October Heinrich was awarded honorary membership of the British branch of PEN and elected honorary president of SDS, Schutzverein Deutscher Schriftsteller, the exiled German Writers' Union. Tirelessly he made the thirty-hour trip from Nice to Paris whenever there were meetings to attend. While they looked for an apartment, Nelly and Heinrich stayed at the Hôtel du Louvre. Their friend Rudi was in a hotel nearby. Heinrich wrote Thomas about the rumour that the *traffic jam* in Germany would last about two years, and then there would be war. He wrote again in mid-October, to thank his brother for sending him his book, and said he would read it when he had more time. He wondered if Thomas had come to terms with living in exile while his books still appeared in Germany. He was dismayed that the rest of the world tolerated what was going on in that country.

Thomas acclimatised slowly; if in France he was plagued by the Mistral, in Switzerland he complained about the Föhn; walking on unfamiliar paths caused panic attacks. He received a long, affectionate letter from his brother. Germany issued racial laws forbidding marriage between Jews and Aryans. While convinced of his absolute rejection of the Nazis, Thomas still had difficulties accepting the idea of exile.

Heinrich told his brother he supported his decision to continue publishing in Germany, that he would have done the same. The French edition of his own book, *La Haine* (Hatred), had appeared, and the German edition, *Der Hass*, published in Amsterdam, would soon follow. It would never reach more than a handful of readers in Germany, while the English were completely disinterested in anything outside their immediate domain. Heinrich wondered if the people left behind in Germany were worse off than those in exile and if this might lead to the regime being overthrown from within; there might even be a Communist uprising. Meanwhile he was upset that his own German publisher Zsolnay, while keeping him under contract, would neither publish nor distribute his books and had not contacted him. He asked Thomas not to talk to their mutual friend Wilhelm Herzog about this, because it might get back to Zsolnay. The letter included greetings from Nelly. In the next letter he praised what he'd read of the first volume of his brother's *Joseph* trilogy; it reminded him of Anatole France's knowledge of angels, their history, their relationship with humans and with god. The work was both intimate and universal, and he admired the great amount of research it had taken to achieve this; he also loved its mix of gravity and humour. He continued to worry about his brother's safety in Switzerland and warned him to be wary of everyone he met. Again he added Nelly's greetings to his own.

On Wednesday 8 November Thomas felt a shake, a sideways shift and heard a cracking in the walls; he wondered if it was an earthquake; the newspapers later confirmed that the quake's epicentre was in Germany. Some of their belongings had been salvaged after all and arrived from Munich; for Thomas, sleeping again under his favourite silk quilt meant that he would not be going back. He and Katia met Wilhelm Herzog for dinner and they talked about Heinrich, his women, his naivety and contradictions, soft-heartedness, hard-heartedness, his work and its weaknesses. A week later Thomas was reading Heinrich's *Der Hass*; he noted that despite its faults, in particular its tendency to slide into unreality, he was deeply affected by its pathos. He wrote to thank his brother for sending him both the French and German editions, and was full of praise. More of the Manns' household goods arrived from Munich.

By Christmas Heinrich and Nelly had moved into 11, rue du Congrès in Nice. He wrote to his brother that he had no desire to return to Germany, not even if he could, not even when this was all over, because it would never really be over. He wished him a few happy surprises for the coming year.

In his diary Thomas Mann noted the welling up of childhood memory and joy on Christmas Eve, the magic. On the last day of the year he felt a little homesick for Munich, but perhaps even more for the South of France, where he'd been happiest most recently: on the stone terrace, sitting in a wicker chair, looking at the starlit sky.

Reading over her old diaries, Virginia had *the sense of all that floating away for ever down the stream . . . of the past swallowing so much of oneself*. She now thought *a very plain narrative might be interesting*.

In February 1932, Klaus Mann was drinking tea at Deux Magots in Paris, when Joseph Roth and Max Ernst passed by. In March he had a nightmare about his father being forced to shoot himself and jump out of a fifth-floor window. In May he was in Venice, reading *Anna Karenina*. In June he visited Alfred Flechtheim in Berlin. In July he cried in a dream about his father's death. In August he feared the dark. In November he was in Berlin again and in a café he ran into his uncle Heinrich. In December he was in London, where Eddy Sackville-West took him for a drive to Knole, the family's magnificent ancestral home, of which Eddy was the heir, thus bypassing the more direct female line of inheritance of his cousin Vita.

January 1933. Klaus was captivated by Heinrich's *Ein ernstes Leben*; when he discussed it with his mother, he found that she disapproved of its manipulation of the facts. He again dreamed of his father's death. In February he woke up one morning, wishing to die and fearless of death. In May, with his family in France, it was strange for him to see the two brothers, his father and his uncle, together; they were very different; he described Heinrich's bearing as *gentle and resolved*. In October he watched a magnificent shower of shooting stars and regretted that it was not the end of the world. That month he dreamed, *I was supposed to sit at the same table as Goebbels and Göring, who were in high spirits; Goebbels was bearable, but when Göring arrived, I left.* In December he dreamed that he was skiing and could not stop, grabbed hold of a small tree that he pulled over; the tree grew on a great mountain of books which he had caused to slide dangerously out of control. The real avalanche Klaus faced was his addiction to drugs: the repertoire included Eukodal, morphine, opium, cocaine, Veronal and ether.

Robert Musil's wife, Martha, once dreamed that she'd read in the paper that Thomas Mann's son was getting married, but the article had left out the fact that his bride was Robert Musil's daughter. Musil thought he could use this material to make a story about someone posing as Klaus Mann, confidence tricksters, plagiarism and the *overvaluing of M[ann] to the extreme of absurdity.*

Part Two

They Dwell in Us

We were miserable, we used no more than a hundredth part
of the gift we received for our long journey.

Moments from yesterday and from centuries ago –
a sword blow, the painting of eyelashes before a mirror
of polished metal, a lethal musket shot, a caravel
staving its hull against a reef – they dwell in us,
waiting for fulfilment.

CZESLAW MILOSZ, 'LATE RIPENESS'

1934: The Forest

Jakob Wassermann was born 10 March 1873 in Fürth, known as the town with a thousand chimney stacks, famous for metalwork and the production of mirrors. It had one of the oldest Jewish communities in southern Germany. He loved his mother, who was kind and beautiful. In his memoir *My Way as German and Jew* (1921) he wrote, *I was often told that strangers who visited the town and got to hear about her beauty, became so intrigued that they would request to see her.* She died when he was nine. Half the town followed her coffin to its grave. Then his father's grief cast a shadow so dark and creeping that it made a place in the boy's mind, where fears grew uncontrollably like weeds. He feared people, objects and ghosts. His father pursued and failed in a number of business ventures, including a toy factory that was destroyed in a fire. Since Jakob was forbidden to write poetry during the day and so wrote in secret by moonlight, he was the first to see the toys go up in flames. He later said he grew up in an atmosphere of misery, mistrust and superstition, where pleasure and learning were regarded with great suspicion. Once, on opening a book that attracted him, he was told that anyone who read Spinoza would go mad. Such was the case, he said, with anything enlightening that came within his reach. We know that when homes become unhomely, children in fairy tales are forced to seek refuge in forests. Jakob's place of escape was his own imagination. *Between the ages of 10 and 20 I lived in a constant state of dreaming, very far away . . . I was told later, that even while I was apparently wide awake, I had to be loudly called into awareness.* His passage back into the world – an apprenticeship at his uncle's factory and a year of military service – was awkward and full of mishaps. When the army asked him for a *curriculum vitae*, he was unworldly enough to present it as a poem. In 1896 in Munich, Wassermann's first published story, 'Finsternis' (Total Darkness), appeared in a new magazine called *Jugend* (Youth). It told how one day while hiking in the Black Forest (a favourite pastime of the author) a man got lost and as night closed in he was overcome with a terror so intense that he lost his mind and had to be admitted to an insane asylum. The man was cured and told his story to a stranger while they both waited at a station for the train to arrive.

You take a wrong turn. In German *sich verirren*, to lose one's way, is closely related to *sich irren*, to make a mistake, as well as the adjective *irr*, crazy, and the noun *Irre*, madman. From a simple *oops, sorry* to total insanity, the kith and kin of error leap through a mindstream of lexical derivatives performing nasty acts like *irreführen*, to lead astray, and its sad consequences, *irrewerden*, to become confused, *Irrtum, Irrglaube, Irrsinn, Irrläufer*, a letter delivered to the wrong address, *Irrgarten*, a maze, and *Irrenanstalt*, an insane asylum. Darkness falls. You pronounce the double-r from deep inside your throat like swallowed mud. Or from the mouth, the tongue purring 'rr' like a modern engine. Walter Benjamin believed in *Irrkunst*, the art of erring, of getting lost.

Caspar Hauser oder die Trägheit des Herzens (1908; *Caspar Hauser. The Enigma of a Century*, 1928) was Wassermann's best-known work. Caspar Hauser (1812–1833) was a real person (the author's grandfather had seen him in the streets of Nürnberg), a homeless foundling rumoured to be a prince descended from a number of European dynasties. He came to be called *the child of Europe*. With this book, Wassermann was among the very first twentieth-century writers to challenge the German obsession with social hierarchy. He said, *I was convinced that I'd given Germans an essentially German book, from the very soul of the nation . . . But the public balked at the fact that such an idiosyncratic book should have been written by a Jew*. Disillusioned, he looked into the mirror to see if he could find the split in himself, as did so many of his generation – Schnitzler, Toller, Polgar, Döblin, Roth – *youths from nowhere* (to paraphrase the opening of *Caspar Hauser*) who had made the leap from humble beginnings to cultural eminence, only to feel isolated from both sides. For Wassermann, German and Jew *was a distinction which I could neither comprehend nor cease to worry about*. In 1933 Heinrich Mann congratulated him on his sixtieth birthday. He said his work was enviable in its perfect fusion of reality and fiction.

On 1 January 1934, the Central Committee of German Jews for Relief and Reconstruction issued a report on Jewish public elementary schools. It began: *The Jewish schools develop a special character as a result of the twofold experience of life of every Jewish child living in Germany: Jewish and German. These two basic experiences are to be equally developed and made conscious; they are to be made fruitful and developed both in parallel lines and in the tension between them.*

Wassermann was a moralist. He was especially drawn to close examinations of injustice, because at its core he discovered not evil pure and simple, but something terribly human, *Trägheit*, a kind of lethargy of the soul, all leathery and repulsive, the hard heart that is the pod, and inside this indifference there is a seed, the miniscule residence of goodness. One imagines it is only tangible, barely audible, never visible. For him, every end point, exhaustion, fading spark, speck of dust, broken tip of thorn, broken word, every sound of something breaking, held a memory of tenderness and wholeness and a yearning that was inextinguishable. If you placed your ear up close, it spoke of new beginnings in a raspy whisper. Jakob Wassermann died Monday 1 January 1934 in Altaussee, Austria.

It's likely that on the first day of 1934 Nelly and Heinrich got up very late, having celebrated too long the night before. She prepared a light meal, perhaps she only heated up some soup. In the afternoon they walked along the promenade, soaking up the winter sun. They sat on a bench and looked out across the Baie des Anges. The painter Edvard Munch once wrote to a friend that it was far more wonderful in Nice than one ever imagined, especially the Promenade des Anglais, which *is imposing with the remarkably blue water on one side, water such an aerial blue that it seems to be painted with Naphtha.* In the evening, several evenings in a row, alone in their apartment, they sipped wine and he called her *mon ange* and they read Thomas's *Tales of Jacob*, published a few months before and already a great success in Germany. *Mes anges*, she called the little birds that hopped in and out of open cages and sang and flew around the room as if it were a room in heaven. Nelly liked to keep moving as she read aloud, holding the book up, chin raised, back straight. The old parquet floor creaked beneath the rhythm of her barefoot stride. Almost a dance. Heinrich was captivated by the gravity of her tone, was suspended in time until it was his turn. He read from the armchair or lying on the bed, propped by pillows. When he put the book down and took off his glasses, she placed her basket of knitting on the floor and picked up the book. A relay of narrative pleasure. When they finished, he wrote to Thomas about the book's richness and . . . what shall I say? He called out to Nelly as she chopped onions and garlic in the kitchen, and against the sudden hiss of vegetables in hot oil she called back . . . say it's poetic. So he wrote that it was *a poetic exten-sion . . . of slender sources.*

The second day of January, Thomas Mann went for a walk in the forest near his house in Zürich, and in the uncanny loneli-ness of an unfamiliar path he was struck with fear. He knew this feeling only too well. He had experienced it before. It was a loss of nerve so intense that it affected his entire physical and mental composure. He thought that he would faint, but somehow man-aged to pull himself together and find his way home, where he was told that his old friend Jakob Wassermann was dead. News of death always gave rise to thoughts of his own mortality, leaving him in a mess, nauseous, shaking, pale, irritable and frightened.

Despite the fact that he had been sent his favourite red silk quilt from the Munich house, Thomas continued to have trou-ble sleeping. In his diary he was still listing the Phanodorm, Luminaletten, Adaline, and chamomile tea that he regularly took to get a good night's rest. Some of these medications increased the potency of alcohol or other medicines taken at the same time; potentially addictive, they caused withdrawal symptoms if they were suddenly discontinued, including restlessness, fear, trem-bling, sweating and – insomnia. It was a vicious circle. For pain, particularly the recurring trouble with his teeth, there was a fur-ther array of drugs. In the months and years to come, he car-ried within him a never empty, often overflowing sense of crisis. When it threatened his hard-won equilibrium, he had a colour-ful vocabulary for what was essentially one and the same condi-tion, calling it *Erregung, Nervenkrise, Herzunruhe, nervöse Irritation, nervöse Verzweiflungszustände, Erschöpfungszustand.* He was deeply af-fected by reading one of Heinrich's essays, about surviving the first twelve months of exile, was devastated by the news that his house in Munich had been confiscated by the political police, sickened by reports of the mistreatment of concentration camp prisoners, and by the hopelessness of reports about the political situation unfolding in Vienna. His wife's talk of menopause released in him a spectrum of emotions from nostalgia to sheer terror at the thought of age and death. On holiday in Arosa, experiencing physical discomfort – a rough track to walk on, an expanse of snow that blinded him with glare – he again faced fear, palpitations, panic.

In Nice, Heinrich opened the briefcase in which he'd carried his manuscript across the border and took out the notebooks that were the work of years of research. His historical novel about Henri IV of France, known as the good king, was conceived during a visit to Pau in 1925, and probably the inspiration had come even earlier, when as a child he listened to stories his father told him, about kings and queens and foreign places. As well as his written notes, Heinrich now looked at the many drawings he'd made, and for long moments, I imagine, he lost himself in the memory of his quest, where he'd been and what he'd seen, how he'd cupped his hands to drink the icy water of the stream that flowed below the castle at Pau, had run his palm along the castle's walls and tapestries, tapped on the large tortoiseshell that had once been Henri's cradle and listened for an echo, as if such husks retained the memory of their seed. How the Pyrenees wind had blown across the castle terrace! Mountains, valleys, the lines of poplars along the ancient roads the king had built; people he'd met, food he'd savoured. And in Paris, the thrill of setting out on cold mornings for the Louvre or the Bibliothèque Nationale, then, once inside, like a visitor to the sixteenth century, how he was always warmed by the intimacies he discovered in portraits, journals, correspondence, miscellanies. When he told Nelly that at Henri's christening the baby's lips were rubbed with garlic and drops of aromatic local wine, she knew just where in Nice she'd find a few bottles of this fabled Jurançon.

Heinrich replaced his briefcase next to its companion, the umbrella. He sat down at the desk and poised his pen against a clean sheet of paper. He was in his early sixties, but often felt older. He was exhausted. Over the past months he'd received too many invitations to travel, most of which he'd declined so he could resume telling the story of this one king's moral vision: Henri IV's fortitude against the political evil that threatened to swamp him and his country. He wanted his readers to feel the physical power of the landscape of Henri's childhood and youth as the source of his conviction, and the adventures that followed, how at fifteen he led his first military campaign, how he came to be a revolutionary king. The parallels that struck him, between that chaotic past and the present, also occurred to others. In 1932 Harry Kessler had seen that *the struggles between the radical movements (Communists and Nazis) have much more affinity with the wars of religion during the sixteenth and seventeenth centuries in Germany, France and Britain than they have with the political struggles belonging to the eighteenth and nineteenth centuries. They are bitter armed disputes between two ideologies which exclude compromise.* But if Heinrich Mann had once believed his readers could be stirred to action by this king, as an historical example of militant humanism, he worried about who his readers would be now. Nelly opened the window and watched him mirrored in its glass, suspended like a painted portrait above the busy street, while outside a bird she could not see sang its plaintive song.

He worried that since his publisher in Germany had blocked his path, by refusing to accept new work or to release the rights on existing titles, and British and American publishers had also backed away from him, the book he'd just published, *La Haine*, arguably the most powerful anti-Fascist book of its time, with its prophecies of global aggression and cultural perversion, would not reach as wide a range of readers as he had hoped. It was published in German by the Dutch Querido imprint, a joint venture of Emanuel Querido and Fritz Landshoff, who in the 1930s supported many authors in exile, and with great personal effort and expense, against all the odds, maintained a distribution network throughout Europe. When Heinrich wondered what difference his book would make, since it could not be sold in Germany, and when he said that his slide into literary obscurity had begun, Nelly told him to pour the wine and cut the bread. The scent of acacia from his glass of Jurançon, the rich complexity of spices that developed on the palate as he sipped, the reward of a pleasant haze at the end of a shared bottle, helped diffuse the problems on his mind. The book was bought by Germans in exile and was reprinted nine times. But the German government cautioned the Dutch never to publish anything like it again. And to avoid the threat to Querido, that if his essays appeared with them, then their firm would be closed down, for his next polemical work Heinrich was obliged to find another publisher, Oprecht in Zürich.

He worried that in exile circles he was recognised too easily; strangers greeted him in the street; sometimes he thought he was being followed, watched; sometimes letters he'd sent or expected did not arrive. It was possible that there were plans to extradite or to assassinate him. He arranged for most of his mail to be sent via the address of his French friend Félix Bertaux. Then he shaved off his signature beard; kept the moustache; refused to look over his shoulder as he went on his errands in town, remembering that in another era even Goethe thought he might be murdered. In Paris, Nice and Sanary-sur-Mer exiled Germans traded rumours, searched the newspapers for daily developments *at home*, clung to the radio. At the end of January 1934 they heard that all political parties in Austria, except the right-wing Fatherland Front, had been banned and all resistance from the Schutzbund, the Austrian Left, was quickly suppressed.

On Sunday 18 February, the poet Max Herrmann-Neisse in

London wrote to Heinrich Mann that he had recently run into the playwright Carl Zuckmayer, who asked him why, since he wasn't Jewish, he didn't go back to Germany; Hermann-Neisse said he was deeply disappointed with people like that, like Gerhart Hauptmann, Gottfried Benn and Oskar Loerke. On the same day Virginia noted in her diary that the Belgian King Albert had died while mountaineering at Marche-les-Dames near Namur and that the previous week's fighting in Vienna *somehow comes closer than usual . . . the people shot down.*

In Denmark a doctor put Helene Weigel's wrists in plaster because she had been typing too many of Brecht's manuscripts and was suffering from a tendon infection.

In Nice Heinrich and Nelly were regulars at the Café Monnot in Place Masséna. He flicked through the *Dépêche de Toulouse*, a paper of the south-west of France for which he wrote a monthly column. When he found his own article he fell silent to consider the weight of his words, always advocating a common cause, the force of reason, and the need for political unity. Occasionally he was vindicated. When the German ambassador to France complained about the appearance of Heinrich Mann's articles in the French press, he was told bluntly that in France politicians did not control the press and that there would be no censorship. But his mood slid easily from conviction to despair. Then he looked like a sad caricature of himself. Put on your Zola face, Nelly might have said to snap him out of it, a reminder that twenty years before he'd fought for the very same ideal. As Heinrich made notes for his next article, his next broadcast, his next speech, Nelly sat by his side and read the second volume of Thomas's *Joseph* epic, published in March. As she turned the pages, she dipped sugar cubes in her glass of port, and he looked up and told her she was already sweet enough.

In 'The Author as Producer', an address prepared for the Institute of Fascism in Paris, April 1934 (but never delivered), Walter Benjamin argued that Heinrich Mann, Kurt Hiller and all those who believed that writers and other intellectuals could still turn the tide of Fascism were naïve.

Dear Tommy, Heinrich wrote his brother at the beginning of March, regretting his own circumscribed routine, *no trips abroad, almost no familiar faces: just the necessary walks and rest. It's becoming monastic . . .* He told him that he did not believe there would be war, that instead, an economic collapse would bring down the dictatorships. He suggested that if Thomas was going to move, he should come to Nice because then they'd both be in the same place, and he, Heinrich, would like that. He mentioned plans for the summer holidays together, preferably in the mountains. The Pyrenees perhaps? They were magnificent and peaceful, in an old-fashioned way. *It's still possible to get those transparent quills there, that our parents used to bring back for us from their holidays.* He signed off with a request for a copy of *Tonio Kröger,* which Nelly wanted to read.

To make writing quills, the longest wing feathers are extracted from living birds, most commonly from geese or swans. For fine drawing quills, crows, eagles, owls, hawks and turkeys provide the best feathers. If you are right-handed, it is the bird's left wing that is best suited, and vice versa.

On Tuesday 27 March, Heinrich Mann received a telegram with birthday greetings from his brother. Nelly invited friends for the evening. A passionate cook, she had already added Provençale specialities to her repertoire. She must have wandered through the Cours Saleya market, under its bright awnings, past baskets and gleaming copper vats, making her choice of herbs, bread, flowers, olive oils, honey, anchovies; bought fish directly from the fishermen's boats on the beach; the birthday dinner would have been a grand affair. In April Heinrich Mann accepted the presidency of the exiled German PEN. They heard that the German police force was now under the command of Heinrich Himmler, that the Italian parliament had granted Mussolini an absolute mandate, and Ludwig Marum had died in Kislau concentration camp.

Marum had been awarded a medal for his services in World War I, he was Jewish, a lawyer, a Social Democrat and a member of parliament who fought for the abolition of the death sentence, for the rights of illegitimate children and unmarried mothers, and for equal pay for women. For many years he had successfully exposed Nazi illegalities. When the alarm bells started ringing, however, he underestimated the danger and refused the chance to leave the country. His attachment to his place of birth and his belief in justice, he thought, could not be undermined. In 1933 he was arrested, together with six other Social Democrats. On their way to prison the men were driven through Karlsruhe in an open truck, while hordes of SA men and groups of locals crowded the streets to shout abuse. On arrival at the concentration camp, under SA guard, the prisoners were photographed: a lineup of middle-aged men in hats and trenchcoats, each with a small suitcase or parcel by his side. The others were eventually released. But Marum represented too great a threat, particularly for the right-wing politician who had already usurped his place in parliament. In the night of 28–29 March 1934 he was strangled and hung from the window bars of his cell to make it look like suicide. Despite the Gestapo's attempts to intimidate them, thousands of mourners and demonstrators attended his funeral.

In his diary on Easter Sunday, a cloudless, wonderfully warm spring day, Thomas noted the news of Marum's death with horror. In France, exiled Germans sat in cafés, subdued, perplexed, looking around to see if anyone was listening to their conversations; because Marum's fate might have been their own. Marum? At

Kislau? He was a good man, a good man, a good man, the words swung sorrowfully, like caged canaries in a pitch-black mine. Someone asked, isn't it a health spa, Kislau near Mingolsheim? A relative had gone there for the sulphur, not so long ago. Someone made a small coughing sound, into his fist, as one did when one was lost for words.

On Friday 4 May, on holiday in Galway, Virginia picked some bright blue gentians on a cliff. On Wednesday 9 May, having been to Stratford, she contemplated the possibility that some of Shakespeare's things could have been sold off after his death and that a long time later – now, for instance – they might *come to light*.

Heinrich poured himself into writing. Articles with contemporary concerns, with titles like 'The Meaning of This Emigration' and 'Youth Taken In', were published as soon as he delivered them. Nelly straightened his bow tie and ran a finger along the links of the golden chain that dropped from his lapel like a fishing line into his coat pocket. He squared his shoulders, kissed her goodbye and caught the train to Paris, where on 10 May, the first anniversary of Germany's book burnings, he opened the German Freedom Library as its president. The library was founded by André Gide, H. G. Wells, Romain Rolland, Lion Feuchtwanger and members of the Schutzverband Deutscher Schriftsteller, an organisation formed for the protection of German writers, whose meeting place was the basement of the Café Mephisto on Boulevard Saint-Germain, where everyone talked about the dust storm that was ravaging America's Great Plains. Since Thomas would soon be going on his first trip to America, Heinrich sent his brother early birthday greetings. He also passed on Nelly's thanks for the copy of *Tonio Kröger*.

On 14 and 15 June, Hitler, who to the horror of his fanatical followers greatly admired all things Italian, met Mussolini in Venice, at the Villa Pisani on the river Brenta, where Napoléon had once lived. The meeting got off to a bad start when Hitler arrived in civilian clothes, hatted, creased, and according to Mussolini, looking *like a plumber in a raincoat*. The Duce was more tightly packaged in a grey uniform decorated with a beam of medals. He did not remove his black leather gloves to shake hands with his visitor. It was a hot summer's day and they were plagued by large mosquitoes. Hitler admired the perspective of the villa's Tiepolo ceiling, an apotheosis of gods gambolling on clouds like ample feather beds. He was less amused by the uncensored art he was shown at the Venice Biennale. Mussolini thought Hitler was a joke. *A silly little monkey*. He resented his long quotations from *Mein Kampf*, his endless chatter, and having to pretend for hours that he understood what was being said. His head ached. Hitler had a great time; he later claimed that he could talk with Mussolini intimately about matters he could not entrust even to his closest associates at home. On their return from America on the Dutch liner *Rotterdam*, Thomas left the ship at Boulogne to buy a newspaper. He read about the meeting between Hitler and Mussolini. Back in Küsnacht, he and Katia talked about being wedged between Germany and Italy, and how Switzerland could become a mouse trap for them.

In June, Heinrich was writing about the marriage in 1572 of the Huguenot Henri of Navarre to Margaret, daughter of Catherine de Médicis, followed by the terrible Massacre of Saint Bartholomew's Day, the mass murder of French Huguenots by Catholics, instigated by Henri's new mother-in-law, who took advantage of the fact that large numbers of leading Huguenot families were gathered in Paris for the wedding. The destruction spread to their homes and businesses, which were looted and burned; some said the Seine was so full of bodies you could walk across them from one bank to the other. The provinces followed suit, and across France for several months, tens of thousands of people were murdered. The king of Spain and the pope celebrated the scourge. When he became king it was this massive continental rift that Henri set out to heal.

Towards the end of June, Thomas received a letter from Heinrich in which he said he'd seen the first page of the *New York Herald* proclaiming Thomas Mann to be *the most eminent living man of letters*. Heinrich thought that if old George Bernard Shaw heard this, he would be jealous. He asked his brother to support the campaign for the imprisoned Carl von Ossietzky to be awarded the Nobel Prize. On 2 July Heinrich wrote to his brother from Pension Les Edelweiss, at Cauterets in the Hautes Pyrenees, where waterfalls and forest paths reminded him of his last holiday in Bad Gastein, in Austria. On 5 July Thomas told his brother that in America people said it was *like a dream* to meet him in person. He was now thinking about becoming an American. In Svendborg, in Denmark, close to the Brechts, Walter Benjamin had settled into the Pension Stella Maris with his newly arrived library of books; he stayed from June until October. Benjamin showed an essay he'd written on Kafka to Brecht, who thought the piece placed too much emphasis on the idea of *essence*.

The massacre scene Heinrich had just completed writing corresponded chillingly with the events in Germany from 29 June to 1 July, the Night of the Long Knives, Hitler's elimination of his rival Ernst Röhm, and nationwide, of hundreds of SA men and others, ambushed in their offices, homes, beds, stabbed or shot on the spot with a single bullet or by firing squad in forests, drowned in lakes, or imprisoned and killed in Berlin at the Gestapo head-quarters at Prinz Albrecht Strasse. In a phone call between Hitler and Göring, the code word that unleashed these paranoid killings was 'Kolibri' (hummingbird). *Unhappy, foolish nation, that has been won over by this shameful rubbish, this swamp of lies, brutality and crime*, Thomas wrote in his diary. *Brutal bullies*, Virginia wrote in hers a couple of days later, that *go about in hoods and masks, like little boys dressed up, acting this idiotic, meaningless, brutal, bloody pandemonium.*

Pandemonium, the poet Milton had written, was the high capital of Satan and his peers.

Then came reports of the death of Erich Mühsam on 10 July at the Oranienburg concentration camp.When Heinrich heard about it, he remembered their Munich days in the Café Stephanie, where a large group of friends who were writers, artists and intellectuals would meet for lunch, and regularly at twelve o'clock a man called Hitler passed their tables to make his way to the telephone. One day someone's chair had blocked his path. Was it Mühsam's chair? And now he had had him killed? As in Marum's case, nobody believed the official claims of suicide. After his arrest in Berlin on 28 February 1933, Mühsam had been moved around, from the prison in Lehrter Strasse, to the concentration camp Sonnenburg, where his teeth were knocked out, where his head was branded with a swastika, where he had to dig his own grave and endure a mock execution, then to the prisons Plötzensee and Brandenburg, and from the beginning of 1934, Oranienburg, where his bones were broken, glasses broken, and his attackers had gobbed into his mouth. With bloodshot eyes, a swollen face, red as fire, a swollen ear, a large blister bulging from the ear canal, he was left for a week, slumped on a sack of straw. Who could endure it? Then he was murdered. *If you hear that I committed suicide*, he had told a fellow prisoner, *you must not believe it.* One of Mühsam's murderers was Theodor Eicke, the commander of the Deathhead Division of the Waffen SS and later commander at Dachau concentration camp, who had killed the SA chief Ernst Röhm during the Night of the Long Knives, and was feared as brutal and evil even within his own SS ranks.

The death of Mühsam and of another writer, Kurt Aram, once again led Thomas to think that in the present climate in Germany he would also have been killed. Friday 20 July was a magnificent summer's day. He was inspired to get up early and resume his old routine of exercising in the nude. Four days later he and Katia arrived in Venice, where he was mesmerised by 14-year-old twins who reminded him of his youngest son. The mosquitoes were huge and numerous, the same breed that had plagued Hitler and Mussolini a month earlier. To sleep, he took half a Phanodorm.

Mussolini spent his summer holidays with his family, and the wife and children of his friend the Austrian chancellor Engelbert Dollfuss, at the seaside resort Riccione. Had he been re-reading Machiavelli, as he did throughout his life, when the Austrian Nazis murdered Dollfuss on 25 July? Mussolini was outraged that the silly man in the raincoat had got the upper hand. The news brought Thomas close to tears; a week later he was still sick with grief about the political situation. He felt pressure to declare himself by writing an open letter of condemnation of the Nazis.

Leonard had acquired a marmoset called Mitz and in his autobiography he describes how *during the day she was always with me, but the moment it became dark in the evening she left me, scuttled across the room into a large birdcage which I kept full of scraps of silk and slept until the next morning.* When Vita visited on Tuesday 17 July, Virginia noted that her friend had *lost her radiance.*

Heinrich continued to write his letters, speeches, newspaper articles and his novel, whenever and wherever he got the chance, at home, at his regular table at the Monnot where the waiter called him Monsieur Henri, and when he travelled, in pensions, bistros and railway-station waiting rooms. Nelly read and typed everything he wrote, she read the papers, listened to the radio, and to Hermann Kesten and Joseph Roth, who had just arrived in Nice with firsthand reports of what was happening in Spain. Kesten was born in 1900 in Galicia; he was a writer who had studied law and literature, and had begun but never completed a dissertation on the work of Heinrich Mann. In the summer, a house with three furnished apartments became vacant at 121, Promenade des Anglais. Kesten and his wife, Toni, moved into the first floor, Roth and Andrea Manga Bell took the second, and Heinrich and Nelly took the top floor. Kesten recalled that in the evenings *we stood on our balconies and watched the sun disappear into the sea and its last rays rouged the waves and the sky and our women's cheeks.*

Nelly became firm friends with Kesten's mother when she visited. Galician-born Ida Kesten, widowed and now in her early sixties, had supported her family as a travelling saleswoman, dealing in eggs, brooms and brushes, textiles and fur, platinum, silver and gold; she sang Mozart's Lieder as she went about her daily chores. She read people well, and in her eyes this younger woman was full of courage, with a profound sense of goodness; Nelly had a rough start, Ida thought, and her end might be just as hard, but in between she was living the best way she could. In fact anyone who shared their life with a man like Heinrich Mann needed to have an enormous capacity for love, both of the affectionate and the deeper kind.

At dusk while the men drank vermouth and talked, the women took long walks together. When they sat down at the water's edge, Nelly pulled a bottle of wine and glasses from her bag, made a point of speaking loudly, switching between High and Low German, and an unembarrassed, error-riddled French, about everything, politics, books, the latest film sensation. A movie producer travelled to Skull Island, she told them, and he captured a giant gorilla and brought it back to New York, where King Kong scooped the heroine high above the skyline. She'd heard that the actress Fay Wray was not a natural blonde. And did they know that the face of the beast's full-scale model was made from the fur of thirty bears, while the smallest model was made of rabbit fur? Having finished her glass of wine, Nelly said that the atrocities being committed in Germany and what was going on in the world made her want to scream like Wray, and in an instant, for a few long seconds, the warm Mediterranean night all around froze with her rendition of that scream.

The group ate their meals together and swapped stories. According to Kesten, *Joseph Roth told a love story from Podolia, Heinrich Mann a love story from Palestrina and Mrs Nelly Kroeger told stories of her younger days on the Kurfürstendamm, uninhibited, one might say stark-naked stories, typically Berlin, inspired more by red wine than by poetry.* And yet it was Nelly's narratives that raised their spirits. *She told of mild summer evenings on the Kurfürstendamm, promenading up and down with a girlfriend, both of them blonde and young and curvaceous,* an image that caused Heinrich to sigh so deeply that all eyes were suddenly on him, and as the outward breath of his great sigh blew out the candle on the table, they exploded with laughter.

The kinship between truth and fiction was the topic of the day. All three men were at that time writing histories. Heinrich worked on his *Henri IV*, Roth on the Napoleonic novel *Die Hundert Tage* (The Hundred Days), and Kesten on the Spanish *Ferdinand and Isabella*. German authors were extremely keen on biography and historical fiction. In 1934 alone, there was Ludwig Bauer's study of King Leopold of Belgium, Max Brod's Heine biography, Paul Gerhardt Dippel's comparison of Wagner and Nietzsche, Lion Feuchtwanger's *Die Söhne*, which was the second part of his trilogy about the Jewish historian Flavius Josephus, Bruno Frank's *Cervantes*, Martin Gumpert's book about Hahnemann's discovery of homeopathy, Emil Ludwig's *Führer Europas*, a study of European leaders, Alfred Neumann's *Neuer Cäsar* about Napoleon III, Karl Tschuppik's book about Empress Maria Theresia of Austria, René Schickele's about D. H. Lawrence, Theodor Wolff's *Der Krieg des Pontius Pilatus*, Stefan Zweig's *Erasmus of Rotterdam*. Over a hundred historical novels appeared in German in 1934 and the number kept rising over the next few years.

Especially in exiled literary circles, where the break with the past was like a gaping wound, discussions about the historical novel were carried on with great intensity throughout the 1930s. When Kesten, Roth and Mann met, they would have dealt the names Zola, Scott, Hugo, Dumas, Manzoni like strong cards as they talked about their own projects, about transporting the reader to another time, making it real, background scenes, foreground action, the devil in the detail, infinity in a grain of sand. If Döblin had joined them, he would have said the historical novel was a contemporary form of fairy tale, raising questions about the purity of genre, and about the epic potential of montage. Heinrich might have said that he augmented history and legend, his work was like a house where successive generations built their extensions, giving the example of the many co-existing layers and styles of the castle at Pau. Anxious about too much change and modern times, Roth often warned that mechanical levers would one day replace human arms, and then there'd be no turning back. He also wanted to discuss *moments*, their disjunction and significance, how one wrote about hearing the song of a nightingale at the very moment that nearby on a park bench a man was dying. If the discussion turned to excess and control, he might have said he liked to simmer and skim his work to a rich, clear broth. And on that note they patted their stomachs and ordered lunch. How much fiction would the form allow? How much research, hauled together over months or years, was enough? The drawing of parallels. Allegory. Past and present in one frame. Double time.

The best writing occurs on a narrow ledge between fact and fiction. That uneasy place the poet Wallace Stevens called *the metaphysical streets of the physical town*.

Maybe it was Kesten who questioned the role of eyewitnesses. Many years later, as the group's survivor, he passed on anecdotes which have in turn been quoted by Mann's biographers as fact.

He told, for instance, how one evening he was sitting with Joseph Roth and Heinrich Mann at the Café Monnod during Carnivale. A full moon, drunken and ghostly white, floated above the Casino. Efforts for political unification among left-wing organisations had failed, the French had started to set up internment camps for foreigners at places like Le Vernet, Gurs, St Cyprien and Les Milles, the number of exiles choosing suicide was rising, a mood of disillusionment and panic prevailed. According to Kesten, on that moonlit night Mann started to reminisce about other writers he'd met, about d'Annunzio, Gide, Rilke, Hauptmann, Wedekind, telling stories from his past that were both sad and funny. He stopped suddenly and said he hadn't heard from Jakob Wassermann for a long time, he wondered what he'd been up to. Kesten said he and Roth looked at each other and told him Wassermann was dead. Really? Mann replied. After a while he started to speak about Kurt Tucholsky, more sad and funny stories, and then stopped. Roth told him Tucholsky was dead. Mann was incredulous. He hesitated, looked at them, and asked about Werner Hegemann. Also dead, was Roth's reply. Heinrich Mann said well, well, tugging his moustache as if he needed something to hold on to. That's going a bit too far, he said. I don't dare ask about anyone else. He complained that they'd killed off more dear friends in an hour than he'd lost altogether over twenty years. He took his leave with great, slow dignity, and nobody saw him for three days.

Presumably the point of this story was to show that Heinrich Mann was living too much inside his own head, that he was out of touch with the world, and not least, that he was getting old. But in fact, Thomas had told Heinrich about Wassermann within a week or two of his death, by mid-January, and in a reply to Thomas on 25 January, he referred to the *painful news* and asked his brother how their friend had died, if it had anything to do with the recent stress of politics and his severely reduced earnings, which Heinrich thought was enough to make anyone sick. Clearly Kesten's allegation that Heinrich did not find out about Wassermann until much later, and that he and Roth were the emissaries, was untrue. In fact, the three deaths of which Heinrich was meant to have been ignorant, occurred over a period of almost two and a half years. Tucholsky died in December 1935. And the architectural historian and novelist Werner Hegemann, whose *Frederick the Great* was published in New York in 1929, died in April 1936. Heinrich Mann travelled, wrote, read, corresponded, and unlike most of the exile community, conversed as fluently in French as German. Far from being isolated, we may assume that he was reasonably well informed. So did that moment under the full moon on the terrace of the Café Monnot ever occur? Or had Kesten the eyewitness embellished history?

In southern France news of betrayal and persecution kept trickling through. A Nazi hit list of literary figures was thought to exist, but nobody had seen it. Those whose names were said to be absent from the list were suspected by the others of spying. With voices low and accents held in check, people often spoke in languages not their own, not only of Hitler's latest murders, but also of Stalin's purges. Millions, it was reported, had been herded like cattle into camps. Millions of Ukrainians had starved to death. Millions. Impossible to tell truth from taunt, because the Communists and Social Democrats were always raking muck into each other's yards. People met in the dark doorways of the narrow street maze of Nice's Vieille Ville. Words were exchanged, tempers stretched on racks until they tore, insults flew, fights broke out. Before the police arrived, however, everyone dispersed, knowing that when foreigners were arrested, they were deported, destined for incarceration or death *at home*.

The joke about Hindenburg, for months already, was that he'd died but that people had forgotten to tell him. When he did die at the beginning of August, there was a grand summer funeral. Hitler merged the titles of President and Chancellor, and after the August elections he gained dictatorial power. People said, I told you so. But it was too late. It had come about that thirty-eight million people voted for this man. Thirty-eight million people had entered the forest. Darkness fell. Before they could find their way home again, they would be transformed or dead.

Thomas Mann sat at his mahogany desk, which had been saved from his Munich study, too distracted by political events to concentrate on the third volume of his *Joseph* books. He grieved for the fate of his country and wrote in his diary that he was ashamed of his own procrastination in speaking out. There were pro-Fascist rallies in New York and London. Heinrich listened as Nelly read from the newspapers in her curiously confident French, about Mao Tse-tung's march, Gandhi in India, Kemal in Turkey, Churchill, Stalin, Hitler. Pied Pipers and their bedazzled crowds. On the Promenade in Nice there was talk of Sholokov; someone had suggested he was the new master of the modern epic. The king of Yugoslavia was murdered in Marseille.

Driven by the conviction that only a coalition of the left could turn the tide against fascism, Heinrich continued tirelessly to write and speak and travel, mostly within France, since he was stateless and had no papers to cross borders. When he accepted an invitation to speak in Czechoslovakia on 19 October for the 175th anniversary of Schiller's death, it took forty hours by train to get there. His anti-Fascist sentiments, loudly proclaimed, did not please the Germans of the Sudetenland, while some Communists he met were appalled that his brother had not yet publicly denounced Hitler or Nazi Germany. They urged him to shame Thomas into action, which he refused to do, knowing his brother's silence was tied to the decision to continue to be published in Germany for as long as possible.

The move to Prague had not been easy for Goschi and Mimi, who had sent him requests and thanks for money, complaints about having to live with Mimi's elderly parents, of illness, a sense of abandonment and premonition; Mimi said she'd predicted the whole catastrophe and in her body she felt there was worse to come. While he was in Prague, Heinrich spent time with his daughter. He had suggested that she might get a job, but she said that as a German speaker she was having problems, and that all she wanted to do was dance. She showed him the bright yellow outfit in which she'd performed a French gavotte, the soft green taffeta she'd worn for an Argentinian tango. She told him how the audience applauded when she did the splits. He used his earnings from the trip to rent an apartment for Goschi and Mimi. These issues of their dependence were never resolved; a few years later Goschi even offered to pay for her dancing lessons by becoming his secretary in Nice.

Writing *Henri IV* made Heinrich feel youthful. As he planned each chapter, he sketched landscapes, battle scenes, and the king's lovers, a gallery of voluptuous peasant girls and noblewomen. He glanced across to the armchair where Nelly was reading. She looked up and smiled. Show me what you've drawn, she might have said. And when he did, she laughed. They're all the same! And she turned back to her book. Queen Margot, Henri's first wife, was also a reader, he told her, Montaigne's niece was her librarian. Then that's how she should be portrayed, Nelly replied. But she knew that Heinrich's sympathies lay less with Margot than with another woman, Henri's beloved Gabrielle d'Estrées, who was only seventeen when she first met the thirty-seven-year-old king. Artists including Titian, Rubens, Giorgione, Tintoretto, Carpaccio and Veronese have painted her, golden-haired, fair-complexioned, red-lipped, blue-eyed, her beauty enhanced by the reputation that all the women of her family were great lovers. The best-known portrait is a *peinture anonyme* in the Louvre, of Gabrielle and one of her sisters, both naked to the waist, one sister pinching the nipple of the other. To Heinrich it was most uncanny, as he thought and wrote about her, that Gabrielle, like Nelly, was a little fearful, a little melancholic, and that the two looked very much alike. So he gave his own words to the king. *Nothing can do me more good*, he has Henri say to his mistress, *than the sight of you*. Henri and Gabrielle had three children; he wanted to marry her but others opposed it; she died in childbirth. A small strip of paper torn from a sheet of music was found amongst Heinrich Mann's notes after his death, showing the title of a *chanson* thought to have been composed by Henri IV; it was called 'Charmante Gabrielle'.

By the end of the year they had moved back to their previous apartment at 11, rue du Congrès, the address *Mme Nelly Kroeger-Mann* had printed on her calling card. One of these cards she sent home to her family in Niendorf, it must have been around Christmas time, with greetings and thanks for the gingerbread they'd sent her. On 17 December Heinrich told his brother that over the last couple of years he'd worked harder than ever before, which had left him feeling increasingly tired and irritable. Nonetheless, he enjoyed writing the novel and hoped the first volume would be published early in the coming year.

On 30 December at Rodmell in Sussex, living next door to a woman who bred fox terriers, Virginia and Leonard found no peace from *those cursed dogs barking*.

That same day in Küsnacht near Zürich, Thomas Mann took his dog for a walk, and at tea he talked with a friend about the vertiginous decline of Europe.

In exile you hear the woodsman's axe but you never see the woodsman.

1935: As Ripe Fruit Falls

The angel said, Put forth thy sharp sickle, and gather the clusters of the vine of the earth; for her grapes are fully ripe. REVELATION 14:18

On Tuesday 1 January 1935 Thomas Mann changed his desk calendar with a measure of excitement; this year he would be celebrating his sixtieth birthday; the next day he was glum again. Wrote a letter to Heinrich about deep despair, declaring the thing that had still held hope, that one had wished to believe in, Communism, was now tainted with the same deceit and brutalities as practised by the Nazis. A week of sleepless nights. Beer, he discovered, disagreed with him by acting as an aphrodisiac. It snowed. He read Pushkin's *Snowstorm* and slept well; of all aesthetic experiences, what he loved best was attenuation. In Pushkin's story, the weather plays havoc with the lovers' plans, driving them apart. The narrative bends its portent like a laden bough until they find each other again, and the tension is eased.

He and Katia travelled to Prague. The Austrian border guard was a reader who recognised him and asked for his autograph. In Prague, Mimi Mann, now settled into her new apartment, cooked lunch for them. When she was married to Heinrich she had inherited and perfected many of the family recipes, and on this occasion she might have served some of the old Lübeck favourites: a fine pea soup, juicy *Frikadellen*, carrots in white sauce with nutmeg, followed by an almond cake with coffee and cream. It was all delicious. With Goschi's help, the hostess bustled between courses, and everyone listened politely to her lament of hard times and ill health. Did she also tell them how often she re-read Heinrich's letters? Did she curse the woman who had taken her place, who – hadn't they heard – had name cards printed on which she called herself Madame Nelly Kroeger-Mann? In Prague, and then Budapest, Thomas was well received with rounds of interviews, speeches, lunches, dinners. In Vienna they visited the National Gallery with Martha Wassermann. Thomas was captivated by Correggio's raincloud painting of *Jupiter and Io*, its hovering kiss, erotic anticipation. On the border between Austria and Switzerland, the face of another guard lit up when he inspected his passport. Thomas returned home pleased with himself. Katia went to bed with a cold.

In her first diary entry for the year, Virginia noted a recent conversation with W.B. Yeats and Aldous Huxley, when the two men claimed *that their great aim in writing is to avoid the 'literary'* . . . *Yeats said that he wanted only to use the words that real people say* . . . *And I said, rashly, that all the same his meaning was very difficult.* Later Virginia noted *a vast sorrow at the back of life this winter.*

Whenever he read Pushkin at bedtime, Thomas found he did not need to take sleeping pills. On Tuesday 5 February he went for a walk in a rainstorm and had difficulty holding on to his umbrella. Later that month he recorded the death of Max Liebermann. The son of a Jewish textile manufacturer, Liebermann was born 20 July 1847 in Berlin, where he studied philosophy until his interest in art took him to Weimar, Paris, Holland, Munich and eventually, with his marriage to Martha Marckwald, back to Berlin. He became one of the country's leading Impressionists; he painted the most seductive dance of light and colour; the sandy paths and sappy greens of high summer were his specialty. In 1931, at Heinrich Mann's sixtieth birthday celebration, Liebermann announced that not only was he the oldest person present, but also Mann's oldest living admirer. In 1932 he was elected Honorary President of the Prussian Academy of the Arts, only to resign the following year, when this institution declared it would no longer support the work of Jewish artists.

Frayed nerves. Thomas and Katia took a holiday in St Moritz. Walked through sleet. The paths were covered with new snow. He had arranged to meet Katia but could not find his way. Visual disorientation, dizziness, a terrible sense of emptiness. News reports of two women accused of spying.

Betrayed by the same man and charged with passing on military secrets, Benita von Falkenhayn and Renate von Natzmer were in Berlin's Plötzensee Prison, in separate cells, in wooden clogs and grey gowns, their hands tied behind their backs. Karl Gröpeler was the executioner, red moustache, tailcoat, top hat, white gloves, black suitcase, the axe in the suitcase. The death bell. One woman fastened in position on a block of wood. Took off his hat and coat and rolled up his sleeves. He grasped the handle of the axe with both hands. The first woman killed at 6 am, the other shortly after, 18 February 1935. Each time, the single blow, the sudden gush and spray of blood, the head dropped into a basket. It is thought that consciousness can remain intact for about seven seconds after a beheading. *Blood fell in big slow drops, as ripe fruit falls from the branches of a tree* (Flaubert, *Salammbô*, 1862). The moaning bell, rung twice. The executioner shot himself, years later.

20 February, Virginia thought about her novel, but *ideas are sticky things: wont coalesce; hold up the creative, subconscious faculty.* 26 February she looked out and saw *a very fine sky blue, my windows are filled with blue for wonder.*

In Küsnacht, early March, on a long walk, Thomas worked his way through wet snow and through his perpetual fear of being lost and alone. Mid-March he strolled in the sun, anticipating summer and his big birthday. At the end of the month he read Nietzsche's letters. Heinrich wrote his brother, he could not believe from day to day what he was reading in the papers. Was it fact or fiction? These extremes of history, these abusive fantasies, he said, they now tainted all works of the imagination. When he passed a café table with visitors from the Third Reich, their proximity made him feel sick. He suggested that any ill health Thomas had been experiencing lately was due to the fact that in Zürich he lived much too close to the German border. He urged him once again to move.

Virginia thought Vita had grown very fat and that their friendship was over, *not with a bang, but as ripe fruit falls*. She had a headache from trying to talk politics in French with André Malraux, *the fluent ideological foreigner*. On 31 March she visited T. S. Eliot and he was so distracted he forgot to offer her a glass of sherry. In London, leaves appeared on the chestnut trees. The blossoming of daffodils, magnolias, cherry trees, the scent of spring.

Monday 8 April, some lines Heinrich read, of Storm or Platen, reminded him of a drawing he'd once placed inside a volume of poetry, when he was twenty and Carla was ten. *Our sister*, he said in a letter to his brother. He saw her clearly, pencil in hand, looking up from the picture of a pink pot of blue violets, with her words written underneath . . . *this is what I always draw and then I colour it in*. On the same day, Thomas remembered a novel he'd been reading in Munich, left there, unfinished on his bedside table. It was *The Dream of the Red Chamber*, a Chinese masterpiece by Cao Xueqin. Thomas resolved to buy another copy and read it to the end. Later that month, while acting rather cold towards an insinuating friend, he reminded himself of his mother, who also became icy when faced with too much unwanted affection. He wondered if now was the time to write an open letter to the German people, to tell them what the rest of the world thought of them. On Monday

29 April, he read a book of fairy tales; they were pleasing, but had lost the magic he experienced in childhood.

Mid-April Virginia wrote that *it is almost settled that we shall drive through Holland and Germany, concealing Leonard's nose, and to Rome*, and that next year she planned to learn German. Towards the end of the month they had a visit from Ernst Toller. He said that they were on the brink of war. *Mussolini, Hitler, Macdonald. All these people incessantly arriving at Croydon, arriving at Berlin, Moscow, Rome; and flying off again*, she wrote. It was time to buy their gas masks. *The usual headache wings its way about me, rather like a fowl soaring and settling and giving me a peck in my back.*

Ernst Toller was born 1 December 1893 in Samotschin, in the Eastern province of Posen; his ancestor had been the only Jew allowed to settle in the town; his father was a grain merchant. Toller volunteered for service in WWI, fought valiantly on the Western Front; was promoted; suffered physical and mental collapse fom the trauma of the war. He was a dramatist and poet, but above all he was a left-wing activist, charged with high treason for his participation in the Bavarian Revolution, imprisoned for five years, 1919–1924. In 1935 he was living in exile in England.

A clear day in May. A great burst of blossoms and foliage. A concert, where from afar Thomas noticed that his youngest son had become a handsome young man. On Tuesday 14 May, he and Katia drove to Geneva, where they left their car and with time to spare before catching the overnight train to Nice, walked to the lake. He smoked a cigar, they ate ice cream. An eagle spiralled down from the Salève. On their way back, at the station end of the rue de Zürich, a young woman who had put a heavy bag of books and shopping down on the pavement, and was opening the door at number 47, suddenly greeted them as if they were closely acquainted. *Thomas? And Katia? How lovely to see you!* They shook hands; the young woman had an unexpectedly strong grip. There was so much she wanted to ask them, but she knew they had a train to catch, so it would have to wait until next time. *Goodbye, goodbye, and best regards to Heinrich and Nelly in Nice . . . Oh, just a minute, you can give them this.* In her arms she was holding two thick folders tied with string and handed one of them to Thomas. *Tell them it's a copy of the manuscript, but of course it's not yet finished.* Smiles and nods and an awkward moving on. So who was that? And on first-name terms? A shrug of shoulders, and slight dismay that they should have been addressed so warmly, so informally, by someone they did not recognise. He must have put the folder down on a bench in the station's waiting room, and forgotten it, because later, looking for it on the train, it was gone. Anyway, people were always giving Thomas their work; it was a burden; he had enough trouble keeping his own papers in order. When the Polish writer Bruno Schulz sent him one of the few copies he'd made of *The Messiah*, a novel he'd worked on for many years, Mann misplaced it, lost it, destroyed it, who knows, and because all other copies have also disappeared, there is no trace of what must surely have been Schulz's major work. Thomas was pleased once more that the train conductor realised who they were.

Nice was overcast. Heinrich met them at the station, looking distinguished with his white moustache and also strange without his beard. He took them to the Hôtel D'Angleterre, where they sat and talked on the balcony of their room overlooking the sea. It rained. Roses for Nelly and dinner for four at the Régence. Heinrich displayed his enormous capacity to enjoy food and drink. Thomas was irritated by Nelly's exuberance, thought her behaviour was common and foolish. The wind was heavy with the smell of the sea. A huddle of umbrellas and Nelly overexcitedly attempting to talk to Thomas about his books as they walked back to the hotel in the rain. One evening she cooked a memorable meal and the visitors seemed more relaxed. Vermouth, wine, bouillabaisse, a walk on the promenade, meetings with old friends, and their son Klaus. An excursion to Monte Carlo. On foot through pine forest to Monts Alban and Boron with grand views of the harbour, as far as Cap d'Antibes in one direction and the mountains around Grasse in the other. Eventually a day of sunshine. The brothers bid each other a fond farewell. Nelly hands over a basket full of delicacies she had prepared for them. Elegant triangles of English sandwiches, tartlets bursting with olives and herbs, paté, a bottle of *vin du pays* – how thoughtful – and madeleines, wrapped in quotations from Proust – how silly. Followed a few days later by letters of thanks and good wishes between Küsnacht and Nice.

From 1 May the Woolfs and their marmoset spent a week motoring in Holland. In her luggage, Virginia had D. H. Lawrence's *Aaron's Rod*, an edition of Katherine Mansfield's letters, Stendhal, Chekhov. They crossed into Germany, where they were caught up in a grand parade organised for Goering and had to drive courageously, ceremoniously, between Nazi flags and banners bearing anti-Semitic slogans. The crowd cheered the little monkey that sat on Leonard's shoulder. *Nerves rather frayed.* 13 May, in Verona, drinking wine. *I don't want to wake up. This is the lust that led many astray, but not comparable to my own private excitements. And it wears off so soon . . . Queer what a part wine has played in human life . . . How all impressions are mixed . . . my honeymoon . . . The sensation is of a tight band round the head tingling in the soles of the feet, hotness, and a spring expanding. What would the writing of a complete drunkard be?* A woman reminds her of a bird. In Rome, her sister drawing. Her niece Angelica lacking the ability to be still and contemplate works of art. Shopping at the markets. And the return journey along the coast, the easy Mediterranean perfection of geraniums and bougainvillea, sea, mountains and bright light. Crossed into France on Sunday 26 May. Midday at Monte Carlo. The Casino, outside lurid, inside dull. Heavy weekend traffic on the way to Nice. Sunday evening, Aix-en-Provence, eating trout. Maps and cigarettes. Getting closer to home, Virginia thought about her work, finishing one book, planning the next. *I can't start a new one till the cage doors are opened.* Then Chartres and *the blue windows blazing in the cold grey night.* And home.

Birthday greetings began to arrive; on 6 June, Thomas Mann turned sixty; the sun shone; the house filled with his family; congratulations flooded in. He noted that this time the tone of letters and articles was more festive, more solemn than ten years earlier. He was now held in highest esteem. Time was ripe. Immortality had shifted into view. Thomas and Katia travelled to America, where alongside Albert Einstein, Thomas was to receive an honorary doctorate from Harvard University. Tuesday 25 June he sat by a river in Connecticut, plagued by mosquitoes, reading Kafka's *The Castle*. At night the river reflected stars and glow-worms. They were invited to dine with the Roosevelts at the White House.

In articles and speeches, Heinrich continued his passionate appeals for political unity in exile. He finished the first volume of his *Henri IV* book on 8 June; Nelly typed the manuscript; an edition of 4,000 was published by Querido in August. In Paris from 21 to 25 June, while his brother was being fêted in America, Heinrich was at the International Writers Congress for the Defence of Culture, organised and attended by supporters from all over the world, including Barbusse, Rolland, Gide, Malraux, Kisch, Bloch, Brecht, Forster, Aragon and Musil. Heinrich Mann delivered the keynote address and six thousand people rose to their feet to applaud his courage and dedication in the fight for humanitarian ideals and literary freedom.

One of the principal organisers of the congress was Egon Erwin Kisch. Born 1885 in Prague, he grew up in a cultured Jewish home. His pacifism and antimilitarism were the result of firsthand experiences during WWI. He became a journalist and was a close associate of Willi Münzenberg, the Comintern's chief propagandist in the West. Kisch joined the KPD in 1925, was arrested after the Reichstag fire, spent ten days in Spandau prison, was deported to Prague and escaped to Paris. In 1934 he was sent to Australia to attend a peace congress, and when he was denied permission to go ashore in Melbourne, jumped off the ship onto the pier, and broke his leg. He defied the authorities, got around on crutches; he appeared to be as ubiquitous here as he was in Europe. Australians love heroic outlaws. With his tattoos that he was always ready to show off – a feather and snake on his right shoulder, a gollywog on his right arm, a bird on his left shoulder, a dagger on the left side of his chest, a wild man with snake-hair and a dagger through his head on his left inner forearm, a tattooed woman disappearing below his belt, and more – and with his tales from all parts of the globe and his ironic humour, Kisch won people's hearts, as he continued with great energy to speak about developments in Europe, the mass arrests, tortures, murders.

In February 1935 he arrived at Sydney's Domain sitting on a table on the back of a lorry, and was carried to a platform, to tell ten thousand people who came to hear him, that Fascism was a terrible form of Capitalism, and that he was an eyewitness of some of its worst deeds. *I saw my friend Erich Mühsam, the poet whose works I translated, made to walk naked, even in winter, and to lick up the spittle of his captors. All his limbs were broken one by one, and he was killed.* Mühsam was a name most of the crowd would not have recognised, but I have met someone who was there on that hot summer day, and he said that all around him people had tears in their eyes and everyone was deeply affected by the speech and the story of Erich Mühsam's suffering. One young man, the journalist John Fisher, son of one-time Australian prime minister Andrew Fisher, was so impressed with Kisch that he accompanied him back to Europe and then continued on to Moscow.

In a café in Paris, after his return, Kisch told his friends about Australia: the infamous dictation test in Gaelic devised to keep undesirables like him out of the country; the Melbourne palazzo that housed the trade unions, *with pillars and a flight of stairs and a sloping terrace, comparable to the houses of parliament in the capitals of Europe*; cricket; the Blue Mountains; black swans; and the beaches of Newcastle where *the waves bear phosphorescent lights, and when the surf breaks on the shore their glimmer falls on the rocks, and the rocks at night are blue.*

One of the people Kisch had met in Australia, the writer and critic Nettie Palmer, was in Paris for the Congress. She noted that, *with daylight saving, and in June, even the most determined late-diner can't dine after dark. So in sunset light you recognise Heinrich Mann in a Boul' Mich' pavement café. He is dining alone, thoughtfully, and with a napkin tucked amply round his neck.* She wondered how the refugee writers earn a living. *Heinrich Mann, I suppose, can keep on with his novels wherever he is, and they'll be translated and published.* She heard that the novelist Anna Seghers lived in the suburbs of Paris with her husband and two children, writing her books, keeping a low profile to protect her parents left behind in Germany, that she had their photos pinned to the inside of her sewing-basket lid. Nettie met another Australian writer, the elegant Christina Stead, and she heard Gide talk at the Mutualité, and attended a reception at the Russian embassy, where she was introduced to a flirtatious Lion Feuchtwanger, who tried to impress her with the information that his books were being translated into numerous languages, even before he had finished writing them, and that he used a card index to choose characters and plots for different historical settings. *What a picture of literary and secretarial activity he called up, this alert little man whose books are published in every country but his own. Surely book-making on this scale has never been carried out before?* On the other hand, it was impossible to ignore the fact that *his novels, basically, are much the same.*

That summer in Paris, it seemed to many that writing really was a form of political action, that the different factions of the left might still be saved from impending fragmentation, and that an alliance might be formed in the fight against fascism. But not everyone was convinced. Aldous Huxley was there and thought it was a farce, a large-scale exercise in Communist propaganda, *a rather discreditable episode in the Comédie Humaine.*

Back from their holiday at the beginning of June, Virginia found that she was unable to work. *Odd how the spring of life isn't to be tapped at will. I can't get into the swim by saying it is Saturday morning and I will write. I can't get into that stream by standing and wishing it . . . nothing surfaces.* But by the end of the month, at the end of her book, she is *wedged – no, buoyant – in a floating storm of scenes.* Bees swarmed, cuckoos called. It was summer.

In July Thomas and Katia returned to Europe on the Cunard liner *Berengaria*. A few days into the voyage, on the high seas, he found it odd that their luxurious cabin, now in an entirely different spot on the surface of the earth, was the exact same place in which they'd drunk whisky and soda with friends, prior to departure, in New York. Sea air was good for him, he thought; as always it stirred his libido. During the voyage he continued reading Kafka, which he found compelling.

While one brother loved the sea, the other loved the mountains. Mid-July, on his way home from Paris, Heinrich spent some time in Briançon in the French Alps, the highest town in Europe; snow-covered peaks, naked rock in magnificent formations, wind. It was a highlight, he told his brother, of his life on Earth. At the end of the month he and Nelly were in Bandol, where for a few weeks they rented a quiet apartment close to the shore. There they received a letter from Thomas regarding the situation in Germany . . . *most terrible is the fact that nobody interferes, that everybody acts as if this is a government like any other.* Heinrich wrote to Willi

185

Münzenberg to say there was no time to lose in their plans to topple the Nazis. In August news of the death of the Queen of Belgium. Driving along a road near Lake Lucerne, King Léopold lost control of the car and it plummetted into a ravine. A small Czech town accepted Heinrich Mann as an honorary citizen, part of the process of bestowing Czech nationality.

The harvest on the hill is positively orange, Virginia wrote. Blackberries ripened, but there were no mushrooms. She was so busy typing up her manuscript, that in her diary she had to leave a lot unsaid. Her head *mildly throbs and can't breed a word at the end of the morning*. Repainted her room and chose some chintzes. Thought she might call her novel *Other People's Houses*. Out walking, Leonard came to meet her, but they missed each other. *War seems inevitable*. The Belgian Queen. *The car ran off the road into a tree, and she was flung out; struck her head. The king kissed her as she died.* Mussolini's advance into Abyssinia. *Everybody talking about Abysinnia, which I cannot spell.*

When Heinrich's *Henri IV* was published, Thomas received a copy and began to read it at the beginning of September. With it came a letter from Heinrich to say that he and Nelly were now back in Nice, that he was hardly sleeping, and was exhausted from the exertion of finishing the book. There was a tone of optimism, the idea that the Third Reich was about to fall, mixed with paranoia. He could not visit them in Switzerland because he had information which he could not discuss, that German spies were operating there. Sunday 15 September, the ugliness of Hitler's voice on the radio. The Nuremberg Laws on citizenship and race. Article 2, section 1: *A citizen of the Reich may only be one who is of German or related blood, and who, through his behaviour, shows that he is both prepared and fit to serve loyally the German people and the Reich.* The applause. It took three weeks for Thomas to finish reading Heinrich's book, which he thought was unusual, superior to any-

thing being published in Germany right now, rich in texture, restless, with a heightened sense of history. Clearly an analogy for the
political errors and stupidities of the present time. The literature
of exile at its best; to receive its highest honours later, when the
crisis is over. He was also relieved to find it was no more than that;
placed it on the shelf with Heinrich's other books; no threat to his
own status in the world of literature. For his tiredness, nervousness and digestive problems Thomas was now prescribed a mix of
herbal and homeopathic remedies. On Monday 30 September, he
entertained the thought that if only his great gifts were matched
with even greater energy, he might have been a true genius. Towards the end of September, Heinrich was again in Paris. He had
begun writing the second volume of his *Henri IV* novel.

Virginia bought some silk for a nightgown and had a dream
of men committing suicide. Decided to call the book *The Years*. She
had trouble writing. *Can't pump up a word . . . shall wait . . . and
let the well fill. It has to be damned deep this time.* She wished experts
knew more about the workings of the brain. Visitors came, with
children. *How quick and hard and unexpected children's minds are . . .
the whole of society in one drop.* Watched a kingfisher fly across the
river.

October. Italian troops crossed into Ethiopia. Thomas read enthusiastic reviews of Heinrich's book, one by Arnold Zweig, another
by Klaus Mann. Misty autumn days. A visit from his son-in-law, the
poet W. H. Auden. A visit from an old friend, the medical superin-
tendent of a German hospital, forced to emigrate, bringing reports
of suicides and heart attacks from stress among the German Jewish population, of the methodical eradication of Jews, hidden from
the world. Thomas wondered when the League of Nations would
step in and stop the criminals. He sent his letter in support of the
jailed pacifist Ossietzky's nomination for the Nobel Prize for Peace
for 1935. Leaves fell, late roses bloomed. News of further execu-

tions. On Thursday 31 October Thomas walked along the road to meet Katia, but they missed each other. To a friend he wrote, regarding Heinrich's contribution to French culture, he thought his brother deserved the rosette of the Legion of Honour. He was upset that instead Heinrich led the life of an ordinary emigrant, with all the annoyances of French officialdom, and made matters worse by sending his mistress along to deal with the bureaucrats.

The following day he was disgusted when he heard that Goebbels had placed wreaths at the graves of Schiller and Goethe. Sunday 3 November Thomas purred as he drank a cup of coffee with whipped cream; it was pure pleasure. Leaves now lay around the base of trees in circles. His son Klaus was unwell, his morphine addiction the cause. Hemingway said that Thomas Mann would be a great writer if he'd never written anything after *Buddenbrooks*. Thomas thought he saw the ambiguity of this. Heinrich was in Paris 21–25 November, staying at the Hôtel Lutetia on Boulevarde Raspail. He chaired a series of meetings with other exiled intellectuals, calling themselves the Lutetia Circle, and planning to establish a German popular front, an alternative government in exile. He wrote to Thomas to say he was on his way to Geneva and from there he would come to visit them. On behalf of those in exile, Heinrich Mann addressed the League of Nations on 29 November.

He arrived in Zürich on Sunday 1 December. The brothers spent the afternoon and evening talking about politics. A storm on Monday, Heinrich reading out his open letter, to be published three days later in the *Pariser Tageblatt*, in answer to the Norwegian writer and Nobel Prize winner Knut Hamsun, who had opposed Ossietzky's receiving the Nobel Peace Prize. Tuesday they walked in the forest through thick snow, drank vermouth in the Grand Hotel. Wednesday they took Heinrich to the train, for his trip via

Geneva, staying overnight in Lyon, back to Nice. A couple of days later a friend told Thomas he thought Heinrich was too gullible, uncritical, childlike in his belief in Communism. On Tuesday 31 December, Thomas Mann and his family stayed up late to watch the burning down of the candles on their Christmas tree.

Brecht was in America and regretted that he could not be with his family for Christmas; he asked his son Stefan to take his place as head of the family.

Tucholsky had a deep yearning for peace and quiet. Sometimes he found it. Ten years earlier, in the South of France, he had described it. *There lie the valleys. Empty of people, no village in sight, just the occasional farmhouse. And finally, finally, that which I have searched for in vain for so long: silence. Here it is silent . . . Happiness, the wise man claims, is something negative. Absolute silence all around. And I am so happy, thankful for what is absent.*

More often, silence had holes barked into it. Noise that swamped the brain until you drowned, helpless and unable to think. *Dogs always bark,* Tucholsky once wrote, *they bark when someone arrives and when someone leaves, they bark in between, and if there is no reason to bark they create one by barking . . . When dogs bark for a long time, they sound as if they're vomiting.* He thought the incessant, monotonous barking of dogs was full of bitterness. *It chops up time like a never-ending striking clock: there, another second has passed, you will die, don't even dare to rise above it all, stay with your feet firmly planted on the ground, because you will die, made of the same stuff as I am, a dog, you belong to us, to me, until the end, bow wow wow.* Now it wasn't just dogs that barked, but dictators and their minions. Kurt Tucholsky took an overdose of Veronal and died on 21 December 1935. *I left the Jewish faith in 1911,* he wrote a few days before his death, *and I'm aware that that's not even possible.*

Virginia listened to the wind, and the barking of the dogs.

Across the continent flocks of birds, intoxicated from eating fermented berries, dropped from their perches, crashed into windows that they mistook for open space, fell from the sky.

Like a drunk on the bald crest of a hill, the old year bobbed out of view.

Guillotining, Musil had once written in his diary, it was *conceivable that, one moment after separation, 'I' functions are present both in the head and in the body (sub-cortically). A 'What is happening to me?' – then the human being is truly double* . . . He was trying to grasp the trauma that preceded miracles of regeneration. *Transitions to formation of buds, finally to procreation.* He decided that in fact *the 'I' does not divide, become extinguished, emerge, but is rather – simply part of the given whole.*

1936: Red Snow

On 20 January a number of exiled German writers held a memorial service in Paris for their friend and colleague Kurt Tucholsky.

The critic Alfred Kerr visited James Joyce. While Kerr told him how much he and others admired his work, Joyce insisted that he had always been maligned; he said he'd called a spade a spade, but *some were enraged by the realistic picture, others by the style. They all took revenge.*

On holiday in Arosa the Manns again met with Wassermann's widow. Thomas had contributed a preface for her biography of her husband; a greeting, he called it, to his dear friend Jakob in eternity, where everyone is equal. He wondered when he would be joining him there. Before sleep he drank linden-flower tea and read Proust. *Presently my aunt was able to dip in the boiling infusion, in which she would relish the savour of dead or faded blossom, a madeleine, of which she would hold out a piece to me when it was sufficiently soft.* Such idylls were rare. He received a deeply troubling letter from his children; Erika and Klaus urged him to stop floating above the torrent and to make a public statement about his political position. He replied that if he'd acted from the start like others, like Heinrich, *my voice would have already sunk into the common pool of exile, my option to take a moral stance would now already be exhausted. But as I've played my cards, I've created a reserve, which could still be useful.* He added that he would never have been as outspoken as Heinrich; what he called the *brother problem* had stood in his way. But he was swayed; pleased with his decision finally to raise his voice and condemn the German government. His open letter to the literary editor of the *Neue Zürcher Zeitung* was published 3 February.

Neatly parted, neatly combed dark-grey hair, brush moustache, double chin, bow tie, monocle chain and pocket handkerchief. The remarkably blue focus of his eyes. Heinrich was in Paris in January and for a week at the beginning of February, at the Hôtel Lutetia, to lead the plenary session of the United Front conference on 2 February 1936. The 118 participants included 23 Communists, 20 Social Democrats, members of other left-wing and religious groups, and many writers. Klaus Mann was there, as were Lion Feuchtwanger and Ernst Toller. Heinrich carried a new diary, inscribed by his daughter. *Sent to you by your Goschi, so that you'll think of her all year.* He dined at La Coupole in Montparnasse and met with friends, including Salomea Rottenberg, who would remain loyal to him and Nelly throughout their years of exile. Others, who had once shared his convictions, like the painter George Grosz, shook their heads at Heinrich's idealism and distanced themselves from the congress; they believed that Communists and Socialists were deadly enemies and would never unite. The Lutetia Circle's central committee was beset with problems from the start; the Communist propagandist Willi Münzenberg, the Social Democrat Rudolf Breitscheid, and Georg Bernhard, an editor and writer whose work had been denounced at the book-burnings of 1933 as *un-German journalism of a Jewish democratic kind*, represented just some of the factions that squabbled within their own ranks and with each other. In any case, without a real constituency, their model for a future German government was like an airship without hydrogen. *In faith we disbelieve* is a quote from H. G. Wells that was found among Heinrich Mann's papers; it's self-cancelling logic fits the mood. In Spain the left won the elections on 16 February, leading to civil unrest and violence.

Purple clouds. Virginia *began the year with 3 entirely submerged days, headache, head bursting, head so full, racing with ideas; and the rain pouring; the floods out; when we stumbled out yesterday the mud came over my great rubber boots; the water squelched in my soles*. She thought of taking sentences from great writers and expanding them. Revised *The Years*; like a bird *I peck and stop; peck and stop again*. Death of George V, King of England, 20 January. Newspapers reported tears around the world. The prime minister said that just before he died the King seemed to be preparing to go on a long journey. *How is the Empire?* These were his last words. Virginia watched the funeral procession and noticed in the crown a luminous pale blue stone.

Brecht stayed in New York until February. He went to the movies every day. Apart from his favourite gangster films, he would have seen *The Bride of Frankenstein*, which was released in 1935. Strongly influenced by German Expressionism, it starred Elsa Lanchester in a dual role, as bride to Boris Karloff's monster (the highlight of her performance is her piercing scream when he tries to touch her) and as the story's author Mary Shelley, who features in the opening scene with the poets Shelley and Byron; she is sewing and Byron is incredulous that *these fragile white fingers . . . penned the nightmare*; she accidentally pricks herself and appears shocked by the drops of her own blood. Lanchester was the wife of the actor Charles Laughton, who later became Brecht's good friend, and while she was critical of Brecht (his petulance, his cheap cigars and his lack of personal hygiene), he was impressed enough with her film and stage performances to ask her, in 1946, to play the title role in *Mother Courage*, which she declined.

Thomas was puzzled that the homeopathic drops he had been prescribed worked as an aphrodisiac. Met his lawyer at the Baur au Lac in the same corner of the hotel lobby where he'd sat with Jakob Wassermann a fortnight before his death. In March, Thomas noted that red snow fell in south-east Switzerland. Thought to be sand from the Sahara. They say sandstorms in Mongolia can fall as red rain or snow over Russia. Blood rain. Wine rain. Watermelon snow. Water vapour condenses on dust in the air; as it falls, each drop or snowflake contains a grain of sand. If one lands in your eye you weep red tears. In Germany a Jewish man was sentenced to four years of prison for flirting with a group of non-Jewish girls. German troops marched unopposed into the demilitarised zone of the Rhineland. There was an uproar. Heinrich Mann's Paris-based Committee for a German Popular Front called for the mobilisation of troops to stop this violation. It fell on deaf ears. Heinrich heard that Querido, fearing imprisonment, would not publish his next book, a collection of essays called *Es kommt der Tag. Ein deutsches Lesebuch* (The Day Will Come. A German Reader); it is a symposium of writings by Kant, Nietzsche, Fontane and other well-known German authors, infused with urgency by the addition of Heinrich's own discursive prose. Friday 27 March was his 65th birthday. A mailbox full of greetings, including one from Else Lasker-Schüler in Ascona, written with her arm in bandages. *Most honourable Mr Heinrich Mann . . .* She said for writers it made no difference whether they're sixty or twenty-six or several thousand years old, that the luminosity of his fight against their enemies would be eternally inspiring. They celebrated the next day with lobster, chicken, Veuve Cliquot. Among their guests were the flirtatious Nietzschean Dr Oscar Levy and his daughter Maud, and Eva Landshoff, whose husband, Dr Fritz Landshoff, was responsible for Querido's German publications.

In London Virginia thought she heard the guns of war.

The political situation worsened, it was closing in on them. She continued writing, *like a doomed mouse, nibbling at my daily page*; noticed that the crocuses were out. Friday 20 March there was a tap on the window; she thought it was the dressmaker's apprentice with a delivery. But it was a girl asking for a drop of water, hardly able to walk or speak, fainting. *I'm hungry*. She took her in, called Leonard to stay with her and went to warm some soup. The girl had been walking all day looking for work, used to be a seamstress, sewing slips, but was suffering from neuritis and now could not sew. Nothing for breakfast but a cup of tea, in a room alone in Bethnal Green. With the soup she regained strength. A little conversation. *You look like brother and sister, both have long noses. I'm a Jewess*. The girl stressed the word. *So's he*, Virginia said, and the girl cheered up a little.

In March Brecht was in London, living in a small room at 148 Abbey Road. In a letter to Helene Weigel he told her to look after her wrists, which were again inflamed from typing his manuscripts. He saw Chaplin's *Modern Times*.

Violets in the woods, hyacinths, crocuses like blue and golden tufts of silk plucked from the soil's unconscious. Sharp needles. Seamstresses sewing slips with saffron threads.

Virginia forgot to play an April Fool's trick on Leonard, and he forgot too. The discovery on re-reading *The Years*, that it required a lot more work, pushed her into *catastrophic illness – never been so near the precipice*. Three months of suffering.

Heinrich was invited by Benjamin Crémieux – beard, glasses, intellect, associated with the French branch of PEN – to embark on a lecture tour to Rio de Janeiro. He wrote to his brother that for as long as he could remember he had wanted one day to visit Brazil – their home before their birth – but that now he was too tired to travel. Crémieux later died in Dachau.

Heinrich acquired Czech nationality on 24 April. In Küsnacht

Thomas noted the yellow sprays of forsythia that defined the spring. His son Bibi's prank with Phanodorm and other drugs; the tense household.

Forsythia is a favourite food source for a moth called The Gothic.

Freud's eightieth birthday brought them all together; a letter of congratulations organised by Stefan Zweig and signed by Wystan Auden, Georg Bernhard, Bertolt Brecht, Le Corbusier, Salvador Dali, Alfred Döblin, Lion Feuchtwanger, André Gide, Aldous Huxley, Alfred Kantorowicz, Marta Karlweiss-Wassermann, Egon Erwin Kisch, Else Lasker-Schüler, Erika Mann-Auden, Golo Mann, Heinrich Mann, Klaus Mann, Thomas Mann, Joseph Roth, Ernst Toller, Ernst Weiss, Leonard Woolf, Virginia Woolf, Arnold Zweig and others.

Italians in Addis Ababa. Germans reoccuppying the Rhineland. Tuesday 12 May, Thomas and Katia were again in Prague enjoying Mimi Mann's cooking. They reported back to Heinrich that though she complained about weight problems, Mimi seemed much better than on their previous visit, free of her earlier premonitions of death. On the train someone took Thomas's hat by mistake. At home, trouble with Bibi, who refused to see a psychiatrist. Pictures of St Sebastian from an acquaintance in Rostock. A visit to Freud's summer house mid-June.

Virginia read Flaubert's letters and in them heard her own voice cry out. *Few people can be so tortured by writing as I am. Only Flaubert I think . . . My brain is like a scale: one grain pulls it down.* One cool, quiet morning she emerged from her pain, only to fall back again soon after. She was unstable for four more months.

Nelly received a letter from Maud Levy in England and replied 13 June 1936, to thank her for the special nibs she'd sent Heinrich, saying that now he'd be able to write again; a chatty letter that mentioned the great number of mosquitoes, that they'd had a lot of visitors, including several of Thomas Mann's children, and that they were looking for a new apartment. It ended with warm greetings, also to the Tollers (Maud Levy was working as Toller's secretary) and a kiss.

At the beginning of July, Heinrich was again in Paris, to attend the International Committee against War and Fascism. He now wondered if all the disparate groups – Communists, Social Democrats, Catholics and others – would ever be persuaded to overcome their differences and form a single anti-Fascist force, but the alternative was too depressing to contemplate and he got on with his tired mission. Thomas read Heinrich's latest book of essays, published in Switzerland by Oprecht's Europa Verlag. He was moved by the naivety and self-assurance of his brother's moral manifestoes, and thought the collection would be appreciated by future generations. Monday 13 July Thomas arranged his volumes of Nietzsche on the new bookshelves in his study. The next day he wrote to his brother about the essays, but tore up the letter. From mid-July until early August, Heinrich and Nelly and their friends, Oscar and Maud Levy, were in the Hautes-Alpes, in St Chaffrey near Briançon. Nelly returned to Nice on her own to undergo treatment that included four weeks of rest and mudbaths. Heinrich had organised for his daughter to spend September with him in the South of France, warning Mimi that it would not be safe for Goschi to travel via Austria where his books were banned. In Sils, at the end of the month, Thomas pinned a bunch of dark red alpine flowers to a plaque commemorating Nietzsche. He and Katia discussed their financial situation and were satisfied that their current standard of living would remain unchanged. News of Erich Mühsam's widow Kreszentia gaoled in Russia for anarchist remarks.

Nettie Palmer and her family were living near Barcelona. 5 July was *a lovely, hottish day, with little striped tents appearing on the beach and the sea full of bathers . . .* On 19 July they *awoke to the dull sound of firing, but took it to be celebrations connected with the opening of the People's Olympiad . . . not till the milkman came did I notice how still everything was – no trains running, no cars on the road, hardly a soul on the beach.* She heard machine guns across the bay in Barcelona. *It was terribly hard to grasp what was happening.*

July 17, civil war broke out in Spain. The writer Alfred Kantorowicz (born 1899 in Berlin) was serving in the International Brigades, made up of 25,000 volunteers from around the world, Communists, writers, young and old idealists, including about 5,000 Germans; a great mix of arms and uniforms and languages; training near Albacete. The Thaelmann Battalion had for its leader the novelist Ludwig Renn (born Arnold Vieth von Goessenau). In his memoir *Deutsches Tagebuch* (German Diary), Kantorowicz explained how *at that time we only saw that the Soviet Union was the one European power supporting the Spanish people in their fight against Fascism – this was what we wanted to believe, not just out of self-interest, but to uphold the principle of international solidarity.* The slaughter. A war in which 300,000 to one million people would be killed. In August the murder of the writer Federico García Lorca. *If I am dying, leave the balcony open.*

Opening ceremony of the 1936 Olympic Games in Berlin on 1 August; sport playing into the hands of Hitler; the self writ large; one of the spectators, later that week, was Jacques Lacan who had delivered a paper on the mirror stage in infant development at a conference of the International Psychoanalytical Association in Marienbad, 3 August.

August 14, the dissident Marxist Victor Serge wrote to Leon Trotsky. *Dear Leon Davidovich: I am worried about you. Write me a few words. What is happening? I wrote to you yesterday. I asked if you'd received one of my previous letters. I believe that they are in the process of preparing the physical liquidation of Zinoviev and the others . . . The passivity of our comrades in the face of the repression in the USSR was a crime*. Confessions by torture; on 25 August, Stalin's executions of 16 senior Communists, including Grigory Zinoviev and Lev Kamenev (Trotsky's brother-in-law); the public face of mass arrests and executions; estimations of the death toll vary between 1 million and 100 million. *Dear André Gide*, Serge wrote. *In the great drama in which we participate it is in reality very little a question of you and me . . . I remember the pages of your journal in which you noted in 1933 your adherence to Communism because it assures the free development of the personality . . . I read the pages of your journal at a period when no one around me would have risked keeping a journal*. He begged Gide not to close his eyes to the disappearances and deaths of so many in the Soviet Union, to the revolution gone terribly wrong.

Tuesday 11 August, Thomas read Robert Louis Stevenson's *The Strange Case of Dr Jekyll and Mr Hyde* at night; heavy thunder, lightning strikes close by. A new pair of kittens called Pizzi and Cato. At the end of August Thomas and Katia drove to Geneva, where they stayed overnight, before continuing on to Avignon, the Hotel de l'Europe, then St Cyr, the grand Hotel Les Lecques. Mornings at the beach, the water calm, clear, warm and very salty, evening visits to friends in Bandol and Sanary. Readings from his *Joseph* epic; admired; his writing was called universal, fugue-like. Vermouth. Mistral. Then on to Le Lavandou, the Hôtel d'Aiguebelle. Forest fires, red clouds, ash-laden winds. Unhappy with the weather, the hotel, the food. Getting a cold. He had begun reading and making notes for his Goethe novel *The Beloved Returns*, later titled *Lotte in Weimar* (published in Sweden in 1939).

Heinrich was in Brussels for the World Peace Congress from 3 to 6 September, in Paris from 7 September. Followed by a family reunion. On 11 September he and his daughter joined Thomas and Katia in the South of France. As soon as he arrived, Heinrich wrote to Nelly. *My dear*. That he had not heard from her for a long time; asked her to send everything to him straight away; not all the old newspapers, only those that featured his articles; asked if she had been looking for a new apartment, or at least temporary lodgings; if her health had improved; said he hoped she'd been resting and that no news was good news; reminded her that in response to her telegram he'd sent her another 700 francs; he hoped to see her soon, looking healthy and beautiful.

Two days later he wrote to her again. *My sweet.* Happy to have received her photo, because she looked so radiant; he was proud of her. Told her that now she had to make sure that above all she was eating well. But not to incur too many other expenses. He was enclosing 1,000 francs. She could not claim that he did not look after her: since 7 August she'd received 1,000 francs, followed by two lots of 700 francs, 2,400 altogether. He thought that after paying for the hospital and the health clinic there should be enough left over to pay for rent and food. Told her rather sternly that she must get on with finding them a larger apartment. Or move provisionally to a small hotel costing about 35 francs. Before settling into a new place and buying furniture, they should perhaps wait to see what was going to happen in Spain; their decisions hinged on that. If they furnished a place and then had to leave the country, it would all have to be abandoned, a repetition of what happened in Berlin. He did not want to frighten her, but it was wise to be careful. She should keep sending his mail, and to give him her new address. He hoped that Rudi, in Spain as weapons master with the 11th Brigade's Edgar Andre Battalion, was okay. Everyone sent her their greetings, he sent her kisses. *My sweet. My beauty.* Told her that he wished that on the photo she'd sent him, she had moved her arm a little so that he could see more of her legs; her face had blossomed. A sexy postscript in the margin, anticipating their reunion.

Some observations. Nelly had been sick, in hospital. What was wrong with her? Was it physical or mental, or both? Did she have a nervous breakdown? It appears that Nelly was left alone in Nice, perhaps to recover, living in hotels – there's a bill for a room at the Hotel Massena, for example, for end September to 5 October, with additonal charge for breakfasts, coffees, water, whisky and port, stationery, medication and a thermometer – while she looked for a new apartment, and Heinrich travelled and spent the rest of the summer with his family on the coast not very far from Nice. Did he have to promise Mimi that he would not introduce their daughter to his mistress? And another thing. How odd to hear the tone of Heinrich's letters shifting between an abundance of love on one side, and on the other, strictness and anxiety, especially about money.

The brothers walked on the beach, swam, shopped, talked politics, drank vermouth. Thomas noted Heinrich's optimism, his dream of a German revolution. Mosquitoes. Linden-flower tea. Overcast days that reminded them of their childhood summers on the Baltic. Disapproving looks from locals when they spoke German in public. Goschi's chatter. After all those years apart there was so much to tell her father. She was twenty, cheerful, still training to become a dancer and therefore trying to lose some weight. But soon she was sick with a sore throat and fever. All four of them were unwell. All stayed in bed, except Thomas. Then he too worsened, with severe rheumatic aches and a high fever, while the others improved. The entire hotel was affected, the dining room empty. As well as fever, the guests suffered headache, nausea, insomnia, neuralgia and angina. Everyone was taking quinine. There were storms, followed by high humidity. A melancholy mood. Thursday 17 September the Manns moved to a friendlier and more sanitised establishment in Le Lavandou, Pension Calanque. Rain and the smell of the sea. The brothers read each other extracts from their works in progress. Thomas and Katia left Monday 21 Septem-.

ber; overnight in Valence, more unpleasant heat and mosquitoes. Relieved to have escaped the oppressive climate of the south – *Heinrich's domain*, he called it – to reach Geneva and the cleanliness and lakeside elegance of the Hôtel Metropole. *Ah!* Thomas threw open his hotel room window and with a deep breath he saluted the heroic solitariness of Mont Salève. Fresh air, good roads and tea with cream. Welcome illusions that were all too easily dispelled.

In the heart of Europe . . . *thunder burst with a terrific crash over my head. It was echoed from Salève, the Jura, and the Alps of Savoy; vivid flashes of lightning dazzled my eyes, illuminating the lake, making it appear like a vast sheet of fire; then for an instant every thing seemed of a pitchy darkness, until the eye recovered itself from the preceding flash. The storm, as is often the case in Switzerland, appeared at once in various parts of the heavens.* (Mary Shelley, *Frankenstein*)

Heinrich and Goschi stayed on at the pension in Le Lavandou for a few more weeks. By early October Nelly had been alone since August. Sunday 4 October Heinrich wrote to her from Le Lavandou. She had telegraphed to assure him she'd get everything organised in Nice. A few hours later she telegraphed again, with the message that unless he and Goschi came to Nice immediately, she would kill herself. He had thought that this chapter of her adventures was well and truly finished. He asked her if it was a relapse. Told her that his and his daughter's presence could not help her if she herself was bent on disaster. That it could not go on like that. He told her to pull herself together. She should go back to their old address at 11, rue du Congrès, and stay in bed if she was still sick. He wanted to look after her and help her to recover. To do that he needed calm. She must realise that it was not only her own nerves that were on edge. He now had to go to Toulon, an arrangement it was impossible to change. He would arrive in Nice on Tuesday evening, by the first train leaving after four o'clock, which would get to Nice around ten. He didn't know the timetable, suggested that she could find it out. Did she want to meet him at the station on Tuesday evening? He'd be grateful if she did. If not, he'd find a hotel, perhaps the Cecil, and would then take it upon himself to search for an apartment. Told her he could no longer stand the continuous crises. It did not have to be like that. He really hoped her latest anxiety attack had passed and her telegram, which he'd only just received, was already obsolete. He was sure that by now she was feeling better and braver. He would be overjoyed. Expected to hear from her by telegram on Monday, whether he would see her on Tuesday at the station in Nice, or at their old place. *Auf Wiedersehen.*

We can assume Nelly met Heinrich's train that night. By the end of October they had settled into number 18, rue Rossini. A note about Nelly's suicidal plea, as an aspect of her life which Heinrich thought she'd overcome: his comment suggests that she had either threatened or attempted suicide before, and her stay in hospital that year was related to this problem. Many years later Heinrich mentioned to a friend that Nelly attempted suicide twice while they lived in France. In that case her first attempt may have been in 1936. He declined an invitation to go on a two-month speaking tour to America.

October. Thomas had been unwell, and the shock of seeing her father looking dark and dreadful, with a seven-day beard, triggered his youngest daughter Medi to have an asthma attack. Recovered from illness and clean-shaven, he returned to his smoking ration of two cigars per day. Goschi stayed with them on her way back to Prague. Bibi's rebellion still caused distress; there were no signs of the father's sympathy or understanding for his son. Thomas wondered if all-out chaos was approaching and the time had come to think about moving to a safer place. He had furious dreams about an authority figure, a mix of Heinrich and his father. They heard on 22 October that martial law had been used to suppress a Fascist uprising in Belgium. Thomas acquired Czech nationality. The news of Ossietzky's Nobel Prize. Thomas received roses from a couple who liked his latest novel so much that they named one of their twin sons after him. They had guests on Sunday 28 November and later another fight with Bibi, who left the house. Katia and Medi tried to find him, without success. At breakfast Katia was in tears. Thomas was keen to keep working on his Goethe novel; he retired to his study while his wife and daughter looked for the boy again; he was found.

Fierce fighting in and around Madrid; the siege would last three years.

In November Leonard read the completed manuscript of *The Years*, and liked it. Virginia was relieved. *I hand my compliment to that terribly depressed woman, myself, whose head ached so often . . . I think she brought it off . . . How she did it with her head like an old cloth I don't know.*

Friday 4 December, Thomas received news of his loss of German citizenship. Gide visited him and expressed interest in Ludwig von Hofmann's Arcadian painting *Die Quelle* (The Source), that hung in the study, depicting three male nudes around a spring. Christmas eve. His presents included a chest of drawers with a large mirror, a recording of Wagner's *Valkyrie*, and more pictures of St Sebastian from his acquaintance in Rostock. Their daughter Moni was suffering from depression and did not want to leave her room to join in family festivities. At the end of December it was rumoured that the Nazis had sanitised Schiller's study by removing a book by Moses Mendelssohn from the shelves. Punch and pancakes to celebrate the new year; Thomas felt unusually happy, eager to know what lay ahead.

In his Paris studio, Mondrian layered white paint very thickly on the canvas. The black lines of his grid are like ladders or maps, or like roads shovelled free of snow, the primary colours of his interlocking planes are there for us to dwell on and move between, like lives. The conspicuous absence of green, the lost dream of Eden, in the house of exile.

James and Nora Joyce were walking around Hamlet's castle at Elsinore. Someone asked him, *Do you like flowers, Mr Joyce?* He answered, *No. I love plants, green growing things, trees and grass. Flowers annoy me.* It started to rain. *Why didn't you bring an umbrella, Nora?* She answered, *I hate umbrellas.*

Virginia walked past Buckingham Palace and noticed lights burning in the upper windows. A few days later she noted that King Edward III was said to be making up his mind, and drinking. Then the abdication. The announcement that he could not be king without the help and support of the woman he loved. *A very ordinary young man*, Virginia thought.

Trotsky, who had tried to expose Stalin's falsehoods, was ushered out of Norway on the petrol tanker *Ruth*, headed for Mexico.

The fist of Italy, Germany and Spain tightened around those in exile in France. People started making plans to move on. Nelly thought she might soon have to learn another language. Perhaps she taught herself English, listening for snippets of it, repeating random phrases she had caught – *gone with the wind, certainly not, joe di maggio is a new york yankee* – over and over again, in the street, entering rue Rossini and crossing the marble mosaic floor of the entrance hall, then in the lift, looking out from the wrought-iron balcony, cooking, a phrasebook propped up against a bowl, as a test mixing the ingredients for plum pudding from an English cookbook she'd found. Heinrich was in Paris for a few days before Christmas. On the last day of the year he wrote to a friend about his excess of commitments and complete absence of leisure. They received New Year cards; one was signed by Salomea Rottenberg and the veteran Marxist Charles Rappoport in Paris. It addressed Heinrich as *Meister* and freedom fighter.

From exile in Paris, Döblin wrote to a friend in Vienna: *I see myself walking from Bellevue station to your place . . . one time Wassermann was there too, sitting in the back room . . . and my home was in Berlin, its streets carried me on my large and small daily rounds.*

The writer Alfred Polgar told a friend he was thinking of going to live in Sydney. The friend thought that was a bit too far. Polgar asked: *Too far? From where?*

1937: The Great Cat

Maybe they moved to a larger apartment because Nelly needed space for her millinery equipment, the ironing board, wooden hat blocks, wire, patterns, straw, fabrics, veiling. And trimmings she amassed from the markets of Nice and surrounding towns; artificial flowers, ribbons, braids and feathers. She had a flair for fashion, and I imagine her studying trends, head shapes, prices, wearing her latest creations in cafés, restaurants, casinos and on the Promenade des Anglais. If someone admired her hat, she would produce her business card, wait for a phone call, and then receive or visit her new client for a measurement; the down payment would always have been welcome. For herself she favoured the bandeau or turban, but for others she must have created cartwheels and cloches, pillboxes and hybrid cocktail hats, to be worn coquettishly. She might even have made felt hats for Heinrich: blocked into shape, sanded, brushed, lined with silk, his name embroidered on the inside rim. Millinery is mainly handwork, and so perhaps this was how they spent the best days of their French exile, she stitching, he writing, the space between them filled with birdsong. Canaries fly freely around the apartment, Yorkshires, Glosters, Norwiches, Lancashire Coppies, like dashes of sunlight in a forest clearing; they're fed delicate portions of apples, pears, turnip tops, lettuce and the young dandelion leaves Heinrich and Nelly bring back from their walks; at dusk her *angels* return to their cages, darkened with drapes.

A timely honorarium of 1100 francs from the sale of books in Russia offset Thomas and Katia's recent spending on Christmas presents; a good start to the year. On 2 January he went to the hairdresser, where a charming young man attended him. Thomas's reading now revolved around Goethe; he marked passages in books for later use. Katia typed up the first chapter of *Lotte in Weimar*. On Friday 8 January they left Zürich for Prague; he noted the dog's *melancholy* at their departure. The train conductor's recognition and extreme politeness. A slice of *gugelhupf* gave him indigestion; Phanodorm for sleep; Goethe's *Wilhelm Meisters Lehrjahre* lay open on his chest. On arrival, the customary evening with Mimi and Goschi, followed by days and nights of receptions and readings, and a visit to the town that had granted him and his family honorary residency. Back in Küsnacht, Wilhelm Herzog sought a meeting to discuss Heinrich's chances for the Nobel Prize. *Hopeless*, Thomas wrote in his diary afterwards. On arrival in Arosa for a winter holiday he felt unwell. *Mountain sickness.* The University of Bonn deprived him of his honorary doctorate; on 24 January his reply to its dean of philosophy appeared in the *Neue Zürcher Zeitung*, and at the same time, for maximum distribution, the letter was also published by Oprecht as a brochure. Thomas Mann's break with Hitler's Germany was complete. Heinrich read the open letter with great satisfaction, and told his brother it said everything there was to say. A Czech newspaper article featured a photo of Thomas and Katia, taken in Mimi's apartment, against the backdrop of Heinrich's rescued library. He was very moved by this scene; he hoped they would continue to visit Goschi on their trips to Prague, because sadly, he could only see her rarely and his books he'd probably never see again.

H. G. Wells, Virginia noticed, had tiny hands and feet; his voice was a *little sparrow's chirp.*

When Katia hurt her leg skiing, Thomas brought her a bunch of lilacs. Their wedding anniversary was the same as the day of their departure from Munich four years earlier. Conversations with family and friends focused on the large numbers of young intellectuals flocking to fight in Spain, the place, Auden wrote, where *Our thoughts have bodies; the menacing shapes of our fever / Are precise and alive . . . Madrid is the heart. Our moments of tenderness blossom / as the ambulance and the sandbag; / Our hours of friendship into a people's army, / To-morrow, perhaps the future.*

News of arrests in the USSR. The Second Moscow Trial. Confessions. Karl Radek (1885–1939), who had helped to write the 1936 Soviet Constitution, was imprisoned but managed to stall his execution. Victor Serge described him as a great intellect and wit; his stories *often had a savage side to them . . . just like an old-time pirate.*

In February, south of Madrid, the Battle of Jarama; the dead of the International Brigades on Suicide Hill were mostly British; a stalemate.

Virginia was fearful that *The Years* would be reviewed unenthusiastically, that it would be taken as *the long drawn twaddle of a prim prudish bourgeois mind.* But to her great relief she soon found that people liked it. One admirer was Christopher Isherwood, *a most appreciative little bird.* With the promise of an income boosted by the sale of books, she strolled through one of her favourite London haunts, the Caledonian Market in Islington, and spent four shillings on some yellow gloves and a pair of stockings. A conversation about Kipling's style, and from his autobiography, the lasting impression of a set of lines he'd written. *When the fog thinned, I looked out and saw a man standing opposite the pub where the barmaid lived. Of a sudden his breast turned dull red like a robin's, and he crumpled, having cut his throat.*

The woman in the bus spread her hands like two fans. Canary-yellow gloves. She might have remembered a red pair she once owned. *When the fog thinned I looked out and saw . . .* wet snow, melting; with Vita in Berlin.

Küsnacht, Wednesday 24 March, *wet snow, snow mush, almost impossible to walk through, snow continues to fall all day, monstrous weather.* Four days later, on Easter Sunday, the breakfast table was decorated with coloured eggs and sprigs of spring green. A letter on the last day of the month from Erika in New York, recounting an anti-Nazi demonstration attended by 23,000 people, where she read out a message from her father and received massive applause *when she mentioned my name.*

Applause, the fruit of the fame tree, the writer's harvest.

At the beginning of March, still unsure of the reception of her work, Virginia wrote of terror. *As if I were exposed on a high ledge in full light. Very lonely . . . No words. Very apprehensive. As if something cold and horrible – a roar of laughter at my expense were about to happen . . . I want to burst into tears, but have nothing to cry for.* She was pleased a few weeks later, when praise for *The Years* referred to her *astonishing fertility. A feeling of glory. Of flight.*

In April, Thomas and Katia travelled to America on the *Normandie*; on board they visited Aldous Huxley and his wife in tourist class. English words now crept into his diary notes, pier was *pear*, and the sherry they drank was *cherry*. Their time in New York brimmed with meetings, interviews, dinners, lectures, and in their hotel room at the Bedford, deliveries of letters, flowers, gifts of books. A busy program, full of high-mindedness. Proclamations. Celebrations. Set against stories of massive unemployment, of people surviving on potatoes, handouts. He noted that he had met the writer Willa Cather. Returning home on the *Ile de France*, while plagued by physical discomfort – ongoing dental problems and neuralgia in his leg – he reflected on the irony of experiencing such pain in the lap of luxury.

Willi Münzenberg was born in 1889 in Erfurt; his mother died when he was very young; his father was an innkeeper and a drunk and reputedly the unhappy offspring of a dalliance between a shepherdess and a baron; when Willi was thirteen his father accidentally killed himself while cleaning his gun. As a young man Willi lived in Switzerland, met Karl Radek and Lenin, became a Communist. In Berlin from 1924 to 1933 he was an influential publisher, publicist and politician, a prominent Communist spokesman and member of parliament. After the Reichstag fire he fled to France, where he was one of the founders of the German Popular Front and numerous other organisations, including the World Committee for the Relief of the Victims of German Fascism; he understood that Hitler was primarily a propagandist, and so he concentrated on developing counter-propaganda. His book *Propaganda as Weapon* exposed the lies of totalitarian régimes. Münzenberg possessed an intriguing blend of charm and toughness; he persuaded the writer Arthur Koestler to go on a dangerous mission to Spain on the side of the Nationalists to discover how much aid General Franco was receiving from the Nazis. He did not smoke or drink, loved good coffee, movies and Karl May's adventure stories. An expert at cards, it was said he played to calm his nerves. He was married to Babette Gross, who would later write his biography. Describing their circle, she said it was easy *to make friends with the open-minded, easy-going bon vivant Heinrich, who unlike his brother Thomas was not in the least bit pompous.* They visited the *4th floor flat in Nice where he lived, surrounded by canaries, with his future wife Nelly*; the two couples holidayed together in Briançon.

Babette's sister was Margarete Buber-Neumann, a writer whose first husband was Rafael Buber (son of the philosopher Martin Buber); her second husband was Heinz Neumann, one of the

highest-ranking members of the German Communist Party and
Münzenberg's good friend. Neumann had been critical of Stalin's
regime. In April, the couple lived at the infamous Hotel Lux in
Moscow, the nightmarish, prison-like place where the secret police
kept a close watch on resident emigrés and foreign Communists,
and where, to save their own skins, comrades betrayed one another. Like so many of its *guests*, Neumann was arrested and shot;
his wife was sentenced to forced labour and was later handed over
to the Nazis. She survived Ravensbrück concentration camp. In
the title of her autobiography she called their links with Moscow
an *Irrweg*: the wrong path.

Increasingly, at meetings and in conversation, Münzenberg
had also criticised the Communist Party for its mistakes and
crimes; privately he suffered from depression. As he was effect-
ing his break with the party, others had already begun to scheme
against him, and after he was called to Moscow in 1936 for questioning, he was reprimanded and counted himself lucky to have
escaped a worse fate. Early in 1937 he rejected requests to return
to Moscow. In April he opened the Paris conference of the German Popular Front, followed by Heinrich Mann's address; it was a
gathering of about 300 delegates; Münzenberg stressed the importance of the unity of anti-Fascist forces. That summer he held talks
with Leo Schwarzschild, Georg Bernhard, the editor of the *Pariser
Tageblatt*, and Heinrich Mann, to create the Deutsche Freiheits
Partei (German Freedom Party). But any chance of unified action
was still hopelessly undermined by infighting and intrigue. When
the KPD in Paris elected Walter Ulbricht as their leader, Heinrich
Mann told his friend Kantorowicz, *I find it impossible to share a table
with someone who suddenly insists that the table at which we're sitting is not
a table but a duck pond and who wants to force me to agree.* Nonetheless,
as the Communists withdrew from other left-wing organisations,
Heinrich continued to try to mend the rifts.

Hell erupted on 26 April when German and Italian bombers destroyed the Basque town of Guernica.

In early May, a performance of Lessing's *Nathan the Wise* (1779) with its powerful plea for tolerance – religious and political – brought Thomas Mann close to tears. On 6 May the airship *Hindenburg*, arriving from Frankfurt, and about to land in New Jersey, exploded with ninety-seven people on board; a third of the passengers died, survivors sustained terrible injuries; an odd mix of circumstances, including an electrical storm, had caused the accident. Later that month Thomas and Katia went to the cinema, where they were horrified by the graphic details of the disaster, the shock of hearing screams. Thomas read Schopenhauer on death.

Leonard and Virginia and their monkey Mitz went to France. They visited the caves at Les Eyzies; the castle at Meyronne; *an old woman shredding salsify*; a little girl collecting snails for Mitz. *The Years* was now a bestseller in America.

On the last day of May, Almería on the coast of Spain was bombarded by the German fleet.

Tuesday 1 June, Thomas wrote in his diary that he began his birth month suffering terrible pain, such as he'd never known. A list of his medications included Alonal, Phanodorm, Veramon and Oktyron. On his sixty-second birthday he was worried about his son Klaus, who was staying at the Siesta Sanatorium in Budapest undergoing rehabilitation treatment for drug addiction; thought that *the boy was morally and self-critically damaged*, that Klaus did not respond well to authority. In a letter to a friend, Klaus described being cured as *exiled from artificial paradises*.

Heinrich received an invitation from Louis Aragon to attend a congress, and in case Mme Mann also wished to come, he was told this could be arranged, as long as other participants did not find out about it, as they might expect similar privileges. Heinrich sent his brother birthday greetings; he said each day now he shook with nervous apprehension on opening the paper; believed, however, that a small chance for peace still existed, if only England acted more decisively. Stalin ordered twelve of his generals to be shot. Franco's forces took Bilbao. In Munich on 19 July, the opening of the exhibition of Degenerate Art. Targeting Expressionism, Dadaism, Surrealism, Cubism, Fauvism and other modern movements, it included work by George Grosz, Ernst Ludwig Kirchner, Max Ernst, Paul Klee, Ernst Barlach. *Tortured canvases, rotting mentalities, sick imaginations, deranged incompetents.* Entry: free.

Virginia was invited but would not go on a lecture tour of the United States.

Another visit in Küsnacht from Wilhem Herzog; they sat in the summer light on the terrace and discussed politics; the need to distance oneself from Stalin, and Heinrich's far too positive view of Russia. Thomas had heard that Hitler was having screaming fits. That the aviator Amelia Earhart (1897–1937) had vanished while crossing the Pacific Ocean; the costly search. Jean Batten, who later that year set the solo flying record between Australia and England – 5 days, 18 hours, and 15 minutes – told people not to send out search parties if she disappeared into the sea. One day Thomas found himself alone at the edge of a forest near Küsnacht, looking across a sunny meadow where butterflies flew in pairs; this was peace and happiness. Happiness also when he slept under the new lilac silk bedcover.

In July the Second International Congress for the Defence of Culture was held from 4 to 17 July in Spain and France; it was a just cause with terrible speeches by honoured guests, standing ovations nonetheless. Despite the show of strength and the spirited singing of anthems, Heinrich in Paris was distressed to witness the breaking up of the Popular Front and the desperate regroupings that were often based on personal rather than political agendas. Non-Stalinist anti-Fascists were shouted down. Konrad Heiden and Leo Schwarzschild, who did not get on with Georg Bernhard, formed a Club of the Clean which André Gide and Klaus Mann had joined, and tried to enlist both Thomas and Heinrich, who advised his brother against it. Heinrich had seen Erika and Klaus when he was in Paris, but was upset that his nephew had not kept one of their appointments; he maintained that although the unity of the Volksfront was now compromised, it was the only effective opposition to Hitler's regime, that there was no room for splinter groups or wishy-washy liberalism. To this effect he wrote his nephew a stern letter, which was not appreciated. He asked Thomas to tell Klaus it was well-meant. This trip to Paris had been long and difficult for Heinrich, too politically intense and emotionally fraught. He needed rest, a holiday with Nelly in the Hautes Alpes, at the familiar Grand Hôtel in Briançon, and the chance to finish the second volume of his *Henri IV*. This book told the story of the Edict of Nantes, issued by the French king in 1598, drawn up to protect religious minorities and to end dissent; its focus was on civil rights and unity. In Heinrich's eyes it was a model of reconciliation that might be adapted for the current crisis.

On Tuesday 20 July, Virginia was told of the death two days earlier of her nephew Julian Bell in Spain. He had been driving an ambulance. The boundless grief that followed; her sister Vanessa submerged in sorrow, *an atmosphere of deep green waters*.

The news that on 28 July, Japanese troops had taken Peking. A thousand people died when the Chinese accidentally bombed Shanghai on 14 August.

Schiller, Liszt, Bach and Nietzsche had lived in Weimar. Goethe lived there from 1775 until his death in 1832. His favourite walk was through a nearby beech forest – *Buchenwald* – on the Ettersberg. When the land was cleared to build the concentration camp, an old oak tree was left standing because it was believed to be the one under which the poet had sat with Charlotte von

Stein, who inspired the *Sorrows of Young Werther* (and the subject of Thomas Mann's work in progress, *Lotte in Weimar*). About eight kilometres north of Weimar, Buchenwald concentration camp was opened by the Nazis on 1 August. From 1937 until 1945 a quarter of a million people were imprisoned there in the most gruesome conditions; over 50,000 died. The writer Jean Améry, the child psychologist Bruno Bettelheim, the writer and Nobel Prize winner Imre Kertész, the leader of the Communist Party of Germany Ernst Thälmann, and the writer and Nobel Peace prize recipient Elie Wiesel were among the inmates.

Early in August, Thomas was reading *War and Peace*. He noted that a long letter from Heinrich about Russia was one-sided and naïve, *as usual*. Mosquitoes. Reports about the persecution of emigrants in Prague. When Thomas read from *Lotte in Weimar* to a group of friends, he looked up to find his publisher Oprecht fast asleep and snoring; in September in Locarno he met Arthur Koestler.

Heinrich Mann was in Paris at the end of September, back in Nice beginning of October. Meanwhile Nelly received a letter from Willi Münzenberg, saying he'd expected her to come too and was sorry she didn't, that he'd armed himself with a bunch of flowers, for a surprise attack. Words that glimmer with a playful mix of sincerity and self-irony from the man whom many believed to be in charge of the Communist plan to overthrow the Western world. He wrote to her again two weeks later, thanking her for her letter, saying that amidst the mountains of mail he received every day, he was always happy to hear from real friends like Heinrich and Nelly, and that he and Babette hoped to spend Christmas with them in Nice. He said he was optimistic about the political situation (though as one of his biographers has pointed out, the political noose was already tightening around his neck). He sent special greetings to Nelly's canary Chrischan, saying that when people upset him, he found solace in reading about animals, had just read a touching story about a bear cub called Michka. He told Nelly he'd love to have animals around him, but his circumstances didn't allow it; he believed animals needed even more love and care than children, or at least as much. Signed, *your loyal and humble friend Willi.*

Thomas told Heinrich he was unwell, troubled by his teeth, but he had a lot of work to do preparing for an American tour scheduled for early the next year.

The Bali tiger was hunted to extinction. The last one – an adult tigress – was killed on 27 September 1937. Sunday 17 October at the zoo, Thomas noticed the thoughtful expression of a chimpanzee, the growing excitement of a wildcat at the nearness of a young child. The following week he quoted Nietzsche, that Germans are a people who had subordinated themselves to a man like Luther! And commented that no, the prominence of Hitler was not a case of rotten luck, but was directly in line with Luther and so *a truly German phenomenon.* He was bothered by the visiting publisher Blanche Knopf's flashy manicure, her *red claws.* Received a letter from Willi Münzenberg, supported by the novelist Romain Rolland, again regarding Heinrich's nomination for the Nobel Prize. Did he toss it in the bin? The discomfort of dentures. A walk in the forest with Katia. Trouble with sleep, and with false teeth while speaking. Received a litre of eau de cologne as a gift from the manufacturer.

The Duke and Duchess of Windsor visited Germany and Hitler. In her autobiography she wrote, *I could not take my eyes off Hitler. He was dressed in his brown Party uniform. His face had a pasty pallor, and under his moustache his lips were fixed in a kind of mirthless grimace. Yet at close quarters he gave one the feeling of great inner force . . . his eyes were truly extraordinary – intense, unblinking, magnetic . . . when I tried to meet their gaze, the lids dropped, and I found myself confronted by a mask. I decided that Hitler did not care for women.*

Virginia planned but then made up her mind not to go to Paris. Overcome with happiness at this decision, she and Leonard *walked round the square love-making – after 25 years can't bear to be separate . . . an enormous pleasure, being wanted: a wife.* She was busy writing all November. Sometimes she said she worked so hard from envy of her sister. *I put my life blood into writing,* Virginia noted in her diary, *and she had children.*

Helene Weigel objected to Brecht's relationships with Ruth Berlau and Margarete Steffin; she wanted a separation.

Shanghai fell to the Japanese; the mass executions and widespread killing of civilians.

Oh this cursed year 1937 – it will never let us out of its claws, Virginia wrote. She worried about Leonard's health. *The great cat is playing with us once more.*

It was a year in which Thomas Mann recognised the *frighteningly Hitleresque* qualities of Wagner, drank a lot of cocoa, enjoyed a fair amount of caviar, as well as words of praise; someone had referred to his *majestic stature* in the literary domain. In Küsnacht he kept reading Schopenhauer; ended the year with fruit punch and pancakes.

Summer hats are dreamed up in winter. On the dining table, Nelly sorted and plaited hunks of raffia. A bird sat on her shoulder, warbling; another trilled to an opera playing on the radio.

1938: War Expected

If I'd given up hope, I'd already be in America. HEINRICH MANN

At the beginning of the year Walter Benjamin was staying with his ex-wife and son in San Remo. He was working on an essay on Baudelaire, which he regarded as a *miniature* of his Arcades Project.

The Mann brothers and their wives exchanged New Year's greetings by mail. In January, Thomas and Katia again occupied their favourite rooms on the third floor of the Waldhotel in Arosa, comforted by its familiar surroundings. He continued work on his Schopenhauer essay, and before going to sleep he once again immersed himself in Proust. The papers reported northern lights across most of Europe and around the globe on the night of 25–26 January, magnificent neon-like displays across the sky, of reds, blues, greens. This phenomenon of solar winds interacting with Earth's magnetic field played havoc with railway signals and disrupted transatlantic radio communication. Londoners thought the city was on fire and called the fire brigades. Scandinavians passed on the folk belief that a profusion of herring had cast its colourful reflections into the sky. The end of the world. For doomsayers this awe-inspiring phenomenon gave credence to their rhetoric. On the last day of their vacation, Thomas slept badly, disturbed by the onset of a cold as well as his perennial existential pain. He took

Phanodorm with chamomile; Katia came to his room. *When she held my hand, I thought, that's how I'd like it to be when I die.* A fierce snow-storm on the day of their departure left him breathless with panic.

Pleased to be back home to sleep in his own bed, with the feel of his own pillow, and the lightness and warmth of his silk-covered eiderdown; porridge, Zwieback, egg and tea for breakfast; fol-lowed by writing on Schopenhauer. Mid-February they travelled on the Cunard liner *Queen Mary* to America. It was their fourth trip. A journey, he wrote, that was overshadowed by the Austrian catastrophe. Thomas registered disgust, and wondered about *the consequences for Prague? The effect on Switzerland? Where to go? Paris? London? America?* Meanwhile they enjoyed caviar, soup, tournedos, ice cream, chablis and coffee in the ship's elegant dining room. At dinner on Saturday 19 February he remembered with shocked surprise that it was their thirty-third wedding anniversary. He felt dizzy at the thought. He told Katia he would not want to repeat his life, because what he called *das Peinliche* – the embarrassment of his homoerotic inclination – had been too dominant. Then he realised that by saying this he might have hurt her. Thomas wrote to Heinrich. He imagined his brother would be devastated by the latest political atrocities. *Who would have thought that Austria's fall would come so suddenly and without resistance.* Disorientation of the media. Of oneself. The need once more to think about emigration. Arrived in New York on Monday 22 February for an extensive lecture tour of fourteen states to deliver a paper titled 'The Com-ing Victory of Democracy'. Speaking about democracy to Ameri-cans, he flattered his audience, saying of course it was like taking coals to Newcastle, because Americans knew that democracy was a universal phenomenon, a basic human right. Most of the venues, seating thousands, were sold out. Tuesday 8 March, Thomas again met Willa Cather. I wonder how well they knew each other's work. Did they recognise similarities in their masterful spinning of narratives around secrets, around that which remains unspoken or unrealised?

The Germans invaded Austria 11 March. The Anschluss was announced 12 March. It was being called the Death of Austria.

In Tulsa, Thomas and Katia discussed the Austrian crisis. They had heard that thousands of people had been arrested, that amongst the intellectuals there had been an epidemic of suicides. He felt tortured, suffocated, at the thought that England did not step in to stop the progression of political crimes and the chaos in Europe. Reports of murders and suicides day after day. He was reading Dostoyevsky's *The Idiot*; was doubtful about their return to Switzerland. Puffed by the applause in Salt Lake City, where he lectured and read from his work to an audience of 2,000. News of a ravaged Vienna, with mass arrests, lowly acts of cruelty, sadism, cowardice. On Thursday 24 March, they settled into the Hotel Beverly Wilshire in Hollywood. He went to the beach, breathed deeply and looked around, taking in the American scale of things, its grandeur and newness, and the light; the heady scent of eucalyptus mixed with the ocean breeze. Listening to the radio, reading the newspapers, talking about Europe, they decided for the moment to stay in Los Angeles.

In a letter to a friend at the end of March, Walter Benjamin wrote, *no matter how wide I cast my gaze, I find the horizon to be just as doomed as the beings who exist before my eyes. Given all of this, I must still consider myself lucky that my son, who until recently was in Vienna, is now with his mother in Italy.* He thought that in view of the fact that it had become impossible even for wealthy Austrian Jews to flee, *we no longer have the petty comfort that whispers to us that you and I would have been smarter in the same situation. For I do not believe that.*

We are not in agreement with the sense of panic of the others, Anna Freud had written in February, suggesting that *it is still too early to judge exactly what is taking place.* She was arrested. In case of torture,

221

her father's doctor had provided her and other members of the family with lethal doses of Veronal. The drug had helped Freud's twenty-three-year-old niece Caecilie, pregnant and unmarried, to end her life in 1922. Freud started choosing books from his library to take with him to London.

Hitler has invaded Austria, Virginia wrote. This fact combined with the latest news of Russian trials and executions was *like drops of dirty water mixing*. Her book *The Years* was selling well and she experienced *the delight of money; buying freely*. On Tuesday 22 March at their house in Sussex she wrote that *the public world very notably invaded the private*, that war was imminent *and England, as they say, humiliated. And the man in uniform exalted. Suicides. Refugees turned back from Newhaven. Aeroplanes droning over the house.* Back in London a walk through the city took her mind off politics. By April she had begun to plan the book that would become *Between the Acts*.

Nelly and Heinrich were good friends with Anna Jaffé, a widow in her eighties, and her nephew, the medievalist Gustave Cohen. The four of them often went for drives in Mme Jaffé's chauffeured car, or took afternoon tea together at her villa in Nice, which housed a magnificent collection of artworks. Mme Jaffé had once hosted a literary salon that included Proust and Henry James. She was especially fond of Nelly.

In March, Klaus Mann wrote to his uncle Heinrich for his birthday, to say he was feeling optimistic that politically the worst was over; that he understood the absolute despair of people like their friend, the Viennese writer and actor Egon Friedell, who had jumped out of a window when the Gestapo knocked on his door, but it was not a good time to take one's life. Klaus was busy with a number of writing projects, including a book co-authored with his sister Erika, about the German emigration. *In a form as dramatic and varied as possible, it will describe the lives of the exiles, the famous as*

well as the unknown. Apart from our text, we want to include the protago-
nists' personal documents, by which I mean diaries, or letters to us, or short
autobiographies. They would feature Stefan Zweig, Bruno Walter,
Lion Feuchtwanger, Thomas Mann, *and you*; he asked Heinrich to
write a contribution for the book, perhaps a diary page – real or
made-up – from the first days or weeks of his arrival in Nice. He
wished they could all celebrate his birthday together in the rue
Rossini, and imagined that *Frau Kröger*, to whom he sent his best
regards, would have cooked a delicious meal and his uncle would
have read to them from his latest work.

At the beginning of April Thomas thought the war in Spain
was coming to an end. In Beverly Hills on Thursday 7 April he
reflected on his childhood holidays in Travemünde, and on his
sister Carla's death. He and Katia continued to discuss the wisdom of returning home, knowing that since their departure much
had changed, even in Switzerland; France, he commented a few
days later, was once again without a government. They walked
in the Hollywood Hills, up to the observatory; were invited on a
guided tour of the Goldwyn-Mayer *trick-world*; strolled along the
beach with the Huxleys, Mrs Huxley pointing out the washed-up
condoms. All were horrified by reports about Vienna. Visiting
friends, Thomas noticed that their youngest son, in a swimming
costume, bore a striking resemblance to his old love Klaus Heuser.
Warm, starlit nights. The silhouettes of palm trees. An evening at
the home of the director Ernst Lubitsch; charmed by the actress
Madeleine Caroll; uneasy with the free flow of champagne and the
increasingly drunken guests. A letter to Heinrich thanking him for
his. Monday 25 April was their last day in Beverly Hills, their journey complicated by the need to decide where they would set up
their next home. Train to Chicago through a landscape of mountains, cactuses, the desert bathed in lilac light.

In Baudelaire's terms, nothing in his own century comes closer to the task of the hero of antiquity than the task of giving form to modernity, Benjamin wrote.

Cleveland, Sunday 1 May, Katia was sleeping badly, worried about the safety of her elderly parents who were still in Germany. The next evening in a grand amphitheatre filled to capacity, Thomas once more soaked up the reverence and the applause. They returned to New York 5 May. Dinner 16 May with Willa Cather and the publisher Knopf. On 19 May, after an official function, they drove home with the mayor, Fiorello La Guardia, policemen saluting the car as it passed through the streets of New York. One day, walking alone, he was greeted by someone he did not recognise. With the building up of political tensions, Thomas's nerves were on edge. A friend offered them a house in Jamestown, Rhode Island, where they had to get used to the constant blaring of the foghorn. Clear, windy days. He was homesick for Switzerland.

Nelly was in Paris to see doctors. Heinrich had stayed in Nice to finish the second volume of his *Henri IV*. He wrote to her on 12 May; asked what was happening, why he had not heard from her; a tone of impatience. He wondered what had become of her good intentions to go to Paris for advice from specialists, for treatment, for a fresh start. What had become of all that? Asked if she was staying in a hotel or in a clinic, and if she'd be back soon. Told her that their doctor in Nice, Dr Barnathan, thought it was a good idea for her to consult German-speaking doctors, but that a change of scenery, a holiday could be just as beneficial as medical treatment. Heinrich cautioned her not to spend too much money. He'd heard from Willi Münzenberg, who wanted to meet her for a meal while she was in Paris. If she did see him, perhaps she could reassure Willi that his real friends were not the ones alienating him from the party, and that it was the Americans who were scheming against him. He told her he'd finally met up with Mme Keun and her fiancé, a French sailor, a decent fellow who missed her terribly since her departure for America. Heinrich asked Nelly once more to write and signed off lovingly.

Irmgard Keun (1905–1982) was a novelist who left Germany in 1936. She'd written the 1932 bestseller *Das kunstseidene Mädchen* (The Artificial-silk Girl). Döblin, Kesten, Kisch, Heinrich Mann, Toller, Tucholsky, Ernst Weiss and Stefan Zweig were her friends. Her two-year relationship with Joseph Roth ended in 1938.

Soon after he posted his letter to Nelly, Heinrich received one from her and replied immediately, on 13 May, to say how relieved he was to hear from her, and wished her all the best for the next few days, and that if she was to have an operation on the following Saturday, she would surely not be able to travel for several days; that she should send him a telegram to tell him when she'd be back. The little birds were well; they hoped she was too and awaited her return. It wasn't doing them any harm to be kept in their cages for a while. On the first day they finished off almost an entire lettuce that was supposed to last much longer; he'd worried that they might get sick; today they had fresh seeds, and got fresh water every day; he'd soon have to buy more bottles; Chrischan had been unusually well behaved. The housekeeper was due to come on Saturday, and then again on Tuesday or Wednesday. He was managing to cook for himself. They'd had an invitation for Sunday from Mme Jaffé, but he'd cancel it, since she would not be back by then. He sent his best regards to Mme Rottenberg, with whom Nelly had been in touch in Paris; it was extremely kind of her to offer help. And a note of caution about Münzenberg. (It seems Heinrich and Nelly knew that Willi Münzenberg had been or was about to be expelled from the Communist Party.) Taking Willi's current state of mind into account, she'd have to decide for herself what to say to him. Heinrich had not answered his last letter, and she could apologise for him, explaining that he'd been very busy. Willi had taken the wrong path and Heinrich advised him to reconcile himself with the party. He looked forward to Nelly's return. She must recover her health and take her time; sent his greetings to all their friends in Paris; told her how happy he was to hear that she would be cured.

Walter Benjamin had started to revise his memoir *Berliner Kindheit um 1900* (Berlin Childhood around 1900, later titled *Berlin Chronicle*), which he hoped *might turn into a noteworthy publishing success*. He believed *it has something to say to thousands of German refugees*, with whom he shared not only an intimate feeling for a place and time now lost, but those flashes of memory, *moments of sudden illumination* that produce the sense of being in two or more places at once.

On Wednesday 1 June, Thomas Mann received an honorary doctorate from Yale. Heinrich wrote to say that he was looking forward to a reunion in Switzerland, though it would have to be in a place below 800 metres because his doctor had cautioned against all kinds of exertions. He was exhausted and needed to conserve his energy to finish his novel, the deadline was the end of August, but a moderate mountain range might do him some good. In Jamestown, Thomas noticed the abundance of a sort of *beetle* – small and tough, that drilled its head under one's skin and once in, was hard to evict. He removed one – it was a tick – by cutting it with scissors; killed several, with great disgust. As usual, the sea air worked as an aphrodisiac. It stirred his sensuality, he noted, especially when it rained. By mid-June he wrote in his diary that life in Jamestown was too dull. He'd received a letter from Heinrich which was optimistic. Walked with Katia to the cliff edge, a loving moment, watching waves roll and froth over the rocks. He read *The Threepenny Opera*; at first he thought the work wasn't bad, but decided that the significance of Brecht's theory of Epic Theatre was inflated. He became increasingly annoyed with Brecht. Some shopping in New York, a blue suit, a straw hat, a silk dressing gown, prior to their departure on the liner *Washington*.

The Freuds were allowed to leave Vienna on 4 June. They arrived in London two days later. Freud said that *the triumphant feeling of liberation is mingled too strongly with mourning, for one had still very much loved the prison from which one has been released*. His brother Alexander had also escaped from Vienna, and his sister Anna was already living in the United States. Remaining behind, his sisters Rosa (Regine Debora), Mitzi (Marie), Dolfi (Esther Adolfine), and Paula (Pauline Regina) were sent to concentration camps, where they perished.

Döblin's friend the German expressionist painter Ernst Ludwig Kirchner had been using Veronal as a sedative since his nervous breakdown while serving in the war in 1915; he was also addicted to morphium. He had become depressed by the news that the Nazis had destoyed hundreds of his canvases and works on paper. He shot himself on 15 June near his home in Davos, Switzerland.

In his reading of Kafka, Benjamin found *there is an infinite amount of hope, but not for us*.

Virginia was writing *Three Guineas* and thought it was *the mildest childbirth I have ever had . . . No book ever slid from me so secretly and smoothly*. She and Leonard travelled to the north of England and Scotland, where they were conscious of looking at the same landscape that the Romans saw. She met a woman whose grandmother had heard Wordsworth *muttering poetry*. At Sir Walter Scott's grave she *picked a syringa in memory but lost it*.

There was a rumour that Theodor Herzl's nephew the Austrian jurist and writer Raoul Auernheimer had been taken to Dachau concentration camp and killed; through international pressure Auernheimer was released and left for America. Thomas thought of Wagner's *Tristan* as their ship passed the coast of Cornwall. After an absence of four months they returned home early in the morning on Thursday 7 July. Golo and Medi met them at the station and chauffered them to Küsnacht in the Chevrolet; a brilliant summer's day and the house full of flowers; bliss. And renewed anxieties. In mid-July the news of Robert Musil's danger if he remained in Vienna; the trouble trying to help him leave Austria. A note from René Schickele, who suffered from eczema on his writing finger. Evening walks and waterlilies. The annoyance of an urgent letter from Louis Aragon asking Thomas to attend an anti-Fascist congress in Paris. All six children came home to celebrate their mother's fifty-fifth birthday on 24 July.

Walter Benjamin spent the summer in *monastic confinement* in Denmark. *I have a large garden at my disposal, in peace and quiet, and my desk in front of a window with a clear view of the sound. The small ships that sail past . . . represent my only distraction, apart from the daily chess interlude with Brecht.* Benjamin rarely won a game. Impossible to beat Brecht when he raged against the Fascists who had stolen his house, his fishpond, his car, his stage and his audience. It was also beginning to dawn on him that the Soviet system had taken a catastrophic turn.

Heinrich and Nelly spent part of the summer in Sanary with Alfred and Friedel Kantorowicz. They walked, talked and ate in inexpensive restaurants. The air was fragrant with the scent of sea and cypress. Towards dusk the heavy heat that lay about all day rose up to drift off with the evening breeze. In his memoirs Kantorowicz described Nelly as amusing, enchanting, stimulating. In his eyes she possessed an extraordinary vitality and an innocent lack of inhibition. Next to his wife, who was small and reserved, Nelly was tall and talkative, and the two women were great friends. Like many in their circle, he was fascinated by the relationship between the elderly and distinguished literary figure Heinrich Mann and his beautiful but uneducated and often uncouth mistress, his Blue Angel, whose lowly origins in a Baltic fishing village explained her propensity to get drunk and swear like a fishwife.

Kantorowicz especially remembered an episode when they had a meal together in a restaurant and the men stayed on to talk, while the women went ahead to a harbourside café for a glass of cognac. All of a sudden they heard the distinctive rolling pitch of Nelly's North German dialect, lashing loud protest and colourful abuse against someone who had told her to speak French. Also in Sanary that summer, swimming off the rocks, meeting at the Café de la Marine, Chez Schwob, or La Pêcheuse were the Feuchtwangers, the Marcuses, the Schickeles and the Werfels, among others. By the end of July Heinrich Mann was in Paris to attend the Third International Writers Congress.

During the last week of July, Heinrich received a letter from his daughter. Goschi and Mimi were staying at an Intourist hotel in a mountain resort in Russia. She wrote to thank him for making the trip possible. Told her father that on arrival in Moscow they were well looked after by the president of the commission for foreign literature, a Mr Apletin. When the two women had medical checkups it was discovered that Mimi was diabetic and that Goschi had a thyroid problem. A translator who was also a doctor accompanied them to Kislovodsk, where they followed a course of massages, baths, exercises and diet. At the end of their vacation Mimi sent Heinrich a telegram to say that they would soon be leaving and urgently needed his advice, presumably with regard to the safety of returning to Prague.

Döblin's sixtieth birthday, 10 August, was celebrated a month later at a restaurant, the Cercle des Nations, with speeches by Heinrich Mann and Anna Seghers. The Döblins had settled in Paris. Their son Wolfgang was a brilliant young mathematician who had already made a significant contribution to the development of probability theory. He received his PhD from the Sorbonne in 1938 and later in the year enlisted in the French army.

Virginia had too many social obligations. *I'm stuck in a bristle of dates*, she wrote, and *it's odd how one's friends torment one.* Someone gave her a gift in a small box: a death's-head moth.

On 12 August, Germany mobilised its armed forces; three days later Chamberlain visited Hitler for crisis talks. Heinrich finished the second volume of his epic novel on 23 August. He had been reassured by Thomas that despite the proximity to Germany it was safe for him to visit them in Switzerland. No one needed to know that he was even there. Heinrich arrived on 26 August. In the cool of the evening the brothers drank vermouth and charted the urgencies of political news, gossip and analysis. They took walks and explored the countryside by car, read each other's latest works, including Thomas's essay called 'The Brother', which argued that one must acknowledge one's kinship with monstrosity, with what one hated most.

Nelly had typed up Heinrich's manuscript. She was tired, emotionally exhausted from the threat of war and the increasing insecurities of life in exile, exacerbated by loneliness whenever Heinrich was away. She had trouble sleeping, sometimes she could not sleep at all from nervousness and fear. Dr Barnathan prescribed Veronal. Nelly picked up one supply of the drug on 23 August, the day Heinrich finished his novel, and another on 29 August, while he was visiting his brother in Switzerland. Veronal was discovered in 1902 and produced by Bayer. It is a barbiturate. In small doses it relieves tension by depressing the central nervous system. In the 1920s and 30s it was used in psychotherapy and marketed as a sleeping drug. Freely prescribed, in some parts of the South of France this highly potent medicine could even be bought without prescription. It became a bestseller. When not followed by sleep, it can cause mental confusion and intoxication, especially if mixed with alcohol. In large doses, or in combination with other drugs, including alcohol, it is lethal. Only decades later will research reveal the high risk of addiction to Veronal, and the great difficulty of withdrawal. By mid-September Nelly must have felt that her condition was worsening and she wrote to a doctor in Paris, once more seeking help. Unfortunately we do not know anything more specific, but the doctor replied that as he understood it, it was an illness that must be examined seriously and asked her to come to Paris for a diagnosis.

Vita brought Virginia a present of a basketful of peaches and a bottle of Château d'Yquem. Harold Nicolson predicted war, *but not this week*. Virginia was happy with her work, alternating between writing the biography of Roger Fry and fiction, *switching from assiduous truth to wild ideas*. The discovery in the nearby river of an old woman who had drowned herself.

Thomas and Katia had finally made the decision to leave Europe; during their last days in Switzerland, Robert Musil and his wife came to tea; Heinrich left Tuesday 6 September. On 7 September after dinner, they had a visit from Dr Max Pulver, whom Thomas knew from the parapsychological sessions organised in Munich by Schrenck-Notzing, and his strange assistant, the graphologist Oskar R. Schlag. The shame of England sacrificing Czechoslovakia. Hitler's Nürnberg speech, barking, provocative, but without specific demands. *That means: no war, which is what I always knew*. Katia received a letter from Heinrich to say how much he valued the time he'd spent with them; he signed off with best wishes also from Nelly. Wednesday 14 September was the Mann family's last night in Küsnacht. The following day they were in Paris, staying at the Hôtel Lutetia, where Heinrich had also arrived to attend a congress. Chamberlain met with Hitler. War was expected. Thomas and Katia boarded the liner *Nieuwe Amsterdam* bound for America. He imagined there were people so distressed by the betrayal of Czechoslovakia – the end of democracy – that they would be driven to suicide. They arrived in New York on 24 September and continued on to Princeton, where a house had been made available for them.

In a race against the war Walter Benjamin completed his Baudelaire project, on which he'd worked for fifteen years. Despite his *choking fear*, he *felt a feeling of triumph* to have pitched *the fragility of a manuscript* against the threat of *the end of the world*. He was especially anxious about the safety of his son in Italy, until he heard that Stefan had escaped to London.

Saturday 10 September. *Sirens will hoot in a particular way when there's the first hint of a raid. Leonard and I no longer talk about it. Much better to play bowls and pick dahlias. They're blazing in the sitting room, orange against the black last night.* Three days later, the broadcast of the Nuremberg Rally where *Hitler boasted and boomed but shot no solid bolt . . . A savage howl . . . Then howls from the audience . . . Frightening to think of the faces . . .* On the one hand Wednesday 14 September was a *fine summer day*, on the other a time of *all slipping consciously into a pit*. They needed to think of gas masks and emergency supplies.

At the beginning of October, Germany annexed the Czech territory of the Sudetenland. Thomas smoked a cigar called Optimo. He was moved by something Heinrich had written about Nietzsche. Friday 7 October was a big day: the furniture and contents of their Zürich household – some of it saved from Munich, and a few items dating back to Lübeck – arrived in Princeton, his grandmother's candelabras, his reading chair and his desk, which he had great pleasure in arranging exactly as it had always been. He gave the overseer of the move, as if this man were the ferryman to a new life, a gift, a copy of *Buddenbrooks*. The next day, on hearing news of the danger to German emigrants in Prague, he phoned his neighbour, Albert Einstein, to discuss what they could do to help. He was emotionally wrecked.

In Denmark at the beginning of October, Walter Benjamin *prepared the several hundred books I have here for shipment to Paris. Now, however, I am increasingly coming to feel that this destination will have to become a transfer point for them as well as for me. I do not know how long it will continue to be physically possible to breathe European air* . . . He worried about his son. When he waved goodbye to the Brechts on 16 October it was the last time they would see each other.

In the autumn Heinrich Mann was in Paris, where he presided over one more attempt to revive the Popular Front committee. Nelly's days in Nice were filled with scrubbing, washing and sewing. The new apartment at 2, rue Alphonse Karr looked lovely. Despite a backache she was happy. She signed her letter to Heinrich with a kiss.

The postman told Virginia that in five years people will say that Hitler should have been killed long ago. Sandbags in Bloomsbury. A friend gave Virginia a copy of a speech by Thomas Mann, 'The Coming Victory of Democracy'.

You turned on the radio, heard a weather report, dance music, then the news flash; you rushed outside and looked at the night sky, expecting war. On 31 October the *New York Times* reported that *a wave of mass hysteria seized thousands of radio listeners between 8:15 and 9:30 last night when a broadcast of a dramatisation of H. G. Wells's fantasy,* The War of the Worlds, *led thousands to believe that an interplanetary conflict had started with invading Martians spreading wide death and destruction in New Jersey and New York.*

In Princeton on Wednesday 2 November, Thomas was puzzled by his increased sexual arousal; he wondered if it had to do with the change of climate. Katia was busy filling out their immigration forms. The news of a massive anti-Semitic propaganda campaign throughout Germany.

When Herschel Grynszpan was told that his parents had been evicted from their home in Hanover, that their business and belongings had been confiscated, and with thousands of others they were forced across the border into Poland, the 17-year-old, who was living with his uncle in Paris, set out on 7 November to assassinate the German ambassador to France, who was not there. In his place Grynszpan shot another embassy official, Ernst von Rath. The act triggered the Kristallnacht pogrom against German Jews. On the nights of 9 and 10 November, throughout Germany, Austria and the Sudetenland, Jews were killed, injured and arrested; Jewish properties, synagogues, cemeteries and schools were destroyed and vandalised. Without a hint of absurdity or shame, the German legal system was adjusted to exonerate these crimes: Jews were to be blamed for the recent events and held legally and financially responsible for damages; they had to hand in all precious metals to the government; they were no longer eligible for pensions; their shares and artworks belonged to the state; they were to live in segregated areas of towns and cities and observe curfews; they could not own carrier pigeons, drivers licences, radios or weapons.

Walter Benjamin's friend Theodor Adorno received the long-awaited essay on Baudelaire. He was disappointed because while it identified a number of significant motifs – panorama and trace, flaneur and arcades, modernism and the immutable – it did not develop them. The work was *demonic* in its resistance to interpretation. It lacked mediation and bypassed theory, which gave it *a deceptively epic character . . . a wide-eyed presentation of the bare facts . . . you almost superstitiously ascribe to the enumeration of materials a power of illumination.* It was as if *you lived in the cavelike depths of your Arcades and therefore shrank in horror from completing the work because you feared having to leave what you built.* At the time Benjamin was living in poverty in Paris, trying to obtain naturalisation papers, and looking after his sister, who was very ill. His friend's criticism came as a great shock.

Heinrich had been supporting his daughter in Prague with

monthly payments. When it wasn't sufficient, he received requests for more to pay bills and debts. At the conservatorium Goschi had some unpleasant encounters with other students, possibly of an anti-Semitic kind. In October she was ill with jaundice. Pulling at his heartstrings, Mimi wrote to say the illness was partly due to the political tensions and partly to the fact that his daughter had not seen him for such a long time. On 8 November Goschi wrote to tell him how much she missed him and to thank him for the money, but also to say that the exchange rate was very bad and they had received much less than usual, they had to buy coal for the winter and had borrowed money from acquaintances which needed to be paid back. She begged him to send more money as soon as possible. She also mentioned that an old friend of Mimi's, who had lived in America for the past twenty years, had visited them.

Heinrich had written to Mimi to ask her for some of their old furniture from Munich, which was taking up too much space in her apartment, including a chaise longue, bookshelves, curtains, a carpet. On 9 November Mimi wrote, *Dear Heini! I hope this letter reaches you*. She was still having trouble making ends meet and organising storage for his books. They looked forward to seeing him soon. She'd been assured that there would be no problems with passports and visas if they had an invitation from him to come to France.

On 9 November Nelly dropped off a blue woollen dress, a floral silk dress, a grey suit and a black silk dress to be dry-cleaned and six silk stockings to be mended. They heard that the Kurfürstendamm and its tributary streets had become rivers of broken glass and the synagogue near their apartment in Fasanenstrasse was in flames. The memory of the newly furnished home they had abandoned in 1933 was now etched against a flaming sky. Defiantly, as if once again compelled to re-create what was being lost, on

235

16 November they went out to buy a second-hand Early Empire writing desk, a nine-piece dining suite and matching sideboard decorated with bronze sphinx heads, altogether costing 5,450 francs, which they paid in cash on 22 November; pleased that it was much cheaper than modern furniture.

Out of the blue Heinrich was told that his daughter Goschi was getting engaged to an American in Prague on that very day, 22 November. He wrote to Thomas, *that's all I know, and can only ask what kind of American gets engaged in Prague in the present situation, and why with my daughter*. He was suspicious and clearly distressed. He wanted Goschi to fly to Cannes, sent her a reply-paid telegram, but Czechoslovakia was under occupation and in disarray, and he did not receive an answer. He told Thomas he'd lost his perspective on the future, on what to say or do next. Meanwhile the second volume of *Henri IV* had come out and he'd sent a copy to his brother. He wrote that if there'd been time for a dedication, it would have been for Thomas – *For the one closest to me*.

Max Beerbohm confessed to Virginia that he always read his own work as Virginia Woolf might read it. Thinking of her friends T. S. Eliot's and E. M. Forster's literary status, she believed their reputation was much higher than hers. *I'm fundamentally, I think, an outsider.* A few days later she was still unhappy, jealous of her sister's children.

Thomas noted with no small degree of pride that his name was being linked more and more with that of Goethe. He was plagued by sexual arousal. In Princeton on Wednesday 21 December he wrote in his diary that most of the time he felt sad and tired, with thoughts of death. His spirits were lifted by the festivities of Christmas Eve, with all the family, all the trimmings, a night that ended at one o'clock the next morning with champagne and *Baumkuchen*.

Heinrich had seen his daughter briefly in Geneva, either just before or after she married 'the American' Dr Aschermann, who did not waste time in asking his new father-in-law to help provide funds needed for his own family to transfer their business to the United States. As for politics, Heinrich told Thomas his hopes were growing old. The letter was dated 29 December, but Heinrich never mentioned what had happened to Nelly over the past weeks.

In Nice between October and December, Madame Mann had run up a bill of 838 francs at A la Cave Saint-Paul, suppliers of fine wines, champagnes and liqueurs. She had bought vast amounts of rum, rosé, red wine, cognac and mineral water. St Paul, she might have told the young man serving in the shop, had found his refuge from persecution in a cave; he was a hermit; ravens and lions kept him company. That's my cave over there, she might have said, pointing in the direction of her apartment. I'm no saint, but that's where I live like a hermit most of the time, with my canaries and my dog Lion.

How safe were they in Nice? Where could they go if war broke out? Nelly lived in fear of what was to come. Increasingly, in the second half of 1938, it is likely that she combined her already well-established drinking habit with her use of Veronal, to calm her down and help her sleep. With continuous use of Veronal, one develops tolerance to the drug, and for it to be effective, the dose has to be increased, while the drug's lethal dose remains the same. On the night of 17 December she was taken by ambulance from her home to a *clinique chirurgicale*, the Villa Constance, Avenue Lorenzi in the Quartier Saint-Barthélemy. Nelly may have taken an overdose of Veronal mixed with alcohol, without understanding the deadly potential of her act. Or she may have tried to commit suicide.

Soon after being admitted to the clinic, she wrote to Heinrich that she was feeling better and would like to exchange this *morgue*, where she was caught amidst a parade of ghosts and corpses, for something more cheerful. She was looking after herself as best she could, but was always terribly cold and hungry. Just like her little birds; she worried that they were properly cared for, with plenty of seeds and cake. What a way to spend Christmas! She hoped to be home for New Year's Eve. Dr Barnathan was very good, though she did not really trust him; he was too stern. It was true that he had saved her life, and for that she was thankful. She preferred to be treated by Mme Jaffé's nephew Dr Gluge, who spoke German. She wondered if Heinrich was managing to eat well enough on his own, and hoped she'd soon be taking care of him again. Heinrich, meanwhile, collected her dry-cleaning and paid the bills at A la Cave Saint-Paul and for the ambulance's *transport de nuit*.

Nelly wrote again a few days later, admonishing, pleading, floating excuses in a large and uncharacteristically untidy hand, with extra comments crammed into the margins. She was upset with Heinrich; she'd heard that he told the doctor that if she were to come home now, he'd move out of their apartment. If that was true, it was very cruel. She explained that prior to her breakdown she had become too weak to go anywhere without assistance. A friend had nonetheless persuaded her to go out, which proved too great a strain. She had become physically and mentally so exhausted that the pain was unbearable. She knew she needed help, but there was never enough money to pay for medical expenses. Then she defended herself against the charge of mixing drugs and drink, claiming that the amount she'd taken was minimal, *a drop of wine from a cup in the kitchen*. Would Heinrich come the next day? He must remember to send season's greetings and flowers to Mme Jaffé and Gustave Cohen. She begged him to pick her up and to find out how much it was all going to cost; underlined at the top of the page was a reminder that she did not have any money with her at all.

The next time she wrote from the Villa Constance, her tone

and handwriting had regained some equilibrium. She assumed
that Heinrich had received her letter and hoped he had overcome
his hostility. She said that he, of all people, must understand why
she was full of fear. When he came to see her, she'd been lying in
this place in terrible pain and without sleep for three days. At times
she'd been so hungry she was reduced to tears and thought she
would go crazy. Her body ached. This was no way to treat people
who'd suffered a breakdown. Each morning when she woke she
was surprised she was still sane. Never again did she want to be in
a clinic where she was deprived of food and warm clothing, where
they did not even give her socks against the cold, where she was
surrounded by the dead and dying and (echoing a scene from *The
Magic Mountain* which she'd been reading), where before daybreak
corpses were carried away on carts below her window. If she had to
endure this much longer she'd rather be dead! A friend had told
her that Heinrich would have her released from this place only
if she was willing to be transferred, in an ambulance and without clothes or money, to another clinic. She asked not to have to
go by ambulance, because that would upset her. The same friend
had described in detail what had happened to her on the night of
17 December. Nelly said it frightened and disgusted her. She went
out into the garden for fresh air as much as possible, in her bathroom slippers, light pyjamas and summer dressing gown; she knew
not to stay in bed all the time as that could bring on pneumonia.
Asked Heinrich how he was feeling; told him she was concerned
about him; asked about the apartment; if the housekeeper was
likely to steal anything, since it had all been left unlocked; whether
the plants were being watered. The birds, her little angels, needed
to be given fresh white bread every morning. And if he was looking
for the bottle of Cinzano, it was in the cabinet on the lower shelf.
She asked him not to use doctors or friends as go-betweens to pass
on messages to her; he should tell her everything himself. Her

nerves were still very raw. If she got upset all over again, it wasn't long before she'd end up in a madhouse. When she was calmer, he could have a serious talk with Dr Gluge to find out how things stood. If they were honest with her and gave her some hope, she would do all in her power to regain her health, would never cause him any more trouble, never drink another bottle of wine in secret. She promised, knew that Dr Gluge believed her and Heinrich must try to trust her too. After all, she was not all bad, but had been through so much, and lately had been overworked. If anyone came to see her, they should bring clean underwear and food. The trip to Paris must be cancelled; she should have gone there for a break before she got sick. What she needed now was sleep, a lot of it. And some light reading, but please, no emigration tragedies or child-murder stories! She sent kisses and pledged to erase all the trouble she had caused with love and kindness. Signed, Your Nell. Adding that she still felt weak.

Barbiturate addiction produced symptoms similar to alcoholism. The effects of withdrawal from both Veronal and alcohol were severe, causing feelings of extreme weakness, tremors, anxiety, seizures. Around the third day, schizophrenia and paranoid delusions could appear, with effects that might last for up to two weeks. Heinrich must have known that Nelly's recovery would take a long time and she must have resigned herself to a longer convalescence. She sent him a list of what she needed. A warm dressing gown, blue trousers (the ones missing a button), wine-red blouse (or any other), warm cardigan, a bra, a pair of panties, colouring for her hair, socks, winter shoes, red scarf, glycerine, soap, face lotion, hair gloss, nail brush, nail scissors and sewing equipment: a needle, wine-red and black thread, some stamps, a lot of writing paper, a lot of nice books, some food, and some money to buy more food to stop her hunger.

Dear Heini! Mimi wrote towards the end of the year. She wanted to let him know that he would receive everything he asked for, but that the mover thought the bookshelves were not worth the cost of transport, and as for the chaise longue, it would be cheaper to buy one in Nice; the carpet was ruined, with burn marks and holes from the time when their Munich apartment was searched, and the yellow curtains never arrived in Prague. Perhaps he'd like the blue ones? She was very ill with a throat infection. He would have to wait a bit longer for the furniture, because if she attended to it now, all the dust could kill her. Everything would be taken care of when Goschi returned to Prague with her mother-in-law. The children were organising their travel requirements in Zürich. It was all very urgent, because it looked like the political situation would deteriorate by March. She hoped to be out of Czechoslovakia by then. She begged Heinrich to help them as much as he could. Goschi and her husband, whom they called Tommy, were very happy. *He loves her very much. The mother-in-law . . . writes to say what a lovely couple they are.*

Virginia tallied what she'd spent, what she'd written. Other things were unaccountable. *Mitz was found dead on Boxing Day . . . her white old woman's face puckered; eyes shut; tail wrapped around her neck. Leonard buried her in the snow under the wall.* Their year ended with snowstorms and freezing temperatures.

1939: Failure of the Written Word

Nelly fought to regain her dignity and balance. She asked Heinrich not to blame her for what had happened. She had not wanted things to turn out this way. They had both been equally careless and must share the blame. It was true that she drank too much and should have known better. All the same, he should have listened to her and let her get help when she told him she was ill. She wanted him to think well of her, to believe her, not to listen to others, not to get agitated. He must not say terrible things about her to their friends; she did not deserve it. Above all she hoped that he would be patient, because she was always so affected by his moods and could easily get upset all over again. Pleading for his trust, she assured him there would not be another breakdown and promised to cooperate with Dr Gluge. Her only wish was to recover quickly and for it to cost as little as possible. A flu epidemic at the hospital made her extremely anxious. She'd prefer to move into a pension in Vence, which would cost half of what she was paying here.

If he did blame her for what had happened, he must remember there were times in the past when he'd treated her unfairly. Friends who'd visited told her they'd noticed how ill she was for quite some time before the breakdown. She was already sick when they were living in rue Rossini, but there was never enough money for her to seek medical attention, because he was always paying for his wife and daughter to stay in expensive health resorts to lose weight. This clinic was such an awful place! Yesterday she was told he was coming to visit and she'd hoped he'd take her home. So she sat in her nightgown waiting for him from six in the evening until midnight. When a doctor told her that her condition was very serious and that she might have died, she laughed and said that her husband would have been pleased. But the doctor did not share her sense of humour.

The next day the doctor had given her a message from Heinrich. This was humiliating and she was furious. It was the worst thing he could have done. How dare he make the doctor their go-between! How dare he tell him that if she were to return home, he would leave! Had he forgotten that she had followed him to France, in good faith, leaving everything behind? That she did not even have a passport? Had he forgotten that for a long time she'd been supporting them both financially? That all her money was now spent? He had no idea what it meant to run a household, what things cost; he'd get a shock if he had to fend for himself.

The doctor had explained everything. She knew what was wrong. She begged Heinrich to get her out of Villa Constance as soon as possible; she couldn't stand it anymore. She'd be extremely thankful and very well behaved. To make matters worse, because her heart needed monitoring, there were nurses looking after her day and night, and she was sure it was all becoming too expensive. She was desperate to move to Vence, a place she loved. Asked about the birds; she often thought of them and missed them terribly. Signed, Nelly Kröger.

In another letter on Villa Constance letterhead, she thanked him for the nice things he'd sent; reminded him that their concierge needed to be paid 50 francs for his garbage duties and an extra 50 as a New Year bonus. She was suffering from a terrible toothache, her face was lopsided from the swelling; the tooth would have to be extracted. She sent him her best wishes, with renewed assurances that this new year would be a better one.

She wrote in French to Dr Barnathan, thanking him for his help, informing him she'd rather not go to Paris for further medical opinions, because she did not want to see new doctors or have to explain herself in French, which in her present condition was too much of an effort. All she wanted was to feel well again, like she did before the emigration, and asked him to refer her to Dr Gluge, so she could communicate in German.

Heinrich told her he'd expected her to be home by now, that she would have recovered and they would have resumed their former peaceful life, but it seemed that three weeks was not long enough to achieve this. He found a safe and pleasant place where she could rest. He hoped she saw his good intentions and that she would stop being resentful. She may not yet have come to terms with the fact that she'd been very ill; the illness was not a new one, but it had become unbearable for both of them. He'd faced the choice of giving her money and leaving her, which would soon have had disastrous consequences, or to try one last time to have her cured. She now had excellent care, in a place that was like a palace. He'd insisted she should have one of the best rooms available; the garden was pretty and there was a healthy mountain climate, just as she'd wanted. The staff assured him that she would have plenty of good food; they all wanted to help her. He asked her not to be mistrustful, but to find the will to improve. He begged her above all to accept him as her true friend. If it were otherwise, it would have been easier for him to ignore his responsibility. He looked forward to visiting her soon, and asked her to write when she felt well enough to see him.

At the new clinic in Vence, Nelly was happy to have one of her birds to keep her company. But she felt frustrated that only some of her belongings had arrived, useless things, a blouse covered in stains, when she had asked for it to be dry-cleaned, trousers with a broken seam and dirty from the recent move to the new apartment; the dressing gown and shoes were dirty too. She was bristling with shame to receive such rags; had no equipment to mend or clean them herself; someone needed to come and collect her dirty washing; the situation was becoming unbearable; she might even return home to fetch what she needed. She couldn't live like a pig! The hairbrush, nail scissors and pen had also been forgotten; and she'd asked for pyjamas, the red ones and the striped ones, as she still only had the chiffon nightgown she'd worn since her arrival. Where did he discover all these torn and grubby things, when her wardrobe was full of clean dresses and blouses? If he looked he'd find more than a dozen pairs of decent underpants in her chest of drawers. To insist that she stay here, under these conditions, was doing more harm than good. She'd had enough of everyone's good intentions; was feeling worse, not better. So could he please send her the following: a clean pair of pyjamas, a bottle of cleaning fluid, her pen, the small pair of nail scissors (kept in her sewing kit, or with the toiletries in the bathroom), a clothes brush and some brown shoe polish; things she'd asked for a month ago. Could he please send all this in a single package or small suitcase as it was demeaning to be handed items one by one, and if their housekeeper Paulette brought them, she must not be intimidated by the staff but come upstairs to collect the washing.

The doctor was allowing her to drink as much white wine as she wanted. Her head had improved, but she had a fever that blurred her vision, as if there was a wall in front of her eyes. She'd been told her blood was weak, too many white and not enough red cells, and was given some medicine to correct this. Could Heinrich ask the doctor if the fever was related to the low blood count? She was concerned about Paulette, who told her that the hatbox in which she'd brought a dress, underwear and her expensive new pen opened on the bus and the pen must have dropped out. But it was impossible for the box to open by itself. Nelly said she could tell by the look on Paulette's face that she'd taken the pen. Certain things – money, clothes – had disappeared too easily, and she now wanted to come home to make sure her jewellery and the little bit of money she still had left did not vanish as well. On top of everything, she'd broken her glasses; could Heinrich please bring her other pair, the black-framed ones. Could he make sure her room, both wardrobes, and the kitchen cupboard were locked; she did not want to lose her linen. And could he come to visit as soon as the weather improved; it was already clearing. She'd like some paté, some fruit, she needed her small travel iron, and cufflinks, which he'd find in her sewing kit (she drew O-O, to explain that by cufflinks she meant two buttons sewn together). How was he feeling? Was he lonely? He must not trust too many people. She looked forward to seeing him soon and signed the letter, *your poor Nell*. A comment in the margin suggested that he should not think she was over-anxious, but was simply telling him what worried her.

Heinrich wrote, *My dear*. He had received all her letters and her lists; thought most of the items had already been delivered. She must ask the staff to make sure all her belongings were transferred from the Villa Constance. He thought the problems she was having with her digestion might be due to alcohol withdrawal and this would soon settle down. It was important for her to remain strong and focused. She could not imagine how much he wished for her complete recovery and for their life together to return to normal. He reassured her of his love and said he was looking forward to his visit.

In one of her letters, dated 16 January, she let Heinrich know that she was not as agitated as he might have thought, but what she wanted to say was not always well served by the way she expressed herself in writing. She still hoped to be picked up to go home on Friday. If not, could he come to visit her very soon, since she was completely unable to communicate with the doctor. Right now she could not speak French at all; did not know how this happened; it was as if she'd lost her memory. Several days of rising fever had made her weak and irritable. She also found it difficult to breathe, as if there was not enough room in her chest for air. She was convinced there was something wrong with her lungs, could not sleep, was always hungry. The portions of food were getting smaller all the time, they were only half the size now than when she arrived. If she asked for more, they smiled politely and that was the end of it. Her pulse was weak, but there was nothing they could do about it. For her heart, the doctor was injecting her with camphor.

The 1920s and 30s saw an increase in the intravenous use of camphor, which was thought to have an energising effect on the central nervous system. There was only a minuscule difference in the doses that would stimulate or paralyse the brain.

Heinrich wrote, *My poor Darling*. Her letters upset him. She must know that she could count on him to support her in every way. He would talk with the doctor, say something about the food, and come to visit on Friday. Meanwhile he'd send Paulette to bring all she needed; would buy her a new pen, for the moment an inexpensive one in case it got lost again. He told her he hoped she'd be well enough to come home soon. They both knew they only had each other and needed to look after their health. But she must not think about leaving while she had a fever and was receiving camphor injections; for now, it was the best place for her. She must keep up her spirit. She was probably only suffering from a cold. It would all be better soon.

Most of Nelly's letters were in pencil. Then her *stylo* arrived. *Dear Heinrich*. It was fairly certain that she had a lung condition and had to see a specialist, since the resident doctor could only treat nerves. Best to speak to the more sympathetic Dr Gluge. The doctor here was useless, it was impossible to communicate with him. The cure-all for anything difficult to diagnose, it seemed, was to lock the patient up. It was infuriating. The previous night she had eaten about eight slices of that soggy bread they serve, just to stop her hunger. It gave her cramps. So she placed a hot-water bottle on her stomach. The doctor asked why she needed it. Did she have her period? She told him no, that she'd simply been hungry. Could she have a slice of cold meat or a piece of cheese instead of celery and lettuce? The diet was becoming unbearable. The doctor replied that surely she didn't want to gain any weight. It was cruel. She was sick and was supposed to get better, but she was always hungry, unable to explain to those in charge that she suffered from a thyroid condition and so was burning up too much energy, which was why she needed to eat properly. Surely this did not make her into a monster. Could Heinrich please come to see her and bring Dr Gluge? She'd like that, because she was still running a fever, still felt weak and hungry. She knew the doctor did not want to work with Gluge. He preferred Dr Barnathan because they were friends. And she knew exactly what Barnathan's diagnosis would be: that she was in excellent health. That would be it! And behind her back, Barnathan said terrible things about her, as if she was worse than a common tramp. She again asked if Heinrich could bring her a slice of paté, some butter and some fruit.

Mid-January a letter from Goschi in Zürich, where she'd just got married. For the moment Heinrich spared Nelly this news. He wrote Thomas that his new son-in-law worked in a chemical factory owned by his father in Vienna and they planned to transfer the business to New York. He'd been told, that for Goschi to be able to follow Aschermann to America, it was first necessary to set up a bank account of $10,000 for her at the National City Bank of New York on Wall Street, with access for her husband, who claimed that the more one paid, the quicker one would receive the visa. Heinrich regretted that he was not able to contribute more than a small fraction of the required sum, and this meant his daughter might be left behind in Europe. More letters from Goschi in Prague to her father, to say she had bought her ticket and was waiting to hear from her husband to send the immigration papers.

Wednesday 18 January. Virginia *often came face to face, after tea, at odd moments, with the idea of death and age. Why not change the idea of death into an exciting adventure?* She was reading books with *steady passion.* Towards the end of the month she made a note that Barcelona had fallen. The Woolfs were Freud's English publishers and visited him at 20 Maresfield Gardens. Leonard thought Freud was both a genius and *an extraordinarily nice man.* Virginia saw *a screwed up shrunk very old man, with a monkey's light eyes, paralysed spasmodic movements, inarticulate, but alert.* Freud loved to present flowers to women. He'd once given Lou Andréas-Salomé pink tulips, lilacs, roses. Virginia received a narcissus. On the last day of the month she took the bus to Southwark Bridge and walked along Thames Street, climbed down some steps to the river and below the rows of warehouses, discovered the strand of the Thames, a *riverine* landscape of rubbish, rats and green slime, wooden pillars and rusted chains. She bent down and picked up *a button hook thrown up by the tide.*

All the Mann children except Monika were now in America. Family and a constant flow of visitors passed through the house in Princeton. Thomas was inundated with requests for support and commentary by the media. He felt homesick for Switzerland, with nervous exhaustion from a deep sense of displacement. Friday 20 January, frost, sun, wind, and a visit from Einstein. Discussions with Erika about the misery and the altogether worsening situation in Europe. Franco's capture of Barcelona. A report that the French had banned a documentary about the global plight of refugees. He was too dispirited to write. A visit from Auden.

A visit from the Princeton physicist Niels Bohr (1885–1962), who would work on the development of the atom bomb at Los Alamos between 1940 and 1945. A visit from Oswald Veblen – Thomas heard the name as Webbles – a Princeton professor of mathematics, a likeable and clever man, interested in fish. On Thursday 9 February, at a dinner in a restaurant, the waiter revealed he'd been in a concentration camp. Thomas Mann's Freud lecture on 13 February. The next day, he and his son Klaus discussed the failure of the written word to deal with the current crisis, the chasm widening between reality and art. Thomas despaired at the uselessness of protest, the feebleness of gestures of denunciation in the face of what was happening; with a sense of impotence and self-loathing. A rainstorm, and the news that the Hungarian Prime Minister Béla Imredy, who had busied himself with the nazification of his country, was forced to stand down when it was discovered that his great-grandmother on his mother's side was Jewish. On 17 February, a visit from Goschi's new husband, Dr Aschermann, who aroused some suspicion. The weather was warmer, windy, with an air of spring. Thomas woke early, took *eine Belebungstablette* (a stimulant) with breakfast, and did a good day's work. Monday 20 February, he received a copy of the second volume of Heinrich's *Henri IV*. Towards the end of the month, while he was walking with Katia, she told him that their daughter Medi and their friend the historian Guiseppe Antonio Borgese intended to marry; she would be 21 that year, he 57. Thomas was unwell, physically and mentally run down, suffering from shingles.

On Friday 17 February, Virginia went out *in the brisk cold to buy note books. I'm starting my grand tour of literature. That is I'm going to write a book of discovery, reading as one pulls a string out.*

27 February the British government announced that it recognised the government of General Franco.

Walter Benjamin was still deeply depressed by Adorno's criticism of his Baudelaire manuscript. In Paris he kept running into people who'd made it out of Germany or Austria just in time.

At the beginning of March, Thomas had trouble writing to Heinrich about his book and about his son-in-law. He said *Henri* had just arrived and he'd been reading it night and day; that it was nothing less than extraordinary, the best, most dignified and spiritual work of this era. One day people will wonder how it was possible to produce such a book in such abject times. It was a great work by virtue of its content and qualities: love, art, courage, freedom, wisdom, goodness, its abundance of wit and imagination and sensibility; absolutely stunning. The synthesis and culmination of who you are, he told his brother, and the life you've lived. It was truly European, and a monument to German culture in exile. Unfortunately, he went on, the matter of Goschi's husband was less pleasant to report. He'd visited and had called Thomas *uncle*; had now gone west, to California, which oddly, Aschermann had referred to as *south*. His ideas about transferring his business – impossible in any case to imagine that you could move a chemical factory – as well as the requirements for a bank account in Goschi's new name, were a little hazy, to say the least, since it was well known that the wives of immigrants were allowed to enter the country without any such financial guarantees. Nor was it clear why he had to go to California. A few days later, a man called Morton W. Lieberman, from South Orange, New Jersey, arrived to warn them about Aschermann. It appeared that Thomas Mann's self-styled *nephew* had been entrusted by a wealthy Jewish woman to take her funds and jewellery out of Germany; she had later managed to leave the country and was now pursuing him; she was going to have him charged with embezzlement; he had done the same with the possessions of many other Jews, who could not press charges, because they were still in Germany or Austria. It seems that when Aschermann visited the Manns in Princeton, he made a good enough impression and they were inclined, for Mimi and Goschi's sake, to give him the benefit of the doubt. But in view of the allegations and the fact that everything had happened so quickly, Thomas and Katia were now worried about the marriage, as well as the money Heinrich had given Goschi, and the furniture from the apartment in Prague, which he'd volunteered to ship to America. Thomas hoped that all their suspicions were unfounded. He was sorry to send his brother such distressing news, but it was necessary to warn him.

A visit from Ossip Flechtheim, the political philosopher, futurologist and incidentally, the nephew of their sister Carla's unrequited love, Alfred Flechtheim. Thomas and Katia went to New York. They stayed at the Bedford Hotel, where he lounged in his silk dressing gown before presenting his lecture, titled 'The Problem of Freedom', at Columbia University. In this lecture he tried to universalise the idea of socialism, to make it more palatable for his American audience. It was followed by an extensive tour with Katia and Erika, and fourteen pieces of luggage, first to Detroit, where they ate cabbage soup and piroshki with a local rabbi in a Russian restaurant. Then on to Cincinnati and Chicago; there he dined at Jacques, his favourite restaurant, amidst exotic plants and birds. The Germans invaded Bohemia and Moravia on 15 March; Slovakia became a German protectorate 16 March; within days Hungary annexed Ruthenia and Germany annexed part of Lithuania. Thomas and Katia heard the news of Hitler's successes in Eastern Europe. He noted that England and France had not reacted and that Russia remained an enigma. It was painful to read the papers, especially about people being hunted down in Prague and the waves of suicides in that city. In St Louis he had lunch with a bishop and a rabbi; drank Coca-Cola with ice. Throughout the trip he took a variety of pills, to liven him up or calm him down. Hitler's triumphal procession through Berlin. St Louis zoo; attractive young men working as porters at the Fort Worth Country Club in Texas; then Kansas City, Omaha. Reading *The Brothers Karamazov*. In Seattle, where 3,000 people attended his lecture, he wrote in his diary on Wednesday 29 March that the capitalist world was being forced into war by Fascism, its pampered offspring.

Franco's troops occupied Madrid on 28 March. It marked the end of civil war in Spain. Half a million dead. To escape the Fascists, hundreds of soldiers fled into France, where they were imprisoned. In April, Rudi Carius was interned at the newly constructed camp at Gurs near Bordeaux in the foothills of the Pyrenees, a cold and windy place. Sanitation was inadequate; the huts were constructed by the prisoners themselves, who were malnourished. Without enough clothing and blankets, some froze to death in their sleep.

Heinrich Mann wrote to his friend Bertaux that he would not leave France until he knew that his daughter was safe.

Beverly Hills, Saturday 1 April, the joy of Thomas's return to this happy and well-tended world of sunlight and sea air. The following day he watched Hitchcock's *The Lady Vanishes*, which he thought was called *Women Vanished*, and found amusing. After delivering a lecture on 5 April, he went with the director Ernst Lubitsch and others to eat pancakes with butter and syrup; *excellent*, he wrote in his diary. The Italian occupation of Abyssinia. On the return train trip east via Chicago, Thomas *dreamed* the ending of his *Lotte* novel and promptly forgot it again. In Washington they stayed at the home of his friend and patron Agnes Meyer, the journalist and philanthropist whose husband owned *The Washington Post*. He stole some of their rose-scented soap. An extensive interview-article appeared in *Life* magazine, proclaiming Thomas Mann as Germany's foremost literary exile. He was still unconvinced that there would be a war. The world waited for Hitler's reply to Roosevelt, who said he himself would not be listening to Hitler. *Neither will I*, Thomas wrote. Wanting to do something, to have an effect on the German people, he and his daughter Erika planned to smuggle the work of exiled writers into Germany. He was told it was inevitable that after Hitler's fall, he would be the country's president. Harold Nicolson reviewed Erika Mann's book *School for Barbarians: Education under the Nazis* (1938) for the London *Daily Telegraph*, and referred to her *amazing family*.

Leonard Woolf once thought an ideal life would be to live with a concubine and read Voltaire. Virginia was touched by Leonard's observation that he loved her more than she loved him. On Saturday 29 April, she thought about what she'd like to be reading ten years hence. *Perhaps literal facts. The annal, not the novel.*

Walter Benjamin lived *in expectation of being overtaken by bad news.*

About his wife, Nora, James Joyce had written thirty years before, *Her soul! Her name! Her eyes! They seem to me like strange beautiful blue wildflowers growing in some tangled, rain-soaked hedge. And I have felt her soul tremble beside mine, and have spoken her name softly to the night.* In May, Joyce's *Finnegans Wake*, a book he sometimes called a monster, was published in London and New York. *Well, Jim*, said Nora, *I haven't read any of your books but I'll have to some day because they may be good considering how well they sell.* He sighed with disappointment when he read the reviews, most of which did not go further than labelling the work as madness, genius or joke.

Dogwood trees blossomed in May. Thomas read *Anna Karenina*, in order to write the introduction for a new edition. He wrote to his brother because someone had told them about Nelly's recent illness and how it had affected Heinrich's own health; they were upset to hear this, and hoped for a fast recovery. He told Heinrich of his plan to establish contact with Germans who did not support Hitler by smuggling brochures written by various exiled intellectuals into that country. He had financial support to commission, print and distribute 5,000 copies of each brochure. It was their duty, he told his brother, to try to urge people to get rid of Hitler, if they wanted to avoid war. Perhaps he was unaware that Heinrich was well experienced in this kind of underground activity. Lunch with Albert Einstein. On Monday 22 May, news of Hitler and Mussolini's pact of steel, and that in New York Ernst Toller, who had been suffering from insomnia and nervous exhaustion, had hung himself; a return ticket to London was found in one of his pockets. Thomas was asked to speak at Toller's funeral, but did not think he could. News of the death of the Hungarian poet Attila Jozsef, whom he'd met in 1937. Oppressed. On Thursday 25 May he felt unwell and for comfort spent the night in Katia's room. On Saturday 28 May, at dinner with three of their children, they all made fun of Zweig, Feuchtwanger and Remarque, wondering who would take the prize in a competition for worst writer.

Heinrich Mann was in Paris again to speak against war and fascism at an international conference. *Dear Tommy*, Heinrich wrote on 25 May, with birthday greetings. He told his brother that he had been involved in smuggling countless propaganda articles into Germany for years, and that he supported any renewed efforts of this kind. It was shameful that Germans had not rebelled against the Nazis. Winter had been hard, with a sick wife and an unhappy child, and his own doubts about the value of his work. He would help his wife by legalising their relationship. After ten often very difficult years together it was the least he could do. She deserved it. He had only waited for his daughter to get married first. But her marriage now looked very sad. He'd found out that even the address of that scoundrel of a mother-in-law was false, that she was an embezzler, just like her son. Worse still, she had persuaded Goschi to travel with her across Germany. It might have suited her if Goschi had been arrested. Mimi was foolish enough to have given the woman an expensive piece of jewellery. He'd hesitated to hand over money before the marriage, but had given it to his daughter, who passed it on to her husband, who then disappeared. Heinrich wanted to add his name to the list of people pressing charges against this man. He'd tried, unsuccessfully, to send some money to Goschi and Mimi in Prague and had been organising for them to escape via Sweden to Moscow, where they would have financial support. Heinrich asked Katia if she'd write to them as well, to stress that this was now their only way out.

When Joseph Roth heard that his friend Ernst Toller had killed himself, he drank so much sliwowitz that he collapsed and was taken to hospital, where he was placed in a straitjacket to control the shock and convulsions he would suffer from alcohol withdrawal. Roth's last article, dated Monday 22 May, was titled *Goethe's Oak in Buchenwald*. With sharp irony, he wrote that too many stories were being spread about the concentration camp at Buchenwald, horror stories, and it was time to tell the truth, for the place was also known for the beautiful old oak tree where Goethe had often met Charlotte von Stein. When the forest was being cleared in order to build a kitchen and a laundry for the concentration camp, the oak was left standing. Roth's incredulity dwelled on the barbarous absurdity of a tree preservation order being granted in a place where human beings were imprisoned, humiliated, tortured and murdered. *Symbolism*, he wrote, *has never been as cheap as it is today*. But so far he had not heard of anyone being tethered to this tree; people were tied to all the other oaks remaining in the forest, but not this one.

From the hospital, Joseph Roth wrote to his friend Stefan Zweig. He said that he had already been interested in the work of

Lessing, Schiller, Goethe and Hesse as a boy of twelve, and could now look back at his own career as a writer with good conscience. That when he and his mother moved to Vienna, he mourned for Brody, the little shtetl they had left behind, and some of his books came from this sense of mourning, to tell the reader what it was like to live in Galicia, and also to keep those memories alive for himself. *Since childhood I inhabited two worlds. One belonging to the great thinkers of the European enlightenment and the other belonging to orthodox Eastern European Jews.* It had made him at once open-minded and religious. His main objectives, which he addressed in his work, were humanity and social justice. He loved Vienna, but had a love-hate relationship with Berlin. He would never get over what he had experienced during the First World War, and this had turned him to drink. His wife, Friederike Reichler, had almost succeeded in curing him. *Oh what a happy time we had to-gether!* But Friedl suffered from schizophrenia and their happiness only lasted about six years. Then Roth began to drink again. *I can never forget her.* From 1933 he lived in exile in Paris, though he said he already saw the horror approaching ten years earlier. He loved writing, but was only interested in the lives of ordinary people. He had once been quite well-off; now he was poor. *I no longer have the strength to battle against alcohol on my own and I feel that it is destroying me.* If he had to describe himself in one line, he'd say: *That's who I am, angry, drunk, but a decent human being.* He expressed his deepest respect for his truest friends, who had stuck by him, and he urged them to keep courage against the evils of oppression. He died on 27 May; the following year at the Steinhof Sanatorium in Vienna, Roth's wife was murdered by the Nazis.

Jewish refugees on board the ocean liner *St Louis* were refused asylum by Cuba, the United States and Canada, and the ship was forced to return to Europe, where many of those who'd made the journey were sent to concentration camps.

On his birthday Thomas and Katia left the United States for Europe on the liner *Ile de France*. Germany signed a non-aggression pact with Latvia and Estonia. Unhappy days on board ship; deep depression, tears and the feeling of shame. In Paris, on Tuesday 13 June, and again the next day, they met Heinrich, who was still tirelessly trying to raise funds and consciousness for anti-Fascist forces. An emotional farewell between the brothers.

Thursday 15 June, from the Hôtel Sainte-Anne in Paris, Heinrich sent Nelly a letter that began with a short erotic rhyme. She could not imagine how much he loved her and needed her. Being away from her made him all the more aware of it. He told Nelly that *their* relatives were very concerned and had asked after her. He would also try to organise help for Rudi, would speak to their friend Budizlawski about him. There were still quite a few meetings for him to attend between now and Tuesday; he'd leave Wednesday if he was not too tired. He told her he'd like to be in bed with her, his sweet wife; that they would always love each other; signed with a kiss.

Friday 16 June, Nelly sent Heinrich a hurried letter, typed, with mistakes and crossings out, exclamations, underlinings. *My dear bien beau.* She'd been bothered by Jewish beggars, had been cleaning the apartment, had a visit from her cousin who ate a lot of cake. Lion the dog was very sweet; she said he must have inherited her character; he was so funny, people stopped in the street and laughed at him, especially since he loved to play with the very biggest dogs and made friends with three Saint Bernards. The terrible news she had to tell him was that now Rudi was suffering from scurvy and had asked to be sent a lot of lemons; she thought he was probably too polite to ask for money. She'd already told Heinrich in a previous letter that some of the prisoners at Gurs had typhoid, and some had gone mad. People had also disappeared from the camp; fourteen so far; they were being deported. One mother from Berlin who thought her son was at Gurs wanted to know why she had received a card from him from Dachau. Nelly had heard that there were Gestapo at the camp who made life hell for people who were already desperate, without anything to eat, no sanitation, behind three layers of barbed wire. Perhaps he could look into this situation, without putting himself at risk, because something had to be done. She begged him to be careful.

Followed by another letter the next day. Almost their wedding day, she wrote, or at least the anniversary of ten years of love, with a few interludes. *Dearest Heinrich*. She said he would have received her last letter. The news of Rudi's predicament made her very sad; he was sick and desperate. With all that misery she could almost understand those poor prisoners who'd been lured by the Gestapo to return home. She said she sometimes wished she could go home too, but home was no longer what it had been. She pleaded with Heinrich to do something, not just for Rudi, to have him released, but for all the people – the brave survivors – now being punished and killed in these camps. She'd spent what little money she had on a wedding outfit and could not even send Rudi 50 francs. Instead of a wedding present she wanted to hear that Goschi had been able to escape to Moscow and that Rudi was free. Signed with kisses and cuddles, his good, hard-working wife. And a PS: that when she played the Marseillaise on the gramophone the dog ran off as if he was being chased. She was feeling melancholy, not at all like she'd felt on the same day – 17 June – ten years ago. She longed for that same experience, for someone to come and take her away from all this, to save her, just as he'd done when they met in the summer of 1929.

In Nordwijk, Holland, Thomas needed red capsules to get to sleep. Friday 16 June he noted the death of *the alcoholic Roth*. He worked on *Lotte* and the *Anna Karenina* introduction, copying out passages he'd annotated. A day in Amsterdam to see the Van Gogh collection: interpreted as dark beginnings and the breakthrough of light; crazy self-portraits. He thought the wheatfield with a dark blue sky and crows was a passionate work, but the famous Yellow Room did nothing for him. In the mail he received a copy of Heinrich's latest publication, the essay collection *Mut*.

On Wednesday 28 June, Leonard's mother fell and broke two ribs. *She will not die, so I assume*, Virginia wrote in her diary. *There is a terrible passive resistance to death in these old women. They have the immortality of the vampire.* But she died a few days later. *It was a bright, showery day . . . I always notice the weather in which people die, as if the soul would notice if its wet or windy.* Virginia found it hard to work, and felt *a regret for that spirited old lady, whom it was such a bore to visit. Still she was somebody: sitting on her high backed chair with the pink cushion, all the flowers around her, a cigar always for Leonard, and plates of cakes which she pressed us to eat.*

War was now inevitable and not far off. Thomas had lunch with the publisher Querido. In Noordwijk on Monday 24 July, Katia's birthday, he finished writing the seventh chapter of *Lotte*; he started to prepare the eighth. It had been overcast and humid. When the sun came through as he was resting on the hotel terrace, he was suddenly overcome with the feeling of terror he'd often experienced; it was as if fire were about to engulf his mouth. He wrote to Heinrich, asking him to read Klaus's book *Vulcan* and to tell his nephew what he thought of it, since he had not sold many copies nor had much feedback and would welcome a response from his *big uncle*.

In July Heinrich and Nelly stayed in the spa and lavender town of Digne, near Grenoble. Many years later, in a letter to Salomea Rottenberg (dated 20 July 1947), Heinrich said that the days he spent with Nelly in Digne in the summer of 1939 were the happiest time of his life.

Virginia wrote letters, cooked dinner and did her embroidery.

She read through the year's diary, and embarked on Gide's *Diaries*; thought it odd *that diaries now pullulate. No one can settle to a work of art.* She and Leonard argued about the building of a greenhouse. *Yet so happy in our reconciliation. 'Do you ever think me beautiful now?' 'The most beautiful of women.'* On the last day of July the downs glowed with corn. *Much to my liking.*

Robert and Martha Musil moved from Zürich to Geneva, where they lived first in rue de Lausanne in the city and later further out in Chêne-Bougeries. He fell in love with the scenery; loved going to the movies, especially to see films with Mae West, or Fred Astaire and Ginger Rogers.

Early August the Manns took the train to Switzerland; the conductor looked at their passports and asked if he was *le grand philosophe.* In Zürich, to their great delight, they were soon driving through a familiar and much loved landscape. *Vertraute Wege, das vertraute Land* – for Thomas this sense of *familiarity* was one of the keystones of security and pleasure. After settling in at the Wald-hotel Dolder, they walked in the nearby forest where they came upon a *sexually active couple on a bench* and discreetly turned back. They visited all their old establishments, doctors, tailors, news agencies. On Wednesday 9 August, Thomas stood in front of their house, and looked up at the window of his study, where the third volume of the *Joseph* epic was written, and much of *Lotte*. Unsettled, grieving, in pain. Political tensions increased, but Thomas doubted that it would end in war. He was reluctant to leave Switzerland. To London by Swissair on 18 August. *Lift-off in that enormous aluminium machine ¾ hour late . . . to Basel . . . Then at great altitude, 2500 meters above the fog. Soft-white cloudscape beneath the sun-lit blue . . . calm, speed . . . Hard-working Swiss stewardess. Mid-day lunch: bouillon and ham sandwich. Cigarettes. Only a moment of palpitations. Above the Channel, small ships below, the English coast in geographic relief.* They were met by their daughter Moni and her husband, Jenö

Lanyi, who were married earlier that year in March; stayed at the Hotel Alexandria; walked across Hyde Park; bus rides and walking over several days; taking in Buckingham Palace, Trafalgar Square, the Thames and its bridges, Parliament, Downing Street, then Richmond Park and Hampton Court. Wild weather on Monday 21 August; six people killed by lightning in Hyde Park. The following day they received the news from Berne that Grete Walter had been shot dead by her husband, who had then turned the gun on himself. Grete was the younger daughter of Bruno and Elsa Walter, the Manns' neighbours and good friends in Munich. Erika and Golo would attend the funeral. Farewell to Moni and Lanyi at St Pancras station, with the assurance that they will be looked after by Harold Nicolson in case of war.

The German-Soviet Non-Aggression Pact was signed in Moscow 23 August, followed by global confusion and outrage at this infidelity. The left had ruptured. For Willi Münzenberg it was a betrayal of Socialist ideals. Stalin was a traitor. Thomas Mann saw it as a great chasm that swallowed all hope in one merciless gulp, as the moment when the past was cut off from the future; he needed red powder to help him sleep. When Heinrich heard about the German-Soviet pact, he locked himself in his study for two days and spoke to no one.

Virginia tried to kid herself into believing that a penholder is a cigarette. *So far I'm taken in.* She thought, as she was getting dressed one day, she'd like to write about *the approach of age, and the gradual coming of death. As people describe love . . . a tremendous experience, and not as unconscious . . . as birth is.* Mid-August Leonard and Virginia and the Hogarth Press moved from 52 Tavistock Square to 37 Mecklenburg Square. *The Russian pact a disagreeable and unforeseen surprise . . . Communists baffled.* Monday 28 August, at Rodmell, Virginia *walked on the downs; lay under a cornstalk and looked at the empty land and the pinkish clouds in a perfect blue summer afternoon sky. Not a sound . . .* She supposed that everyone everywhere was writing about this last moment of peace. A swallow flew into their sitting room. Wednesday 30 August, she delighted in the brilliance of the light, *very evanescent*, and watched some *red faced boys in khaki guarding Rodmell Hill*. Two days later she wrote, *war is on us this morning*.

German soldiers, dressed in Polish uniforms, staged the attack on the radio station in Gleiwitz. Reprisals. At dawn on Friday 1 September, news of the bombing of Warsaw and other Polish cities; the advance of German troops into Poland; the bombing of Gdansk. Virginia imagined that *the bombs are falling on rooms like this in Warsaw. A fine sunny morning here, apples shining*. On Sunday 3 September, she spent two hours sewing blackout curtains.

The day war was announced, Thomas delivered a lecture in Saltsjöbaden; Bertolt Brecht and his wife were in the audience. They heard that in Germany there had been mass confiscations of radios, to prevent people from listening to foreign broadcasts. Thomas and Katia flew to England and continued by ship to America; it was a kind of homecoming. Thomas now hoped that Germany would become the battleground of the fight between Russia and the West, resulting in Hitler's defeat and Communist revolution. But if not that, then at least the fall of the Nazi regime. You could hear Hitler's madness in his words. *When I have Poland, I'll stop. I'm much more of an artist than a politician, and it is as an artist that I'd like to spend the last years of my life.*

On 3 September, Great Britain, Australia, New Zealand and France declared war on Germany, South Africa followed on 6 September, Canada on 10 September.

Exiled Germans, Austrians, Czechs, Slovaks and Hungarians between the ages of seventeen and fifty, including large numbers of intellectuals, were no longer safe in France. Many were interned or handed over to the Germans. Walter Benjamin was arrested on 3 September and with hundreds of others was taken to a stadium in a Paris suburb. A young man looked after him, carried his suitcase for him when they were moved to a *camp des travailleurs volontaires* in an old castle in Nevers, in the Loire Valley. Benjamin collapsed on the walk from Nevers station to the camp.

While Heinrich had a Czech passport, Nelly had no valid papers. She was stateless. In Nice on 9 September, Luiz Heinrich Mann, aged 68, married Emmy Johanna Kröger, aged 41.

On Wednesday 6 September, Virginia and Leonard experienced their first air-raid warning . . . *an empty meaningless world now . . . I took up my watch this morning and then put it down . . . my mind seems to curl up and become undecided . . . It's the gnats and flies that settle on non-combatants . . . all the blood has been let out of common life . . . all creative power is cut off. Perfect summer weather.* They had days of *pitiless fine weather*. Nerves on edge. HMS *Courageous* torpedoed and sunk in the British Channel. By Saturday 23 September, Poland had been *gobbled up*, divided between Russia and Germany. There was no petrol for their car, so they rode bicycles; discussed their income and *once more we are journalists . . . My old age of independence is thus in danger . . . Then one begins stinting paper, sugar, butter, buying little hoards of matches. The elm tree that fell has been cut up. This will see us through 2 winters. They say the war will last 3 years.* Freud died the same day. Virginia had trouble concentrating on her work. *Yet if one can't write . . . one may as well kill oneself . . .* She read Stevenson's *Jekyll and Hyde* and did not like it.

The last book Freud read before he died was Balzac's tale about a magical shrinking skin, *La Peau de chagrin*.

October. Germany annexed western Poland; Polish Jews were deported to the Lublin ghetto.

Nora and James Joyce moved out of their Paris apartment and into the Hôtel Lutetia. Joyce was upset that the publication of *Finnegans Wake* had been upstaged by the war.

Far from reading the latest books, people were listening to Hitler on the radio. Thomas thought it was *a humiliating farce, the world's listening to the voice of this idiot, who determined everyone's fate.* The Manns acquired a poodle. After three years of research and writing, Thomas finished *Lotte* at the end of October. He said it was *a rich fabric of references, much of which is compilation and appropriation, exploiting of sources.* On the last day of the month Katia's parents finally managed to leave Germany for Switzerland.

Virginia's nerves were on edge, her hand trembled, and she tried to compose herself by tidying up her room. Driving to London, *it seemed as if we were driving open eyed into a trap.* The city was eerily empty. *At night it's so verdurous and gloomy that one expects a badger or a fox to prowl along the pavement. A reversion to the middle ages with all the space and silence of the country set in this forest of black houses . . . People grope their way to each others lairs . . . profuse unbridled medieval rain.*

Walter Benjamin was back in Paris, suffering from nervous exhaustion. He looked for someone to teach him English, in case he went to America.

On Wednesday 8 November, Thomas recorded the assassination attempt on Hitler; and that the invasion of Holland was imminent. The family purchased a new radio and gramophone set. They were in New York Thursday 16 November, for an emotional reunion with the Walters, who passed some of their murdered daughter's things on to Erika. End November, radio reports of the Russian invasion of Finland. Thomas and Katia congratulated Heinrich and Nelly on their marriage, and reported that their daughter Medi had married her *anti-Fascist Professor.* Postal services between Europe and America had slowed down considerably.

Virginia wondered how one could compete with the brevity and clarity of Gide's Journals . . . *Well, the plain truth is I can't.* Hitler's *strangled hysterical sobbing swearing ranting* on the radio.

On Saturday 9 December, Thomas wondered at the impossibility of knowing what Germany and the rest of the world would look like after the war. Sunday 24 December, guests, family, a champagne Christmas dinner by the light of his grandmother's candelabras.

From Paris, Salomea Rottenberg wrote to Nelly that she was worried about her sisters and brother in Poland. Heinrich wrote to his brother, with good wishes for the New Year, congratulations to Medi on her marriage, and to Thomas on finishing his novel. Happy to hear that he and Katia had a safe passage back to America, and that her parents had also made it safely to Switzerland. It was his first letter written in German for a long time; these days he only sent cards to people, in French. His wife was more secure now that she had a Czech passport; she was happy knitting for French soldiers. Hermann Kesten in Paris wrote to tell Nelly that in such difficult times her friendship and letters were a great comfort, especially for his wife.

Heinrich and Nelly felt fenced in. He remembered a nightmare he had had during the last war, of being caught in a crowd between two barriers and being pushed forward towards a checkpoint knowing that he did not have a passport and could not go any further. At that time it must have been Italy he wanted to reach, and even now he regretted all the places in Italy he had not visited; he had to be content with listening to Italian opera on the radio.

His greatest worry was the fate of his daughter. If only he'd stopped her marriage, but it had all happened so quickly. All the money he'd given her was gone and she was left behind in Prague. The Nansen Aid organisation in Stockholm had done their best and he'd appealed to the Red Cross, all without results. A friend told him that amongst the German exiles, his name was now the only one that carried any weight because he stood above politics; Heinrich knew it wasn't true. Writers in concentration camps were asking for his help and there was nothing he could do, neither for his own daughter nor for them.

Goschi's husband – Traugott Max Aschermann, who called himself Dr Aschermann – had disappeared. It seems that he was born 14 September 1918 in Vienna (though he usually claimed the year was 1912), the son of Prague-born Maximilian Aschermann and Franziska Josefine née List (though Mimi referred to her 'American' friend as *Suzanne*). His family may have owned a chemical factory; in one document I've seen, his father is listed as a director of the national energy consortium VIAG. At this time he'd travelled to the United States at least twice. First on board the SS *Normandie*, leaving Le Havre 10 August 1938. The immigration form gives his age as 22, single, occupation lawyer, born Vienna, travel documents issued June 1938, last residence Prague. The second time on board the SS *Champlain*, leaving Le Havre 8 February 1939. This time his age was given as 26, occupation lawyer, married, born Vienna, travel documents issued in Washington September 1938. As his nearest relative he cited his father-in-law Heinrich Mann, giving an erroneous address in Nice. As his American contact he named his 'uncle', Professor Thomas Mann at the University of Princeton. Among other falsehoods, he had lied to Goschi and her family about his citizenship, since on the ship's passenger list he was not classified as a US citizen but as an alien.

I tracked down Izzy Lieberman, whose father, Morton, had visited Thomas Mann to warn him about Aschermann. He told me that in 1939 a cousin, Ludwig Zachlupnik from Vienna, asked the Liebermans for help to get to America. *My brother who was only eight at the time seems to remember more than I do, though I was thirteen. We didn't know what to do until one day my mother was talking to this German lady named Mitzi who owned a bakery in South Orange who had a daughter who knew Heinrich's daughter and told my mother*

*they had set up some sort of organisation to get people out of Europe –
presumably Aschermann was part of this organisation . . .* and presumably his connection with the Manns made him seem trustworthy.
The Liebermans paid him to arrange their cousin's escape and
Ludwig arrived in America in January 1939 with nothing but
the shirt on his back. He had been persuaded by Aschermann to
send his overcoat with valuables sewn into it, separately. Izzy be-
lieves that when the coat did not arrive, his father set out to warn
Thomas Mann. He remembers that eventually the coat turned up,
full of treasure, while his brother Daniel argues that it never arrived and that his brother might have imagined *the vivid discharg-
ing of the hem loaded with diamonds.*

On Friday 8 December, Virginia was *gulping up Freud.* Above all
she applauded his savagery against God. She received a fan letter
from a soldier in the trenches. Sunday 17 December, *the* Graf
Spree *is going to steam out of Monte Video today into the jaws of death.
And journalists and rich people are hiring aeroplanes from which to see the
sight . . . several people will lie dead tonight, or in agony. And we shall
have it served up for us as we sit over our logs this bitter winter night . . .*
Snow and frost. Leonard went skating on the last day of the year.

One of the most significant literary works of all time, *Finnegans
Wake* had failed to win critical applause. James Joyce told Samuel
Beckett, *we're going downhill fast.* His health had deteriorated. He
was drinking too much. Both his daughter and daughter-in-law
were in clinics for the mentally ill. There was a war. According
to his biographer Richard Ellmann, *if spoken to directly he gave the
shortest possible answer and lapsed back into silence, staring blankly ahead.*
Almost blind, he tapped his way with his stick through the streets
of Saint-Gérand-le-Puy, hitting out and throwing stones at the village dogs. His heroine Anna Livia Plurabelle asked, *Is there one who
understands me?*

1940: No Time to Think

They had returned to Australia and lived at Florida Flats, St Kilda Road in Melbourne. At the Victorian International Refugee Emergency Committee, where Nettie Palmer had been working as a teacher, she was known as the Angel of the Refugees. When she asked her husband on 1 January for a prophecy for the year, Vance replied that *1940 seemed likely to be difficult.*

Nettie liked to imagine bookshelves where the works of Australian writers stand alongside novels by Virginia Woolf, Willa Cather, Sigrid Undset and Rahel Sanzara.

Princeton, 1 January 1940. It was very cold. Thomas and his poodle Niko walked along the avenue. An ice storm a few days later. The art historian Erwin Panofsky's *bad poodle* attacked Niko. Thomas read Indian literature for his novella *Die vertauschten Köpfe* (The Transposed Heads). A letter from Heinrich, politically resigned. Thomas and Katia packed for another lecture tour. He was nervous and unwell, needing a red capsule and Phanodorm, the largest dose he'd ever taken, to sleep. The oriental beauty of the ice-flowers forming on the windows of the train. In Ottawa he walked around the Parliament, the temperature 29 degrees below zero, it was the most extreme he'd ever experienced, though oddly it felt the same as temperatures half as cold. Then Toronto and

Detroit; lectures, book signings, interviews. Mild winter weather in the Midwest, windy. In Toledo he received mail with reviews of *Lotte in Weimar*, pleasing, but he wrote in his diary that the book was special and most critics lacked the intelligence to look into it. A cigar, coffee, and thinking about the moral seriousness of Tolstoy's *Family Happiness* (1859) in the train back to New York; sleep with the help of a red capsule and Phanodorm. He was preoccupied with his Indian novella; thought its inherent surrealism was very far from Tolstoy. News of air raids and the English coast under attack. On Wednesday 31 January he noted that one-twelfth of this suspenseful year had already passed.

Letters to Nelly from Salomea Rottenberg, written in Paris on 12 January and 5 February, worried that she hadn't heard from her for a long time.

It's a long bitter winter frost . . . 22 below freezing . . . hard white snow; and the street like glass . . . Virginia wrote in her diary on Wednesday 3 January. She was trying to work on her biography of Roger Fry, but was distracted by other ideas: a book on women and peace. A few days later she read the obituary of a man called Wolfe or Wolff with whom she'd once shared a packet of chocolate creams and who told her he was often asked if she was his wife. The silence, when she took a walk on Saturday 20 January, matched her sense of emptiness. Six days later she made notes to herself, that in future, during *moments of despair – I mean glacial suspense – a painted fly in a glass case*, she must try to relieve the pressure through *flight*, an upward motion of the mind, an ecstasy. These were *travellers' notes*, in case she ever got lost again. On Tuesday 30 January she was unable to go to London *because of the worst of all frosts . . . everything glass glazed . . . ink frozen . . . a great flight of wild geese . . . now and then the wireless reports a ship sunk in the North Sea.* She wrote that she tried to hug the present moment in which the fire was going out.

Walter Benjamin's apartment in Paris was so cold that he

stayed in bed most of the time. The gas mask hanging on the wall looked *like a disconcerting replica of the skulls with which studious monks decorated their cells.* He had always been mesmerised by *the incomparable language of the death's-head: total expressionlessness . . . coupled with the most unbridled expression.* If he went for a walk, he needed to rest every few minutes. In *The Origin of German Tragic Drama* he had suggested that the *continual pausing for breath* was *the mode most proper to the process of contemplation.* Now the doctor diagnosed myocarditis. Nonetheless, he managed to get to the Bibliothèque Nationale to renew his reader's card.

Exiled Germans living in Sweden were being interned. With one eye on the door, Brecht read Thomas Babington Macauley's *Life and Writings of Addison* and thought about the continuity of the English literary tradition.

Virginia Woolf had once observed the durability of Addison: *Two hundred years have passed; the plate is worn smooth, the pattern almost rubbed out, but the metal is pure silver.*

On Monday 5 February, Thomas and Katia saw a production of *Mise and Men* [*sic*], got a parking ticket, and received the painful news of their friend René Schickele's death. They packed for yet another lecture tour. In Delaware, Ohio, they were invited to the home of a young professor who had a dog called Schmutzi; Thomas was always a keen recorder of the dogs he met. Monday 12 February, he received a letter from Schickele, written without a hint of premonition two weeks before he died. To Iowa, puzzled at the ingrained religious culture of this region, the commonplace assumptions of Christianity. He noticed people's friendly greetings, their assurances that they enjoyed his talk *so much*, and he doubted their sincerity. In Minneapolis, Minnesota, he was haunted by the impossibility now of thanking Schickele for his letter; the passing away of his friends. Newspapers brought close the catastrophes of this European winter and the fear that spring would reveal thousands of unburied Russian corpses. He thought the world was now divided into two fronts, the totalitarian and the democratic. They travelled to Kansas and Texas. In Houston he needed half an Ermutigungstablette, an upper he called *Heiterlein* (Cheery) to get through his lecture. An audience of 2,000 attended, there was great applause, and he was pleased with his performance. On the night train to San Antonio, the effects of *Heiterlein* took some time to be extinguished by his usual sleeping potion. San Antonio sunshine. While walking with Katia in a park, his eye caught the Mexican beauty of a young shoe polisher. He was upset to hear that it was Emil Ludwig, the biographer of Goethe, Napoléon and Beethoven, and not as he'd suspected, his old enemy Alfred Kerr, who had written and distributed a satire about him, titled *Tommy in Weimar*. A generous letter from Heinrich about *Lotte*. Thomas dreamed about his dog; he was now homesick for Princeton. A red capsule and Phanodorm in the train to New York, and sleep.

Virginia wished she could *conglobulate reflections like Gide . . . they occur at breakfast, or when I'm up to my knees in mud. The lost thoughts . . . the thoughts I've lost on Asheham down, and walking the river bank.* While living in the country she thought lovingly of the city, her favourite walk to the Tower of London, and *if a bomb destroyed one of those little alleys with . . . the river smell and the old woman reading I should feel – well, what the patriots feel.* She was glad not to be on a warship or a plane raiding the German coast, glad to be reading Freud instead. On Sunday 11 February she noted that Leonard had seen a grey heraldic bird while all she'd seen were her own thoughts. Later that month she noticed snowdrops growing on the graves.

Hermann Broch came to lunch and, discussing dental problems, was advised against having seven teeth pulled out. On Wednesday 20 March, Thomas read through his Swiss diaries, feeling homesick again, or rather, the sickness that comes from thinking of the past. Six days later, in a letter from a friend, he received horrifying accounts of war atrocities and the recently released details of Mühsam's death by torture.

Nelly was busy responding to letters from friends, acquaintances and strangers asking for help. For some she found work, found a cheap room and free milk for a penniless couple with a newborn baby; she sent parcels to prisoners in internment camps. On 3 March she received thanks from the Communist activist and writer Hans Marchwitza, imprisoned at Huriel in Auvergne. He asked politely if she could also send him something to read; he said that despite everything, he tried to keep his spirits up, which was helped by the onset of spring.

By the end of March, Virginia had finished writing the biography of Roger Fry and given it to Leonard, who was extremely critical, telling her it was all wrong, too much analysis, too few facts, worse still, that it was dull to read. He was *so emphatic, that I felt convinced: I mean of failure; save for one odd gleam, that he was himself on the wrong tack.* Others praised the work. She was reading Tolstoy; welcomed as she always did, the crocuses and daffodils; remembered *the sudden profuse shower one night just before the war which made me think of all men and women weeping.* Her spirits lifted and on Friday 29 March she looked forward to baking a cake *now and then.*

Germany invaded Denmark and Norway. The Brechts left Sweden for Finland on 17 April. As always Brecht got the best room in their new apartment, while the children shared a room and Helene Weigel made a curtain to separate her bed from the kitchen.

In a list headed by Marx's *Das Kapital*, Thomas was pleased that *The Magic Mountain* was named one of the twenty-five most influential books of the first half of the twentieth century. A German ship carrying soldiers and horses was torpedoed by the

English in Norwegian waters. Thomas had tea, bacon and eggs for breakfast, smoked Personality cigars, observed that the English presence in Norway was a disaster.

Virginia bought silk for sewing vests. She visited the London Library and made notes. Thoughts of war, especially the German invasion of Norway, stretched *the back curtain of the mind*, while in the foreground it was a day *luminous* with daffodils.

The British Prime Minister Chamberlain resigned on 10 May and was replaced by Churchill. On the same day the German land and air attack on Holland, Belgium and Luxembourg occurred; five days later the Dutch army surrendered; the German army took Amiens and Arras in France on 21 May; seven days later Belgium surrendered. In London, the Norwegians and the Dutch established governments in exile.

Magnolias in bloom. Thomas was reading the letters of Gustav and Alma Mahler and found them embarrassing. He was concerned about the safety and whereabouts in Europe of his son Golo, and hoped the Dutch writer Menno ter Braak had been able to escape in time. In England his daughter Monika and her husband were fearful of the worsening situation.

Leonard says he has petrol in the garage for suicide should Hitler win. Virginia made some buns for tea. *Apple blossom snowing in the garden.* Planes overhead. George Bernard Shaw wrote to tell Virginia that when he first met her, he fell in love with her, as he supposed every man did. The terror of war, but *no, I don't want the garage to see the end of me. I've a wish for 10 years more . . . it's all bombast this war. One old lady pinning on her cap has more reality.* She read Coleridge and Wordsworth, *untwisting and burrowing into that plaited nest.* Watched a hospital train go past, *heavy laden and private,* and imagined the wounded looking out. She was becoming increasingly irritated being beaten by Leonard at their evening game of bowls.

The French government left Paris on 10 June to save the city from being destroyed; the same day Italy declared war on Britain and France. From Tours on 13 June the French Prime Minister Paul Reynaud begged the Americans to help stop the invasion. The Germans entered Paris on 14 June. Marshall Pétain, aged eighty-four, became the new French leader on 16 June; he would collaborate with Hitler to arrest or hand over all Germans living in France. Refugees from Paris and the North headed south. There was a heatwave; water, food and beds became scarce in the towns through which they had to pass. The Russians invaded Latvia, Estonia and Lithuania on 17 June; France made peace with Germany 22 June; Russia invaded Rumania 27 June.

Walter Benjamin joined the exodus. He left his papers and belongings in Paris and escaped to Lourdes. He was waiting for an American visa.

Willi Münzenberg was interned at Chambarran near Lyon. When France capitulated, the internees were dispersed, some by bus to other camps, some on foot towards the South. He died on 21 June in a forest near Saint Marcellin in the Val d'Isere. His corpse, with a rope around its neck, was found four months later, covered by autumn leaves under a tree. It was either suicide or murder; the mystery of his death has not been solved.

German women living in exile in France were interned at Gurs, including Münzenberg's wife, Babette Gross; Marta Feuchtwanger; Nelly's friends Friedel Kantorowicz and Toni Kesten; and the political theorist Hannah Arendt.

On Saturday 1 June, Thomas received birthday greetings from Heinrich, sent at the beginning of May. His brother sounded old and calm. On 6 June, Thomas described his sixty-fifth birthday as a clear, fresh summer's day, on which he awoke with his usual regularity at seven-thirty, much like Goethe in chapter VII of *Lotte*, he observed. He noted the battles being fought in France, the Germans closing in on Paris and that by Sunday 16 June, the collapse of France was complete. He was reading Kafka's *Castle*. There was uncertainty about their safety in America. It's what they always talked about, the doubts. He noted that until Churchill was elected, England sold oil to Germany; that America had facilitated the Japanese war against China. Wondered if he would survive this chaos. There were renewed attempts to find out if Golo and Heinrich were safe. The purchase of a dark blue Buick, with heating and a radio. Gruesome reports that Himmler had arrived in Paris, and had organised the hunting down of German emigrants in the city and surrounding forests; that Bordeaux, full of refugees, was bombed. When he heard the *Lohengrin* overture one night, he cried, because it seemed as if in his demise, he was listening to his favourite piece of music from his youth. Emigrants in America sought each other's reassurance about those left behind in Europe. The phone never stopped ringing. He thought that Heinrich might be hidden by friends or that he might make it across the border to Spain. Then he heard that Golo had been interned, and wished that a giant wave would sweep his son to safer shores. It now looked like French and German fascism would join forces against England.

Kafka's friend the doctor and writer Ernst Weiss was born in 1882 in Brno, Moravia; in 1914 they were travelling to the Baltic together just before the outbreak of war; Weiss later lived in Berlin and from 1938 to 1940 in Paris. As a student he'd written medical reports for his mentor, the Swiss surgeon Emil Theodor Kocher, who was awarded the Nobel Prize in 1909. He claimed that this early experience of scientific observation shaped the documentary style of his literary work; his favourite book was W. M. Thackeray's anti-heroic novel *Vanity Fair*, which he'd read seven times. In his novel *Der Augenzeuge* (The Eyewitness), written 1938–1939, Weiss relates the story of a crazy but charismatic blind man who believed he was telling the truth while he lied. It was 1918. The man had served as a corporal in the war; he'd received the Iron Cross Second Class but forged the records to read First Class. Suffering from the effects of a mustard gas attack, he was in a ward for the emotionally disturbed at the Pasewalk military hospital in Pomerania, where his anti-Semitic ranting intimidated his fellow-patients and the staff. The doctor treating him narrates the story. *I had to understand this man through my imagination . . . he was an incorrigible fantasiser in his delusions of grandeur. I had to approach this man not with logical premises but with a tremendous lie in order to conquer him; for he lied, probably not in the single detail with deliberate purpose, but in his being . . . he was really one gigantic lie for whom there was no absolute truth but only the truth of his imagination, his striving, his urges.* The narrator was in fact a Dr Edmund Foster and the patient, whose blindness he had cured with hypnosis – whom he told *you have to have a blind faith in yourself, then you will stop being blind* – identified in the book as A.H., was Adolf Hitler. The doctor was later horrified to witness his ex-patient applying the lesson he'd learnt: how with endless repetition and *by the narrowing of the mental field of vision*, he hypnotised an entire nation. Dr Foster realised he had created a monster. And the monster pursued his master. Foster was killed in 1934.

The medical report of Hitler's treatment at Pasewalk diagnosed him as a psychopath with hysterical tendencies. Before the document was destroyed by the Gestapo and only weeks before his death, Dr Foster had shown the report to his colleague Ernst Weiss, who used the material to write *The Eyewitness*, in which fact was only thinly disguised as fiction. In exile in Paris, Weiss received some financial support from friends, including Thomas Mann, but mostly he lived in great poverty, bad health, isolation, with no opportunities to earn money, neither as a doctor nor through his writings. His partner, the actress and writer Rahel Sanzara (who had changed her name from the Germanic Johanna Blaschke), had died in 1936. Despairing, he killed himself on 15 June, unaware that Thomas Mann had persuaded Eleanor Roosevelt to grant him a visa to the United States and that travel arrangements had already been made. It was thought that all his manuscripts and personal papers were lost. But a copy of *The Eyewitness* came to light years later because he had entered it in a literary competition – offered by the American Guild for German Cultural Freedom for the best German novel by an exiled author – which he did not win. But the manuscript was preserved in the competition's archive and *The Eyewitness* was finally published in 1963.

The great battle which decides our life and death goes on. Friday 7 June there was an air raid, and the *question of suicide seriously debated . . . in the gradually darkening room.* If London is destroyed and the country surrenders, it *will mean all Jews to be given up. Concentration camps. So to our garage.* What everyone feared most was the precedent, that Paris should fall. Virginia thought the first person singular – the I – was now irrelevant, without audience or echo. This signified a kind of death. Paris fell. *I have my morphia in my pocket,* she wrote. And wondered, if this was the end, whether she should be reading Shakespeare. *The corn was flowing with poppies in it,* and she thought it might be her last walk. People were killed in night raids on the English coast. *We pour to the edge of a precipice . . . I can't conceive that there will be a 27th June 1941.*

The Brechts spent the summer in Finland. On 1 July, Bertolt Brecht wrote in his journal, *the world is now changing by the hour.* The first German daytime air attack on London took place on 2 July. The Battle of Britain. The British bombarded the French Navy. Dunkirk was evacuated. The Vichy government broke off relations with Britain. Bombing raids on Germany by the RAF began on 9 July.

The Manns moved to California. Soon after arrival in their temporary home in Brentwood, Los Angeles, and still without servants, Katia cooked a chicken which the poodle stole and ate; when

Thomas went for a swim in the pool the poodle surprised him by jumping in too. A volley of news and rumours reached their ears, that Golo was in Le Lavandou, that Lion Feuchtwanger had been captured by the Nazis, that Walter Hasenclever, at the French internment camp Les Milles, was dead from an overdose of Veronal. Golo was in fact in hiding at the American vice consul Harry Bingham's villa near Marseille; he'd written to Nelly to thank her for her efforts in trying to find him and stayed in correspondence with her over the next months. On Wednesday 31 July the Manns heard that their first grandchild Fridolin had been born, the son of Michael Thomas (Bibi) Mann and Gret Moser (married in 1939). Thomas noted the child was an American by birth, with a mix of German, Brazilian, Jewish and Swiss blood.

The reviews of her Roger Fry biography were good and Virginia was satisfied. Friday 26 July, when she won two games of bowls, was a warm summer evening. Two days later she lost and wondered why she minded losing. *I think I connect it with Hitler.*

They walked by the beach at Santa Monica almost every day. He changed his cigar brand to a Santa Fe. To facilitate Heinrich's escape from France with exit and entry visas, the Czech consul in Lisbon was put in touch with the American consul in Marseille, and the scriptwriter's contract Thomas had organised for his brother in Hollywood was confirmed. They were told that Golo was again interned, that Franz Werfel and his wife, Alma Mahler-Werfel, were in trouble in Lourdes. Air raids along the English coast. Thomas was reading Dostoyevsky's *The Devils*. He took Evipan to get to sleep. Friday 16 August he noted that the RAF had bombed Munich, which was exactly what that rotten lair deserved. On 21 August Trotsky was assassinated at his home in Mexico. Increased attacks on England.

By the end of June, Heinrich Mann had instructed his lawyer to pay his debts by disposing of his remaining possessions. But the exact moment when Heinrich Mann stopped believing that the Nazi regime would soon fall cannot be pinpointed. It seems as if he was one of the last to let go of his wishful thinking. Perhaps Golo persuaded him of the extreme urgency to leave France, or perhaps it was Nelly. There was now the fear that at any moment the borders would be sealed. Just as she had done seven years before in Berlin, Nelly took on the practical tasks of paying bills, closing bank accounts, selling their furniture. She found homes for her pets, it must have been a tearful parting. She was aware that they would have to travel light, and packed their bags with a minimum of essentials. Books were sent off separately. The concentrated effort of reaching a safe haven in America had begun. They moved into the Hôtel Normandie in Marseille to wait for their exit visas. Opposite, the Hôtel Splendide was the temporary residence of Varian Fry, head of the clandestine Emergency Rescue Committee, who knew that Mann, Feuchtwanger and Werfel were at the top of the Gestapo execution list. He would help them escape. Marseille was no longer a safe place; it was a bureaucratic hell. The Vichy government had agreed to turn in to the Gestapo all Germans who applied for exit visas. Foreigners without a local permit were being arrested day and night. People killed themselves; some climbed to the highest point of the bridge over the harbour and jumped off. When Heinrich was stopped by the police one night, he remembered that he was often mistaken for the prefect of the Bouches du Rhône, and so he avoided arrest by impersonating him.

She was working on the book that would become *Between the Acts*. On Friday 16 August, Leonard and Virginia lay down under a tree and *the sound was like someone sawing in the air above us. We lay flat on our faces, hands behind head.* On Wednesday 28 August German planes flew overhead again, *circled slowly out over the marsh and back, very close to the ground and us. Then a whole volley of pops (like bags burst) came together . . . It would have been a peaceful matter of fact death to be popped off on the terrace playing bowls this very fine cool sunny August evening.* A few days later she had a phone call from Vita to say she could not come because there were bombs falling all around her, and Virginia felt she was *talking to someone who might be killed any moment.* Vita told her it was comforting to speak with her.

The joys of walking by the sea at Santa Monica included sightings of youthful male bodies striking poses. Despair on hearing news of repeated attacks on London, the city in ruins, as if destroyed by earthquake. Thomas was deeply disturbed and unable to write. He worried about Erika, who had gone to England to work for British intelligence. At midnight 10 September the news of an air raid on Berlin. The Manns bought land in Pacific Palisades, with the idea of building a house. The New York *Herald Tribune* featured a letter critical of the quality of translations of Mann's work into English. (And these translations, by H. T. Lowe-Porter, which an entire generation of readers has now depended on, were indeed awful.)

Golo, Heinrich and Nelly were to leave Marseille from Gare St Charles at dawn on 12 September. There are mixed reports of what happened that morning, that Golo was late, that Nelly became hysterical for fear that they would miss the train; on the other hand, that she was never anything but calm and helpful. With them were Franz Werfel and Alma Mahler-Werfel, who had American visas but not the required French exit visas or travel passes.

To distinguish themselves as tourists rather than refugees, the group travelled first class. Heading west towards Spain it was a twelve-hour trip, already hot in the outer reaches of the city, across the Camargue, via Nîmes and Sète, beautiful open country marred by the recent proliferation of internment camps, each of which Golo knew by name and reputation, pointing them out in all directions. At Perpignan they had lunch and waited for the connection to Cerbère. The Werfels' dozen or so suitcases, which Alma insisted were all essential – containing Mahler's scores, the original manuscript of Bruckner's third symphony, and her husband's work in progress, as well as her extensive wardrobe – had been sent ahead. The Werfels told the others about their recent series of dramatic escapes across France, always just a step ahead of the Germans, and how they had met Walter Mehring and his wife, Hertha Pauli, who confessed they were so afraid of falling into German hands that they considered suicide, but could not find a pharmacy that would sell them poison without a prescription.

When the group arrived in Cerbère, they may well have wondered at the irony of the town's name. The original plan had been to continue by train across the French-Spanish border to Portbou, but they were now told that it was as unsafe to continue as it was to stay, and that their only option was to cross the mountains. That evening, with their last French meal, they drank a 1912 burgundy. The next day, on Friday 13 September, Varian Fry would go ahead by train with their luggage and a supply of Gitanes and Gauloises for the Spanish guards. When he said goodbye to them and Heinrich raised his hat, Fry noticed the initials HM stitched into the hatband, and since this might cause him trouble – Heinrich Mann was travelling in disguise as Heinrich Ludwig – he cut off the initials with his pocketknife.

They met up with their guide and carried only rucksacks, to look like holiday-makers going hiking in the foothills of the Pyrenees. The only incongruity was Alma's voluminous white dress. They made their way over slippery rocks, up steep goat tracks and ancient smugglers' paths, where low-growing thorny bushes caught on their trouser legs and tore the women's stockings to shreds. Sunburn, sweat and thirst. At some point they became separated from their guide and feared getting lost. But despite the women's bleeding ankles, Werfel's obesity and heart problems, and the almost 70-year-old Heinrich being supported and sometimes almost carried by Nelly or Golo, they were all determined to keep going. When they reached an altitude of 2,000 metres, buffeted by a fierce wind, they were discovered by their second guide. Some *gardes mobile* suddenly appeared and they thought bad luck had caught up with them, but instead they were politely shown the path leading towards Spain. At the border the Spanish guard asked Golo if he was the son of Thomas Mann and told him he was honoured to make his acquaintance. Meanwhile Fry, with seventeen pieces of luggage that might have been hard to explain if he'd been stopped, had an easy twenty-minute train ride through the mountain tunnel into Spain. It was a close escape. The hounds of hell, the German agents pursuing the group, arrived in Cerbère the next day.

In Portbou they celebrated as inconspicuously as possible, with a meal and Spanish wine. On Saturday they went by train to Barcelona, from there a further fifteen hours to Madrid, and then on Monday 16 September, incognito, they flew by Lufthansa to Lisbon, where immediately Nelly joined the bureaucratic battle to secure their passage to New York. Amidst rumours that the Gestapo were picking refugees off the streets of Lisbon, they were not yet safe. Before leaving Portugal, Nelly and Heinrich had dinner with Varian Fry.

On Friday 20 September, the Manns in America received a telegram from Golo and Heinrich in Lisbon, where they were waiting for a ship. Thomas was relieved, but unhappy about the fact that the *Mrs* – he could never bear to write or say Nelly's name – would also be coming. On Sunday 22 September they heard the tragic news of the sinking five days earlier of an English ship, the *City of Benares*, that was evacuating children to Canada. On Monday they heard that Rudolf Olden and his wife, the psychoanalyst Ika Halpern, were dead. He was the writer, publisher and lawyer who had defended Carl von Ossietzky and was responsible for organising Musil's escape to Switzerland, and Goebbels claimed to have targeted the ship because he knew that Olden was on board. A year earlier, writing from Oxford, Olden had congratulated Heinrich and Nelly on their marriage, which he'd read about in the *Times*; he suggested a meeting of international writers to show the world that *literatures . . . have no war among each other*. Thomas and Katia had dinner with European friends, commenting afterwards that too many of these emigrants lived in the past; for him the best part of the evening was meeting an Irish setter called Athenia. The following morning, Tuesday, they were shattered by a telegram from Erika that informed them Monika and Lanyi were also on the *City of Benares*. Monika was in a Scottish hospital. Her husband had drowned. Katia and Thomas were now worried about the safety of Heinrich and Golo travelling to America.

A heat wave in England. The night of Thursday 5 September was so hot that Virginia walked in her nightgown on the marshes. She thought that all writers were unhappy, that the world of books was too dark. She equated real happiness with wordlessness. Saturday 7 September, around 4 o'clock in the afternoon, hundreds of German bombers and fighters began their raid on London. The Blitz would continue for fifty-seven consecutive days, and then intermittently until May 1941, when the German airforce prepared for the invasion of Russia. On Monday 9 September they went to London, where a house near theirs had been hit by a bomb; she wondered who had lived there. They drove through the city and saw the destruction, gaps where buildings had been crushed, glass and rubble, *the cinema behind Mme Tussaud's torn open: the stage visible; some decoration swinging*. Back in the country, with hundreds of German planes streaming overhead at night, there was *a strong feeling of invasion in the air*. On Wednesday 18 September she wrote that their London house had been destroyed, windows broken, ceilings fallen down, china smashed. In Sussex that day she picked black-berries, gathered apples, bottled honey. Towards the end of the month a bomb dropped so close that *the pen jumped from my fingers.*

About a month earlier, in the last letter to his friend Adorno, Walter Benjamin had written that *the complete uncertainty about what the next day and even the next hour will bring has dominated my existence for many weeks.* Crossing the Pyrenees from France to Spain on 25 September, he carried a provisional American passport and a Spanish transit visa, but did not have a French exit visa when he was stopped by the Spanish border guards. Because he looked ill they allowed him to spend the night in a Portbou hotel before he was to return to France the next day. According to Arthur Koestler, who had met Benjamin just before, he had a stock of fifty morphine tablets and had given half of them to Koestler. On the night of 25–26 September, Benjamin swallowed fifteen of the tablets. He died around 10 pm on 26 September. There are speculations that he may also have suffered a heart attack. The death certificate identified him as Benjamin Walter.

From May to July, when the risk of invasion seemed imminent, male German refugees living in security-sensitive coastal areas of England were arrested and interned as *friendly enemy aliens.* Kurt Schwitters had arrived in Great Britain from Norway on an ice-breaker and was arrested in Edinburgh on 18 June, to spend more than a year as an enemy alien in British internment camps, where the conditions were harsh and he suffered relapses of his childhood epilepsy. When he was moved to the Hutchinson Camp in Douglas on the Isle of Man, he began work on a new Merzbau using plates, scraps of lino, chair legs, and instead of plaster, porridge, which grew mould.

Walter Benjamin's son Stefan Rafael Benjamin, aged twenty-two, was another internee. His *place of capture* was London and the date 28 June 1940. On 10 July he was put on board the HMT

(Hired Military Transport) *Dunera*, which sailed out of Liverpool at midnight with 2,542 German and Austrian, mostly Jewish, internees on board (including traumatised survivors from the *Arandora Star*, torpedoed and sunk on 2 July), as well as 200 Italian Fascists and 251 Nazis, about 1,000 people above the ship's maximum capacity of 1,600. Their possessions were confiscated, they endured fifty-seven days of hunger, and cramped and unsanitary living conditions, they were mistreated by the troops escorting them, often with great cruelty, and were not told where they were heading. They assumed it would be the United States or Canada. It was said that the orthodox Jews survived on cheddar cheese and prayer. The men ranged in age from sixteen to seventy. The long list of occupations included doctors, lawyers, rabbis, publishers, editors, actors, archaeologists, engineers, tailors, farmers, watchmakers, waiters and cooks; there was one tea taster. Among the names there was Broch, Cassirer, Feuchtwanger, Freud, Heine, a Karl Kafka, Kantorowicz, a Josef Roth, and Wittgenstein. When Lieutenant-Colonel William Patrick Scott, the commander of the ship's escort troop, issued a report at the end of the voyage, he wrote that the Nazi Germans' *behaviour was exemplary. They are a fine type, honest and straightforward, and extremely well-disciplined . . . [if also] highly dangerous.* The Jews *can only be described as subversive liars, demanding and arrogant . . . not to be trusted in word or deed.*

The *Dunera* arrived in Sydney in bright sunshine on 6 September. Blue sea, blue sky, it was spring in the Southern Hemisphere. The police boat that accompanied the ship into the harbour was called *Nemesis*. From Sydney they were taken to internment camps in Hay on the vast treeless plains of western New South Wales. Stefan's identification number was E 39130; his surname was given as *Benjamini* (perhaps because he'd been living in Italy); his occupation as student; religion Jewish; brown hair, blue eyes. He was kept in the Hay camp for about six months; then he was transferred to another camp at Tatura in Victoria. Despite their imprisonment behind layers of barbed wire, and the harsh conditions aggravated by summer heat and dust, many of the Dunera Boys, as they came to be called, liked this latest place of exile and remained in Australia after their release. Stefan Benjamin was released in December 1941 and according to Defence Department documents, left for the United States; he eventually returned to England, where he later managed an antiquarian bookshop that specialised in books about London, opposite the British Museum. He died in 1972, survived by his wife and two daughters.

Lion Feuchtwanger escaped from Les Milles internment camp in a kidnapping stunt organised by the American consular official Myles Standish, who bundled him into a red Chevrolet and gave him a woman's coat and scarf to wear on the way to Harry Bingham's villa. Unfortunately, arriving in America on the *Excalibur* on 5 October, Feuchtwanger revealed the story of his dramatic rescue and thus compromised the safety of Varian Fry's underground organisation.

It was night when the Greek passenger liner TSS *Nea Hellas* departed Lisbon for New York at the beginning of October with 678 passengers, mostly Jewish refugees from Italy. As they steamed out of port and down the Tagus river, Heinrich Mann looked back at Lisbon's unbelievably beautiful harbour, his last view of Europe, with great sadness. His whole sense of himself was inextricably connected with this continent and this moment of time. He said it was an emotion far more intense than parting from a lover. He carried with him the catastrophic defeat of intellectual politics. And a more personal failure. With the help of the Swedish writer Amelie Posse (-Brázdová), he had tried to organise Mimi and Goschi's escape from Prague, but now had no idea if this had been successful. Sick and angry, he mostly stayed in his cabin, drawing Titianesque nudes on the blank end pages of a book by Anatole France. Also on board were the writers Walther Victor and his wife, Maria Gleit; political activists Victor and Hermann Budzislawski; the publisher Leopold Schwarzschild; and the Werfels, Döblins, and Polgars.

Alfred Polgar was born Josef Polak, 1873, in Vienna. Hermann Broch said that as a writer and critic Polgar was so remarkably astute, he *could catch deep sea fish on the surface of things*. He was a friend of Bruno Frank and Joseph Roth; was disliked by Schnitzler. At the beginning of March 1933 his life was saved by Bertold Viertel, who one day phoned him before dawn in Berlin and ordered him to come immediately *to visit* him in Prague. Like many others on board ship, he now made earnest attempts to learn English. With books like *1000 Worte Englisch* in their hands, they paced the decks, glancing at the phonetic guide and repeating their lines. *Vott immpjudennss! Ai vont tuh rihd ohl dsihs pehpers maisself! Iff ewwrivönn kömms tuh rihd dse pehpers inn dse kaffeh, hau ahr dse pöhblischers gohing tuh inkrihss dsehr ssörkjulehschen?* Some words needed more attention than others; they were calling each other *mai löw* instead of *mai dihr*; others – *ssohssedsches, wedschetebls* – had them in hysterics. Polgar later said that the nicest person on the ship was Heinrich Mann, despite the fact that he seemed *very tired, profoundly affected and hurt by the European situation*. Everyone was aware of the danger of submarines. It was a tense journey. Alma Mahler-Werfel, who once claimed she had no use for *Madame Bovary* and went to bed with the work of Nietzsche, found the sea monotonous. During their ten-day crossing, Mussolini invaded Greece.

The first day of October brought the belated news that the Dutch writer and critic Menno ter Braak had killed himself when the Germans invaded Holland, in the night of 14–15 May; Thomas speculated that his friend's essay on *Lotte* may have been the last he wrote, and that his own letter of thanks would have arrived too late. *Friends fall. The wasteland expands.* What was to become of his daughter Monika? And how would he handle the proximity of

Heinrich's wife? Now back on the east coast, Thomas, Katia and Klaus were waiting at Hoboken pier when the *Nea Hellas* docked, ramming another ship, around nine o'clock on Sunday 13 October.

Later in the war, the ship was used as an Allied troop carrier, affectionately called the Nelly Wallace by soldiers, and for a time was commissioned as transport for refugees by the Australian government.

Klaus recorded in his diary that on arrival Nelly *inexplicably dissolved in tears*, but then recovered from this emotional outburst, and was well behaved and cheerful. Also at the dock was Kadidja Wedekind, who called herself Heinrich Mann's adopted niece and would later tell him that this day, when she knew he was safe, was one of the best moments of her life. They all went to the Hotel Bedford, where they drank vermouth, as was the brothers' custom, followed by lunch, and the trip to Princeton, where the newly extended family took up residence. They talked about the Germans' barbaric fantasies and the irrevocable damage across the entire continent, the heroism of the English, the dubious compromise struck by France, the suicides. Hearing about Walter Benjamin's death in Portbou, Klaus said, *I could never stand him, but still . . .* Already the next day, at least for Thomas, a certain routine was established; breakfast with Heinrich or Golo, writing, a walk with Katia and the dog, coffee on the terrace, visits and visitors, and after dinner his favourite music: Wagner, Brahms, Verdi. The weather was autumnal, some light snow, a brief return to summer heat, and then a cooling off, with rain. On 19 October Klaus had lunch with Heinrich and with *aunt Kröger*, realising that his uncle had aged, that his energies were spent. He wondered what had happened to the nervous tension that had once produced the wonderful novella *Pippo Spano* or the wickedness of *Professor Unrat*, and he concluded, citing Gide, that old people are not very useful.

Soon after his arrival Heinrich received a request from Helen

Keller, to sign a petition for an American rescue ship to be sent to France to evacuate Spanish freedom fighters from internment camps. He also lost no time to write to the European Film Fund to highlight the danger for the writer Emil Alphons Reinhardt, who was left behind in France, for them to sponsor his visa to America. Ernst Lubitsch replied, saying they would do their best. But Reinhardt was taken to Dachau, where he volunteered to care for typhus patients and died. He also wrote to the Emergency Rescue Committee on behalf of the Rottenbergs, *waiting anxiously to be rescued from Europe*.

Heinrich and Nelly made short excursions to New York. In the bookshops, Thomas Wolfe's *You Can't go Home Again* was a bestseller. Their friends Julius and Eva Lips came to see them in Princeton. Thomas received the good news that more than 25,000 copies of the English translation of *Lotte* had been sold. And that Erika had returned safely to America. On Monday 28 October, Katia drove to New York, where Monika arrived by ship and was brought home and put to bed, everyone feeling great sympathy for *the poor little widow*, who seemed delicate. The next day – at a distance, one might say – Thomas was moved by the newspaper photographs of his wife and daughter embracing.

Nelly's sister Elsa, her husband, Wilhelm Bodenhagen, and their two sons lived in Johnstown, Pennsylvania. On the last day of the month Nelly left Princeton early for New York to travel by train to visit her family. Her nephew Harry Bodenhagen was aged about ten when he met his aunt this first and last time; he only remembers that he sat on her lap and she was very affectionate, stroking his cheek and calling him her little *Schmusekerl*. Now a retired chemist, he makes blackberry wine and leads birdwatching expeditions.

Thomas and Katia accompanied Heinrich to New York later that day. Reading from his speech, typed in English with phonetic markings in the margin, Heinrich expressed his heartfelt thanks at a dinner for the Emergency Rescue Committee. *For to get a man over a mountain, who hadn't climbed one for thirty years, was an athletic feat. Three thousand feet and more, steeply upwards, over paths that were none, where even the goats slipped – not everyone can manage that . . . the most difficult part is not the traveller's, who lets himself be lifted and propped, but the work of his helpful companion . . .* and he described the desperation of those left behind, of whom already *too many have succumbed to the temptation to put an end to their lives.*

They all stayed the night at the Bedford, and on 1 November they took Heinrich to the station, where friends had gathered to say goodbye. Eva Lips handed him a thermos of chicken soup. Then he was on his way to California. Thomas and Katia returned to Princeton. Nelly did not stay long with her family, and must have gone to Chicago or St Louis to meet up with Heinrich. Together they continued on the two-day trip to Los Angeles. In the dining car, as she later wrote to her friends, they were amused by their first taste of American food, especially the salads made of large chunks of hard lettuce called *iceberg* covered with a thick orange-coloured sauce. Speeding across the continent in the Super Chief, Nelly looked out at the moonlit desert, closed her eyes and dreamed of what it would be like in California: of living in a small house with a garden; with dogs, canaries in an aviary, and peacocks to roam free.

Virginia thought she should look at the sunset rather than write in her diary. *A flush of red in the blue; the haystack in the marsh catches the glow; behind me the apples are red in the trees . . . our pear tree swagged with pears.* Should she think of death? The previous night another bomb had dropped close to the house. She told Leonard that she was not ready to die; tried to imagine what it would be like, the painful and terrifying process of *putting out the light . . . a swoon; a drum; two or three gulps attempting consciousness – and then, dot*

dot dot. She regretted that she would not be able to record the act of dying. A few days later, when a German plane flew over just as she and Leonard were out walking, she moved close to him, *prudently deciding that two birds had better be killed with one stone*. Life was full of small pleasures: *October blooms; brown plough; and the fading and freshening of the marsh . . . the mist . . . breakfast, writing, walking, tea, bowls, reading, sweets, bed*. In London on Friday 18 October, they inspected the damage, first to their old house at Tavistock Square – *a piece of my studio wall standing: otherwise rubble where I wrote so many books* – and then Mecklenburg Square, where amidst the mess she looked for her diaries, salvaged some books, crockery and silver, and her fur coat.

The flow of letters from emigrants continued to be a nuisance. At midnight 5–6 November Thomas heard the news that Roosevelt had been re-elected as president. The excitement of this result was so great that he had to take a red capsule to get to sleep. It was the best news he'd heard for many years. A visit from W. H. Auden. A trip to Chicago, where their daughter Medi was expecting her first child. He wrote to Heinrich, who was now living in Beverly Hills. On 16 November Heinrich started work as scriptwriter at Warner Brothers, earning $500 per month. He knew very little English, and so in German he developed a script based on his 1932 novel *Ein ernstes Leben*. Someone suggested – or perhaps even promised – that the part of Nelly's alter ego, Marie Lehning, would be played by Bette Davis, and one of the supporting roles would go to Ida Lupino. In the last note Heinrich made for this script, hero and heroine escape the corruption of twentieth-century city life and return to their fishing village. The wish for a happy ending.

As the Brechts prepared to go to America, Feuchtwanger made his Russian bank account available to them.

Virginia re-read some of her memoirs and thought that *real life has no crisis . . . It must lack centre*. On Tuesday 5 November she wrote, *never have I been so fertile . . . the old hunger for books is on me: the childish passion. So that I am very 'happy'.*

Thomas read Rimbaud. For Christmas Agnes Meyer sent him an expensive silk dressing gown and he was annoyed by its elaborate and wasteful packaging. Their evening walks were now lit by the neighbourhood's electric Christmas decorations. To Chicago on Saturday 28 December to greet the new baby. Anxiety and insomnia, and the question whether he'll ever be free of these two torturing demons.

The Döblins had moved into a small flat at 1842 Cherokee Avenue, Hollywood. Palm trees, bougainvillea, lawns, billboards, doughnuts, hot dogs, the scent of jasmine and of Cashmere soap, comedians cracking jokes on the radio. The European emigrants perceived their new *home* as only a thin layer of civilisation laid across the folds and faults of the Earth's crust. They were struck by the intensity of the sunlight and the emptiness of the streets. Döblin said that in Los Angeles *pedestrians had become extinct . . . people are born as drivers . . . LA is the opposite of a place I'd choose to live in, since I happen to love walking amongst crowds.* Heinrich and Nelly had settled in at 264 South Doheny Drive, Beverly Hills. She had cards and stationery printed with her name, anglicised as Nell Kroeger-Mann, and the new address. They soon realised that they would need to buy a car. On the dining table, an envelope addressed to Mrs Heinrich Mann, inside it a brochure. *BORROWING MONEY can be as simple as ABC. A is for At once, B is for By phone, C is for Miss Clark. Ask for her when you telephone.*

On Friday 6 December for Virginia *what they call real life broke in.* It rained and the miscellany of their London household arrived and had to be stored or unpacked. *Real life is a helter skelter . . . I can't climb up to the other life in a hurry. I see what a working woman's life is. No time to think.* Sunday 8 December was cold and windy, and Virginia had only five minutes to spare to write in her diary that the war continued, that *it dribbled out in such little drops. One can't always catch them*. The Greeks were driving the Italians out of Albania. On Monday 16 December, *the year draws to an end . . . So cold often. And so much work to do. And so little fat to cook with. And so much shopping to do. And one has to weigh and measure*. Her hand had begun to shake. *Italy is being crushed*. On Thursday 19 December, *1940 is undoubtedly coming to an end*. No sugar to make puddings, hardly enough milk to share it with the cat. Pickled eggs. Petrol rationing meant there were fewer visitors. The daily drudgery of blacking out the house. Fewer bomb attacks, but renewed fear of an invasion soon. On Sunday 29 December, Virginia ended her diary for the year with the thought of food. *I make up imaginary meals*.

Alfred Polgar thought that *here, in California, it's beautiful, warm, the country and the people more than friendly; and if <u>inside</u> me it did not look as bad as it looks, then it would be very pleasant to live here*. He thought that unfortunately he was incurably European. His life now consisted ninety-nine per cent of memories. His aim was to live long enough to *enjoy the end of the awful mess made by that monstrous arsehole*.

1941: The Window

A few light taps upon the pane made him turn to the window. It had begun to snow again . . . His soul swooned slowly as he heard the snow falling faintly through the universe and faintly falling, like the descent of their last end, upon all the living and the dead. JAMES JOYCE, 'THE DEAD'

Brecht wrote plays that he knew might never be performed. Norwegian newspapers published recipes for cooking crows and seagulls. About twelve birds for four portions, stewed or baked. It was time to move on. In America, Feuchtwanger went to great lengths to organise visas for the Brechts.

On Tuesday 14 January, Thomas and Katia stayed at the White House as guests of the Roosevelts. *Murder and anarchy in Rumania.* Walks in the snow. He was bored with writing the last volume of his *Joseph* books; too much history.

The German campaign in North Africa was called Operation Sunflower. It's been said the naming of military operations is an art. Churchill tried to ensure that *operations in which large numbers of men may lose their lives* would not be given boastful code names like Triumphant, or frivolous ones like Bunnyhug, or common ones like Flood or Sudden.

The European Film Fund, set up to help exiled writers recently arrived in Los Angeles, provided work at Warner Brothers or Metro-Goldwyn-Mayer for Heinrich Mann, Leonhard Frank, Alfred Neumann, Friedrich Torberg, Alfred Döblin, Walter Mehring, Alfred Polgar. The wives learned English, took care of everyday business, cooked European meals with American ingredients for their homesick husbands. Nelly dealt with their application for American citizenship, the gathering-in of documents, appointments with lawyers. She wrote letters to keep in touch with friends and family. Mornings she drove Heinrich to the office, where he continued his adaptation of *Ein ernstes Leben* as a screenplay, *The Hill of Lies*, and later, with another film script in mind, he started work on a novel, *Empfang bei der Welt* (Global Reception); in the evening she brought him home.

Snow fell in Sussex and around Monk House and it was very cold. Leonard and Virginia went to London, where they *wandered the desolate ruins of my old squares: gashed, dismantled*, and went to a restaurant where she decided *to eat gluttonously. Turkey and pancakes. How rich how solid.* Back in the country *the house is damp. The house is untidy . . . we live without a future.* Another battle with depression had begun, but *this trough of despair shall not, I swear, engulf me.*

Asked in 1940 if he had plans for another book, James Joyce said yes, he'd now write something very short and very simple. His first application for permission to live in Switzerland had been rejected, because the police handling the documents thought he was Jewish. After endless wrangles over affidavits, expired passports, French exit visas and Swiss entry visas, bicycles, cars and trains, the Joyces arrived in Zürich on 17 December 1940; he died there on Monday 13 January 1941. When a deaf man at the cemetery asked who was being buried, the undertaker shouted that it was Herr Joyce, Herr Joyce. When his daughter Lucia was told of her father's death she did not believe it. *What is he doing under the ground, that idiot? When will he decide to come out? He's watching us all the time.* Virginia Woolf was told about his death and noted that they were about the same age, he was two weeks younger.

Their new beginnings did not get off to a good start. Heinrich heard that his boxes of books had only reached Spain and was worried that he'd never see them again. It would be the third library he'd built up and lost. At the end of February he wrote to his brother requesting an affidavit for himself and Nelly, to complete their immigration requirements. Thomas agreed, conditionally. Since he had already taken financial responsibility for his own children and several other emigrés, he could not extend the favour to Nelly; she should ask her American relatives to be her guarantors, which she did. They were unsettled by a barrage of anonymous phone calls telling Heinrich to go back where he came from. They discovered that their phone was tapped and their house was under surveillance, but they could not have known the full extent of these activities. The FBI was especially concerned about his involvement with the Free Germany Movement based in Mexico, and other anti-Fascist organisations, which were believed to be Communist fronts. The FBI file makes curious reading: there's a lot of repetition and mindless detail, blanked-out informants and sources, and some informants are referred to as both *reliable* and *unreliable*. It was as if blindly, foolishly conscientious, the agents felt their way along the outer membrane of Mann's life, looking for an entry point to this foreign territory, tracing his phone calls, reporting the cars parked outside his house, the deposits made into his accounts, and oddities, such as the fact that he *is about thirty years older than his wife NELLY MEMMY JOHANNA KROEGER MANN* [*sic*], whose place of birth they misread as *Thrensboch* in Germany.

In Geneva, Musil made himself keep an exact diary of every cigarette he lit, in order to discourage his smoking habit. In Los Angeles, Polgar had a heart attack, that he described as a time bomb. He was forbidden to smoke; continued with his struggle to learn English; read his own work and found it boring.

Leonard and Virginia believed the Germans would invade England in March. On Wednesday 26 February she finished writing *Between the Acts*. They'd had too many visitors. Food, she said, was becoming an obsession; the example of a spice bun that she wanted to eat and not to share. She wondered if it was to do with age or the war. Then she told herself that it was all part of the adventure of being a writer. *But shall I ever write again one of those sentences that gives me intense pleasure?*

Thomas thought a large part of the world supported Fascism only because it pitted itself against Socialism. Walks in the snow. He and Katia talked about Heinrich as they walked. His brother cast a shadow over their plans to move to California. They worried about living too close to him and his wife, and other needy emigrés. News of Germany's horrific plans to invade England; of the mass castration and mass murder of thousands of people who were mentally ill.

The movers came. Monday 17 March was Thomas and Katia's last day in Princeton. In New York their friend Broch escorted them to the station. They visited their daughter and her family in Chicago. Stopping en route in Colorado Springs, they were served a meal that was prepared according to Goethe's lunch with Lotte in Thomas's novel. On the train he was upset by a child sitting opposite, who made a mess stuffing ice cream and large pieces of sugar into its mouth without parental intervention. As they neared their destination, he welcomed the clarity of light, the palms and hills and tidy towns. Reaching Los Angeles on Wednesday 26 March, he was annoyed that there was no one to meet them at the station. Heinrich and Nelly arrived while Thomas was getting changed in his hotel room, and Nelly then drove them to the Wilshire Theatre, where Thomas delivered a lecture to a full house. Great applause, and afterwards people encircled him, moving him from introductions to interviews to book signings. Nelly took them back to the hotel in her car. The next day, 27 March, Heinrich's seventieth birthday, Thomas was in San Francisco to receive his seventh honorary doctorate, this time from the Faculty of Law at Berkeley. His brother-in-law Peter Pringsheim, a scientist who had been interned in Australia at the outbreak of World War I, showed him the laboratory where experiments to split the atom were taking place. Their son Klaus wrote to his mother, asking about the plans for Heinrich's birthday celebrations, hoping that they were just postponed, not cancelled altogether; he'd heard that *old Heini* was rather isolated, and was *struck down with Frau Kröger as with an infectious disease.*

On his birthday Heinrich began writing *Zur Zeit von Winston Churchill* (In Winston Churchill's Time; not published until 2004). Part manifesto, part melancholy monologue, the book was based on the diary he kept from 8 September 1939 until 22 August 1940, when he abandoned it because suddenly preparations for escaping from France were more compelling. It also included a *Rückblick*, a look back to that brief period from the vantage point of his present moment, between March and June 1941. He spoke of broken dreams, of dreams still breaking, of his ideological blindness in relation to the Soviet Union, and the painful turning to face the truth about Stalin, as well as the tragedy of the Vichy régime in France. *I kept on collecting fragments of hope that already contained the seeds of their own destruction.* But he did not want to hide his mistakes, nor excuse them. Rather, he aimed to show his personal struggle in interpreting the forces of history, his advances and false tracks, his disorientation. Carefully, somewhat incredulously – because as he admitted, his interest in England had always been minimal – he now pinned his battered optimism on Winston Churchill, not as an individual but as the representative of a culture that included the wider concept of the British Commonwealth, which he thought could be a model for a future European Confederation. Central to his new allegiance was his identification with England in its fight against Nazism. His manifesto: amidst his political adjustments and reorientations, he never lost the focus of his profound hatred of all nationalisms and of Nazism in particular, believing that *a real Antifascist does not have to be a Communist, but he cannot be an Anticommunist.* His melancholy monologue: at the end of the book Mann said this was merely *a preface, a quiet tune sung to keep courage on the path into darkness.*

Nonetheless, birthday greetings from friends who expressed their relief that he'd made it to safety in America, because (as Leo Lania wrote from New York) Heinrich's dedication to overthrow Fascism had set the highest standards for an entire generation. On 29 March, in accordance with one of the more absurd procedures for immigration, Heinrich and Nelly had to travel south to cross the border at San Ysidro, in order to recross back into the United States from Mexico. And Thomas was not the only one asked to help other emigrants; some thought that since Heinrich Mann now worked for Warner Brothers, he had the contacts and the power to assist his desperate friends. The anthropologist Julius Lips, for example, was hoping he would help him get a job in the movie industry as a production consultant on ethnological background material.

On Saturday 8 March Virginia went to Brighton to hear Leonard lecture on 'Common Sense in History' to the WEA. She saw *a pretty hat in a teashop* and thought *how fashion revives the eye!* She had been deeply affected by the sight of London as she saw it last, in ruins, but she was determined to *conquer this mood.* She tried to avoid introspection. And then to follow Henry James's advice to observe everything and write it all down, his idea that depression was good for genius. By 18 March, Leonard noted that Virginia was unwell. She thought she was going mad again and that this time she would not recover. Her last entry in her diary was on Monday 24 March. *Leonard is doing the rhododendrons . . .* On Friday 28 March, Virginia drowned herself in the river Ouse. Her walking stick was found on the riverbank, signing the spot where she had entered the water, her pockets filled with stones. Her body was not discovered for three weeks; her ashes were buried at Monks House beneath an elm next to the bowling lawn. *The window was all sky without colour. The house had lost its shelter. It was night before roads were made, or houses. It was the night that dwellers in caves had watched from some high place among rocks.* And then the last lines of *Between the Acts* . . . *the curtain rose. They spoke.*

They visited their son Bibi and his family in Carmel, Thomas taking chamomile, Phanodorm and Evipan to get to sleep. He noted the total nazification of Hungary; the situation in the Balkans, a catastrophe; the Berlin Opera House and State Library, hit in the latest bombings. On Easter Sunday, walking on the promenade at Santa Monica, they met Heinrich and Nelly, whom they visited for tea three days later, Thomas noting in his diary for Wednesday 16 April that Heinrich's wife was an awful trollop (*schreckliche Trulle*). It's not known what Nelly did that day to deserve this derogation, and as *Trulle* can be a slut or whore, whether he meant it in the sense of slovenliness, or in the moral sense. The outburst underlined his extreme disdain for what he perceived as her lowliness.

Trulle comes from *troll*, the giants or dwarves or other misfits in Nordic, including North German, myth, that have supernatural powers and live in caves. *Die Unterirdischen*, the subterraneans. They live below us and watch us through an opening, a *wind eye*. They are the custodians of humble things, jugs and bowls, household vessels made of earth. It's said they shudder at the sound of something breaking.

News on Saturday 19 April of the Greek prime minister's suicide. The next week they again met Heinrich and Nelly by the beach, and invited them for lunch on the weekend. On 24 April, perhaps in view of his advancing age, Heinrich gave his wife power of attorney. At the end of April Thomas spent a couple of days preparing his speech for his brother's seventieth birthday celebration. Friday 2 May was overcast; that evening there was a party for Heinrich at the scriptwriter Salka Viertel's place, at 165 Mabery Road, Santa Monica. Nelly and Alma Mahler-Werfel had been feuding; the Werfels and their friends were crossed off the guest list, but just in time the Feuchtwangers managed to engineer a truce between the two. About fifty people attended, including the Werfels, Feuchtwangers, Mehrings, Polgars, Döblins, Franks and Marcuses; the wives were the chauffeurs. After soup and trout meunière with parsleyed potatoes, Thomas delivered an hour-long speech on his brother's literary achievement, which he later offered for publication in a journal. Heinrich's reply was just as long and generous about his brother's work. In a moving tribute he then described the ordeal of their recent escape from Europe and thanked his wife for her courage, a sentiment lauded by Marta Feuchtwanger, who proposed a toast to Nelly. It was obvious that in Heinrich's deepest affection, Thomas and Nelly were placed equally, side by side. The *médaillons* of veal and beef were overdone and cold, the *pommes frites* soggy. But the party was in full swing, the atmosphere rippling with anecdotes and laughter, so much that a button popped off the decolletage of Nelly's red velvet dress to reveal the splendid contours of her lacy bra. I like to think that the little red velvet button described a perfect arc across the table and landed right on top of Thomas Mann's *Charlotte surprise*.

The blazing sun and hot dry desert winds often made it difficult to go for walks. On such days, members of the German colony could be seen standing like castaways in the shade of palm trees along the promenade. When he watched a black man in swimming costume playing beach ball with two white men, Thomas was shocked to see that the man wiggled his toes at him and flashed a smile; he called it *an obscenity*. On Thursday 15 May a wonderful meal had been prepared for Thomas and Katia at Heinrich's place, but Nelly was nowhere to be seen. Had she drunk too much of the cooking wine and fallen asleep before the visitors arrived, or had she gone out deliberately to avoid them? Heinrich and Nelly, Lion and Marta Feuchtwanger, and the artist Eva Hermann (Lion's lover) were invited to dinner at the Manns' on Monday 26 May; it was hard to escape Feuchtwanger's endless stories about French internment camps. News that the battleship *Bismarck* had sunk the *Hood*, and then that the *Bismarck* had been sunk.

In May, with Margarete Steffin and Ruth Berlau, the Brechts set out for America via Leningrad and Moscow, where Steffin, who was dying, was left behind. Brecht inquired about friends in Soviet gaols, including Asja Lacis and Herwarth Walden; he tried to seek assurances that they would be released. The group travelled for ten days on the Trans-Siberian Express to Vladivostock, where they boarded a Swedish liner that took them via Manila to Los Angeles, arriving there on 21 June.

Sunday 1 June, Thomas wrote, was the beginning of *his* month, this time in an alien environment. The following Friday he turned sixty-six, with birthday greetings and a letter from his son Klaus in New York, asking to be kept informed about the progress of their new house, the servant problem, his mother's well-being, the poodle's behaviour, relations with the *Kröger* household, his sister Monika's future, Feuchtwanger, Polgar and the weather. Heinrich came to dinner Friday 13 June, with no mention of Nelly; the brothers listened to Tchaikovsky. Later that month, Heinrich was ecstatic that Russia had finally declared war on Germany, but Thomas was sceptical.

Nelly must have poured out her troubles in a letter to Eva Lips, who replied reassuringly that when they first arrived she and her husband had experienced the same frustrations with language, tensions with other emigrants and feelings of ambivalence about America. Eva agreed that it was indeed a tough place for anyone not prepared to master the dreadful art of self-promotion, but she pointed out that Hollywood and New York were not the real America; the heart of the country was the Midwest. She was sure that Nelly's energy and confidence, and her sense of humour, would see them through.

Thomas read *Faust*. He was homesick for Zürich, saying that even if he was condemned to live in America, he wanted to go back to Switzerland to die. The two brothers and their wives continued to meet for walks and dinners. Heinrich prophesied that the Russians would put an end to Hitler. It was wishful thinking. Moods plunged when the Germans appeared to be making progress at the Russian front.

In July Nelly received a letter in English from their friend Hermann Budzislawski. Once the editor of the influential Paris-based German newspaper, *Die Weltbühne*, in America he worked as secretary for the journalist Dorothy Thompson. He wanted to warn Nelly, because he'd heard that she had helped his sister-in-law Erna Budzislawski, *a dangerous character* who'd abused his hospitality during the war years in France and extorted money from his wife while he was out of the way in a concentration camp. In emigrant circles this woman was now trying to benefit from being a Budzislawski. She was *extraordinarily selfish, grasping without any respect of the law and regardless of the rights of other people, and unmercifully making use of everybody*. He was sorry that he didn't alert them sooner and that this person, a liar and a thief, had now stirred up so much trouble for *the most irreproachable character I ever met, the famous writer and model of virtue Heinrich Mann . . . [who] . . . is more than the intellectual leader of the anti-Nazi movement: he is the symbol of honour and truth for our whole generation*. The letter was co-signed by a public notary. As for the trouble she was causing, for about ten days in May, Erna Budzislawski had taken over the typing of Heinrich's *Churchill* manuscript from Nelly and there must have been an argument over her payment.

Thomas received a letter from Pamplin, Virginia, questioning the authenticity of his presentation of Goethe's thoughts in *Lotte*. At a Hollywood dinner they met *the fat producer Hitschcock [sic] and his blonde wife*; after coffee Alfred Hitchcock fell asleep in a chair and snored. For the Russian winter, sleighs were ordered and five million fur coats were distributed to German soldiers. Goebbels announced that Germany had no choice other than absolute victory or total destruction. Thomas thought victory was unlikely, and instead of annihilation there would be *Entmachtung*, demilitarisation. The place would be left completely impotent. He thought that after the war being German would be no joke. He heard that in collusion with the Nazis, the French had arrested 40,000 Jews. It had become clear that Heinrich's scriptwriting contract would not be renewed. Thomas worried about the consequences and went to see Harry Warner; he came away thinking he'd been successful in persuading him to keep Heinrich on. On Thursday 25 September the Germans had arrived in Leningrad and what was being called the bloodiest battle in world history had begun.

Brecht heard about Walter Benjamin's death the previous year. In a poem he wrote for his friend, he chose the word *Freitod*, suggesting freedom – of choice, in one's own death, and in the sense of self-liberation – rather than the more brutal *Selbstmord* (self-murder), to describe the suicide. *I hear that you've done away with yourself / Outwitting the butcher. / Eight years of exile, of watching the enemy rise up / Finally forced into an impossible border crossing / They say you made your own passage . . .*

On 25 September Nelly wrote to her friend Salomea Rottenberg in New York. Their last letters had crossed. *We must have been thinking of one another at the same time.* She was happy to hear the Rottenbergs had acclimatised a little, which in the circumstances was the best thing one could do. It was doubtful that they – the emigrés – would ever be able to go back. And even if she could, she would not want to. Nelly said she and her husband were badly off, but that she was trying to find work so that Heinrich could continue writing. They had to abandon their plan to return to New York; for one thing there were already plenty of European intellectuals in that city, and for another, at Heinrich's age the harsher climate would be a risk. But above all, they did not have enough money for the trip and would have to travel by car, which for her would have been a great adventure, but her husband could not bear even to think about it. So they'd remain where they were. *We have finished two books, one has been with Knopf for three months, with Mme Knopf eventually deciding to accept one of the books, but setting conditions and making many changes. Heinrich Mann rejected this, believing that as a writer he knew best what to do.* Nelly supported him in this decision. They were negotiating with another publisher. And the second book, a novel, was being sent to his friend Dr Landshoff, who had arrived in America and would see if anyone was interested. She was close to despair; wished they had enough money to live peacefully and for Heinrich to have the freedom to write whatever he wanted to. It was hard for him. At present they did not even have enough to buy food for the next day. She had sold all her jewellery. The rent was paid until the beginning of December, after that they needed a miracle if they were to have a roof over their heads. And everyone around them was so greedy and unwilling to lend a hand. How different from the America she'd imagined! On top of everything, their boxes of books had arrived in New York and they would now have the expense of transporting them across the continent. She apologised for not being able to pay back straight away the money they owed Salomea.

In exile, husbands often did not have the flexibility or good health required to find work in a new place, and so came to rely on their wives. The architect Karola Bloch, for example, supported herself and her husband, Ernst Bloch, as an insurance saleswoman and waitress. Others got jobs cooking, sewing, cleaning, looking after children. Sometimes the men took on the family's domestic duties, sometimes not, and the women carried the burden of working both in their own home and elsewhere.

The reader's report for Knopf, on *Zur Zeit von Winston Churchill*, suggested that the title was misleading since it set up the expectation that it dealt with Churchill. It also proposed Heinrich Mann should drop the diary form and include more personal experiences, in other words, a complete reworking of the text.

Warm sleepless nights for Thomas in October. Family dinners; occasionally with Heinrich and Nelly. The Germans were pushing on towards Moscow, with Russia calling for help and England turning a deaf ear. Thomas wondered if the English were unable or unwilling to respond. Their holding back seemed shameful. A dinner at Heinrich and Nelly's on Sunday 12 October, where it was confirmed that all the emigré scriptwriters had lost their contracts. Two days later Thomas and Katia set off on a lecture tour, for San Antonio and Austin, Texas, where he needed to take half a Benzedrine to make his speech; to New Orleans, where they heard the Germans were closing in on Moscow in the middle of a great snowstorm. More Benzedrine to face his audience. Then Washington, Chicago and New York, with other places in between. On 25 October in Mobile, Alabama, he'd written to the Soviet ambassador in Washington, Konstantin Oumansky, to let him know about Heinrich's financial predicament. In Princeton they visited their old house, with a feeling of timelessness and sadness. They returned home via San Francisco and were back in Los Angeles by the end of November.

Nelly had a letter from Friedel Kantorowicz, who said the heavy burden of emigration, including the time in French concentration camps, had left its mark on her; she was recovering from an operation at the home of Ernst and Karola Bloch in Marlboro, New

Hampshire, and reminded Nelly of the wonderful time they had together in the South of France; she hoped for a reunion in New York. Nelly and Heinrich had to move by 20 November, but had not found a new place. They had no money to pay for the transport of their books from New York to Los Angeles. Two days before their move, Nelly suffered a haemorrhage and was admitted to hospital. She was grateful to neighbours who gave her husband a room and looked after him. That month the Döblins also had to move to a cheaper flat. To many of their circle, the Döblins' poverty and sense of dislocation, and their turning to Catholicism for spiritual comfort, epitomised the crisis of exile.

Heinrich and Nelly came to dinner on Saturday 29 November and had to be given a cheque for five hundred dollars so that they could pay their bills. Walking on the promenade the next day, Thomas and Katia discussed *the Heinrich Problem*. It was agreed that they would give them an extra three hundred dollars immediately, and one hundred per month from then on. There were hopeful rumours that Hitler had had a nervous breakdown. Thomas was reading Goethe's *Dichtung und Wahrheit* and Laurence Sterne's *Tristram Shandy*. They had a house full of children and grandchildren and did not invite Heinrich and Nelly for Christmas or the New Year. On 30 December, Thomas wrote *Dear Heinrich, we haven't seen each other for a long time*; had he been unwell, he asked, or was it the bad weather that had kept him at home. He sent New Year's greetings to them both.

Salomea wrote to Nelly in her flamboyant French-textured German. *Meine Teure, my dear*. She had so much to tell but did not know how to begin. She wished she could send her some money, but since she and her husband had all their money stolen in Portugal, they were still trying to work out how to support themselves. She'd asked their friend Kesten, discreetly, to see if the PEN organisation couldn't come to Heinrich Mann's rescue, but had heard that the Kestens themselves were not well-off, Toni Kesten was looking for work. Everyone she knew had problems. She was worried about her family in Europe, especially her relatives in Poland and Russia. Heinrich was trying to raise money by selling his work, and in a separate letter, addressing him as *Highly Revered and Valued Master*, Salomea told him she'd delivered one of his manuscripts to the Russian consul, who would send it on to Moscow. At the end of November, Salomea said she was deeply distressed to hear about the recent deportation and murder of thousands of Polish Jews, that her own family lived near Auschwitz and she could not bear to think about what was happening.

The London Blitz, North Africa, the Eastern Front, the Germans within sight of Moscow, news reports intensified every day, sometimes by the hour. Japan attacked America at Pearl Harbor on Sunday 7 December, destroying 12 warships and 188 aircraft and killing 2,471 people. The next day America declared war on Japan. Germany and Italy declared war on America on 11 December. It was what you read about and heard on the radio and talked about. You took out the atlas to locate the latest war zones. The curtain rose, and asleep or awake, your nightmares took place in any one of these so-called theatres of war. *Los Angeles Gets Ready, Time* magazine headlines on Monday 15 December proclaimed in an article about the county's civilian defence committee, which boasted a force of 200,000 *operatives* including policemen, Boy Scouts, actors, *an air squadron of civilian flyers, who furnish their own planes* and a fleet of twenty-five station wagons.

My dear friend, Salomea wrote. She was sure that by now Nelly had made a full recovery, that she was out of hospital, and would stand by Heinrich Mann in these terrible times with fresh courage. Her own husband was also ill and unable to find work. She received news of the death of one of her sons. She cried all the time. Told herself that sometimes the Red Cross made mistakes, that people who were reported dead might be found alive. This is what she wanted to cling to for a while, her own miracle. She had never experienced the feeling of being a mother as deeply as now. She told Nelly to be strong. There was no immediate reply, and again she inquired anxiously about Nelly's health. At the end of December she sent best wishes for the New Year. Salomea wrote that her husband, who had done nothing but work hard for forty years, was still at a loss to know what he should be doing now. She distracted herself with housework, though she often stood in her kitchenette with tears dropping into the food she was cooking. No beam of light had entered their lives for a long time.

With his New Year's greetings Alfred Kantorowicz hoped 1942 would see the end of Hitler. He hoped that they, people like Heinrich and himself, would have the chance to participate in what was being played out on the world stage. It upset him to realise that those who had fought most vehemently against the Nazis were now, in America, the most ignored and isolated group. He said his wife had recovered from her operation and had returned from staying with the Blochs. They were renting a small flat, which friends had helped them furnish. He was writing an article on the strategies of anti-Nazi propaganda, these last years had been too exhausting for him to attempt to write anything longer; he was still recovering from all their ordeals. Friends of theirs had arrived in Mexico, but he feared these latest arrivals would be the last. In France many had been handed over to the Germans. He worried about those who'd remained in Sanary, and about thousands of others for whom it was a hopeless situation.

Before the end of the year Heinrich and Nelly had moved to 481 Holt Avenue, West Hollywood. Together they wrote to their friend Salomea to thank her for her efforts with publishers and with the Russian consul on their behalf. Nelly said the worry of not having enough money to live on and their loss of dignity was hard to bear. Heinrich had been sick with flu for two weeks. This year had been the saddest of her life.

Alfred Flechtheim had escaped to London, where he died in 1937; his wife, Betty, had stayed behind in Berlin. On hearing that she would soon be deported to the East, she killed herself with an overdose of Veronal.

1942: Vanishing Points

People were confused. They looked into themselves. *I only hope I'm not distracted by my dangerous habit of being all too many-sided, adaptable to all things, forever alien to myself and with no central core inside me*, the Portuguese poet Fernando Pessoa had once written. Not finding meaning in the present, writers looked for it in the future, in the past. They re-read the classics and found works that offered illusions of depth, like those created by looking through the black silk threads of a Renaissance draughtsman's net, vanishing points, distances, estrangements. The predicament Robert Musil had once claimed for himself – *I write for people who aren't there* – was now shared by many others.

The Nazi security chief Reinhard Heydrich called a meeting to be held on 20 January for high-ranking officers, in a villa on Berlin's Lake Wannsee, to decide on the Final Solution of the so-called Jewish Problem. The organised, widespread mass murder of Jews was already taking place. At the Wannsee conference, the genocide became official policy. A lot of time was spent discussing the fate of half Jews, quarter Jews, those married to non-Jews, and those Jews honoured in the First World War.

Sounds like *Wahnsinn*, madness.

Early that year, in Nice, André Gide wondered about his place *in the new universe that is confusedly taking shape.*

On 2 January, Heinrich and Nelly took out a loan to buy their 1941, used, two-door Plymouth sedan: $574.44 to be paid in 11 equal payments and one part payment; their desk diary was a gift from the National Automobile Insurance Company. He continued to be watched by informants, some of whom were members of the exile community, coordinated by the FBI. The reports were signed off on by J. Edgar Hoover himself. Increasingly nervous about who would control the balance of power in postwar Germany – America or the Soviet Union – they scrutinised everything that might enlighten them about the health and wealth of Communist fronts, and so they were interested in Heinrich Mann's Communist contacts. One source, for example, *advised that on March 19, 1942, an Associated Press photograph appearing in the Los Angeles Examiner portrays LION FEUCHTWANGER and BERT BRECHT studying a manifesto which they wrote with Heinrich MANN as an appeal to the German people to force Hitler to abdicate. The caption below this picture states that the manifesto will be broadcast by short-wave radio and dropped in leaflets from planes over Germany.* A few months later, in June, it was noted that Heinrich Mann could be a contender for the leadership of the Free Germany Movement in both North and South America. In July he was observed attending a dinner at the Beverly Hills Hotel *under the auspices of the Joint Anti-Fascist Refugee Committee . . . known to be a Communist front organisation.* Heinrich Mann wrote to Kurt Hiller in London, that he'd always thought Socialism would come about as a direct consequence of moral behaviour, plain and simple, but he now knew that it was more elusive.

Brecht lamented that the American movie industry only wanted stories with messages. And that left-wingers were idealising Lenin's *inconspicuousness.* He thought Lenin was above all a functionary *and proved his worth by functioning.* Like other refugees, Brecht, the master of alienation effects in epic theatre, now had to register as an enemy alien. He said the cultural vacuum in which he lived made him feel like St Francis of Assisi in an aquarium, like a chrysanthemum in a coal mine, like a sausage in a greenhouse.

Thomas thought his *Joseph* books were sometimes funny, even bizarre. On the other hand they had become a kind of universal epic. He liked to play with greatness, to associate with it. In keeping with this idea, he had been reading *Faust*. Heinrich and Nelly came to dinner on Wednesday 14 January. On 23 January, Thomas noted the Japanese threat to Australia; two days later, the German retreat from Smolensk to Minsk. He noted the brilliance of *Tristram Shandy*, where he found affinities with his own work. Thursday 29 January he wrote that enemy aliens were being evacuated from American coastal regions, but assumed that he and his family were not in this category. Like many emigrés, he and Katia sought comfort in food that was familiar; they often lunched at a restaurant called Schweizer Haus.

Writing to Heinrich and Nelly, Eva Lips thanked them for their last letter, which was so positive it had made her forget her own troubles. She likened them to a two-towered fortress that would one day be taken as a symbol of survival in these troubled times. She looked forward to their return to New York.

In the first week of February, Thomas and Katia moved into the house they'd been building at 1550 San Remo Drive, Pacific Palisades. On Friday 6 February he wrote that he'd spent his first night in the new bedroom under his favourite silk cover and had slept well. The next day he was melancholy, listening to *Il Trovatore* as he sat on the sofa with Katia, resting his head on her shoulder. While Thomas wrote, rested or went for walks, everyone else was busy setting up the new household. On Sunday 8 February he looked through his old diaries, which filled him with horror, sadness and anxiety. He thought about his separation from Germany and was amazed that since then he had produced anything of significance. He thought about the false, harmful and compromising aspects of keeping a diary. It was the shock of going into exile which had made him take it up again, the challenge of relating history to everyday existence. It was a regrettable habit. Almost two weeks later he was still preoccupied with his journals, dwelling on his old love for Klaus Heuser, and their kiss.

In Petropolis, Brazil, Stefan Zweig was suffering from depression. On 18 February he wrote in English to his first wife, Friderike, in New York. *There will be never return to all bygone things . . . I am continuing my work but with a quarter of my strenght* [*sic*]. He now had few pleasures, he told her, except for the rereading of old books. Over the next few days Stefan and his young wife, Lotte, put their affairs in order. Papers were burned, letters written, envelopes stamped, the names of their owners attached thoughtfully to borrowed books. On Sunday 22 February they swallowed large amounts of Veronal. The news that the Zweigs had committed suicide was a shock for many who thought they were far worse off than they were and had still managed to avoid such a desperate act. Thinking about the mysterious chemistry of couples, Alma Mahler-Werfel believed that if Zweig had stayed with Friderike, he'd still be alive. The playwright Carl Zuckmayer appealed to fellow exiles to make a pledge to outlive Hitler.

Singapore fell on 15 February 1942. On 19 February, 242 Japanese warplanes attacked the northern Australian town of Darwin, the first of 64 raids over a period of nearly two years.

Salomea wondered why she hadn't heard from Nelly. With her letter she included a newspaper notice regarding the murder in Paris by the German military of two Russian-born doctors who had lived in France for twenty years, and the suicide of a third. Nelly was the only one, she said, who would share her grief over the death of their mutual friend.

Alas, Poor Gottschalk was the title of an article in the March issue of *Time* magazine, reporting the death in October 1941 of the German actor Joachim Gottschalk. The Nazis had demanded that he divorce his wife, the actress Meta Wolff, because she was Jewish, with the likelihood that she and their son would then be sent to the Terezin concentration camp. The three died together in a suicide pact. I have heard, but wonder if it's true, that Gottschalk, well known for his role as Hamlet, bequeathed his skull to the German Theatre in Berlin, to be used for future performances in the gravedigger scene.

Thomas was writing his last volume of *Joseph*. He read Harry Levin's *James Joyce: A Critical Introduction*, which he thought was excellent and that his own work had rarely received such an intelligent response. On Tuesday 3 March, they had Heinrich and *his terrible wife* to dinner. There were phone calls from Heinrich two weeks later: he was worried about Nelly, something about having hurt her head, and heart problems. Thomas was disdainful. They sent Golo over to find out what was going on. Returning from a drive-in movie, Thomas had hot chocolate and bread with cheese, which reminded him of his childhood suppers. He wished Heinrich and Nelly would move back to New York, not just for their sake but also for his own. On Friday 27 March they celebrated Golo's thirty-third and Heinrich's seventy-first birthdays, and for a present he gave his brother three bottles of burgundy. They did not hear until a few days after it happened, that on the night of 28–29 March the Royal Air Force Bomber Command claimed its first great success against a German target – Lübeck. With 400 tons of bombs, mostly incendiaries, the damage was extensive: 3,400 buildings were destroyed, there were more than a thousand dead. Nothing but the façade of their grandparents' house in Mengstrasse, the setting for *Buddenbrooks*, was left standing.

Gide made plans to leave France. *I have the soul of a migratory bird and think only of setting out.* He wondered about migration, about the Huguenot ancestry of many Germans and if anyone had ever listed *the exiled families . . . the gifts that France made to foreign countries through the Revocation of the Edict of Nantes.*

During the last weeks of his life, Musil assured his wife that he'd keep working to the age of eighty. On the morning of 15 April, Martha thought she saw death on his face for just a moment. He recorded smoking two cigarettes and died at midday. His wife had a death mask made, which she kept in a small suitcase. She carried the suitcase wherever she went and took the mask out at night. She believed in her husband's continuous presence and omnipresence: perhaps he was up there *with the last rays of the sun on the mountaintops, something he could never have done when he was alive, since he suffered from vertigo.* In July 1946, before moving to America from Geneva, she spread his ashes at the foot of the Salève and threw the urn into the river Arve.

On Wednesday 1 April, Thomas and Katia were invited to a dinner party at the Werfels'. Heinrich and Nelly were also there. They had recently moved to 301 South Swall Drive. He was suffering from a gum inflammation; she, according to her brother-in-law, behaved badly. Heinrich wrote to thank Thomas and Katia for the cheques they'd sent, but he was concerned about two that had not arrived. He said he sometimes found his mail scattered in the street in front of his place or in a neighbour's garden. Meanwhile they owed rent and only opened the door to people they knew. Thomas told his brother he'd heard Heinrich would be receiving $750 for the sale of his books in Russia and advised him to use it for his move to New York. On 15 April, Heinrich wrote to thank him for his concern. Regarding the question of how far the funds would stretch, he said it would get them to New York, with a little left over, he hoped. But he needed to pay the dentist, who had removed not just a cyst, but teeth as well, and he was now waiting for a new set of dentures that cost $225, which he could pay in instalments, though he knew from a similar method of payment for the car, this only caused further anxieties if their money ran out. They still owed $300 on the car. Of the $750 just $225 would be left. If they sold the car once they got to New York, they'd have enough for the next few months. He worried that he'd made so many miscalculations in the short time he'd been in the country, and he was afraid this would keep on happening. He pinned his hopes on his three unfinished manuscripts, and told Thomas he knew it was too much to ask of him to be supporting his brother as well as looking after his own family. He would try to find ways to support himself. Heinrich feared that if he moved to New York they would be too far apart, that even now they saw each other too rarely, though he always had plenty of time. He didn't know why, but he'd started reading *Buddenbrooks* again. Thomas was touched.

On Tuesday 21 April, *the Heinrich Problem* was discussed first on the terrace with Erika and then continued on the Promenade with Katia. They talked about what they perceived to be the impossibility of his life with Nelly, and his health problems. They decided that it was necessary to separate Heinrich from Nelly, which meant that he would have to come and live with them for a while. When they suggested this to him, they thought he showed a willingness to go along with the idea. But Nelly, they knew, would protest. That evening Thomas read Maeterlinck's *Mysteries of the Universe*. The talks developed over the next days, with Golo and Erika sent to their uncle's place as emissaries.

Heinrich arrived at Pacific Palisades on Monday 27 April. On the same day, some might think rather melodramatically, Nelly made her will. Name: Nelly Emmy Mann. Age: forty-four. She left all her property to her husband, Heinrich Mann, who was also her executor. *I hereby declare that I have no issue of my body, and I expressly disinherit any person who may claim to be related to me except my beloved husband*. He seemed to enjoy his holiday with his brother, their walks, visits to the Döblins, the Reinhardts, the cinema. He sketched and read *Buddenbrooks*. But he made it very clear that he did not intend the separation from Nelly to last very long. After two weeks, on Saturday 9 May, he returned home.

Brecht could not write poetry, because no matter how topical it was, it made no difference, the war raged on. *Reader's Digest* returned his story about his and Feuchtwanger's meeting with Hitler in a Munich café in 1922. Visiting the Feuchtwangers at the Villa Aurora, sitting in their beautiful garden, he heard about hormone injections being given to homosexual soldiers and commented that now even they would not enjoy life in the army anymore.

Salomea wrote Nelly that they were still living in a hotel in New York, and despite their extensive efforts, had not found work. It was all so difficult and depressing that it had made her sick. She was trying to learn English. Heinrich and Nelly received some money from their friend Kantorowicz. They wrote to thank him for his generous help.

Thomas was reading *Effi Briest*. He told Heinrich he was pleased the Russian money had arrived, and agreed that he should postpone going to New York until a good opportunity arose. He did not like to think of Heinrich in a small flat in the humidity and heat of a New York summer. Golo suggested Heinrich might like to move to Mexico instead; it offered mountain air, the Spanish language and a more sympathetic political atmosphere. They all understood that for the moment he just wanted to stay where he was, especially since some people thought the war might be over by the autumn. On the last day of May they heard about a massive air attack – the so-called Thousand Bomber Raid – on Cologne that destroyed most of the city. It was said the flames could be seen as far away as Holland.

Near Prague at the end of May two British-trained Czech resistance fighters attacked Reinhard Heydrich in his car and he died a week later. On 10 June in retaliation the Nazis massacred the citizens of Lidice, a suspected partisan stronghold, and razed the village.

Thomas was often recognised in public. He enjoyed being told that he was famous. On his birthday a few visitors came for tea, including Heinrich and Nelly. But at dinner some weeks later, Nelly was drunk, loud and quarrelsome, interrupting Heinrich's reading from his work in progress about Frederick the Great. Thomas vowed she must never be invited again, and retired to his room without saying goodnight to them.

At Pacific Palisades the Mann family argued about the war and Thomas said he was not afraid of Communism, that he would be loyal and subservient to a dictatorship, if that was the only way to beat Fascism. Reports of terrible battles being fought in Russia. On Sunday 19 July Heinrich gave another reading, which Katia and Erika attended, reporting back to Thomas that Heinrich's text was *problematic*. They talked about Nelly late into the night, without resolving anything. For Katia's birthday, Heinrich and Nelly phoned to say they were coming over, but did not turn up; they came the next day. On 31 July Thomas wrote to Heinrich, to say that from now on his monthly cheque of $100 would be issued by the European Film Fund, and that they were having trouble with their servants, but once that was sorted out, they would ask them to dinner.

Heinrich was still waiting for his eight boxes of books to be transported from New York to Los Angeles. In her letters to Salomea Rottenberg, Nelly expressed concern for her friend's health and suggested that Salomea and her husband should move to California for the climate. Maybe they could even take a leasehold on a farm together. It was a good life, always sunny, and relatively cheap; she told her that they lived on about $120 a month, had a big car in which she drove Heinrich to the doctor, the barber, or just to buy cigarettes and a paper. He always waited for his daily walk until she returned home from work.

The brothers Klaus and Golo argued about politics and history. On Sunday 29 August, Thomas recorded half a dozen battles being fought simultaneously in Russia.

In Sidi-bou-Saïd, Tunisia, Gide endured the heat and *for the first time in my life, probably, I am making the acquaintance of what is called nostalgia. I think of the mysterious forest interior at La Roque in which the child I was could not venture without trembling* . . .

Salomea hadn't been in touch because she did not want to burden them with her problems. Her husband had become so anxious that he could not be left alone. The air in New York was so polluted that she always felt unwell. Nelly responded, and Salomea replied. She was full of fear about their situation, and what was happening in the world. She read books in order to forget and admired Nelly for going out to work. But Nelly was still finding it hard to make ends meet. While their rent was relatively low, she had trouble paying their debts; the doctor's bills alone amounted to $50 a month. For the moment she'd given up her job because Heinrich had completed a novel, *Lidice*, which she had to type. She hoped that when it was published, they could pay back the money they owed Salomea. A number of emigrés were working on farms. The composer Paul Dessau had a job weighing eggs at a large chicken farm in New Jersey. Nelly dreamed of renting a house with some land in the San Fernando Valley, where they could make a modest living and lead a quiet and healthy life. For Heinrich, who was still recovering from his last bout of illness, it would be the best thing. Paradise! With their books, now that they'd heard the boxes were on their way, and sunshine, and a car with plenty of petrol to explore the country. You didn't need much more than that. She urged Salomea to consider sharing the house and farm with them. They could put their plan into action in December, when the rains stopped. In this letter of 3 September, she said that she was exhausted from typing for fourteen hours. It appears that she had also found a temporary job, perhaps in a hospital or sewing uniforms, because she mentioned returning to work on Monday. They needed the money; they could not exist on a diet of oats and rice forever.

On Sunday 6 September, Heinrich came to tea and Nelly arrived later. Thomas was rereading Goethe's *Dichtung und Wahrheit*. The following week he noted that no one was helping the Russians fight the battle of Stalingrad, which had dominated the news for months. Blood ran through the streets of Stalingrad. On Sunday 20 September, Munich was bombed with such force that people in Switzerland could hear the explosions. Thomas thought that Munich was a ridiculous place and these reprisals were historically justifiable. On hot days he wore his white suit. Much of his time was spent writing and recording messages to be broadcast into Germany.

Thomas studied an article on the ambiguity of Henry James. The battle of Stalingrad continued. Hot weather, dry winds, forest fires in a valley not far from their home. He read Baudelaire in the garden.

On a radiant morning in North Africa, Gide tried to recall Baudelaire's 'Morning Twilight'. He noted that *the Siamese cat, fed almost exclusively on fish in peacetime, now is quite willing to eat bread*.

The Döblins depended on financial assistance from funds and friends. When these sources dried up, and the stresses and humiliations of exile were too much to bear, Erna Döblin suffered a nervous breakdown. Two months later, Alfred Döblin survived a heart attack.

Brecht worked on a film script. He felt sick when he thought how much of it had to be changed to produce a bestseller. His wife, Helli, gardened; he watered the plants.

The Rottenbergs decided not to come to California and Nelly's dream of farm life came to nothing.

Every time you turned on the radio you heard Bing Crosby singing the Irving Berlin hit "White Christmas." On Sunday 1 November, Thomas saw the film *Bambi*, which he absolutely loved. The German army was in retreat in Africa; the Russian defences were strong. According to Thomas, the danger now lay in the Allies' mistrust of one another, and in the American boast single-handedly to win the war in 1944. On Monday 9 November, on the train to Chicago, he was deep in *Crime and Punishment*, and needed Phanodorm and Evipan to get to sleep; sun, snow and desert flashed by the next day. Annotations, reading Stravinsky's memoirs. A brief stay in New York. By 11 December Thomas was in San Francisco, where he again saw *Bambi*, again heard the fatal shot ring out across the snow, and we might imagine, emerged from the cinema shaken and tearful. Throughout the journey the train compartments, which he called *roomettes*, somehow felt like home.

Franz Werfel's novel *The Song of Bernadette* was published and became an instant bestseller. He'd written it in gratitude for the refuge he and his wife had found two years earlier in Lourdes, when he made a vow that if they escaped from the advancing German army, he would honour St Bernadette with a 'song'.

Kurt Döblin, Alfred's brother, had already died in Majdanek concentration camp. Georg Benjamin, Walter's brother, died in Mauthausen. In his hometown of Drogobych, Poland, the writer and artist Bruno Schulz was killed by Nazis. Heinrich Mann's first wife, Mimi – listed as Marie Mannová – was transported from Prague to Terezin in September 1942.

I no longer cling much to life, Gide wrote, *but I have this fixed idea;*

to last. To make myself and my dependencies last a little while longer: linen, clothing, shoes, hope, confidence, smile, graciousness, make them last until the farewell. To this end he was becoming parsimonious.

A brochure in the mail from the New York Life Insurance Company, for Mrs Nellie Mann, announcing that you don't have to be rich to start an annuity, for $1 a week there's a savings plan that works 3 ways: *IF YOU LIVE . . . IF YOU DIE . . . IF YOU QUIT.*

1943: Phosphorus

Phosphorus is found in rocks, plants, and animals, in teeth and bones; the molecules of DNA contain phosphorus. Discovered in Hamburg by the seventeenth-century alchemist Hennig Brandt, in its solid form phosphorus is waxlike and colourless; it glows in the dark; it ignites spontaneously when exposed to air; for the dangers posed by its misuse it has been called the devil's element. In its Greek etymology it means *bringing light*.

Heinrich and Nelly received New Year's greetings from their disillusioned friends the Lipses, who said that for them too, 1942 had passed under the motto *Just survive!*

On Friday 1 January, as he did almost every day, Thomas went for a walk. The weather was fresh and sunny, and he *marched* along Sunset Boulevard and Amalfi Drive, where Katia picked him up and drove him home. On Monday 4 January, just as he was being called to lunch, he placed the punctuation mark at the end of *Joseph the Provider*, the fourth and final volume of his *Joseph and His Brothers* epic. It was a moment full of melancholy. He saw these books as a personal achievement, more than a literary one, a private monument to perseverance. He read the ending with great ceremony to family and friends gathered at the house that evening. On Sunday 17 January, they heard the news that Berlin had been bombed twice in quick succession. The following Sunday, Thomas wrote that he dreamt he was about to die, that he was performing dance steps while tumbling through space. The war in Russia was reaching a climax; the harbour-quarter of Marseille in flames; 40,000 people arrested in France, with many others collapsing or committing suicide. On the last day of the month Thomas made preparations for a broadcast to Australia, part of a BBC series called *America Talks to Australia*, in which he pointed out that he was *not-yet-American*.

They heard that despite international protest, Max Liebermann's widow had been deported to Poland. The rumours that reached them were often false or oblique. Martha Liebermann, still living in Berlin and in her eighties, had a stroke that winter and was bedridden. On 5 March she received a deportation order. Five days later she took an overdose of Veronal. As she lay dying, she was taken away by the Gestapo.

Thomas delivered his Australian message on Friday 12 February. The following Monday, despite their limited means, there was a *soirée* at Heinrich's place, a buffet dinner for eighteen guests, which possibly included Gregori Kheifets, the Russian vice consul in San Francisco, *known to have engaged in espionage on the West Coast, and . . . to be interested in political as well as in military information.* The FBI files on Heinrich Mann note that Kheifets attended such a dinner some time in early 1943. The FBI continued to be concerned about Heinrich's contact with the Latin American Committee for Free Germans and its publishing arm El Libro Libre, and they continued to intercept his mail. They reported that on 11 March he accepted the honorary presidency of this committee and that on 12 March he was to address a meeting of the Joint Anti-Fascist Refugee Committee . . . *a known Communist front organization* . . . at the Philharmonic Auditorium in Los Angeles, but did not show up. There were rumours that Thomas had been called to Washington, to be nominated as the future president of Germany.

On 26 February, Nelly had been arrested for drunk driving. She spent a night in jail, was bailed for $250 the next day, sentenced by Judge Charles Griffin on 9 March to sixty days in jail with the sentence suspended for two years on the condition that she abstain from liquor. In a sober state she was mortified by her alcoholic misdemeanours.

Reports in March of a massive air attack on Berlin, the fires continuing to burn; the sinking of a Japanese convoy of ships heading for Australia; in London over a hundred people killed in the panic to enter a shelter during the last German raid. Thomas started to look through his old notes on *Faust*, based on the anonymously written *Faustbuch* and the many literary interpretations, including Marlowe's and Goethe's, of the legendary sixteenth- century German sorcerer Dr Johann Faustus who made a pact with the devil in exchange for infinite knowledge and power. A difficult subject, combining the pathological with folktale elements. It took him back to the early days of exile and his anxiety attacks. The loss of a lot of his *Faust* research when he left Germany; the journey of the rest of the file with him from Munich via Switzerland and France to America. He remembered in each place, in which drawer of his desk he kept the notes, and thought how they would now be brought forward, actually and in time, to replace the *Joseph* papers in his filing system and his mind. There was trepidation about approaching this topic, which he always thought would be his last work. The shocking news from France of the German bombing of groups of refugees who'd been rounded up for deportation. A rumour that Hitler was ill and his generals had taken over. On Monday 22 March, there was a dinner at the home of friends, with Heinrich and Nelly, who was drunk. The following weekend it was Heinrich's birthday and they went to his place for tea, bringing

two bottles of burgundy, an odd gift, considering Nelly's problem
with alcohol. Then on to the Hotel Ambassador for cocktails with
his patron Agnes Meyer, dinner in a nightclub with a tropical island theme, palm trees and jazz, good food and bad champagne,
the unwelcome intimacy of having to dance with Mrs Meyer. A
CBS radio broadcast on 23 March, about Heinrich Mann as the
intellectual leader of the German anti-Fascist movement. Berlin
bombed twice in two days at the end of March; Rommel facing
defeat in Africa.

Terrible reports about the devastation of Berlin and the dead.
Forwarding a letter to Heinrich from a friend who had gone to
Brazil, Thomas told his brother that when the war was over they
might travel there together. Heinrich and Nelly came to dinner
on Monday 12 April, when Heinrich read the Dresden scenes
from his *Frederick the Great* manuscript. In mid-April the news that
Australia was once again threatened by Japanese invasion, which
the British treated with scepticism. Dinner at Heinrich's place,
apparently without incident. Thomas was now reading the *Malleus Malleficarum*. This hair-raising handbook on witchcraft and
Satanism was written in 1486 by two Dominican monks who were
inspired by Pope Innocent VIII's 1484 document against the faithless. The pope had declared, *It has indeed lately come to Our ears, not
without afflicting Us with bitter sorrow, that in some parts of Northern
Germany* and elsewhere in that country, *many persons of both sexes,
unmindful of their own salvation and straying from the Catholic Faith,
have abandoned themselves to devils, incubi and succubi, and by their in-
cantations, spells, conjurations, and other accursed charms*, have committed a long list of terrible offences – *enormities, foulest abominations,
filthiest excesses* – and must be tried and punished. With the pre-
cept of bringing light to people and places of darkness, the pope
sanctioned a universal war against satanism and paganism and in-
cited his inquisitors to action. In Thomas Mann's preparations for

his *Doctor Faustus* novel, the *Malleus* illuminated the tragic parallels of past and present massacres.

In April they heard that Erna Döblin had suffered another breakdown. On Friday 14 May, Thomas read a short piece praising Heinrich in a German-American newspaper. It aroused his old jealousy of his brother, and was followed by depression and feelings of aversion. He was calmed only by the thought that *there are many rooms in our father's house*. Then on Sunday 23 May he began to write *Dr Faustus*, though the fictional date given on the first page of the book is 27 May 1943. This concern for dates, dropping anchors in the sea of time, was significant not only for securing the book's historical moment, but also because calendar making (astrology) was one of the original Faustus's occult skills. A few days later, at another gathering that included Heinrich and Nelly, Kafka was read aloud.

They knew their houses had been secretly fitted with telephone surveillance by the FBI, and Brecht and other emigrants mocked the listeners with cryptic conversations. Helene Weigel and Marta Feuchtwanger, for example, read long excerpts from cookbooks to each other in languages they themselves did not speak.

Heinrich and Nelly came to dinner on Friday 2 July and they talked about the political situation. Heinrich read a further section from his *Frederick* work, interrupted by a cough. Thomas thought that Heinrich had produced a series of eighteenth-century grotesques, concise but empty scenes that lacked a connecting thread. No doubt he kept this criticism to himself. When Katia went out one evening, Thomas warmed up some soup, cooked semolina porridge and had raspberries for dessert. Many years later his daughter Monika revealed that he ate non-solids because of the constant trouble with his teeth. An article appeared, claiming that the majority of emigrants believed that when a new government was formed in Germany, Thomas Mann would be its head.

Northern Germany was in the middle of a heat wave when Operation Gomorrah, the British-led Allied firebombing of Hamburg, began just before midnight on 24 July. On approach, the planes cast out aluminium strips to fool German radar, a technique which Bomber Command called *Window*. They dropped a massive cocktail of explosive and incendiary tonnage. People were crushed, buried under the rubble of entire districts, or they were burnt to death. The worst damage was caused by phosphorus bombs. Over the next nine days the harbour city burned with such intensity that waterways and stones were set alight, and roads became deadly rivers of tar on which no person attempting to escape ever took more than one step and great stretches were studded with the bodies and body parts of those who had tried to flee. The fire consumed all the oxygen. For many survivors of the bombings there was not enough air left for breathing. People immersed themselves in water, but covered in white phosphorus, they started to burn again as soon as they emerged. The heat rose to 1500 degrees Fahrenheit. Firestorms raged across the city at speeds of 150 mph, tearing people and objects into the air and casting them, still glowing, across great distances. Some say half-burnt books dropped from the sky as far away as Lübeck. It has been estimated that more than 40,000 people died (some estimations were as high as 200,000). The majority were women and children. Tens of thousands were injured. About a million were left homeless. Of the built environment, two-thirds of the city was destroyed. There was black rain. In California Brecht wrote, *Hamburg sinks. Above the city rises a pillar of smoke twice as high as the highest mountain in Germany, 6,000 metres.*

On 23 July the Dutch publisher and book lover Emanuel Querido and his wife were killed in the Sobibor concentration camp, where 260,000 Jews perished between May 1942 and October 1943.

Early August a meeting took place at Salka Viertel's house, with Thomas and Katia, Heinrich and Nelly, the Feuchtwangers, Brechts, Franks, Marcuses and the composer Hanns Eisler, regarding the drawing up of documents and plans for democracy in postwar Germany. Discussions were long and tedious. The women served sandwiches and beer. According to an FBI informer, the meeting was a Communist front. Thomas was irritated the next day and decided not to remain part of the group. He believed the Allies were right to punish the entire German nation. Brecht, on the other hand, was more compassionate and was angry with Mann for withdrawing his signature. At home Thomas read some of his friends the beginning of his *Faust*, which he called his *devil* book, and he enjoyed their reactions to the darker parts. On Tuesday 3 August he heard about the air attacks on Hamburg, and over the next days, the reports of the total devastation of that city. On Saturday 14 August there was a birthday celebration for Döblin at El Pablo Rey Playhouse, a small theatre in Santa Monica. Heinrich made a speech, there were musical dedications by Eisler and Schönberg, readings by the actors Alexander Granach, Fritz Kortner and Peter Lorre, chansons by Blandine Ebinger. Helene Weigel read out a contribution from Brecht, which acknowledged that he'd learnt more about epic literature from Döblin than from anyone else, especially his methods of bringing together fact and fiction. The event was well attended by members of the exile community, though many became annoyed or embarrassed by the references to religion in Döblin's reply. Newspaper stories about the hysteria of women attending a Frank Sinatra concert at the Hollywood Bowl. On 18 August, Thomas was visited by FBI agents. They questioned him about people he knew, including Brecht, who were in contact with German Communists in Mexico, and their connection with Moscow.

Until recently Brecht had been planning to publish books by

exiled authors, which he hoped would then be dropped over Germany from Allied bombers. Now he said his heart stood still when he read about the bombardments of German cities, that the end of the war was nowhere in sight, just the end of Germany. He heard that Thomas Mann had been criticising him for differentiating between Hitler and Germany. He thought Mann was repulsive, reptilian. Isherwood came to dinner and they discussed English writers. When Brecht said he thought Huxley had sold out, Isherwood got up and left. Brecht commented: *I have the feeling a surgeon must have when his patient stands up during an operation and leaves; I only wounded him.*

The black comedy of Mussolini's abduction by the Germans in September. On Sunday 19 September, Thomas wrote that the only style left to him now was parody, which he had in common with James Joyce. At the end of the month they were visited by the Adornos and their monkey-like dog. They talked about the inherent dialectic – humanism against barbarism – of the Faust legend, and discussed Thomas's novel *Doctor Faustus*, its striking correlation between the life of the protagonist, the composer Adrian Leverkühn, and Germany's monstrous destiny. Visited Heinrich briefly on Wednesday 6 October, to say goodbye before leaving on another lecture tour. Phanodorm to sleep while travelling. On the last day of October, the shocking news that their friend the great theatre director Max Reinhardt (born Maximilian Goldmann, in Baden, Austria, 1873) had died in New York.

Heinrich Mann's novel *Lidice* was published in Mexico. FBI reports stated that the Soviet Vice Consul Kheifets visited the Manns for about an hour at midday on 25 October; the purpose of the visit was not known, but it was noted that afterwards Kheifets visited Brecht, who was described as *an associate of Heinrich MANN*. Apparently the Russians were asking Heinrich to speak at a Soviet anniversary function in New York, and he declined the invitation, though the FBI remained unsure if he actually went to New York or not. They could confirm, however, that he was one of 300 guests at a reception held at the Russian vice consulate in Los Angeles on 7 November. They also noted on 24 November that he had been asked to contribute articles to a leftist magazine on the following topics: *How can questions of the day be handled in a novel?; the influence of the films on the novel and vice versa; the status of the poet in 'emigration'; troubles of a dramatist; relationship of the American short story to the German novel; influence of emigration upon indigenous leaders and the influence of the country receiving the emigrants upon the literature of 'emigration'; what tasks will the end of the war leave to the author.* It seems that Kheifets visited the Manns again on 29 November, arriving by a suspiciously *circuitous route.* And in December informants found Heinrich Mann's name in the confiscated address book of Louise Bransten, an American Communist and Kheifets' mistress.

Between 1923 until he went into exile in Norway in 1937, Kurt Schwitters had built his first Merzbau in the rooms of his home in Hanover. Made up of found objects and materials, *The Cathedral of Erotic Despair*, as Schwitters called it, was a work in progress that presented the artist's world as a series of interior spaces, where ceilings and floors soared and dipped, like moods or fortunes, where big and small ideas were grafted onto columns, secrets were hidden in grottoes. By the time the house was destroyed during an Allied air raid in 1943, Schwitters had left behind a second Merzbau in Norway, and was living in exile in England.

There was a Swall Drive in Los Angeles and another in Beverly Hills; Heinrich and Nelly experienced anxiety all year about mail that was misdelivered or had disappeared, including envelopes containing cheques. It's difficult to say exactly where Nelly found work, and for how long she was employed. She was a member of the Milk Drivers and Dairy Employees Union and of the Brotherhood of Teamsters, Chauffeurs, Warehousemen and Helpers. There are paychecks made out to her, June to the end of August, from a dairy company called Arden Farms, where she had worked as a driver. On 10 November Nelly was arrested for reckless driving *after her machine assertedly struck a car* near the entrance to the National Military Home at Sawtelle in West LA, the veterans' home and hospital where she worked at that time. No one was hurt. She pleaded guilty and was asked to appear in court for sentencing on 4 January 1944. On 30 December, she took out another loan on her car, for $414 to be repaid monthly for a year.

Friends in New York once again assumed Thomas Mann would lead the German government after the war. He asked God to spare him from this fate. He was re-reading Marlowe's *Faust*. They returned to Los Angeles on 8 December. Thomas wrote to Heinrich on 21 December, that they'd expected to see them a few days before, but they heard that Nelly was sick and had been in hospital. He hoped it was nothing serious and that she'd made a full recovery. (It's not known why and for how long she was in hospital and if it was related to the car crash.) Roast pigeons and champagne for their Christmas dinner.

Brecht was worried about Döblin and Heinrich Mann, who were both ill and did not have enough money to pay for doctors. He was angry that Thomas Mann did not do more to help. At the end of the year Brecht and Thomas Mann engaged in a brief correspondence. Brecht asserted the difference between Hitler and the Germans, that Hitler's reign of terror had crippled the nation spiritually and morally, and was committing atrocities against its own people. Brecht reminded Mann that hundreds of thousands of Germans had died or were imprisoned for their fight against the regime. He wanted him, as spokesperson for the exiles, to persuade Americans that rather than punishing the nation as a whole, it would be better to help those Germans who were still fighting to keep democracy and dignity alive. Thomas, however, believed that the German people, as much as their dictator, were implicated in the war, and that democracy could only be resurrected when the war was over, when Germany was defeated and its crimes accounted for.

There were rumours of a false spring having occurred in parts of Hamburg in the autumn: charred trees sprouting new green leaves and then blossoms, the scent of lilac on the edge of dusty wastelands where people walked like ghosts, searching for any remnants of their lives.

The last book Edvard Munch read was Dostoyevsky's *The Devils*. The protagonist of this novel hangs himself with a strong silk cord thickly smeared with soap, and *the doctors' verdict after the postmortem was that it was most definitely not a case of insanity*. In December 1943 an explosion broke the windows of Munch's house near Oslo, and sitting for several hours in light clothes in the stairwell to the basement, undecided, wondering if he needed to take refuge, he caught a cold. He died of a heart attack on 23 January 1944.

1944: Drunken Angel

I n the *Los Angeles Times* on Wednesday 5 January, readers found the headline *Heinrich MANN WIFE VICTIM OF DRUG OVERDOSE. Scheduled to appear in court for sentence on a reckless driving charge, Mrs Nellie Kroeger Mann, 45, wife of the German writer, Heinrich Mann, was in an unconscious condition at General Hospital yesterday after taking an overdose of sleeping tablets, police reported.* The article revealed that her husband had told Officer Kenneth Schmidt of the Beverly Hills Police Department, it was her worry over her court appearance that led her to attempt suicide, followed by a reference to the Manns' escape from Nazi Germany, and the fact that Heinrich was the brother of Thomas Mann. It gave details of the incident, which occurred on 10 November 1943, mentioning that it was the second of its kind and that next Friday she was scheduled to appear for a probation hearing regarding a drunk-driving charge dating back to 26 February 1943, for which she had been arrested, charged and given a suspended sentence.

A telegram in French from Nelly's friend Nadine Appling (born Nadine Rose Rivers, 1898), sent to General Hospital Los Angeles, ward 7200, on the evening of 5 January: God refused to accept you in heaven; so did the devil; your husband and all your friends are relieved. Nadine said she and her husband, Grady, would bring Heinrich to visit Nelly on Sunday; she asked her to get some rest now and to be good. Thomas found the newspaper article about Nelly embarrassing. He and Katia went to Heinrich's place that day, knocked on the door, but no one answered. They wrote a note and pushed it under the door. On 13 January, FBI informants mentioned that Gregori Kheifets, the literary agent Barthold Fles and his wife Ruth, the actress Blandine Ebinger, and someone who resembled either the writer Erich Remarque or the literary agent Otto Clement were at Heinrich Mann's residence for two hours in the evening. Surveillance continued throughout the year, with special interest in further visits by Kheifets and others, items of mail, telephone conversations, bank deposits, manuscript negotiations. The name Salomea Rottenberg was misread as Salonica Kottenberg. The FBI visited Thomas on Saturday 29 January, for information about the actor Ernst Deutsch (best known for his role in *The Golem*, 1920). Who was spying on whom? I've seen copies of Brecht's FBI files that mention Marion Bach (Salka Viertel's secretary), Franz Werfel, Mrs Ludwig Marcuse and the director Douglas Sirk, among others, as *Sources of Information*.

My dearest wife. Heinrich told Nelly he was overjoyed to hear her life had been saved. The doctor at the hospital had battled all night to keep her alive. For this they could never be grateful enough. He begged her to be patient, that at present nothing mattered except that she should stay calm and recover her health. This time, he assured her, she would be completely healed, and he made the point that this included her head. It is now difficult to know if he meant this psychiatrically or physically or both, and what kind of treatment she was receiving. He said the doctors had given him their word, only she had to make an effort and must not resist them. He begged her to cooperate. Out of love for him. He'd suffered more for her than she knew; he was profoundly affected by what she had to endure. He asked her, please, to let them help her. The hospital did not allow him to visit every day. But on Sunday morning he would get a lift from Nadine's husband. He hoped that by then she would be rested. There was no need to be ashamed of what had happened; he'd had phone calls from people asking how she was, including Mrs Döblin and the Feuchtwangers, everyone was very concerned. And their lawyer Dr Kolts was doing what he could. Heinrich reassured her of his love.

Dr Johannes M. Nielsen, who later became head of the Department of Neurology and Psychiatry at USC, was Nelly's doctor. At some point she must have been moved from General Hospital to the Southern California Sanitarium at 3261 Overland Avenue in Los Angeles. From there she wrote to Heinrich, saying she would soon be leaving this place, and she might even leave him and LA altogether. She was in a rage. Over the last weeks she'd been seen by about thirty different doctors, her head had been X-rayed three times and nothing abnormal was found; even the doctor for the police department agreed that she was in perfect health. It appears, however, that (perhaps to keep her out of jail) they found (or needed to find) a very small *Verdichtung* – a benign growth that was (or could be cited as) the cause of everything that flared up in her head, her depressions, her impulsiveness and drinking. It would also be necessary to argue that she had suffered a complete nervous breakdown and had not been able to act rationally. She was upset about this, because now they would claim that she was an alcoholic, that she was crazy, and that her drivers licence must be withdrawn. She felt that Kolts, instead of defending her in court, had betrayed her; nonetheless, he sent a bill for $100 for his services. She was angry with Heinrich for cancelling his appointment to speak with the doctor, when he might have used the opportunity to vouch for her sanity and influence the outcome of the medical inquiry. She was also unhappy about what it was costing them. Some of the bills have survived: one from

9 to 16 January for hospitalisation, medication $5.02 and Kotex $0.33, was for $55.35; from 16 to 23 January $50; another issued on 30 January for hospitalisation, medication, tissues, bobby pins, stationery, tooth powder, cigarettes and matches was $54.84. She told Heinrich, in English, she would *take it easy*, but since she wasn't getting any sleep she'd soon be coming home. On the back of an envelope she'd made a list of all the things she needed: ten envelopes, the red address book, her turban headband, and the *Shekbook* because *I have to paye matsch.*

There is an undated letter from Nelly to her sister-in-law Katia, in which she mentions operations on her head and a course of injections. Could the doctors have considered brain surgery? In the Heinrich Mann Archive in Berlin, on a single sheet of paper, there is an undated drawing of a cranium with a small bump and the handwritten words Endostosis Frontalis, such as a doctor might have sketched, to help the patient visualise and better understand a medical condition. It raises but does not solve the question, whether Nelly's doctor(s) suspected she suffered from lesions of the frontal bone of the skull, also called frontal lobe syndrome or Morel-Moore syndrome, a condition associated with disinhibited and impulsive behaviour, distraction, disorientation, an inappropriate sense of humour, euphoria, emotional sensitivity and poor judgement. Or if this was something the doctors and lawyers tried to establish for her defence in court? Since medical files are protected by privacy laws, or perhaps they no longer exist, my attempts to find out more about Nelly's condition have failed.

On 31 January, Bozzani Motors' repair bill for Mrs Mann's smashed-up Plymouth came to $492. In addition to towing and labour costs, it itemised a long list of parts that had to be fixed, front bumper plates, the radiator and its shell and grill, the front motor support and insulator, fuel pump, gasket, hood, panels, lights and paintwork, nuts and bolts. That day Nelly wrote to Heinrich from the hospital. She wanted to make sure that he'd sent off the $40 cheque to the Crown Loan office; it was urgent as it was already three days late. She said she had always made sure that all the bills were paid on time and reprimanded him for forgetting and thus possibly losing her credit facilities. She'd given the hospital stay a lot of thought and was now sure that she would leave on Sunday. He shouldn't wonder that she was anxious and didn't want to stay there. She didn't need a doctor anymore and the whole thing was costing them money they did not have. So either he would come to pick her up or she would leave of her own accord. In another letter written at that time, Nelly promised Heinrich that she was feeling healthier than ever, and all she needed was a normal life and enough money, a modest amount, to get by. Doctor Nielsen had agreed that she could leave if she returned for checkups on a weekly or fortnightly basis. She hoped that Heinrich would not object. After all, when he was sick and there was no money, not even enough to buy food, she did not put him into a clinic. This was a place for people with serious mental illnesses and she did not belong there; she needed a wholesome environment. And she was resolved never again to get a job like her last one, where she had to clean floors and scrub pots and pans; doing that kind of work was just too awful. She was troubled by everything she'd been through over the last couple of years and agreed she was too quick to turn to alcohol for comfort. That when she found herself in the pit of humiliation, she always had one glass of wine too many, and was often drunk. But that did not mean she had lost her mind. *Now I want to live!* He must help her put their life in order, without too much of a fuss. She had spent the day reading and had not had any wine at all. She asked him not to come with Nadine, who was spreading stories about her. After her release Dr Nielsen wrote to Nelly, suggesting that the only solution to her present dilemma was to get away from home for a few weeks, to a place in the mountains like Lake Arrowhead; he told her to go to her local ration board and ask if they would allow her enough gasoline for a trip to drive there and back.

Döblin taught himself to type. The Russians advanced into Estonia and Poland. There was upheaval on Wednesday 9 February, with an anxious phone call from Nelly, who had left the hospital. Thomas referred to it as an institution and said that she had run away. When she got home she was in a panic to find that Heinrich wasn't there, although he'd only gone out for a walk. On Saturday 12 February, Thomas received another visit from the FBI – you could imagine them saying, 'Let's drop in on the Manns, we're sure to be offered a good cup of coffee and some delicious cake with whipped cream' – this time to ask about the publisher Felix Guggenheim (who appears to have doubled as a suspect and a source). The Americans bombed Berlin. Monday 13 March Thomas read about a Heinrich Mann celebration held in February in New York, and thought the significance of his brother's work was exaggerated. On Wednesday 5 April, he received a phone call to say that Bruno Frank was ill with heart problems, which worried him so much that a few days later he had a medical checkup, to be told that he was in good health. With his doctor he discussed the high incidence of coronaries among the emigrés. There'd been five in the past week.

Salomea wrote to Heinrich that she'd seen de Gaulle compared to Henri IV in the newspapers, and it reminded her of the great impact of his novel when she first read it. She never understood what people meant when they said that his *Henri* was a book of the future. She also mentioned that a friend of theirs was destitute when he died recently, and that the exile community should be ashamed of their lack of compassion for one another.

Brecht went to the cinema to see cowboy and gangster movies, and Charlie Chaplin. He followed boxing matches. By his bed he kept two piles of crime novels, one of books he'd read, the other unread; each day he finished one book and smoked one cigar. He was as deeply affected as ever by music, loved listening to Bach, but at present Beethoven was too much for him. In front of his desk he had a map of Europe marked with the military movements of the war. He was good friends with the actor Charles Laughton and they read Shakespeare together. Chunks of Laughton's garden at Corona del Mar kept falling into the sea. In March, Brecht wrote to Heinrich about the Council for a Democratic Germany; the FBI was keeping a close watch on both of them.

On 3 April, Nelly received a letter from her attorney Oral R. Finch (presumably replacing Donald Kolts), saying he had a copy of the letter sent to her by the attorneys for Mr Edwin G. Roberts, whose 1940 Pontiac she had damaged in November, making a claim for $750 for loss of the use of the car and inconvenience caused by the accident, with $100 now and the rest in monthly payments. Finch wrote, *I think their demand is exorbitant and I do not believe you should pay Mr Roberts any more than his repair bill amounting to $560.* But he pointed out, if Roberts took the matter to court, that would cut out the option of paying in instalments. On 29 April Nelly wrote to Dr Nielsen, asking him to send proof that he'd seen her three times since 9 February *and that you found me perfectly healthy.* Perhaps temporarily, she had been allowed to keep her driver's licence, which cited her height as 5 feet 6½ inches, her weight as 150 pounds, her eyes as grey-blue.

Thomas and Katia went to Heinrich's place, believing they were expected for dinner, but were told there had been a misunderstanding. They went home again. Continuous bombing of the European continent. On Friday 12 May they visited Heinrich. Nelly wasn't there. Later that evening, on their way to a restaurant with the Werfels, a policeman told them it was forbidden to speak German.

Nelly had gone to stay at Ananda Ashrama at La Crescenta, a spiritual retreat in the foothills of the Sierra Madre mountains of Southern California. It was run by followers of its founder, Swami Paramananda, a monk of the Ramakrishna Order. The entrance to its Temple of the Universal Spirit is inscribed with *Truth is One*, and the interior includes shrines dedicated to all the major world religions. Many of its guests were European emigrés, the cost was optional, the idyllic setting, with its woodland paths, stone-built terraces and gardens, must have reminded them of the sanatoriums in which they'd stayed in Germany or Austria. The retreat still exists; a current brochure describes the resident community as one *composed of women monastics and householder men and women* who share the daily domestic and spiritual routines.

In 1944, one of the devotees, Sister Amala, kept a diary and for Friday 9 June, she noted that *Mrs Heinrich Mann* had arrived at lunchtime and had eaten with the other guests, but had gone to sleep early and missed supper. The following week Sister Amala noted that Nelly had attended the afternoon class on Thursday 15 June. Friday 16 June was *a busy day. I went down to the guest house and served the luncheon. Mrs Heinrich Mann gave me a German lesson . . . I read the paragraph from the story 'Schauspielerin – Actress.'* (Did Nelly tell her that it was a portrait of her husband's sister Carla?) *I gave Mrs Mann an English lesson. She read Swamiji's poem 'Silence'. I feel it is a privilege to have this opportunity.* There was another lesson on Saturday. *Nice day at Ashrama* on Sunday 18 June. *Both services held out of doors in Temple Patio. Mrs Mann's friend Henry Hudson* (unidentified) *came to see her. Mrs Mann's husband is ill. She will return home tomorrow afternoon.* Monday 19 June, *Mrs Mann went home today to her husband*. But she came back for the memorial service for Swami Paramananda, ate lunch and stayed for one night at the Guest House on Sunday 25 June; told the sisters that she and Heinrich wanted to live there for three months. As one of its *Un-*

developed Leads, the FBI was trying to *ascertain the identity and possible connection [of] Heinrich MANN's Free German activities, if any, with ANANDA ASHRAMA*. The bureau noted that *one CHRISTOPHER ISHERWOOD* was a student of the ashram's founder.

During her stay Nelly wrote to Heinrich that the retreat had been good for her, that the sisters had travelled the world, were highly educated, discussed Freud and Einstein, and were well connected; they were very fond of her; she had English lessons from Sister Amala and religious instruction from Sister Vimala. She liked the fact that they believed in life after death. She had made friends with a woman who was the daughter of an English governor and had led a dissolute life. She noted that the translation of his *Professor Unrat* had been published, titled *Small Town Tyrant*, and she mentioned that she'd seen a very good review of it in the *New York Times*, but nothing in the local papers, no advertisements, and that it couldn't be found in shops; she'd asked for it in a big bookshop yesterday. *With love, your Nell.*

Heinrich finished writing *Ein Zeitalter wird besichtigt* (Revisiting an Era) on 17 June 1944. This book-length essay was the closest he came to producing a memoir. It followed his lifespan, which he must have thought was reaching its completion, with a panoramic view of Europe, taking in Napoléon, Bismarck, Hitler and Stalin, revolutions and wars, an evaluation of the bigger picture: of an era. There are sweeping generalisations about Russian patience and British resilience, imagined dialogue between German and Russian soldiers, and utopian perspectives, where the USSR resembles the British Commonwealth in the way each rallies its troops to fight for a common cause. He saw it as a period when common destinies took precedence over individual ones, and he was merely an eyewitness, of events and of himself. He identified himself not by name, but in the third person, as Jx. Sounds like *Jux*, a joke. He suggested that both Jx and his era hardly understood themselves. And this was true, especially regarding his anti-Fascist stance, which depended all too earnestly on what he wanted to believe as the good intentions of the Soviet system. He was at his least persuasive when he chewed over the differences between Hitler and Stalin.

Zeitalter gave only a few glimpses into Heinrich's private life. He remembered his puppet theatre, and looking over his father's shoulder to read the newspaper. A Europe through which one travelled without a passport, where poisons could be freely bought but no one thought of using them to commit suicide, trains with individual reading lamps, in French cafés the small complimentary carafes of cognac that were served with every cup of coffee, and the excellence of even the simplest meals in French restaurants. All his old books; he wondered where they were now. A time when the thrill of seeing his plays performed was greater than knowing his novels were being read.

And the turning points. How as a child he made the frightening discovery that there were holes in the Milky Way, like windows into infinity. How as a young man, this transformed into the even more terrifying thought of an open-ended future, *the responsibility for everything that was not yet achieved, that lay ahead*. The fear of getting sick that made him sick. Anecdotes and judgements and opportunities, including ones he'd missed: of challenging Hitler and being elected instead of him.

He thought that in his life, as in his work, he had often been too impulsive, but that this was also the source of what he valued most – love as a higher form of intelligence. The counterpoint to an era marked by hate. At the pinnacle of human aspiration, he placed love even above faith and hope. He loved the friends with whom he'd shared meals and wine, the Austrian writer Arthur Schnitzler, the French critic Félix Bertaux, the brave young German Communist (Rudi Carius) who with his comrades broke up

Nazi gatherings, the sculptor Ernst Barlach, the artist Max Liebermann, among many others. About himself and Schnitzler, he wrote: *We walked together. It was as if the act of walking inspired the art of writing . . . As a young man I probably spent as much time walking up and down mountains, as I did writing.* He loved music. Puccini above all. Of all the women he loved, all were held dear, none was forgotten. His beloved sister. And Goschi, left behind in occupied Prague. He said his two greatest moments of happiness were the birth of his daughter, and Nelly's arrival in France, to share his exile.

On Saturday 3 June, American troops in Italy were close to Palestrina, and Thomas's thoughts returned to the time he lived there with his brother. On 6 June, his 69th birthday, he spoke with Heinrich on the phone. The beginning of Operation Overlord, the landing of Allied troops in Normandy. Thomas received an invitation to go to Sydney for a conference on freedom; Aldous Huxley had also been asked. He met with a literary agent to discuss Heinrich's situation and further possibilities of reprinting a selection of his brother's work. On Tuesday 20 June he started to destroy some of his diaries. Perhaps because on Friday 23 June he and Katia became American citizens. They were photographed by the media, and interviewed in a newspaper office hung with pictures of naked women. Reading an article in the magazine *Freies Deutschland*, which presented Heinrich Mann as a true public intellectual who continued to pursue his democratic goals from the isolation of his Californian exile, the old rivalry surfaced and Thomas brooded once again about what he called the glorification of his brother's literary reputation to the detriment of his own. At the end of June Thomas and Katia bought a new cream-coloured Ford convertible.

On Thursday 6 July, Thomas received the news of the death of his old friend the poet Karl Wolfskehl in New Zealand. In fact, Wolfskehl would die four years later, in 1948. He was buried in

Auckland at the Waikumete Jewish Cemetery; *exul poeta* carved on his tombstone.

The alarming increase in the massacre of European Jews. On Wednesday 12 July, Thomas noted that the Russians were forty miles from the East-Prussian border. There had been an attempt by Claus von Stauffenberg to assassinate Hitler at his Wolf's Lair in Rastenburg near the Eastern Front on 20 July. On Sunday 22 July there were reports of bloody goings-on in Germany, Gestapo rage, well-known generals killed, an entire regiment executed. Thomas was preoccupied with his *Faust*, in particular with Adrian Leverkühn, confessing that this was the character he loved most, of all the ones he'd ever created, that he did not simply love Leverkühn but was in love with him: his arrogance, his coldness, his distance, his lack of soul, his despair, his conviction that he was damned. Thomas noted that Heinrich had had an attack of bronchial asthma and had been taken to a sanatorium in the mountains. He thought that his brother would recover. He read a book just published about Joyce's *Finnigans Wake*, by Joseph Campbell and Henry Morton Robinson; conceded that next to Joyce his own work looked like drab traditionalism, and that Joyce might indeed be the leading genius of the era. It never crossed his mind that Virginia Woolf was also a contender. Mid-August Thomas decided to have his Faustian devil appear in three disguises, as a pimp, a musical scholar, and an icy demon. They received news that Bruno Walter's wife, Elsa (who had always verbally abused her husband), had a stroke and had lost the ability to speak.

From Sister Amala's diary, we know that Heinrich and Nelly arrived at La Crescenta on Friday 21 July, and that he stayed there – he even had the *Los Angeles Times* delivered – while she sometimes returned home. That month Nelly received an advance of $50 from Heinrich's New York–based agent, Barthold Fles; she heard from him again in August; perhaps she had complained to him that he wasn't doing enough to promote her husband's work. Fles told her she could expect to receive payment soon for some republications and he was also trying to interest a publisher in Heinrich's *Zeitalter*, there was even a possibility of film rights for *Small Town Tyrant* being negotiated, although this would take a while to come through. On Wednesday 9 August Nelly brought Heinrich's nephew Bibi, his wife, Gret, and their four-year-old son, Frido, to visit him at the ashram. The following week the sister's diary noted that *Mrs Mann came to Ashrama to be here indefinitely*, though she continued to run errands and commute between the mountains and the city by car, often with passengers, like Erna Döblin, who also stayed at La Crescenta at that time. Reports of Royal Air Force bombings of Königsberg, the historic centre in flames for several days. It was rumoured that the only vertical structure left standing was the statue of Immanuel Kant. The Allies were making advances on many fronts and on Monday 11 September, Churchill and Roosevelt met in Quebec to discuss the next stage of the war.

It seems that Nelly made good friends at the ashram. Barbara, who was probably one of the retreat's *householders*, wrote to say, *I washed and ironed your dress and red and white scarf you wear on your head also Mr Mann's shirt sleeping clothes socks and handkerchiefs, I hope I ironed them good enough for you . . . I am taking good care of him for you . . . I never once told him I saw you drinking not anybody else every one here is asking after you everybody loves you. Sister said she hopes you come back soon.* The letter was full of support, encouraging Nelly to go out and enjoy herself, offering to come to Los Angeles to help her with the housekeeping there, and enclosing vitamin tablets for her to take. On 12 September, Nelly donated blood.

Heinrich told his brother he was reading the last volume of the *Joseph* books. On Thursday 21 September, a beautiful day, Thomas and Katia drove to visit Heinrich at his *Indian* sanatorium, where they ate lunch together, happy to see him looking so much better.

Then Nelly's stakes declined. On 27 September, she received a telegram from her friend Nadine, warning *You lie about me or talk about me to my friends once more and I will go to Mr Griffin* [the judge] *and tell him the truth and to your friends . . . and tell them what you said about them I have had enough of that nonsense you do it once more and I will give you a lesson you will not forget.* The threat of going to speak to Griffin, who was known to be a harsh judge in driving and alcohol-related cases, must have angered Nelly. She drafted, and perhaps sent, a letter to Nadine's husband: *I regret that your wife has caused me so much mental suffering wherefore I am forced to take steps which may seem against you. I am two woundet of her acusation* [*sic*] *. . . Please Grady I hope you will understand and remember that I and Mister Mann are your friends but I have to teach your wife a lesson . . . verry trully* [*sic*] *your . . .* In another draft Nelly wrote that Nadine *even went so far as to say I stole two thousand dollars from her . . .* And on 4 October, she received a telegram in Los Angeles from her friend Barbara. *Dear Nellie you have lost the best friend you ever had I am sorry you tell stories so it can only hurt you. I will never forget what you did you forget that I have first-class friends in LA and the best of references I have already forgiven you but I can never forget you can get into trouble some day doing things like that. Be careful. Please do not give me any more gifts, as from this on you are a stranger to me. Good luck.* The reasons for these outbursts are not known.

According to Heinrich, throughout the year Nelly endured a number of physical and psychological crises, when *her bright eyes lost their spark,* her entire body and face were distorted with her suffering, and she wanted to die. He mentioned *her poor painful head* that was getting worse all the time, implying headaches or migraines. She cried a lot. At one stage she mourned the death of her sister, who was in fact alive and well.

Thanks to FBI investigations, we know that on 16 October Heinrich was visited at La Crescenta by the Soviet vice consuls of

San Francisco and Los Angeles. He left the retreat on Saturday 21 October; he'd been there for three months. When Heinrich and Nelly came to lunch at Pacific Palisades, Thomas noted that his brother was looking much better. Regarding the progress of his own work, gathered over many years from a great variety of sources, Thomas was as always fascinated by the widespread practice of literary appropriation. In his diary he gleefully quoted Stendhal's quotation of Molière's confession after raiding Cyrano de Bergerac, that *I take what I want wherever I find it.* On Tuesday 24 October he received another visit from the FBI *gentleman* regarding information about yet another member of the exile community.

The German field marshal Erwin Rommel was forced to commit suicide. They brought him the poison and then they gave him a state funeral.

Gas, water, electricity, telephone, doctors – the accounts kept coming. Nelly handled all their finances and she was clearly overwhelmed. In October, the Rosslyn Loan and Jewelry Company, 459 South Main Street, issued her with a receipt for $17.50 for a camera, a typewriter and a chair. She had also written to the Joint Anti-Fascist Refugee Committee, of which Heinrich was a national sponsor, to say that her husband had been ill and in hospital, and that for several months they had not been receiving their cheques. She got an apology, with concerns for Heinrich's health, and a cheque for $150 enclosed. Another cheque for $50 arrived in November.

Thomas was unwell at the beginning of November, plagued for the rest of the month with dental problems. On Saturday 18 November, Heinrich and Nelly came to lunch. He noted that she was now working as a nurse. On Friday 24 November the brothers had a long telephone conversation about their time in Palestrina.

Klaus Mann had become an American citizen the previous year and was serving with the Psychological Warfare Branch of the American Army in Italy. Heinrich sent him a Christmas card printed with a rhyme. *It's a joy to sing of all the things a merry Christmas ever* [at this point Heinrich inserted: *not ever, but this year and tout particulièrement pour mon cher neveu*] *brings, And make each note ring glad and clear, With wishes for a bright New Year.* A short note, alternating between English, German, French and Italian, included avuncular advice about staying committed to the cause of peace, and birthday greetings.

Brecht said that now and then he forgot a German word, and only now and then remembered English. Never a drinker, he started to have an occasional whisky. Read Gide's *Journal*, listened to the radio. Helene Weigel told a friend that her reason for living, already very much reduced, was vanishing. That she was no longer able to take herself seriously. She sewed jackets and nightgowns for presents and baked Christmas *stollen*.

In December Thomas still felt tired, unwell, depressed. On Thursday 7 December he was upset about an article in the *Author's League Bulletin* pointing out it was the books of Heinrich Mann, and not those of his brother, that the Nazis despised and burned. On Tuesday 12 December, a hot day, Thomas began to write chapter XXV, the devil's chapter. He was reading Kierkegaard.

It was Sunday, 17 December 1944. He was at home – alone – at 301 South Swall Drive, Los Angeles. In the not yet broken darkness before dawn, the outline of a bowl of fruit on the windowsill, its curves, a hand of bananas that Nelly had bought earlier in the week, grapes, some pears . . . backlit by a grey gauze of curtains. He had stopped sobbing. Shrinking from this terrible night, from this grief that was too much to bear, he was an old man who hunched very deep inside his body, far below the folds of his own soft skin. Feeling minuscule, like a grain of sand.

Later that day Thomas received a phone call to say Nelly had died from an overdose of sleeping pills. He and Katia went to Heinrich's place, talked to him, gave him money to cover the funeral costs, and promised to look after him.

On page 12 of the *Los Angeles Times*, Monday, 18 December 1944, there was the following headline: *THOMAS MANN'S SISTER-IN-LAW KILLS HERSELF*. The article said it was the second suicide attempt by Mrs Nellie Kroeger Mann, that she died the previous day at General Hospital. *Her husband found Mrs Mann unconscious in the bedroom of their home at 301 S. Swall Drive, Saturday. After treatment by their physician, Dr W. A. Swim, she was taken to the General Hospital where she died at noon yesterday.* The article then mentioned Nelly's previous suicide attempt and her reckless driving charges. *Yesterday, however, Mann told investigators that he could think of no motive for Mrs Mann's act.* At the bottom of the page, an ad for children's clothing, a drawing of a boy in a sailor suit.

On Monday 18 December, Sister Amala noted the conjunction of the moon and Venus in the evening sky, and that she had read Nelly's death notice in the paper. *I feel very sorry for Heinrich Mann.* She wrote to him and quoted from the Bhagavad Gita, chapter II, verse 20. *This Self is never born, nor does It die, nor after once having been, does it go into non-being. It is never destroyed even when the body is destroyed.* She added, *you were so kind and gentle with all of us at Ashrama. I consider it a great privilege to have met you.*

Heinrich notified Salomea, saying it was usually his poor, dear Nelly who wrote to her, but that she had died. She had suffered periods of depression in the past, as Salomea was aware, and several times had tried to end her life. She finally succeeded. Although the doctor told him she would survive, in fact her body was too damaged from the previous poisoning, and she did not make it through the stomach pumping procedure. She died just past midnight on 16–17 December in the ambulance on the way to hospital. He excused himself for writing so briefly, saying he was exhausted from the pain this loss had caused him and fearful of the profound loneliness in which he now found himself. A couple of weeks later he admitted there had been two suicide attempts in France, and two in America, and it was the third attempt that was successful.

Heinrich later said that when he found her unconscious, she looked peaceful and beautiful. If his version is correct, Nelly died at 12.30 am on Sunday 17 December, the very same date on which she nearly died in Nice in 1938. One has to wonder if this date had conscious or unconscious significance for her, and if not the exact date, then the season, since at least one other attempt also occurred around that time, in early January.

Marta Feuchtwanger contributed her own interpretation of events. That Nelly was often drunk; the car accidents; the loss of licence; driving without a licence; taking tablets so she'd be taken to hospital rather than jail; combining alcohol and tablets on the day of her death. She said that Heinrich Mann found her unconscious, tried to rush her to hospital in a taxi, but that several clinics refused to take her because he had no money, that he finally found a clinic, her stomach was pumped, but it was too late. Rather ungraciously, she thought the most remarkable thing about Nelly was Heinrich Mann's extraordinary love for her.

The obituary in the *Los Angeles Times* for Mrs Nellie K. Mann said she was the wife of the German writer Heinrich Mann and sister-in-law of the Nobel Prize–winning novelist Thomas Mann.

Thomas recorded that on Wednesday 20 December, he, Katia and their daughter Medi went to the cemetery at Santa Monica for the funeral of *Heinrich's unhappy wife, who had brought him a lot of trouble.* They had sent a floral spray of large bronze *mums* (the florist's shorthand), arranged around a cluster of white ones. They greeted other mourners. Heinrich arrived in the company of a friend of Nelly's. A young attendant uttered some words of spiritual comfort. Heinrich was in tears over the death of his ruinous wife.

A slightly different list of mourners is to be found amongst Heinrich's papers, mentioning Brecht, Feuchtwanger, Eva Hermann, Liesl Frank, Ludwig Marcuse, the artist Ernst van Leyden, Döblin, Salka Viertel, and a nameless friend. Viertel provided another variation: of Thomas and Katia Mann, Helli Brecht, Ludwig Marcuse, the Döblins and Liesl Frank gathered around the grave. She described how Heinrich was the last to arrive, bowed with grief. With him was an elderly, heavily made-up lady wearing an enormous black hat laden with flowers, like a funeral wreath. She was Nelly's best friend and immediately took on the role of hostess, placing Heinrich next to his brother and sister-in-law, introducing people to each other even though she was the one who was the stranger in this group. After a brief service, with no one taking up the invitation to say a few words, and after a quick and monotonous Lord's Prayer, the ceremony was over. Blandine Ebinger arrived late. Heinrich sobbed, covering the pain on his face with a handkerchief, and stumbled away. Katia ran after him, took him by the arm and led him to their car. The coffin was lowered into the ground after the mourners had dispersed, and the grave was filled with soil. The flowers sent by friends, including a spray of lavender *mums* from Nadine – *To my dearest Nellie* – were placed on the grave, her last house of exile.

Heinrich was driven back to Pacific Palisades. They talked, lunched, and then he rested on the sofa in the living room. Before taking him home, they gave him some wine, food, and money to retrieve his furniture from the pawnshop. Thomas believed Heinrich did not have a cent because Nelly had spent all his money, and on top of that, had incurred debts. In the evening, Thomas continued reading Kierkegaard.

On the day of the funeral Brecht sent Heinrich a handwritten copy of his *Gedichte im Exil* (Poems in Exile), regretting it was not a proper book, printed and bound, but since their current situation was a throwback to the early Middle Ages, there was not much to be done, except to make do.

In early December Heinrich had written to Eva and Julius Lips, telling them how difficult it was for him to see Nelly going out to work and coming home exhausted. Not knowing she had died, they replied on 25 December, saying they understood their hardship and hoped the situation would improve in the new year.

From Dr Aron Schwartz, a bill for $150 for Nelly's dental treatment, dated 21 December.

For Heinrich Mann this would be the loneliest Christmas. He found a card Nelly must have purchased but never signed. *Merry Christmas to My Husband*, with *Husband* spelled out in checked, striped, spotted and plush ties, and inside *A loving Merry Christmas / To that man I'm wild about– / That swell guy that I'm married to / And couldn't do without!*

Their friend the Danish novelist and feminist Karin Michaelis, who had just visited them and was now back in New York, had not heard about Nelly's death and had sent him and his *dear and lovely wife* a Christmas card, thanking them *for the beautiful evening I spent in your home*, adding that she'd just heard that the Nazis had confiscated her own *beautiful home* and belongings in Denmark.

Heinrich sent many thank-you notes to friends who had expressed their sympathy. One of the first letters he received was from Ferdinand W. Kahn, a Munich lawyer who was now working in a Los Angeles pottery and who would later learn that his mother had died in Terezin. Kahn wrote that in all his years of exile he had never met anyone who was as warmhearted and helpful as Nelly. On 27 December Heinrich wrote to Hermann Kesten to say that he had reminded him of good times and sunny days, but that the storms and dangers were equally significant and now filled his mind with memories. *Because we were together, she and I, and now I'm alone.* On 3 January 1945 he wrote to Salomea, *Dearest Friend of my Beloved.* Remembering Nelly's courage during their escape from France, he said that surely anyone who crossed the Pyrenees on foot and then travelled to such a distant place of exile must have had the will to keep on living. That she yearned for strength, but could no longer summon it. Her illness – her *head* – made it impossible for her to go on. She embodied all his memories, the best and worst, and if he was unable to keep her alive, she remained beside him in death.

A letter dated 31 December and addressed to the Estate of Nellie Mann offered *immediate cash for everything.*

Klaus Mann wrote to his mother on New Year's Eve, that he'd heard about *the Kröger desaster* [*sic*]. *What a shame! What an embarrassing, superfluous, ugly tragedy! It must be an awful blow to poor old Heini – who is likely to follow her soon. Couldn't she wait a few years? What deplorable, objectionable lack of consideration and self-control! Yet I feel sorry for her. She should have stayed in Germany with people of her own kind. He has ruined her life by transplanting and uprooting her. But then, that's what she wanted. I suppose it was completely on her own account when she followed him to Bandol, or wherever he was at the time. Stupid thing she was! But back in Nice she used to cook really delicious suppers for us. It's all very sad. (I'll try to write a few lines to the Uncle. But there is nothing to say, really . . .).*

Klaus wrote to Heinrich, who replied in January 1945, in English. *My dear Klaus, you wrote me a wunderful* [*sic*] *letter about my poor wife: I thank you for the fine words and the true feelings. She did'nt* [*sic*] *know what she was doing. Or she knew it before and wanted never to do it. When the bad hour came, all was forgotten. Despite of the terrifying last time, I had then the hope to see her restabilised* [*sic*]*; now I can't hope anything, and I am alone.*

The FBI tried *to develop possible information of interest concerning the reason for Mrs MANN's suicide* and *the file of the Los Angeles County Coroner, No. 17943, was reviewed on January 23, 1945. This file reflects that the cause of death was phenobarbital poisoning due to barbituric acid – suicidal. The reason for the suicide was 'unknown'*; the coroner's file suggested that Mrs Mann was *'despondent'*, the basis for this reason was not shown, Mr Mann did not see Mrs Mann commit suicide, and there were no suicide notes left by the deceased.

It might be said that Nelly was the kind of heroine who possessed what the philosopher Tzvetan Todorov calls *ordinary values*.

In Germany, at the Sachsenhausen concentration camp, a group of prisoners, veterans of the Spanish Civil War, had formed resistance groups and planned escape. One of them was Rudolf Carius. He'd been interned there since 1941. Records show that he *liberated himself* in 1945. When he returned home, he was amazed to find intact the desk and matching chair, the marble writing set and many books he had salvaged from Heinrich's apartment in 1933. He placed a photograph of Heinrich Mann above the desk.

The Bird

And a bird sang, slender arrow. / . . . And I knew that death was an arrow / let fly from an unknown hand / and in the flicker of an eye we die.

OCTAVIO PAZ, 'THE BIRD'

Eva and Julius Lips wrote to say they were shocked to hear about what had happened and that they shared Heinrich's grief. For them Nelly was all in one, childlike, womanly and motherly, and the memory of her brought back Mediterranean sunshine and palm trees, her caring nature, her little birds in Nice.

In the mail for Mrs Heinrich Mann, a question: *WHY WALK When you can Ride?* From the Kelley Kar Co on Figueroa Street, suggesting she could sell her car and drive it too, because Kelley would pay today's highest market price for the car and loan it back for ninety days. An accumulation of bills, including the attorney's, and Dr Nielsen's for professional services for Mrs Mann. Nelly's sister and brother-in-law in Pennsylvania thanked Heinrich for his letter informing them of her death. They told him he must not keep asking himself if he'd done enough to help her. Elsa thought she remembered that as a young girl Nelly had already talked about suicide, for no apparent reason. That she'd been troubled for a long time and was now resting in eternal peace, to be remembered as someone who was good, who was too often too good.

Three weeks after her death Heinrich wrote a note to his dear wife, *May the Lord watch between me and thee, While we are absent one from another.* He stayed in contact with Salomea Rottenberg. She wrote to say that Nelly frequently appeared to her in dreams. On 30 January 1945, he told her that he worked every morning and spent the rest of the time thinking of Nelly. A month later, he said that now he thought of time only in relation to the moment of her death. To those who sent their sympathies belatedly, he said it didn't matter, since his grief was as great as on the first day.

Salomea found it impossible to comprehend the devastating news that all her relatives in Poland had perished. And it was hard to believe that Nelly had also died. She asked for a photo, which he sent her. Told her, months later, *I keep thinking about her inner battles, her kindheartedness, how she cared for me, and how she lost her way and at the end left me alone. She was unique, she was mine, but I could not hold on to her any longer, and I'm still perplexed by the enigma of the woman who died.*

An old friend of Nelly's from Berlin, with whom she'd corresponded until 1940, wrote to say that when they were young Nelly was like a ray of sunshine wherever she went, but later she was frequently worried by the homesickness and deep sadness in her letters.

The firebombing of Dresden on 13–14 February. In March, American and British forces crossed the Rhine. Buchenwald concentration camp was liberated in April and the citizens of Weimar were marched into the camp and forced to view the horrific evidence of atrocities committed there, where over 50,000 people had been killed. President Roosevelt died on 12 April 1945, just weeks before Hitler's suicide on 30 April.

The *Cap Arcona* and two other ships, carrying about 8,000 concentration camp prisoners, were attacked by the RAF and sunk in the Bay of Lübeck. Many of the survivors who tried to swim ashore were shot either by SS troops or British pilots.

The end of the war. On 24 May 1945, a letter from Klaus. *Dear Uncle Heinrich, I am writing this in a rush, just to confirm and repeat what I cabled the other day: that I have seen Goschi and Mimi in Prague.* He said that Goschi was all right. She was thinner. As a so-called *Mischling*, and as his daughter, she'd had a hard time under the Nazi occupation. Forbidden to work, she'd survived by selling everything she could, except her father's books and papers. Mimi's condition was very bad. She had suffered terribly during her internment at Terezin. He said he almost didn't recognise her, since one side of her body and face was paralysed from a stroke, her hair was grey and she was extremely thin. Klaus thought that with Goschi's care, she might get better. But the two women were destitute, and he'd ask his mother to send them a parcel; suggested that Heinrich might want to make the royalties from his book sales in Russia available to them. He warned his uncle that when he wrote to Goschi and Mimi, he must not write in German. *It's an unpopular language.*

Goschi was an eager and loving correspondent, constantly urging her father to write more often. An angry tussle ensued when she and Mimi wanted to claim ownership of a painting by the Renaissance artist Giulio Clovio that belonged to Heinrich and had been kept safe by a friend in Stockholm.

Hiroshima and Nagasaki.

An hour before his death, Franz Werfel talked with his wife about their return to Europe, whether it was better to fly or travel by ship; they decided to fly. Werfel died on 26 August 1945. His wife did not attend the funeral, claiming that she never went to those sorts of events.

Comforted by the perfume and texture of Nelly's clothes, Heinrich did not give away anything that had belonged to her. He said that she'd already lost too much. In a letter to Egon Erwin Kisch on 18 June 1945, he wrote that since the human capacity for empathy is very small, it must be nurtured. That when it came to discovering our feelings for others we needed first to look into our selves. Literature wasn't much help, he now thought, it could only have a limited effect on us. Between one book and the next, he tended to forget much of what he'd just read. It's not known if he responded to a request from the chaplain at the Ohio Penitentiary for copies, soiled or damaged, of his *Small Town Tyrant*, which had been requested by several prisoners.

Else Lasker-Schüler had once written *Oh I'd like to leave this world! / But even after my departure / I'd still be circling God's grave. / A flickering flame.* She died in Jerusalem in 1945. The writer S. Y. Agnon recited the Kaddish.

The Rottenbergs' situation improved. They purchased the Sylvania Lumber Company in North Bergen, New Jersey (named after their Silva lumber business in Paris, itself an offshoot of the family's *Holzgrosshandlung* in Tarnopol). Salomea asked Heinrich for his daughter's address in Prague, so she could send her parcels of food and essentials. For Christmas she sent Heinrich Mann a pair of gloves and asked him, as she would every year, to take flowers to Nelly's grave on her behalf. She remembered their time together in Paris. How often Nelly had told her that she was happiest when she was with him, her husband. The pure joy of Nelly's laughter when the doctor told her she was cured. She thought that if she were alive now, she would have laughed like that when she heard the war was over. Remembered also their time in Portugal, when the Rottenbergs, waiting with thousands of others for a passage to America, had all their money stolen, and Nelly was the only one who helped them get through the worst predicament of their lives.

Honouring Heinrich Mann's seventy-fifth birthday in the German-American newspaper *Aufbau*, Ludwig Marcuse wrote that to his great credit, unlike his brother Thomas, Heinrich had cut his ties with Germany a long time ago, because he had seen, already before the First World War, what was happening. Heinrich had sensed the rising catastrophe, what he called *European provincialism gone mad*. From Kurt Hiller, heartfelt good wishes to the living founder of literary activism. From Kantorowicz, an article in *The New Republic*, with the wish that in Germany this year Heinrich Mann would be welcomed back as the country's spiritual leader, that his presence and wisdom were never more needed than right now, to rebuild the moral and material mess left behind by Hitler. From Kesten, the memory fifteen years earlier of Heinrich Mann's sixtieth, when they'd drunk a hundred-year-old cognac together and how reassuring it had been during these dark years in exile, to know he was nearby.

Heinrich suffered from sleeplessness; Dr Rosenthal prescribed Bellargal, one capsule before bedtime.

After her husband's death on 13 March 1947, Salomea's first priority was to travel to France to find her two sons' graves. On her return she decided to continue managing the mill, despite the fact that she had no experience of running a business, and told Heinrich Mann that since nobody expected to see a woman in that position, the hardest part was persuading people that she was now in charge. She felt she was once again fighting for her existence. For Christmas he received a selection of cravats from her. The flowers for Nelly's grave were never forgotten.

On 14 December 1947, Heinrich Mann received a letter from Rudolf Carius in Berlin, saying he'd replied several times to Heinrich's sad news sent in June 1946, but that his letters must have been lost. He asked where Nelly's grave was, because he wanted to show his gratitude, even belatedly, to the person who had meant so much to him and who had done so much for him. That she had saved his life. He also thanked Mann for all his help and if there was ever anything he needed, he must let him know. He said life in Germany was tough and seemed to be getting worse; he wished for better times in the new year. Carius died in 1971.

A telegram from Goschi dated 22 April to say *mother died nineteenth*; Mimi had died from the consequences of her internment in the concentration camp.

Goschi married the Czech writer Ludvik Askenazy; they had two sons. She died in 1986. Her first husband, Traugott Max Aschermann, did his best to leave no trace. Goschi would not have known that he is on the Yad Vashem Central Database of Shoah Victims' Names, where his death on 31 December 1945 is a legal rather than an actual date, and that as Mr Thomas Asherman (and other variations of his name), he spent several years in refugee camps in the Philippines and Italy, and was still alive in 1950 in Santo Domingo.

For many years Heinrich sent care packages to friends in Germany. His old friend Maximilian Brantl, living in Bavaria, wrote to tell him that at the moment Kafka was all the rage, at least among intellectuals, and asked for some cocoa. To Nelly's family in Niendorf, he sent eggs, butter, bacon, tinned peaches, plums and apricots, Hershey's chocolate. His lease was terminated, but he wrote a note, that *Mr Mann will not give up this place, because he does not want to and because he does not have to.* Reluctantly, on 15 October 1948 he moved from 301 South Swall Drive, Los Angeles, to Apartment B – 2139 Montana Avenue, Santa Monica, horrified that the new place had an eating nook instead of a dining room. It was closer to his brother's house and would make their weekly visits easier. For his sleeping problems his doctor prescribed chloral hydrate to be mixed with cherry syrup, two teaspoons in half a glass of warm water. He had a housekeeper who shopped, cooked and cleaned. For his health he sometimes visited the Hot Springs at Glen Ivy. He wrote letters. Many of his correspondents were women, including the writer and political activist Elisabeth Freundlich and the novelist Irmgard Keun. He may have pursued a number of flirtations, as is evident in his correspondence with the Russian writer Sophie Pregel-Breyner. One young woman, a ballad singer, thanked him for encouraging her singing venture. Nelly's friend Nadine, living in San Francisco, sent him cigarettes and foldout postcards from her travels. On 17 December 1948 they visited the cemetery together. The following year she thanked him for his Nietzsche, saying that he destroyed a myth on every page and she particularly liked the amusing way he disposed of the Socratic dialogues. When things weren't going well for her she wrote that she was very tired and wished for *a well ventilated tomb, a soft coffin (with a bed lamp above for reading* and *no memories)*. Nadine died in Los Angeles in 1984.

Keun wrote to him from Cologne, telling him how she had returned to Germany with false papers in 1940 and lived there in hiding until the end of the war. She said the first years, when Germany seemed to be winning, were the worst, and it was only when the bombings started that, despite the devastation and terror, she felt great relief at the thought that the end might be in sight. She was now taking care of her elderly parents in the ruin of their burnt-out house. Life in postwar Germany was grotesque, bizarre, a serious business. She was afraid of memories, the good ones even more than the bad, as they left one aching with a hopeless yearning for what was past. She told him it was reassuring to her to know he was still alive.

From 1948 to 1949 he was in touch with an old Berlin acquaintance of Nelly's, a cheerful prostitute who once again plied her trade on the Kurfürstendamm. He sent her food parcels and money for a new leather handbag, sometimes he telephoned. She offered to become his housekeeper – and more – when he returned. If he brought Nelly's lace dressing gown, she offered to wear it for him.

A hand-knitted scarf from Karin Michaelis. And another gift of cravats and fine linen handkerchiefs from Salomea. She wrote to him on 6 April 1949 from Tel Aviv. *I am visiting the land of my oldest and newest dreams.* In his last novel, *Der Atem* (Breath, 1949) – a work that is gaspingly surreal, elliptical – Heinrich Mann created another *blue* angel: Kobalt is a heroine who, like Nelly, complains about her head. She has led many lives. She has the natural poise of an aristocrat, has been an activist for Communism and survived a number of assassination attempts, has lost a fortune and towards the end of her life keeps going to the bank in Nice to reclaim it. Then she runs out of breath. She dies like a fighter who has no choice but to lay down her sword. This was the last sentence of Heinrich Mann's last book: *From its nights of catastrophic violence, the world had sunk into a stupor, and we too are exhausted and lay down our word.*

Heinrich was suffering from shortness of breath and had to have oxygen delivered to his home.

When he sent the book to Salomea, she instantly recognised it as a portrait of Nelly. She said that the fair-haired angel she used to conjure in her imagination as a child became real the moment she first met Nelly, and that's how she remembered her, as an incarnation of goodness. *She possessed something very unusual, and left some of it behind, for those who loved her.*

Sarah (Salomea) Rottenberg (née Awerbach), born 17 October c.1890–1894 in Kopyszynce, Poland, died 2 November 1988, New York.

There are fates worse than death. Klaus Mann had long been tortured by deep personal and political despair. In 1949, depressed about the rift between the USSR and America, he wrote an essay in the form of a dialogue with a young philosophy student from the University of Uppsala, proposing that the *lethargic* masses might be woken by *a rebellion of the hopeless ones . . . I'd like to see hundreds, thousands of intellectuals follow the example of Virginia Woolf, Ernst Toller, Stefan Zweig, Jan Masaryk. A suicide wave among the world's most distinguished minds.* He took his own life on 21 May 1949.

Heinrich had been increasingly unwell, with bronchial problems and angina. Despite prizes and generous invitations from the Eastern Sector he seemed reluctant to return to Germany. He declined a request to send greetings for Stalin's seventieth birthday. When he was sent money for the trip, he tried to use it to pay back his debts to his brother, which Thomas would not accept. Ultimately he made a list for himself, of things to organise before departure: passport, visa, ship tickets, medical examination, and packed some of his personal belongings into boxes. On 6 February 1950, Lion Feuchtwanger in California wrote to his friend Arnold Zweig in Berlin that he had visited Mann, who seemed much better and was ready to travel to Berlin for the opening of the new Academy of the Arts. *I think he'll make it.* A passage was booked for April on the Polish ocean liner M/S *Batory*.

Heinrich suffered a brain haemorrhage and died on 12 March 1950 in Santa Monica. The evening before his death he was listening to one of Puccini's operas on the radio. In his diary and in letters, Thomas described the circumstances of Heinrich's death. How his brother's heart kept beating for twenty-four hours even after his brain had stopped functioning. A movement from Debussy was played at the funeral and Thomas followed the coffin across *the warm lawn* of the cemetery. A month later he wrote to a friend, *I am hurt and angry that from Munich as from the rest of West Germany (Bonn, Frankfurt, his hometown Lübeck) not one word of official sympathy . . . has reached me concerning the death of my brother Heinrich. It seems they have no idea in the Federal Republic of West Germany who it is that has died.* Towards the end of his life he told Alfred Kantoro-wicz that *stupid Germans* kept arguing about which of the brothers Mann was the greatest. He thought a really great writer would have been one that combined both of them.

Zweig told Feuchtwanger that Mann's death had thrown him out of the saddle. But he would not be sending Thomas Mann a letter of condolence, since letters he'd written him for his seventi-eth birthday and when Klaus died brought only printed reply cards with a couple of handwritten words, and he'd spare him the effort; it was odd, he thought, since they'd been friends for fifty years.

After Heinrich's death, his family discovered his desk drawers full of sketches of voluptuous nudes. Thomas complained about it in his diary, that every day his brother had drawn *fat naked women*. He thought this was due to the family's problematic manifestations of sexuality, as it affected their sisters Lula and Carla, as well as Heinrich and himself. He asked his daughter Erika to destroy the drawings.

Heinrich usually sketched in a rough, urgent, distorting, at once highly personal and Expressionistic style, and amongst the drawings that survive it is touching to find some portraits of Nelly that are interpreted more gently, with greater care to capture her likeness. If finished works possess certitude, if they draw attention to themselves, and even compete with and sometimes become al-most as real as the reality they reflect, sketches, on the other hand, are more intimate and tentative. They're improvisations; they have something of flirtatiousness, compulsion, of new beginnings – of the hint, the gaze, the touch, the deferral – which finished works must forfeit. It's in the very act of sketching, and in the materials, the common use of pencil, charcoal, pen on paper, to trace an out-line, to explore resemblance, to dwell on an idea.

Heinrich also left unfinished what he'd been working on since early 1940, and believed might have become his most important work – an anti-national, anti-military, anti-heroic tragedy – *Die traurige Geschichte von Friedrich dem Grossen* (The Sad Story of Frederick the Great). From a very different perspective, it had been a subject close to his brother's heart, as in 1915 Thomas had started to write, and left unfinished, a patriotic novel, *Friedrich und die grosse Koalition* (Frederick and the Great Coalition).

Broken by the desolation of exile, Döblin sought comfort from a higher order. God had entered his house, he said, and since He was co-owner of the place, he let Him stay. He continued writing, with no hope of getting published. When the youngest of their four sons joined the French army at the beginning of 1945, Döblin and his wife were left alone in Los Angeles, where he walked with Zita the cocker spaniel along Hollywood Boulevard. Their world collapsed completely when they found out that their eldest son Wolfgang had been dead all those years, after taking his own life as a French soldier in Housseras in 1940 to avoid being taken prisoner of war by the Germans. They returned to Europe in October 1945 and moved restlessly between Germany and Paris. In his autobiographical writings he mourned his *dead*, especially those who had gone into exile with him, the actor Alexander Granach, Franz Werfel, Ernst Toller, the clear-headed and honourable Heinrich Mann. He was also scathing about that *creature* Thomas Mann, who had just *abdicated* from life; he thought of him as an emotionally detached, self-appointed patrician who had raised the perfectly ironed crease of his dust-free pants to an aesthetic principle and who had an insatiable hunger for the honours that were heaped on him. There was obviously no love lost between Thomas Mann and Alfred Döblin, Germany's two greatest twentieth-century novelists. Döblin died in 1957; Erna Döblin committed suicide a few months later.

Döblin's view of Thomas Mann seems to be based on the

protagonist of *Death in Venice*, Gustav Aschenbach, who aimed to achieve congruence between his own destiny and that of his generation, and who was *with his whole nature intent from the start upon fame*. His success was to force his work *into a semblance of greatness*. But with Thomas Mann, it must be said, the most disconcerting and thrilling aspect of his work is always its self-critical awareness. He had studied *greatness*, which he called *the aristocratic problem*, and learned to discriminate between its finer points, to be able to tell the difference, for example, between Goethe and Schiller, Tolstoy and Dostoyevsky. Not long before his death he wrote that he considered the nineteenth-century American writer Herman Melville to be superior to Shakespeare, because his character Billy Budd possessed a greater capacity for pathos than characters like Shakespeare's Desdemona. By pathos he meant a concern for morality that draws us in, mediating between text and reader: mediation, the *pathos of the middle*, whose other face is irony. He believed that, if for no better reason than their geographical position, Germans were *a people of the middle . . . the bourgeois world-middle . . . that moves between extremes* with cosmopolitan ease and trickery and *semblance*. He even entertained an etymological link between *die Deutschen* and *die Täuschenden* (deceivers), as if Germany was inescapably tied to its shadows.

Thomas Mann suffered increasingly from arteriosclerosis. With a hint of Goethe on his deathbed asking for light, Thomas asked for his glasses before he fell asleep and died at his home in Switzerland on 12 August 1955.

In 1961 Heinrich Mann's body was dug up at Santa Monica's Woodlawn Cemetery, cremated, and the urn was relocated to East Berlin's Dorotheenstädtischer Friedhof, with the General Secretary of the Socialist Unity Party of Germany (and later that year, the wall-builder) Walter Ulbricht triumphantly declaring that *He belongs to us.* Nelly's grave remains in Santa Monica, but a plaque has been placed at the base of Heinrich's headstone in Berlin, in memory of his *brave companion, Nelly Mann née Kröger.*

There's a bird I've seen, the eastern curlew (*Numenius madagascariensis*), a wader that flies over 10,000 kilometres each year from Siberian marshes to coastal New South Wales. It's not known to what extent the navigational instincts of migratory birds are inherited, or guided by celestial maps or magnetic fields, by the heavens or the earth, or all of these co-ordinates combined.

We live in a place that is not our own (Wallace Stevens).

Note on Sources

Acknowledgements

Note on Sources

House of Exile is a collective biography set in an age of fragmentation and flux. In revisiting this terrain, I have drawn on a wealth of published and archival material, as well as personal communications. In the text, quotations are set in italics. Translations from German are my own.

For the portraits of **Heinrich Mann** and **Nelly Kroeger-Mann**, my sources included the following books.

Heinrich Mann's novels: *Die Jagd nach Liebe* (Munich, 1903); *Professor Unrat oder das Ende eines Tyrannen* (Munich, 1905); *The Blue Angel* (London, 1931); *Die kleine Stadt* (Leipzig, 1909); *The Little Town* (trans. Winifred Ray, London, 1930); *Der Untertan* (Leipzig, Munich, 1916, 1918); *Man of Straw* (trans. Ernest Boyd, London, 1947); *Ein ernstes Leben* (Berlin, Vienna, Leipzig, 1932); *The Hill of Lies* (trans. Edwin and Willa Muir, London, 1934); *Die Jugend des Königs Henri Quatre* (Amsterdam, 1935), and *Die Vollendung des Königs Henri Quatre* (Amsterdam, 1938); *Henri Quatre*, 3 vols. (trans. Eric Sutton, London, 1937, 1938, 1939); reissued as *Young Henry of Navarre* and *Henry, King of France* (New York, 2003); *Lidice* (Mexico, 1943); *Der Atem* (Amsterdam, 1949); *Empfang bei der Welt* (Berlin, 1956); *Die traurige Geschichte von Friedrich dem Grossen* (Fragment of a novel; Berlin, Deutsche Akademie der Künste, in *Sinn und Form*, vol. 10, nos. 2 and 3, 1958).

Novellas, short story and essay collections, plays: *Das Wunderbare und andere Novellen* (Paris, Leipzig, Munich, 1897); *Das Kind* (ed.

Kerstin Schneider, Frankfurt/Main, 2002); *Schauspielerin* (Vienna, Leipzig, 1906); *Novellen* (Berlin, 1953); *Eine Freundschaft. Gustave Flaubert und George Sand* (Munich, 1905/6); *Macht und Mensch* (Munich, 1919); *Geist und Tat. Franzosen 1780–1930* (Berlin, 1931); *Der Hass. Deutsche Zeitgeschichte* (Amsterdam, 1933); *Es kommt der Tag* (Zurich, 1936); *Mut* (Paris, 1939); *Schauspielerin* (Leipzig, 1911); *Die grosse Liebe* (Berlin, 1912); *Madame Legros* (Berlin, 1913).

Memoirs and correspondence: *Ein Zeitalter wird besichtigt* (Stockholm, 1945); *Zur Zeit von Winston Churchill* (Frankfurt/Main, 2004); *Thomas Mann. Heinrich Mann. Briefwechsel 1900–1949* (ed. Hans Wysling, Frankfurt/Main, 1995); *Heinrich Mann. Briefe an Ludwig Ewers 1889–1913* (Berlin, 1980); *Heinrich Mann/Félix Bertaux: Briefwechsel 1922–1948* (Frankfurt/Main, 2002); Günter Berg, Anke Lindemann-Stark, Ariane Martin (eds.), 'Briefe einer Liebe. Heinrich Mann und Inès Schmied 1905 bis 1909. Teil I: 1905 bis 1906' and 'Teil II: 1907 bis 1909', in Helmut Koopmann and Hans Wisskirchen (eds.), *Heinrich Mann Jahrbuch 17/1999* and *Heinrich Mann Jahrbuch 19/2001* (Lübeck, 2000, 2003); 'Die Briefe von Carla Mann an ihren Bruder Heinrich 1899 bis 1910', in Helmut Koopmann, Ariane Martin, Hans Wisskirchen (eds.), *Heinrich Mann Jahrbuch 21–22/2003–2004* (Lübeck, 2005).

Drawings: *Die ersten zwanzig Jahre* (Berlin, Weimar, 1984); *Liebschaften und Greuelmärchen. Die unbekannten Zeichnungen von Heinrich Mann* (ed. Volker Skierka, Göttingen, 2001).

Biographical and critical material: André Banuls, *Zum erzählerischen Werk Heinrich Manns* (1976); Nigel Hamilton, *The Brothers Mann: The Lives of Heinrich and Thomas Mann 1871–1950 and 1875–1955* (New Haven, 1979); Christopher Hampton, *Tales from Hollywood* (London,1983); Jürgen Haupt, *Heinrich Mann* (Stuttgart, 1980); Ekkehard Blattmann, *Heinrich Mann. Die Bildvorlagen zum Henri Quatre-Roman* (Frankfurt/Main, New York, 1997); Heinrich Breloer, *Unterwegs zur Familie Mann* (Frankfurt/Main, 2001); Manfred Flügge, *Heinrich Mann: Eine Biographie* (Reinbek, 2006); Felix Höpfner (ed.), *Taube und Franzbrot. Das Lübecker Hauskochbuch der Familie Mann* (Heidelberg, 1995); Willi Jasper, *Heinrich Mann und die Volksfrontdiskussion* (Bern, 1982), *Der Bruder. Heinrich Mann. Eine Biographie* (Munich, Vienna,

1992) and *Die Jagd nach Liebe* (Frankfurt/Main, 2007); Helmut
Koopmann, Peter-Paul Schneider (eds.), *Heinrich Mann. Sein Werk in
der Weimarer Republik – Zweites Internationales Symposium. Lübeck 1981*
(Frankfurt/Main, 1983); Helmut Koopmann, *Thomas Mann – Heinrich
Mann: Die Ungleichen Brüder* (Munich, 2005); Marianne Krüll, *Im Netz
der Zauberer. Eine andere Geschichte der Familie Mann* (Frankfurt/Main,
1993); Anke Lindemann-Stark, 'Heinrich Manns Nena. Biographisches
zu Inès Schmied', in Helmut Koopmann, Hans Wisskirchen (eds.),
Heinrich-Mann Jahrbuch 19/2001 (Lübeck, 2003); Jindrich Mann, *Prag,
Poste Restante* (Reinbek, 2007); Stefan Ringel, *Heinrich Mann: Ein
Leben wird besichtigt* (Darmstadt, 2000); Wilfried Schoeller, *Heinrich
Mann. Bilder und Dokumente* (München, 1991); Klaus Schröter (ed.),
Heinrich Mann in Selbstzeugnissen und Bilddokumenten (Berlin, 1967);
Joachim Seyppel, *Abschied von Europa. Die Geschichte von Heinrich und
Nelly Mann dargestellt durch Peter Aschenback und Georgiewa Mühlenhaupt*
(Berlin, Weimar, 1975); Peter Stein, *Heinrich Mann* (Stuttgart, 2002);
Dieter Strauss, Maria A. Sene (eds.), *Julia Mann* (Lübeck, 1999); Hans
Wisskirchen, *Spaziergänge durch das Lübeck von Heinrich und Thomas
Mann* (Zürich/Hamburg, 2003), and *Die Familie Mann* (Hamburg, 1999).

Present editions of Heinrich Mann's work are published by
S. Fischer Verlag and Fischer Taschenbuch Verlag.

Lion Feuchtwanger based the character of the philosopher Jean-
Jacques Rousseau's mistress Thérèse Levasseur on Nelly, in his novel
Narrenweisheit (Wisdom of Fools; 1952). In 1960 Ludwig Marcuse wrote
a newspaper article about Nelly and Heinrich Mann. She was a girl
from the country, and later a Berlin barmaid, he said, *blond, attractive,
full of humour and good cheer . . . kind, helpful, funny – and she was as
outgoing as he was reserved. They were probably one of the strangest couples
that ever existed.* After reading Joachim Seyppel's biographical fiction or
fictional biography *Abschied von Europa – the story of Heinrich and Nelly
Mann*, I have been in correspondence with the author about several
dubious points. In *Die Verführbaren* (The Seduced), a 1977 film based
on *Ein ernstes Leben*, the part of Marie Lehning was played by the
Brechtian actress Gisela May. In Christopher Hampton's play *Tales from
Hollywood*, first produced in London in 1983, Nelly was played by Billie

Whitelaw, and in the 1992 TV version, by Sinead Cusack, with Alec
Guinness as Heinrich Mann. In the widely screened German television
film, *Die Manns – ein Jahrhundertroman* (2001), scriptwriter/director
Heinrich Breloer cast Veronica Ferres as Nelly, and she stole the show.

I reject the premise of Kirsten Jüngling's recently published *'Ich bin
doch nicht nur schlecht'. Nelly Mann* (Berlin, 2008): a negative depiction
of Nelly Kroeger-Mann, it arranges scant and often ambiguous
or dubious biographical evidence in a pattern that reinforces an
already existing stereotype. Jüngling focuses on Nelly as a poor and
promiscuous young woman who marries into a higher social class
and who is pathetically, embarrassingly, out of her depth in the Mann
family's milieu.

My portrait of **Thomas Mann** is composed of material from his major
works, predominantly his diaries, *Tagebücher 1918–21, 1933–34,
1935–36, 1937–38, 1940–43* (ed. Peter de Mendelssohn, Frankfurt,
1991–1992) and *Tagebücher 1944–46, 1946–48, 1949–50, 1951–52,
1953–55* (ed. Inge Jens, Frankfurt/Main, 1986–1995). I have
also drawn on: Klaus Harpprecht, *Thomas Mann. Eine Biographie*
(Hamburg, 1996); Volker Hage, *Eine Liebe fürs Leben. Thomas Mann und
Travemünde* (Frankfurt/Main, 2002); Ronald Hayman, *Thomas Mann*
(London, 1997); Anthony Heilbut, *Thomas Mann. Eros and Literature*
(London, 1995); Jürgen Kolbe, *Heller Zauber. Thomas Mann in München
1894–1933* (Berlin, 1987); Hermann Kurzke, *Thomas Mann. Das
Leben als Kunstwerk. Eine Biographie* (Munich, 1999); Donald Prater,
Thomas Mann: A Life (Oxford, New York, 1995); Michael Maar, *Das
Blaubartzimmer. Thomas Mann und die Schuld* (Frankfurt/Main, 2003);
Marcel Reich-Ranicki, *Thomas Mann and His Family* (London, 1990);
Karl Smikalla, Dirk Heisserer, *Thomas Mann und die Engel von Dresden*
(Berg/Starnberger See, 2005); Frido Mann, *Achterbahn* (Reinbek, 2008);
Erika Mann, *Briefe und Antworten*, 2 vols. (Munich, 1988).

The following books were important to *House of Exile*: **Walter
Benjamin**: *Selected Writings*, vols. 1 and 2 (Harvard 1996, 1999), and *The
Correspondence of Walter Benjamin 1910–1940* (London, 1994); Gerhard

Richter, *Walter Benjamin and the Corpus of Autobiography* (Detroit, 2000); Martin Jay, Gary Smith, *A Talk with Mona Jean Benjamin, Kim Yvon Benjamin, and Michael Benjamin*, transcript from the International Walter Benjamin Association First Congress: Amsterdam, 24–26 July 1997. **Bertolt Brecht**: *Tagebücher 1920–22* and *Autobiographische Aufzeichnungen 1920–1954* (1954), *Arbeitsjournal 1938–1955* (1973), and *Briefe* (Frankfurt/Main, 1981); Werner Hecht, *Brecht Chronik 1898–1956* (Frankfurt/Main, 1997); James K. Lyon, *Bertolt Brecht in America* (Princeton, 1980). **Alfred Döblin**: *Berlin Alexanderplatz* (Berlin, 1929), *Destiny's Journey* (New York, 1992), and *Autobiografische Schriften und Letzte Aufzeichnungen* (Olten, 1977); Armin Arnold, *Alfred Döblin* (Berlin, 1996); Jochen Meyer, *Alfred Döblin: 1878–1978. Eine Ausstellung des Deutschen Literaturarchivs im Schiller-Nationalmuseum* (Marbach/Neckar, 1978). **Lion Feuchtwanger**: *Narrenweisheit* (Berlin, 1953); Volker Skierka, *Lion Feuchtwanger. Eine Biographie* (Berlin, 1984); Wolfgang Jeske, Peter Zahn, *Lion Feuchtwanger* (Stuttgart, 1984). **Marta Feuchtwanger**: *Nur eine Frau* (Berlin, Weimar, 1984). **Sigmund Freud**: Peter Gay, *Freud: A Life for Our Time* (New York, 1988). **André Gide**: *Journals 1889–1949* (Harmondsworth, 1967). **Wilhelm Herzog**: *Menschen denen ich begegnete* (München, 1959). **James Joyce**: *Exiles* (New York, 1951); Richard Ellmann, *James Joyce* (London, 1966); E. H. Mikhail (ed.), *James Joyce: Interviews and Recollections* (New York, 1990); Willard Potts (ed.), *Portraits of the Artist in Exile: Recollections of James Joyce by Europeans* (San Diego, 1986). **Franz Kafka**: *The Diaries of Franz Kafka 1910–23* (ed. Max Brod, Harmondsworth, 1964); Max Brod, *Franz Kafka* (USA, 1960), Nicholas Murray, *Kafka* (London, 2004). **Immanuel Kant**: Arsenij Gulyga, *Immanuel Kant* (Boston, 1987). **Alfred Kantorowicz**: *Deutsches Tagebuch* (München, 1959), and *Spanisches Tagebuch* (Hamburg 1979). **Egon Erwin Kisch**: *Australian Landfall* (trans. John Fischer, I. & K. Fitzgerald, 1937); Marcus G. Patka, *Egon Erwin Kisch* (Vienna, 1997), and *Der rasende Reporter* (Berlin, 1998); Heidi Zogbaum, *Kisch in Australia* (Melbourne, 2004). **Else Lasker-Schüler**: Sigrid Bauschinger, *Else Lasker-Schüler* (Heidelberg, 1980). **Elisabet Christina Linnaea**: 'The Gaze of the Nasturtium', in *Kongl. Vetenskaps Academiens Handlingar*, 1762, vol. 23 (Stockholm). **Klaus Mann**: *Der Vulkan* (Berlin, 1956); *Briefe und Antworten* (Munich, 1975);

Tagebücher 1931–33 (Munich, 1989). **Erich Mühsam**: Chris Hirte, *Erich Mühsam* (Berlin, 1985); Heinz Hug, *Erich Mühsam* (Glashütten, 1974). **Willi Münzenberg**: Babette Gross, *Willi Münzenberg* (trans. M. Jackson, Michigan, 1974); Sean McMeekin, *The Red Millionaire* (New Haven, 2003); Stephen Koch, *Double Lives* (New York, 1994). **Robert Musil**: *Der Mann ohne Eigenschaften* (Hamburg, 1952), and *Diaries 1899–1941* (trans. Philip Payne, ed. Mark Mirsky, USA, 1998); Karl Corino, *Robert Musil* (Hamburg, 2003). **Alfred Polgar**: Ulrich Weinzierl, *Alfred Polgar* (Vienna, 1985). **Joseph Roth**: *The Legend of the Holy Drinker* (trans. Michael Hofmann, London, 2000); *What I Saw: Reports from Berlin 1920–33* (trans. Michael Hofmann, London, 2003); David Bronsen, *Joseph Roth* (Köln, 1974). **Vita Sackville-West**: Louise De Salvo, Mitchell A. Leaska (eds.), *The Letters of Vita Sackville-West to Virginia Woolf* (New York, 1985); Victoria Glendinning, *Vita* (Harmondsworth, 1984). **Kurt Schwitters**: John Elderfield, *Kurt Schwitters* (London, 1985). **Daniel Solander**: *Daniel Solander: Collected Correspondence 1753–1782* (ed. and trans. Edward Duyker, Per Tingbrand, Melbourne, 1995); Edward Duyker, *Nature's Argonaut* (Melbourne, 1998); Lisbet Koerner, *Linnaeus: Nature and Nation* (Cambridge, MA, 1999). **Ernst Toller**: *I Was a German* (London, 1934); Richard Dove, *He Was a German* (London, 1990). **Kurt Tucholsky**: *Gesammelte Werke*, 2 vols. (Hamburg, 19—); *Ausgewählte Briefe* (Reinbek, 1962). **Jakob Wassermann**: *Caspar Hauser* (trans. Michael Hulse, Harmondsworth, 1992); Rudolf Koester, *Jakob Wassermann* (Berlin, 1996). **Leonard Woolf**: *Downhill All the Way: An Autobiography of the Years 1919–1939*, and *The Journey Not the Arrival Matters: An Autobiography of the Years 1939–1969* (London, 1967, 1969); Victoria Glendinning, *Leonard Woolf* (London, 2006). **Virginia Woolf**: *Diaries 1915–1941*, 5 vols. (Harmondsworth, 1977–1984); Hermione Lee, *Virginia Woolf* (London, 1997). **Karl Wolfskehl**: Friedrich Voit, *Karl Wolfskehl. Leben und Werk im Exil* (Göttingen, Wallstein Verlag, 2005).

Books by or about the following authors and artists were also consulted: Ernst Bloch, Hermann Broch, Joseph Brodsky, Margarete Buber-Neumann, Willa Cather, Gustave Flaubert, Theodor Fontane, Johann Wolfgang von Goethe, Heinrich Heine, Franz Hessel, Kurt Hiller, E.T.A. Hoffmann, Christopher Isherwood, Alfred Kerr,

Hermann Kesten, Irmgard Keun, Ernst Ludwig Kirchner, Alma Mahler-Werfel, D. H. Lawrence, Federico García Lorca, Emil Ludwig, Golo Mann, Julia Mann, Katia Mann, Ludwig Marcuse, Edvard Munch, Friedrich Nietzsche, Edward Said, René Schickele, Arthur Schopenhauer, Bruno Schulz, Anna Seghers, Victor Serge, Theodor Storm, Leo Tolstoy, Bruno Walter, Frank Wedekind, Ernst Weiss, Franz Werfel, Arnold Zweig, Stefan Zweig, among others.

Further background material about **Germany** was gleaned from Katharina von Ankum (ed.), *Women in the Metropolis: Gender and Modernity in Weimar Culture* (Berkeley, 1997); Karl Baedeker, *Berlin and Its Environs* (London, 1923); Bruce M. Broerman, *The German Historical Novel after 1933* (Pennsylvania, 1986); Blandine Ebinger, *Blandine* (Zürich, 1985); Jörg Friedrich, *The Fire: The Bombing of Germany, 1940–1945* (trans. Allison Brown, New York, 2006); Otto Friedrich, *Before the Deluge: A Portrait of Berlin in the 1920s* (New York, 1972); Volker Hage (ed.), *Hamburg 1943. Literarische Zeugnisse zum Feuersturm* (Frankfurt/Main, 2003); Peter Jelavich, *Berlin Cabaret* (Harvard, 1996); Ekkehard Kaum, *Oskar Troplowitz* (Hamburg, 1982); Siegfried Kracauer, *The Salaried Masses* (London, 1998); Wolfgang Leppmann, *Rilke: A Life* (New York, 1984); Jan Petersen (pseud. for Hans Schwalm), *Unsere Strasse* (Berlin, 1947); Anthony Read, David Fischer, *Berlin: Biography of a City* (New York, 1995); Alexandra Richie, *Faust's Metropolis* (New York, 1998); Klaus Schöffling (ed.), *Dort wo man Bücher verbrennt* (Frankfurt/Main, 1983); Jörg Wollenberg, *Ahrensbök* (Bremen, 2001); *Chronik des Niendorfer Fischereihafens anlässlich der 75 Jahr-Feier* (Gemeinde Timmendorfer Strand, 1997).

These books were useful to my understanding of **the era**: Kenneth Anger, *Hollywood Babylon* (New York, 1975); Armin Arnold, *Prosa des Expressionismus* (Stuttgart, 1972); Sybille Bedford, *Jigsaw* (London, 1989) and *Aldous Huxley: A Biography* (London, 1974); R.J.B. Bosworth, *Mussolini* (London, 2002); Vincent Brome, *The International Brigades: Spain 1936–1939* (London, 1965); David Cesarani, *Arthur Koestler: The Homeless Mind* (New York, 1998); Otto Friedrich, *City of Nets: A Portrait of Hollywood in the 1940s* (1986); Neil Gabler, *An Empire of Their Own*

(London, 1988); Harry Count Kessler, *The Diaries of a Cosmopolitan 1918–1937* (London, 1971); Hans-Christian Kirsch (ed.), *Der Spanische Bürgerkrieg in Augenzeugenberichten* (Munich, 1971); Ralph Jentsch, *Alfred Flechtheim und George Grosz* (Bonn, 2008); Eva Lips, *Zwischen Lehrstuhl und Indianerzelt* (Berlin, 1986); Alma Mahler-Werfel, *Mein Leben* (Frankfurt/Main, 1963); Deborah L. Parsons, *Streetwalking the Metropolis* (Oxford, 2000); Joachim Radkau, *Das Zeitalter der Nervosität* (Munich, 1998); Jasper Ridley, *Mussolini* (New York, 1998); Jonathan Rose (ed.), *The Holocaust and the Book* (2002); Mark Roseman, *The Villa. The Lake. The Meeting* (London, 2003); Reinhard Rürup, *Topography of Terror* (Berlin, 1989); Ute Scheub, *Verrückt nach Leben* (Hamburg, 2000); Erhard Schütz, *Romane der Weimarer Republik* (München, 1986); H. G. Scott (ed.), *Soviet Writers' Congress 1934* (London, 1977); Thea Sternheim, *Tagebücher 1903–1971* (Göttingen, 2002); Tzvetan Todorov, *Facing the Extreme* (London, 1999); Hermann Weber, 'Hotel Lux', in *Spuren – Deutsche und Russen in der Geschichte*, catalogue for exhibition at Haus der Geschichte der Bundesrepublik Deutschland, Bonn, 3 December 2003 – 12 April 2004. Patrik V. Zur Mühlen, *Spanien war ihre Hoffnung* (Berlin, Bonn, 1985).

For the **experience of exile**: Daniel Azuelos (ed.), *Lion Feuchtwanger et les exilés de langue allemande en France de 1933 à 1941* (Berlin, 2006); Elazar Barkan, Marie-Denise Shelton (eds.), *Borders, Exiles, Diasporas* (Stanford, 1998); Stephanie Barron, *Exiles and Emigrés: The Flight of European Artists from Hitler* (Los Angeles, New York, 1997); Paul R. Bartrop, Gabrielle Eisen, *The Dunera Affair* (Melbourne, 1990); John Baxter, *The Hollywood Exiles* (New York, 1976); Hanna Diamond, *Fleeing Hitler: France, 1940* (Oxford, 2007); Lisa Fittko, *Escape through the Pyrénées* (Evanston, 1991); Varian Fry, *Surrender on Demand* (Boulder, 1945); Anthony Heilbut, *Exiled in Paradise* (Berkeley, CA, 1997); Erika Mann, Klaus Mann, *Escape to Life: Deutsche Kultur im Exil* (München, 1939); Andy Marino, *A Quiet American: The Secret War of Varian Fry* (New York, 1999); Jean-Michel Palmier, *Weimar in Exile* (London, 2006); Cyril Pearl, *The Dunera Scandal* (Sydney, 1983); Helmut F. Pfanner, *Exile in New York* (Detroit, 1983); Sibylle Quack (ed.), *Between Sorrow and Strength: Women Refugees of the Nazi Period* (Washington, D.C., 1995);

Michael Seidel, *Exile and the Narrative Imagination* (New Haven, 1986); Louis Stein, *Beyond Death and Exile: The Spanish Republicans in France, 1939–1955* (Cambridge, MA, 1979); George Steiner, *Extraterritorial* (London, 1972); Alexander Stephan, *Communazis: FBI Surveillance of German Emigré Writers* (New Haven, 2000); Susan Rubin Suleiman (ed.), *Exile and Creativity: Signposts, Travelers, Outsiders, Backward Glances* (Durham, 1998); W. G. Sebald, *The Emigrants* (New York, 1996); John M. Spalek, Joseph Strelka, *Deutsche Exilliteratur seit 1933* (Bern, 1976); Peter Viertel, *Dangerous Friends* (London, 1993); Salka Viertel, *Das Unbelehrbare Herz* (Hamburg, 1979); Hans-Albert Walter, *Deutsche Exilliteratur 1933–1950* (Darmstadt, 1974); Heinke Wunderlich, Stefanie Menke (eds.), *Sanary-sur-Mer. Deutsche Literatur im Exil* (Stuttgart, Weimar, 1996).

I have visited or received information from the following **archives**: Heinrich-Mann Archiv, Deutsche Akademie der Künste, Berlin; Research Library, Buddenbrookhaus, Lübeck; Heinrich Mann Archive, Feuchtwanger Memorial Library, University of Southern California (especially for the correspondence in the 1930s–40s of Heinrich Mann, Nelly Kroeger-Mann, Salomea Rottenberg and their fellow exiles); Deutsches Literaturarchiv, Marbach; Stiftung Archiv der Parteien und Massenorganisationen der DDR im Bundesarchiv, Berlin; the Bertolt Brecht and Heinrich Mann files of the Federal Bureau of Investigation, U.S. Department of Justice, Washington D.C.; Gedenkstätte und Museum Sachsenhausen, Oranienburg; Archiv, Magistrat der Stadt Wien, Vienna; Hall of Names, Yad Vashem, Jerusalem; Institut für Geschichte der Juden in Österreich, St Pölten, Austria; National Archives of Australia, Canberra; Research Centre, Australian War Memorial, Canberra; Jewish Museum, Melbourne; *Los Angeles Times* (especially for 5 January 1944 and 18 December 1944); unpublished diary of Sister Amala, June–December 1944, Ananda Ashrama, La Crescenta, California; unpublished diary of Nettie Palmer, 1935, 1936, 1940, National Library of Australia.

Acknowledgements

For their help and generous support, I'd like to thank: Harry and Joan Bodenhagen (USA), Loma Bridge and Joanne Burns (Sydney), Andreas Brüning (Schwules Museum, Berlin), Veronique Cahen (Paris), Julia Casterton (dec., London), Ken Chotiner (Los Angeles), Jacqueline Cooper and Haig Beck (Stradbroke Island), Ottfried Dascher (Dortmund), Dorothee Dennert (Haus der Geschichte der Bundesrepublik Deutschland, Bonn), Britta Dittmann (Buddenbrookhaus, Lübeck), Robyn Dryen (Sydney), Veronika Dünninger (Berlin), Claudia Edler (Staats- und Universitätsbibliothek Hamburg), Susan Faine (Jewish Museum, Melbourne), Norbert Fick (dec., Ahrensbök), Sieglinde Fiedler-Lorenzen (Bonn), Manfred Flügge (Berlin), Bob Friedman (CJH Genealogy Institute, USA), Helen Garner (Melbourne), Renate Gerlach (Hamburg), Cathy Gowdy (Marin County, CA), the Grunseit family (Sydney), Sonja Hamacher (Berlin), Chris Hirte (Berlin), Marian Houston (USA), the Indyk family (Sydney and USA), especially Benjamin Juers Indyk and Samuel Juers Indyk, Antoni Jach (Melbourne), Kerry Jeffrey (National Archives of Australia, Canberra), Gail Jones (Sydney), Nicholas Jose (Sydney), Mireille Juchau (Sydney), Erich (dec.) and Ursula Juers (Leura), Eric Kaufmann (London), Ekkehard Kaum (Bad Krozingen), Martha Keil (Institut der Geschichte der Juden in Österreich, Austria), Antigone Kefala (Sydney), Gisela and Walter Knoop (Niendorf), Helmut Koopmann (Germany), Michelle de Kretser (Melbourne), Marianne

Krüll (Bonn), Hermann Kurzke (Germany), Konrad Kwiet (Sydney), Elaine and Isaiah Urial Lieberman (Los Angeles), Daniel Liebermann (USA), Anke Lindemann-Stark (Germany), Fritz-Bernd Leopold (Deutsches Literaturarchiv, Marbach), Rimma Lerman (Yad Vashem, Jerusalem), Ulrich Luckhardt (Hamburger Kunsthalle, Hamburg), Harald Lützenkirchen (Hamburg), Roger Lustig (Argentina), James K. Lyon (USA), David Malouf (Sydney), Mariette Manktelow (Uppsala), Charles Markey (The New Jersey Room, Jersey City Library), Jindrich Mann (Prague), Ludvik Mann (Berlin), Peter Marmorek (USA), the Mietz family (Ahrensbök), Beate Meier (Austria), Sonja Miltenberger (Archiv, Heimatmuseum Charlottenburg-Wilmersdorf, Berlin), Christina Möller (Literaturarchiv, Akademie der Künste, Berlin), Jerry Nathans (The Jewish Historical Society of New Jersey), Jenya Osborne (dec., Sydney), Mary Osielski (Archives, University at Albany), Gudruna Papak (Sydney), Michael Rakusin (Sydney), Julia Rickers (Berlin), Otto Rönnpag (dec., Germany), Jacqueline Rose (Sydney), Renate Rueb (Berlin), Ulrike Almut Sandig (Germany), Hans-Jürgen Sarfert (Germany), Angela Scherres and family (Berlin), Karin Schick (Kirchner Museum, Davos), Sam Schoenbaum (Melbourne, Sydney and Berlin), Ingrid Schories (Germany), Susan Schrager and Marietta van den Berg (La Crescenta, California), Marje Schuetze-Coburn and Michaela Ullmann (Feuchtwanger Memorial Library, University of Southern California, Los Angeles), Norbert Sedghi (Germany), Joachim Seyppel (Hamburg), Ursula Seeber (Österreichische Exilbibliothek, Vienna), Kerstin Sharpe (UK), Amanda Simons (Sydney), Jennifer Slatyer (Cooma), Gary Smith (Berlin), Vivian Smith (Sydney), Shirley Stark Wein (USA), Andrea Stretton (dec., Sydney), Per Tingbrand (Sweden), Daniela Torsh (Sydney), Anne Summers and Chip Rolley (Sydney), David Weissman (USA), Harry Williamson (Federal), Jörg Wollenberg (Bremen), John Wolseley (Leatherarse Gully), Claude Zachary (Los Angeles), Roswitha Zick-Boegemann (Germany). Special thanks for the research grant from the Feuchtwanger Memorial Library at the University of Southern California. Also to Imants Tillers in Cooma for permission to feature a detail from his painting on the cover. And very special, loving thanks to Ivor Indyk.